D0984682

Gandhi's Peace Army

Syracuse Studies on Peace and Conflict Resolution
Harriet Hyman Alonso, Charles Chatfield, and Louis Kriesberg
Series Editors

Gandhi's Peace Army

THE SHANTI SENA AND
UNARMED PEACEKEEPING

Thomas Weber

With a Foreword by *Elise Boulding*

SYRACUSE UNIVERSITY PRESS

Copyright © 1996 by Thomas Weber

All Rights Reserved

First Edition 1996
96 97 98 99 00   6 5 4 3 2 1

Citations to the A. J. Muste Papers of the Swarthmore Peace Collection are to the microfilm edition from Scholarly Resources of Wilmington, Delaware.

The paper used in this publication meets the minimum requirements of American National Standard for Information Sciences—Permanence of Paper for Printed Library Materials, ANSI Z39.48-1984. ∞™

Library of Congress Cataloging-in-Publication Data
Weber, Thomas, 1950–
    Gandhi's peace army : the Shanti Sena and unarmed peacekeeping /
Thomas Weber ; with a foreword by Elise Boulding. — 1st ed.
        p.   cm. — (Syracuse studies on peace and conflict resolution)
    Includes bibliographical references and index.
    ISBN 0-8156-2684-3 (cloth : alk. paper).
    1. Peace—India—Societies, etc.—History—20th century.
2. Peace—Societies, etc.—History—20th century.   3. Peace
movements—History—20th century.   I. Title II. Series.
JX1908.I4W43   1995
303.6'9'0954—dc20   95-20364

Manufactured in the United States of America

If we are to make progress we must not repeat history but make new history. We must add to the inheritance left by our ancestors.

—Mahatma Gandhi

Virtue lies in taking up only an impossible program.

—Vinoba Bhave

I have said that nonviolence is a simple thing: I am not saying that it is easy.

—Shantidas (Lanza Del Vasto)

Thomas Weber teaches Legal Studies and Peace Studies at Melbourne's La Trobe University. His primary research interests are centered on Mahatma Gandhi's thought and campaigns and, in particular, on Gandhian nonviolence. He edits the journal *Pacifica Review* (formerly *Interdisciplinary Peace Research*) and is the author of *Hugging the Trees: The Story of the Chipko Movement* (Penguin, 1989) and *Conflict Resolution and Gandhian Ethics* (Gandhi Peace Foundation, 1991). He is a regular contributor to scholarly and activist journals. With his wife and young daughter he lives in the wooded hills on the outskirts of Melbourne.

Contents

Tables

Figure

Foreword

Elise Boulding

It is an old dream of peacelovers—an unarmed, nonviolent army to keep the peace. The dream is still alive, perhaps now more than ever. Recent failures of the blue-helmetted UN peacekeepers to end fighting in war-torn areas, in spite of courageous and persistent efforts, are leading people to look for another way. In this book Tom Weber is telling us about another way, Gandhi's way of the Shanti Sena. The Shanti Sena is a civilian people's army. This is a time when the role of the civil society and its transnational form as multiplying networks of international nongovernmental organizations (INGOs), are being re-examined as states and the United Nations itself become increasingly aware of their dependence on non-state actors for problem-solving skills in a problem-ridden world. In such a context, the possibility of civilian peacekeeping takes on new meaning. This timely and well-researched book tells a little-known story of how the Shanti Sena actually worked. Conceived by Gandhi, the Sena did not come into existence until after his death, but it has been a moral inspiration and has been treated as an action model for Western peace brigades and peace service teams for the past half century.

Weber, having studied the experience of the Shanti Sena from the founding of the first Sena in 1950 to the present, interviewed many sainiks, and studied translated Sena documents, asks a very pertinent question: Can the Shanti Sena really serve as a model for international peace brigade projects, given that most international efforts are being organized by westerners in a very different cultural context? To answer this question Weber explores how well the Shanti Sena actually worked within India, and how well the few international projects outside India's borders worked. In short, image is contrasted with reality. The growing number of INGOs that already administer peace service teams or are thinking about doing it, and those who are trying to create networks and coordination among these groups, need to read this book with great care. There is much to learn!

Weber alerts us to the common misconception that the Shanti Sena/ Peace Army concept is primarily international—that it refers to a set of rapid response teams that can go to troublespots around the world at a moment's notice. On the contrary, the Shanti Sena was conceived as being made up of locally based units whose members were committed to constructive social service locally, thus winning the trust of citizens; *in addition* sainiks were trained to act nonviolently to restore peace and order when riots broke out, or other emergencies (fire, flood, earthquake) arose. Only when riots got completely out of hand, beyond the capacity of local sainiks to manage, were units from other communities called in. The key to Shanti Sena success was in knowing the community, and being known. Great emphasis was also placed on local mapping, knowing where people and resources were. The effort to go international in the Cyprus Resettlement Project was profoundly unsettling to the participating sainiks because, although they were trained in nonviolent action, constructive service, and emergency aid, they did not know languages and customs, or the "lay of the land". Having no adequate contact group, they had difficulty relating effectively to the Greek-Turkish conflict situation they had gone to help resolve. They were dogged by the same problems that today's peace teams projects face: inadequate planning, logistical and supply problems, and lack of funds and personnel in relation to the scale of the problems faced.

Although the more experienced contemporary peace brigade projects are well aware of the importance of local contact groups, there is still a regrettable tendency on the part of outsiders from the West to want to jump in and do peacemaking in conflict hotspots. Weber is very clear here, and his words should be posted wherever peace-team planning is taking place: "International nonviolent ready-response teams may prove to be a waste of time if there is no local nonviolence network already in place which the outsiders would merely supplement" (p. 165).

Weber also points out that Indian sainiks, although holding divergent views on ways of working in India, are in complete agreement "that an effective nonviolent peace force can only be formed through a networking of peace centers around the world. If a local peace center feels the need it may then call on workers from other centers. The outsiders would then assist and obey the directions of the locals" (pp. 165–66).

In other words, the Shanti Sena *can* be a model for international teams if they first gain experience in their own communities, and then respond to international calls as helpers, as assistants to local groups in other conflict areas. Although Indian cities are in many ways very different from European and North American cities, one is struck, in reading about urban violence in India, by increasing parallels with urban violence in the West. This means that for westerners to gain local experience at home is a more relevant preparation for working abroad than might have appeared to be the case fifty years ago. To the extent that this message is taken to heart by newcomers to the peace-teams field, this book will have served a very important purpose.

Weber provides a sensitive and in-depth treatment of the Shanti Sena experience of conflict between the gradualists and those who seek immediate change, a conflict that many readers will recognize as familiar in their own activist circles. He points out that for Gandhi, satyagraha was both deeply spiritual and involved concrete action for change, but the change was to be based on an inward conversion of the opponent. He also points out that Gandhi frequently took political shortcuts of nonviolent coercion (such as fasting) that put political pressure on opponents to change their behavior, but that did not change their basic attitudes. After Gandhi's death, Vinoba Bhave became his spiritual heir, the peace *builder,* working primarily for longterm change, eschewing politics, his method to be "gentle, gentler, gentlest." Jayaprakash Narayan, on the other hand, became his political heir, the peace *maker,* engaged in nonviolent confrontation and political action for change. In the absence of charismatic leaders like Gandhi (and in the United States Martin Luther King), peace groups have to work out their own balance between seeking long-term social transformation based on individual transformation, and political action for structural change. In India the conflict greatly weakened the Shanti Sena over time, but that weakening was by no means only due to faults in the movement. It had much to do with the about-face made by the Congress Party under Nehru after Gandhi's death, turning Indian development toward high-technology industrialization, in the opposite direction from the Gandhian vision of *sarvodaya,* thus creating a very difficult climate for the Shanti Sena to work in. In any case, the challenge for Shanti-Sena type action elsewhere is clear, as governments and peace groups rarely have common visions of the preferred social order.

Since the Shanti Sena experience is the most important fund of practical knowledge we have about what is essentially a triad of civilian peacekeeping, peacemaking, and peacebuilding, the stories of Sena actions heighten the importance of this book. To westerners, peacekeeping action usually seems most exciting—getting between parties in combat and stopping hostilities. Next most exciting is peacemaking, doing the mediation work that brings parties to a solution. Last in the triad is peacebuilding, the slow work of building patterns and structures for communication and problem solving in divided communities, developing trust that will make it easier for opposing groups to deal with conflicts as they arise. This is what the Shanti Sena accomplished, over and over again, sometimes with teams of young girls and boys aged fourteen to twenty-one. The Tarun Shanti Sena, formed in 1969 with this age base, had by 1973 nearly two thousand members in thirteen Indian states. More often, sainiks were eighteen or over. Wherever they went, they were easily identified by their saffron scarves—and they were *welcome*. A model for youth gangs in the United States?

Reader, be sure to study the appendixes on Shanti Sena training, the sainik pledge, and organization and coordination of local groups. They are invaluable, and not at all difficult to translate from the Indian setting to other continents. Note also the discussions on centralization versus decentralization. These will be very helpful as other initiatives move forward to create an international network of INGOs and local peace groups committed to the support of peace teams. Like the long-term versus immediate change issue, the centralization-decentralization question has no one right answer. The future of unarmed civilian peace team services as complements to United Nations peacekeeping forces and as possible models for future unarmed United Nations forces, depends very much on the intellectual and spiritual maturity, social inventiveness, and communication skills of peace team activists on each continent. Organizational formats, training for action, and actual deployment patterns for peace teams will have to allow for people with strong views and a range of preferences and talents. Most of all, it will have to allow for the possibility of a continuing, creatively shifting balance between peacekeeping, peacemaking, and peacebuilding, rooted in human capability in local communities.

I would like to think that every reader of this book is a potential Shanti Sainik for the twenty-first century.

Acknowledgments

In late 1982, I was in India researching Gandhi's Salt March to Dandi and regularly visited my good friend, the late A. K. Bose, then manager of the Gandhi Book House in New Delhi. When Bose was busy with customers in the public sales area, I often browsed through dusty volumes in the storeroom. During one of these times I picked up two small books that interested me, Vinoba Bhave's *Shanti Sena* and Charles Walker's *A World Peace Guard: An Unarmed Agency for Peacekeeping*. I had not known of Walker's work in this area and was barely aware of the Sena. Having these two sources in hand at the same time first raised the questions of the link that I attempt to investigate in this book. My initial debt, therefore, is to Bose, Vinoba, Walker, and serendipity.

Thanks are due those who read and suggested improvements to earlier drafts of parts or the whole of this work. They include Robert Burrowes, Rod Church (who generously shared with me his typescript of the early minutes of the Sarva Seva Sangh meetings dealing with the Shanti Sena), Narayan Desai, Piet Dijkstra, A. Paul Hare, Robin Jeffrey, Louis Kriesberg, Lester Kurtz, Theodore Olson, Mark Shepard, Allan and Wendy Scarfe, and especially my Ph.D. supervisor, Roger Douglas. Geoffrey Ostergaard was kind enough to detail the methodological pitfalls he encountered in his study of the Sarva Seva Sangh and to point me in a less problem-fraught direction.

In Australia I also owe thanks to the Peace Research Institute at La Trobe University and later the La Trobe University Research Committee. Their financial assistance in the form of the first La Trobe University Peace Research Scholarship and a La Trobe University Research Scholarship helped fund the fieldwork content of my dissertation (which formed the basis of this book) and enabled me to write full-time. The librarians at La

Trobe University Borchardt Library were unfailingly helpful in ensuring that obscure interlibrary loan documents and microfilms reached me with minimum fuss or delay.

In India I was fortunate to have willing and competent translators without whose help I could not have deciphered various important Hindi and Gujarati books and especially Sarva Seva Sangh pamphlets and minutes of meetings. Included in this list of translator friends were Kisanbhai Trivedi at the Sabarmati Ashram in Ahmedabad; A. B. Bharadwaj of "Gandhi-in-Action," New Delhi; and Parsaiji (R. D. Parsai), Prasun Latant, and Gautam Varma at the Sevagram Ashram.

Many others, most of whom I am honored to call friends and, in some cases, surrogate family, helped make my stay in India a pleasant and rewarding experience: in Bombay, Dr. Usha Mehta, Smt. Licykutty Bharucha, and Manibhai of Mani Bhavan; in Matwad/Karadi Ganeshbhai, Pushpabehn, Kamubehn, Vallabhbhai, and Babubhai; in Ahmedabad, Laxmikant Nanalal and his family and the local half of the Meghani family who looked after me and Amrutbhai Modhi, who offered me the facilities of the Sabarmati Ashram; in Bhavnagar, the other half of Mahendrabhai Meghani's family; in Mangrol village, Mahendrabhai Bhatt and the others at "Prayas"; in Delhi, Rajiv Vora and N. Vasudevan of the Gandhi Peace Foundation and A. B. Bharadwaj; in Varanasi, the family of Arun Kumar; and at Sevagram, all the ashramites, especially Kanakmal Gandhi and Kusumtai Pandey.

I owe the greatest debt to those Shanti Sainiks and experts on the Sena who invited me into their homes or ashrams and gave unstintingly of their time, answered my numerous questions, and went out of their way to ensure that I had access to all available information on the organization. These "informants" included Dr. K. Arunachalam, Ashok Bang, Thakurdas Bang, Ashok Bhargava, Arunbhai Bhatt, Nirmal Chandra, Manmohan Choudhuri, Nachiketa Desai, Narayan Desai, Achyut Deshpande, Dilkhushbhai Divanji, B. N. Juyal, Arun Kumar, Jagdishbhai Lakhia, Amarnathbhai Mishra, Sombhai Patel, Devi Prasad, Radhakrishna, Acharya Ramamurti, Indrasingh Rawat, Hemnath Singh, Badriprasad Swami, and Chunibhai Vaidya. Without them I could not have written the following pages; nevertheless, responsibility for the way the information thus gained has been presented and the conclusions drawn from it are entirely my own.

I am also grateful to the examiners of the original dissertation. Ralph Summy of the University of Queensland, Chadwick Alger of the Mershon Center at Ohio State University, and Harvey Feit of McMaster University, while pointing out several grammatical indelicacies and typographical errors, were positive about the work and offered the encouragement needed to get the work to publishable standard.

Finally, I thank Marja for her patience and support and our daughter,

Hanna, who was born as I started this project, who forgave me for deserting her for fieldwork in India just as she was learning to talk and who gave joy to our lives through these years while leaving me enough of the space that is necessary for writing.

Introduction

Interspersed throughout the literature on nonviolence in action are repeated allusions to the Indian Gandhian Peace Army (the Shanti Sena). In fact, the Sena has been regularly held up as a model for most recent major unarmed peacekeeping attempts. An examination of the Sena, therefore, should allow some conclusions to be drawn about the viability of using the Shanti Sena as a blueprint for these ventures and might allow some judgment to be made about the entire concept. Surprisingly, the history of this organization has never been chronicled. The actions it has engaged in have not been documented in any detail, and the philosophical foundation on which it rests has received scant analytical attention.

The Idea of Peacekeeping

This book is primarily concerned with third party intervention in situations of violent conflict. States, especially as they take on the characteristics of what Myrdal has called the "strong" or "hard" state,[1] jealously guard their monopoly of this process within their borders. Therefore, it is not surprising that the most celebrated instances of third-party peacekeeping and the most ambitious (non-Indian) attempts at nonviolent/noncoercive peacekeeping/peacemaking have occurred in the international arena where at least one of the contending parties welcomed such assistance.

When, during the middle of the twentieth century, peacekeeping forces finally took to the field, the reality fell far short of the aspirations of various ambitious schemes, proposed since antiquity, for an international organization to preserve peace. Although the operation of United Nations peacekeeping forces is limited in scope, it is still beset with problems and contradictions. It may be difficult for peacekeepers to retain enough trust among warring parties to bring them together to effect settlements of their disputes if the peacekeeping force itself has been shooting at them. There may be a contradiction between the duties of guarding, observing, and separating conflicting groups, on the one hand, and attempting a long-term solution to a given conflict by trying to build a new social structure that considers the needs of the antagonists, on the other. Norwegian peace researcher Johan Galtung, the most significant writer in this area, notes that the first role, while not very effective, is easy to implement. The second may be very effective but is exceedingly difficult to implement.[2]

For Galtung the solution is to add peacemaking (negotiation and mediation) and peacebuilding (social change through socioeconomic development and reconstruction) components to the peacekeeping role. That this is rarely achieved, Galtung explains, is because the nature of conflicts can vary so greatly. Peacekeeping may be practical where the conflict is horizontal, that is, where it is between equals and over goals rather than interests, but *not* in a vertical conflict where the parties are not equal (e.g., where oppressed groups are trying to free themselves from domination). The problem is that most conflicts are vertical and, consequently, a peacekeeping force ends up merely preserving (an often unjust) status quo.

If the structural forces that give rise to conflict are not tackled, the likelihood that peace will be lasting is minimized, yet the grafting of aid-agency duties onto a trained fighting force is likely to be unworkable, both in practical and ideological terms. However, peacekeeping (and possibly its nonconsensual and sovereignty-disregarding heir, peace enforcement) could in theory be used by itself to gain time for the introduction of these added functions by other organizations.

The Shanti Sena and the Problems with the Peacekeeping Idea

Although the arguments against this "traditional" model of peacekeeping vary from ones that focus on minor problems to those that see it as fundamentally flawed, a major body of thought rejects this approach altogether and insists that peacekeeping can be carried out by private as well as public bodies and that it can be done within a framework of Gandhian nonviolence. Given the rapidly changing international political situation, the 1990s may be an opportune time to investigate alternatives to the accepted model.[3] In this work I attempt to carry out such an investigation by examining the unarmed nonviolent model as epitomized in the Shanti Sena.

The Shanti Sena was conceived (and because of historical circumstances was able to act) as an intrastate nonviolent force rather than as a nonviolent army with international duties. Nevertheless, because most of its peacekeeping activities were undertaken during bouts of intercommunal violence, its experience corresponds at least as closely to that which can be expected of a scaled-down international peacekeeping force as to that of a domestic police force. Although lessons may be learned from the Shanti Sena experience by those who are interested in an anarchist polity and are concerned with the withering away of the state,[4] in the main it is various international unarmed peacekeeping initiatives that have looked to the Sena for direction.

During the twentieth century several such initiatives (in particular, Maude Royden's Peace Army, the World Peace Brigade, the Cyprus Resettlement Project [CRP], and, most recently, Peace Brigades International [PBI]) have attempted to combine various elements that Galtung pointed out would be necessary for the effective long-term resolution of group or international conflict. All of these undertakings either looked to Gandhi or his philosophy for inspiration or had a significant contingent of Shanti Sena members involved in their founding.[5]

These alternative methods of peacekeeping are readily dismissed by those to whom they seem politically absurd; they appear easily advocated by that (perhaps utopian) minority who have a strong bias toward nonviolence. By most measures these recent noncoercive Gandhian attempts could only be seen as failures. Although in part the failures can be attributed to a lack of expertise, organization, public support, and funding, their objectives, according to Galtung's analysis, may have encompassed contradictions that doomed them to failure. The various peace brigade proposals have tried to combine peacemaking and peacebuilding with peacekeeping to achieve lasting solutions to the conflicts on which they concentrated. According to Galtung, however, these approaches are probably mutually incompatible.

The champions of the Gandhian peace brigade approach to conflict resolution maintain that those making these criticisms do so because they do not understand the operation of Gandhian philosophy. One should be able to answer whether it is possible to undertake all these approaches simultaneously, that is, to be peacekeeper, peacemaker, and peacebuilder at the same time, and to work concurrently at technical assistance while siding with the oppressed and reducing violence by examining the Shanti Sena, at least if the Shanti Sena has not failed in its aims, which combine these approaches. (If one deems the Sena to have failed in achieving its aims, the failure may, of course, be the result of factors totally unrelated to this premise of unworkability.)

The Shanti Sena, first mooted by Gandhi and finally established some ten years after his death, operated in India, on and off, for the next thirty-five years. It was unarmed, nonviolent, and its members preferred to die rather than kill when fulfilling their peacekeeping duties. I examine whether the experiences of the Shanti Sena can provide an answer to criticisms such as Galtung's and try to discover whether the foreshadowed contradictions are real and, if they are, whether they can be resolved.

To this end, I argue that Gandhi's philosophy in action itself may suffer from a fundamental contradiction that was papered over by the towering personality of the Mahatma. After Gandhi's death, when the mantle of leadership fell to his heirs, the leaders of the Shanti Sena, Vinoba Bhave and Jayaprakash Narayan (JP), these contradictions became obvious and their underlying incompatibility surfaced.

The "spiritual heir," Vinoba, adopted a "gradualist" approach to achieving the Gandhian nonviolent revolution, and his gentle/gentler/gentlest form of political action, which it has been argued is the only applicable form in a democracy, is totally in keeping with Gandhi's spiritual ideals. Vinoba's primary task was peacebuilding.

Gandhi, however, often compromised his spiritual ideals because of the "need of the hour." JP followed Gandhi's techniques rather than his ideals, and his more "immediatist" approach was concerned with "this worldly" political results and had a far stronger bias toward peacekeeping.

The contradictions in the underlying philosophy that these divergent paths seem to exemplify may also mean that the Sena was not founded on one coherent ideology and that, therefore, unarmed peacekeeping operations based on what have been characterized as purely Gandhian lines are based on an illusion.

I further ascertain the definitions of the concept of success employed by sainiks and, if there is consensus about these definitions, whether they are especially culture specific. I conclude with an evaluation of whether the experiences of the Sena can provide a viable model for unarmed peacekeeping ventures attempted in different social/philosophical settings.

Gandhi was primarily concerned with the use of correct means and advised that concern over the ends (which in any case, according to him, are not in the actor's hands) should be disregarded. Related to this primacy of means philosophy is an apparent ambiguity in Gandhi's thought between nonviolence as an instrumental and as an intrinsic good. For the Mahatma the ambiguity may have been more apparent than real. He saw a nonviolent lifestyle, even if it leads to the death of the adherent without immediate tangible results, as existentially the life worth living and further believed that a pure sacrifice in the cause of nonviolence would eventually awaken the conscience of the world. In the persons of the Sena leaders, however, the possibly contradictory strands seem to have been distilled into reasonably pure form and provided the seeds for the destruction of the Shanti Sena; they may also point toward problems for the model as a whole. If this analysis is correct then, as a corollary, there is no ready-made philosophical infrastructure that can be borrowed as a blueprint by others wishing to set up Sena-like organizations. In this case, the Shanti Sena experience, rather than providing answers, may warn of problems that require consideration by those seeking to investigate nonviolent solutions.

A further question is raised. If the Shanti Sena primarily views "success" in existential or optimistic terms, is the experience relevant to the setting up of international peacekeeping operations that may want to measure success in a more narrowly defined cost/benefit way? In other words, are the calls for "internationalizing the Shanti Sena idea" (if such an idea can be discerned at all) in reality calls for internationalizing very personalized and possibly misguided views of what the Shanti Sena idea is?

A Summary of the Argument

The main argument is divided into eight chapters. In the first three I detail the history of peacekeeping of both the United Nations and of the alternate unarmed variety, including attempts by Gandhi to set up peace brigades in India.

In chapter 1 I trace the development of the peacekeeping idea and ascertain why peacekeeping forces, when they finally took to the field, did so with the brief and problems that characterize the U.N. Blue Beret forces. This chapter includes an examination of possibly inherent difficulties and contradictions in this approach.

Given that the future of this model is currently in a state of flux, a survey of alternative models is appropriate. To this end I examine the unarmed model that looks to Gandhi's nonviolence for inspiration and of which the Indian Shanti Sena is the primary example.

In chapter 2 I examine the major, generally Gandhi-inspired yet non-Indian, unarmed efforts at peacekeeping attempted in the twentieth century. The arguments over whether this model is viable depend on whether Gandhian nonviolence can fulfil the promises that the advocates of this model hold out for it. To establish this, I discuss the successes and failures of these attempts and examine inherent contradictions that may exist in this model.

The clues to answering some of the questions raised lie in the history of Gandhian attempts to implement the unarmed model. In chapter 3 I chronicle Gandhi's experiments with the setting up of peace brigades. I argue that although Gandhi's reasons for setting up his Shanti Dals were at least in part political, a careful reading of his intentions shows that this was by no means the sole reason. These attempts, like the model advocated by many Western champions of unarmed peacekeeping, encompassed a strong peacebuilding element.

To make the connection clear and to put the Shanti Sena in context one must examine the underlying Gandhian philosophy on which the Sena is based. To this end, in chapter 4 I explore the definition and importance of nonviolence in Gandhi's philosophy and explain *satyagraha,* Gandhi's method of using active nonviolence to resolve conflict. I note the possible ambiguity between nonviolence as an instrumental and as an intrinsic good and stress the importance of the "constructive program" (technical assistance) element. The debate about the feasibility of the unarmed model, to a large degree, revolves around differing interpretations of this philosophy.

One may discover whether the philosophy has a practical application in unarmed peacekeeping from the history of the Sena, which was ostensibly founded on Gandhi's philosophy by the Mahatma's philosophical heirs. To this end, in the next three chapters I examine the Shanti Sena itself. In chapter 5 I trace the history of the Indian Shanti Sena from its founding by Gandhi's spiritual heir Vinoba Bhave in 1957 to the present.

The peacekeeping work of the Sena is far easier to document than the grass-roots peacebuilding undertaken by dedicated Gandhian workers, who often acted alone in tiny and unexceptional villages. And it is this peacekeeping activity of the Sena that has been the main focus of the advocates of unarmed peacekeeping. In chapter 6 I examine the modus operandi of the Shanti Sena by detailing several of its campaigns. The survey of these activities provides some practical guidelines for unarmed peacekeeping.

Although the type of actions chronicled in chapter 6 are the epitome of the "Shanti Sena idea" for those who champion the internationalizing of the Sena, the real question is whether this *is* the Shanti Sena idea.

The history of the Sena shows that Vinoba and JP interpreted Gandhi's philosophy differently. This difference does not bode well for the model as a whole and raises the questions of whether at least one of them misunderstood the teachings of their guru and whether, if these teachings had been better followed, the Sena and the Gandhian movement as a whole could have been more effective.

In chapter 7 I investigate Vinoba and JP's interpretations of Gandhi, their moral and political worldviews, and consequent ideology, which guided the functioning of the Shanti Sena. Further, in this chapter I examine the ideological basis for the operation of the two current Shanti Sena factions that, as a generalization, owe allegiance to either Vinoba or JP. That the two factions are now, since the death of their leaders, moving closer together, back to the more centralist position occupied by Gandhi, seems to indicate that Vinoba and JP took overly extreme positions in their interpretations of Gandhi's philosophy.

A closer analysis of Gandhi's thought in light of the interpretation by his closest followers should help to clarify further the viability of the model if it is to be based entirely on what can be termed traditional Gandhian philosophy. I examine the calls to internationalize the Shanti Sena idea in light of this ideological background.

In the concluding chapter I answer the questions posed in the historical and philosophical chapters from the perspective of this further ideological discussion. I evaluate whether an inherent contradiction in Gandhi's philosophy ensured the demise of the Shanti Sena. I discuss the degree to which the Shanti Sena experiment has managed to overcome the problems associated with peacekeeping in vertical as well as horizontal conflicts, has managed to combine technical assistance and second and third party approaches to conflict resolution, and has been able to combine peacekeeping with peacemaking and peacebuilding. I also investigate the division that sees peacekeeping as either an instrumental or as an intrinsic good.

Further, I analyze the contradictions in the Sena itself, for example, the debate about the degree to which Gandhians should be involved in power politics, whether the Sena should primarily serve in a "fire-brigade" role or actively engage in the creation of a radically new society through nonviolent revolution. More simply put, should the Shanti Sena engage in immediate or long-term actions? Finally, I assess the prospects for, and relevance of, the Shanti Sena in today's India and as a model for international peace brigades.

Gandhi's Peace Army

1

Mainstream Peacekeeping

The *Peacekeeper's Handbook,* published in 1978 by the International Peace Academy as a practical manual for those engaged in peacekeeping operations, defines international peacekeeping as "the prevention, containment, moderation and termination of hostilities between or within states, through the medium of a peaceful third party intervention organised and directed internationally, using multinational forces of soldiers, police and civilians to restore and maintain peace."[1]

The academy was set up in 1970 by senior officers who had been commanders of United Nations troops to develop skills and techniques for greater efficiency within peacekeeping forces. Their definition, at least as far as it relates to interstate disputes, conjures up the image of the blue-bereted or blue-helmeted soldier of a U.N. peacekeeping force.

Whereas the U.N. approach to peacekeeping is relatively modern and more the product of circumstances than philosophical design, the plans for world peace that preceded it have an extremely long and distinguished tradition in the Western world.[2] Churchmen, scholars, and royalty put forward countless proposals for the enforcement of a peaceful international world order long before the first United Nations Emergency Force soldiers arrived in the Middle East.[3]

These earlier proposals often included provisions for international peacekeeping armies. Generally, however, they were mainly concerned with international law and international organizations, with considerations about the balance of power between major blocs and, in some cases, with securing advantages for the proposing nation. It is, therefore, more fruitful to view them as precursors of the diverse international forums and regional defense pacts that presently abound than as precursors of the currently prevailing model of third-party intervention peacekeeping as embodied in the forces of the United Nations.

The Advent of Peacekeeping

There is no explicit mention of "peacekeeping" in the U.N. Charter. The idea of an unbiased force, without enemies, had not been considered by its framers[4] and first seems to have emerged in response to the Suez crisis of 1956. After the Anglo-French attack on Egypt, the Security Council was unable to adopt effective measures because of British and French vetoes. The procedures suggested by the "Uniting for Peace"[5] resolution were used to call an emergency special session of the General Assembly. On 2 November 1956, the Assembly called upon the parties to cease fire and to withdraw to their previous positions.[6] Two days later, the secretary-general was asked to submit to the Assembly "within 48 hours a plan for the setting up, with the consent of the nations involved, of an emergency international UN Force to secure and supervise the cessation of hostilities."[7] And finally, on 7 November, the Assembly expressed its approval of "the guiding principles for the organization and functioning" of the force as detailed in Dag Hammarskjöld's report and authorized him "to continue discussions with the Governments of Member States concerning offers of participation in the Force, towards the objective of its balanced composition."[8]

The force, made up of soldiers from ten nations, none of them a great power, was assembled within a few days. The first units of the United Nations Emergency Force (UNEF) were flown into Egypt on 15 November. As the Anglo-French and Israeli forces withdrew, the U.N. force moved in to act as a buffer. It occupied positions along the Israeli border and undertook the tasks of patrolling and preventing raids.

This force was not intended to take sides. It was neither designed nor equipped for fighting (except in self-defense). It was merely deployed to prevent incidents of renewed fighting while negotiations resolved the problems. It relied solely on its presence to produce a deterrent effect, and the outcome proved successful. The dispute was contained and the UNEF "was widely hailed for its beneficial properties."[9] Such actions came to be called *peacekeeping*.

The Aims of United Nations Peacekeeping

A survey of U.N. peacekeeping operations shows that no set formula governs the degrees of coercion or use of force. Peacekeeping can be completely noncoercive (with the set tasks limited to mediation, conciliation, and observation) or aggressively coercive (where armed troops are deployed). U.N. forces have been mandated to observe, investigate, and report (Kashmir, Lebanon, Yemen), aid in mediation (Greece), police a demarcation line (India/Pakistan, Iraq/Kuwait), patrol a demilitarized zone (Sinai), maintain law and order and normalize conditions (Cyprus, Somalia), secure peace and stability in one area (Congo), deliver humanitarian aid (Bosnia, Somalia), and effect a transfer of authority (West New Guinea, Namibia, Angola, Cambodia). In some operations U.N. troops have had no authority to threaten force to accomplish or frustrate an action and have worn only side arms, and those solely for use in individual self-defense (Middle East). At other times they have forcibly disarmed soldiers or irregulars while keeping military actions to very low levels (Cyprus). They have also engaged in sporadic military operations, usually in pacification efforts (Congo, Somalia), and have even undertaken full-scale military operations (Korea).[10]

Given political realities, until very recently, a Korean style operation could not have been envisaged[11] and the likelihood of a Congo-style action was also doubtful. Many commentators have charged that "no pure question of peacekeeping was involved in the Congo. Rightly or wrongly, a military movement for secession was put down by military means without any reference to the population involved, for purely political reasons."[12] The questions about the validity of the Congo action[13] and the ensuing financial and constitutional crisis when the Soviet Union and several other states refused to pay for the operation[14] almost ensured that such large scale coercive operations were unlikely until the Berlin Wall came down.[15] During the 1990s, since the improvement of superpower relations and the joint U.S./Soviet condemnation of Iraq after Iraq invaded Kuwait, this is no longer the case.

Still, what is now recognized as a peacekeeping force bears little resemblance to the international armies proposed over the centuries by the likes of king George Poděbrad of Bohemia in the mid-fifteenth century[16] and French king Henry IV one hundred and fifty years later in his *Grand Dessein*.[17] Peacekeeping forces have generally been far more modest in size and ambition, their functions usually more akin to those of police forces than those of the military. Some saw these forces merely as part of a "facesaving manoeuvre" to be used at the point in an unending war by proxy between the two superpowers when neither could afford to let its client be defeated or allow the conflict to escalate to the point that their own armed forces may have to intervene.[18]

Bidwell provides a restricted but more positive definition of peacekeeping forces than the one given above. Although he notes that the term *peacekeeping* is an ambitious description because "the presence of 'peacekeeping' forces has never *kept* the peace, for the simple reason that they have neither the authority nor the military ability to do any such thing," he adds that "their function is restorative. What they provide is a pacific, disinterested, impartial agency which, at the moment when the belligerents feel so disposed, or are under pressure from their sponsors, can separate the two sides, demarcate truce lines, arrange the exchange of prisoners of war and report infractions of . . . truce agreement[s]. They can exert a calming influence at the psychological moment when both sides are mentally and physically exhausted and only too ready to call a halt to combat."[19]

This description ascribes a very restricted role to peacekeeping forces; but Bidwell's portrayal appears reasonably accurate. He does, however, add that "these are very valuable functions in themselves."[20]

Although peacekeeping forces may be used as mobile "fire brigades," which could act quickly to prevent the spread of local conflicts and extinguish local eruptions with the use of force if necessary,[21] historically, they have been far more likely to occupy the position of guard forces or observation corps (which provide information to U.N. agencies about the observance of agreements).[22]

Peacekeeping, then, eschews force in what may be termed "consensual" exercises. The U.N. force becomes an impartial intermediary in local wars or tense situations that threaten stability in a way that hopefully will ensure an atmosphere conducive to constructive negotiations.[23] In theory this paves the way for diplomatic settlements that would be absent if the parties were either allowed to fight it out or a full-scale intervention on one side had resulted.[24] Further, the forces have no responsibility for settling the underlying problems; they merely provide a stable and moderating influence.[25] During the early 1990s, in Cambodia and to some degree in Somalia, U.N. peacekeepers have taken over the administration of complete countries affected by war. This move into peacebuilding is far beyond the original concept of traditional peacekeeping, and the experiences seem to suggest that U.N. peacekeepers may not be the most suitable group to undertake such tasks.[26]

The impartiality of a peacekeeping force means that it can be invited in by the disputants and can then undertake control services the parties would not trust each other with and would not accept from other outsiders who they did not consider equally impartial.[27]

Although peacekeepers may look like soldiers, they rarely fight because generally they have no foe to destroy or to defend themselves against.[28] The preferred tactics are moral pressure ("neither side to a dispute wants to shoot at the U.N. nor do the parties to a dispute wish to be charged with aggression," which would invariably happen if they did),[29] patience, persuasion, and compromise. Fabian notes that although there are good philosophical reasons for such a choice of action (the use of force that has recently been attempted rather unsuccessfully in Somalia makes peacekeepers collective enforcers who are neither impartial nor consensual), there are also strong practical arguments for such an approach, the main one being that "it plainly works best."[30] Brian Urquhart, the U.N. under general-secretary for Special Political Affairs, adds that the moment a peacekeeping force "descends into the arena of conflict or becomes a party to the conflict it is likely to be lost. The importance of a peacekeeping force does not lie in its numerical strength or military capacity. It lies in the international political will which it represents and in the capacity of its members to conduct a 24 hour-a-day exercise in conciliation and de-escalation. A peacekeeping force should never get into the position of regarding any party as an enemy."[31] Fabian continues the argument for the nonuse of weapons (except in self-defense) by pointing out that such restrictions "are logical, inescapable corollaries to impartiality and consent, because above a certain point in the scale of coercion, a point that moves with circumstances, the parties will no longer cooperate voluntarily. The intermediary will then have changed from collaborator to adversary."[32]

When quoting a senior U.N. officer, he presents a further argument against a greater ability to use force: it would be counterproductive because the peacekeeping contingent may be "pressed by each disputing party to use force against the other." This situation could lead to a U.N. force being maneuvered to act, or be seen to be acting, on behalf of one of the parties.[33] In this way the U.N. Protection Force established in 1992 in the former Yugoslavian republic of Bosnia was severely frustrated in its operations.

Problems with the United Nations Peacekeeping Model

Since the days of the UNEF, at least one U.N. force generally has been on duty somewhere in the world and some five hundred thousand soldiers, from the armies of fifty-eight separate nations, have had experience with peacekeeping. The U.N. model, as it has evolved, however, is still beset by many problems, unresolved contradictions, and doubts about its effectiveness and, among some thinkers, even about its desirability.

There are fundamental problems with the ad hoc assembling of a force from disparate sources. Although U.N. troops come from various countries, there is always the possibility that they could be controlled, at least to some degree, from their home states (or, perhaps, pulled out of a U.N. action at a crucial and/or propaganda-rich time). What would happen if U.N. troops went into action against friends and neighbors of some of the units that comprise the force? Does it matter if some nations are willing to commit troops to certain tension spots but not to others?[34] And the problems of political control can also come from the other side. It is up to the host state to accept or reject the force (as Egypt did in 1967, leading to a fresh outbreak of hostilities), but should it have any say about the composition of the force sent, where it will be stationed, what duties it will perform and when it will be withdrawn? Further, what if the host state is not recognized by the United Nations?[35]

At the most basic level problems with internationally composed forces can include the feeding (various contingents can represent radically different eating habits), equipping (different contingents may have different vehicles, causing problems supplying spare parts, or equatorial troops may be called into action in cold mountain regions),[36] and paying of forces (Swedish soldiers can be paid ten times the amount of Indian soldiers and such differences in pay scales can lead to morale problems).[37]

Problems are also present at a far more fundamental level. After a survey to determine how U.N. peacekeepers see themselves, Galtung concluded that the role is one of *keeping* the peace, not of making or building it.[38] The *Peacekeeper's Handbook* points out that

> it is important to recognize that international control of conflict em-
> braces a wider horizon than the purely military aspect; for it is not
> simply a military responsibility but a combined operation encom-
> passing all the agencies that have a contribution to make to the peaceful
> containment and ultimate settlement of a conflict, the reestablishment
> of stability, and the rehabilitation of community life. When therefore
> one is considering peacekeeping, it is necessary to consider the parallel
> dimensions of peacemaking (negotiation and mediation) and peace-
> building (social change through socio-economic development, rehabili-
> tation and reconstruction); for together they comprise the three
> dimensions of peace construction and as such are interrelated.[39]

Despite relatively long tours of duty, Galtung's survey of Norwegian U.N. peacekeepers revealed that they rarely if ever made friends with the local population or mixed with them except when requiring a service, as from merchants or servants,[40] and that their dislike of the local population greatly increased during their stay.[41] Galtung concluded that "the closer one comes to a conflict scene, the more difficult it is to maintain any kind of 'balanced attitude' to the sides the forces were keeping at peace."[42]

Galtung points to a dilemma: "On the one hand there is a relatively clear minimum role definition in terms of guard and observation duty, keeping the parties apart with a very modest display of arms, showing behavior rather than attitude. On the other hand there is another type of role: being involved, being a part and party to the entire conflict system, showing attitude as well as behavior, but trying to mediate and trying to help build a new social structure encompassing the antagonists. The former role," he concludes, "is possible but not very effective, the second is very effective, but not very possible."[43]

The solution would be "to build into the role peacemaking and peace-building components."[44] For this to occur specialist peacekeeping training courses would have to be established. Such courses could also overcome other problems: for example, the difficulty professional fighters have when suddenly expected to become peacemakers, to suppress their combative instincts. Indarjit Rikhye, military attache to U.N. Secretaries-General Hammarskjöld and Thant and later chair of the International Peace Academy, adds that the possibility of success of even the basic task of "putting out brush-fire conflicts" (peacekeeping) is increased "if the firemen are already trained, equipped and prepared."[45]

The point, however, is that even these things will be unlikely to occur in the near future. When sovereign states are so reluctant to earmark troops of their own armies to train in the techniques that would make them the best possible U.N. peacekeepers, they will scarcely agree to their troops being trained by a central authority. Some, like Salstrom and Waskow, have proposed setting up a peacemakers academy, which, when it has proved its usefulness, could be co-opted by the United Nations.[46] This proposition has almost as little chance of coming to fruition as have the proposals by Grønning and others for individually recruited U.N. soldiers who would have U.N. citizenship and carry U.N. passports.[47] Without vast shifts in political will these problems will remain.

Difficulties with the concept of peacekeeping go beyond even these political and logistical questions to politico-philosophical issues that question the validity of the peacekeeping idea itself. The very act of suppressing violence, it has been argued, can have negative consequences. Peacekeeping without peacemaking and peacebuilding "may generate even more unmanageable conflicts later on."[48] Wars have occurred between India and Pakistan over Kashmir and in Palestine between Egypt and Israel even though U.N. forces had kept the peace there previously. As Bloomfield notes, it has been suggested that "perhaps the fighting had been stopped prematurely."[49] Although this argument may be defeatist or may smack of cynicism, there is probably a great deal of truth to the argument that peacekeeping can be a mere "band-aid" measure or a device that perpetuates inequalities and structural violence,[50] that it is a palliative rather than a cure. Yet Fabian asks whether peacebuilding by an outside force is possible and whether disputants' ends as well as their means can be adjusted. And then, what will be the measures of success?[51]

Galtung, again tackling some of these more difficult issues, explains that in normal peacekeeping operations time is gained—time that could be used for peacebuilding and peacemaking. Why this is so difficult to do and why it is rarely successful when it is attempted is not only because the Blue Berets are not trained in peacebuilding techniques but also because conflicts themselves can be fundamentally so different.

Galtung maintains that a good case can be made for peacekeeping in *horizontal* conflicts, that is, conflicts between equals in which there is no element of dominance, in which the conflict is over goals rather than interests. In such cases peacekeeping cannot, either by design or by chance, become the means of maintaining a structure of dominance. It remains truly a third-party effort. The problem, however, is that only a fraction of violent disputes are horizontal. If a peacekeeping force intervenes and freezes the status quo in a *vertical* conflict, one in which dominated groups are trying to free themselves of dominance that dominating groups are trying to maintain, then, wanting it or not, "it is simply a party to the conflict, siding objectively with the side most interested in preserving the status quo."[52]

Preventative peacemaking faces similar problems. If requests for U.N. intervention depend on requests from sovereign governments, they are unlikely to be made in cases in which the underlying issue relates to a popular revolt against that government. Questions of who decides what preventative or conciliatory measures should be taken, and, further, when and where they should be taken have not been addressed.[53]

Until very recently international peacekeeping has had a rather limited role. It could not be used in internal situations (because, the recent shift to a more assertive system of peace enforcement notwithstanding, these are precluded by the doctrine of nonintervention) and, generally, in regional wars the region has near monopoly on peacekeeping inside its domain of jurisdiction. And there is still one other filter. According to Galtung, international peacekeeping "is intended for the weak not for the strong." This is not merely because the United Nations itself is weak but because the use of peacekeeping forces in disputes between big powers would mean that "the big powers would no longer be big." He concludes that "the target of peacekeeping is reduced to wars between periphery nations from different regions."[54]

Where a horizontal conflict exists, a symmetric relationship can be maintained with the disputing parties, and the impartial third party, the peacekeeping force, can add *peacemaking* to its *peacekeeping* function. In this way the time that is gained by "keeping the lid on" a conflict can usefully be employed to ensure the possibility of a more lasting peace. Even with this Galtung sees the possible danger in taking the conflict out of the hands of the actors themselves, and this may be "alienating and impoverishing."[55] Even when peacemaking efforts are seemingly successful, they may not hold in the long term; new actors may not feel bound by the decisions of the old, and the structural forces that support the system may not have been built.[56] Galtung concludes, therefore, that deeper-lying factors in the relations between the parties must be tackled to arrive at ideas about how a self-supporting conflict resolution could be achieved. In other words, what is necessary is *peacebuilding*.[57] And this is way beyond the scope of any force that can be envisaged going into action wearing the blue berets of the United Nations in the foreseeable future.[58] It may, however, conceivably be undertaken by a more independent organization with a different philosophy governing its operations.

Conclusion

Since the end of the cold war, deployments of U.N. peacekeeping forces have greatly increased around the globe[59] as have experiments with far larger, more complex, and more lethal versions of peacekeeping. Although the U.N. peacekeeping model has been the product of historical forces, those forces are rapidly disappearing, and any consideration of the future role of peacekeepers must be considered in light of the new emerging world order and not merely through past U.N. peacekeeping experiences. Even the argument that, at least in the foreseeable future, nonearmarked troops will continue to be called together from disparate small nations to undertake peacekeeping operations in the name of the United Nations may no longer be the case. And any consideration of future peacekeeping operations must take the thaw (and possible overt friendliness) in superpower relations into consideration.

Because of costs and the other issues discussed above, the prospects for a standing U.N. army are still very small (and so the philosophical implications of such a development need not be discussed here); however, united Security Council operations of the type that saw action in Korea are again being entertained. The unanimous Security Council decision to blockade Iraq in 1990, after its invasion of neighboring Kuwait, seems to have been the start of a new enforcement role for the council. During 1992, without the request from a specific host country, United Nations troops were deployed in Somalia and in the former Yugoslavia. And, increasingly, the deployment of Article 43 troops (that is those drawn from the permanent Security Council members rather than exclusively from small powers)[60] is becoming a reality. Although this development may mean a far stronger emphasis on peacekeeping and nonconsensual peace enforcement within the United Nations, any such move may also be symptomatic of a confusion in assumptions about the nature of conflicts that should be reevaluated.

Burton claims that the thinking behind the U.N. Charter reflected a fictitious domestic model in which disputes are handled by a central authority that has a monopoly of power and in which domestic conflicts do not exist. The flaw in this analysis, he claims, is that conflicts, whether domestic or international, that are about "ontological needs of identity and recognition, and associated human developmental needs" rather than negotiable interests,[61] and are therefore not open to compromise, are quite distinct from disputes. Although peacekeeping forces can end disputes, they cannot contain or suppress conflicts while basic human needs remain unsatisfied.[62] The rapidly changing face of global politics may have eliminated factors that previously determined the scope of peacekeeping and now provides the opportunity to experiment with new techniques of achieving peace, and a realization that different processes are required for the resolution of conflicts than for the mere settlement of disputes, that is, for peacebuilding, makes the task critical.

In a study "on the perspectives for the future uses of the armed forces in the 1990's," Brigadier Michael Harbottle notes that involvement in paramilitary actions such as peacekeeping and disaster relief is viewed by the military as "temporary deviations from the norm and an interruption of their primary function to train for war."[63] With East/West confrontation at an end, the role of the military, he believes, needs reorientation. He suggests that military thinking and doctrine must change, that "proper soldiering" should encompass the prevention of conflict by assisting in "the *peaceful* settlement of disputes, and preempting the manifestation of conflict violence by contributing to the resolution of the structural causes of violence."[64] Echoing some of the concerns of analysts of mainstream peacekeeping, Harbottle points out that the qualities a peacekeeper needs (patience, restraint, advocacy skills, approachability, tact, fairness, persuasiveness, a broad perspective of the situation, impartiality, flexibility, and humor) are not traditionally part of a soldier's makeup.[65] Repeating Galtung's observations, he also notes that soldiers are generally alienated from civilians. By establishing peacekeeping forces composed of a combination of professional soldiers (who are well trained and disciplined) and conscript/reservists who are really civilians in uniform, the peacekeepers can better relate to the community in which they are stationed.[66] Without explaining how soldiers can undertake peacebuilding work, his evaluation begs an important question: Should this type of activity be left to soldiers at all?

Although prospects for the originally envisaged U.N. peacekeeping forces seem to be improving, this is, perhaps, fortuitous, and, in any case, that model is just as unsuitable for effective conflict resolution as the one generally still employed. The need to devise methods of peacemaking and peacebuilding continue. Past and, indeed, continuing experiments in this area may provide the key or, at least, valuable pointers to possible directions that this process may take.

There has been a long, yet little-recognized, parallel history of unarmed attempts that goes beyond narrowly defined peacekeeping. The alternative model, the one that I examine in this book, has strong roots in the philosophy of Mahatma Gandhi and promises a method of peacekeeping that aims at long-term solutions to the problems of violence by taking the task of peacebuilding seriously.

2

Unarmed Peacekeeping

In his introduction to the the *Peacekeeper's Handbook,* Harbottle notes that although some forms of military intervention may stabilize a conflict to the degree that other agencies are provided with an increased opportunity to deal with the political and socioeconomic formations that were the root cause of the discord, international peacekeeping, without resort to the use of force or enforcement measures, is, nevertheless, theoretically possible. He continues by pointing out that "there are those, military practitioners and peace theorists among them, who believe that force has to be met by force; that in certain circumstances enforcement can prove an effective purgative and as such is good for the system. However, it is a fact that, taken in the context of both interstate and intrastate conflict, force and enforcement tend to extend and prolong a conflict rather than reduce it; and that military counter measures in an internal security situation can stiffen rather than lessen resistance."[1]

As Bidwell, a reviewer of the *Handbook,* correctly notes, "It begins with a perfunctory genuflection in the general direction of the non-violent theory of peacekeeping, but such airy stuff is dismissed by page 2: thereafter it is pragmatic and practical."[2] Thus, when discussing "interposition" (the "physical act of placing a 'buffer' force between two opposing armed forces in order to prevent an outbreak or renewed fighting among those forces")[3] in the *Peacekeeper's Handbook,* Harbottle points out that "the self-defence principle of the use of force applies very directly to the peacekeeper." In such situations "he places himself in the direct line of advance and line of fire of one side or the other, or both. For the interposition to be credible, the principle permitting the use of force in self-defence and the defence of one's position has to be firmly recognised by those who might attempt to attack or pass through the position held by the peacekeeping force.

11

Without such a credibility, the interposition would be non-viable and non-effective."[4]

Although the *Peacekeeper's Handbook* is about settling disputes peacefully, it was written by military men with military experience for other military personnel. Despite his long-standing support for various unarmed peacekeeping attempts, Michael Harbottle, the editor and person apparently responsible for most of the writing, was chief of staff of the United Nations Forces in Cyprus (UNICYP) from 1966 to 1968. This line of reasoning is, therefore, understandable and, given the presumable brief of the editor, probably inevitable. There has, nevertheless, also been some debate from the inside about whether peacekeeping forces should be armed. Gilpin, former deputy chief of Civilian Operations in the Congo, while wanting to recommend an unarmed U.N. peacekeeping force, eventually echoes Harbottle's feelings and can only bring himself to support a lightly armed force trained in nonviolence techniques. He believes that occasionally the backup provided by weapons exercises a restraining influence on armed groups and can give necessary confidence to the peacekeeping force itself which, while not actually carrying weapons, would know that it has them in reserve should the situation demand their use.[5] Even the effectiveness of such a force "must depend on the *will* of the opposing factions to stop fighting and to seek an acceptable, peaceful solution to their quarrel." Where this does not exist Gilpin, too, becomes pragmatic: in these situations "an international force would have to *enforce* peace; in that case it would have to be greatly superior militarily to the warring parties and be ready to fight, not necessarily 'in the last resort.' "[6]

Most writers in this area, when not calling for a world army, accept the arming of peacekeeping forces as a matter of pure logic. Some, like Gilpin, have tried to have it both ways. Others have come up with novel suggestions by recommending that international police forces be armed with the technological ability to engage in nonlethal violence. Nunn, for example, contends that although warring parties such as Arabs and Jews may reject methods of fighting that do not hurt the opponent, "it seems incredible that United Nations forces should ever consider using any other type of weapons."[7] This approach would provide goodwill from the peoples of the world and considerable military advantages. Further, it would overcome the problems faced by trained U.N. soldiers who have to act as police and who cannot fight until attacked. The use of weapons such as nonlethal chemical agents would, in other words, not only preserve life but would also remove the tactical military disadvantages under which U.N. forces have traditionally operated.

The voices for a completely unarmed peacekeeping force, however, have also been heard regularly throughout the twentieth century. Pacifists who believed in a world government could scarcely have done otherwise but call for such a force if they wished to maintain consistency.[8] But there were practical reasons also. Charles Walker, the Quaker advocate of a World Peace Guard, suggests that the military may not be the best instrument for securing peace.[9] He criticizes the proposals of some military veterans of U.N. missions who have been pushing the concept of a military agency that includes peacemaking and peacebuilding functions.[10] A peace force that has been engaged in military operations will find it difficult to talk to the party it has been shooting at (and this became painfully obvious during 1993 in Somalia). If violence is used, then a peacekeeping force may in critical situations "become a paramilitary force with aspects of an occupying army" in which case community relations programs, even those attempted by dedicated officers, cannot hope to overcome or mitigate the community's hostility.[11] Perhaps, as Walker notes, it is an inevitable consequence that "the effect of a military force will be estimated in military terms."[12] And finally, following a survey of peacekeeping possibilities in a world not yet disarmed or disarming to any significant degree, he concludes that "peacekeeping missions by military forces are likely to serve primarily the interests of the superpowers; and threaten to isolate, exploit or dominate smaller and weaker nations, particularly in the Third World."[13] Walker and other advocates of the unarmed alternative see these problems as inherent in military forces, especially those under the control of a supranational authority where the superpowers dominate and have rights of veto.

The alternatives to the mainstream style of peacekeeping are not merely theoretical; there have been many attempts to think through a nonviolent and unarmed approach, and several examples have been attempted in practice.

Early Attempts

During the sixteenth and seventeenth centuries the spread of religious wars in Europe and the establishment of standing national armies were accompanied by the rise of pacifist sects. Practical examples of what may be called peacekeeping forces (or more accurately, peace emissaries) were abundant in Quaker dealings with the Indian population in the American Colonies.[14] Although peace missions were undertaken by John Easton,[15] Caleb Pussey,[16] and John Woolman,[17] as with the mainstream idea of peacekeeping, the history of nonviolent, unarmed peacekeeping forces only really commenced in the twentieth century.

In 1910, with the publication of psychologist-philosopher William James's influential article, "The Moral Equivalent of War," a new era in the development of unarmed peacekeeping forces was born. The work was given wide publicity by pacifists, and, although it did not lead directly to the formation of peace brigades, it encouraged the development of voluntary peace-camp movements that undertook peacebuilding activities.

Pierre Ceresole, the Swiss Christian pacifist and first secretary of the

International Fellowship of Reconciliation, for example, was inspired by James's writings and so shocked by the destruction of the Great War that he set up the International Civilian Service (Service Civil International). This independent organization aimed to bring about the replacement of national military service by an international civilian service. Ceresole sought to organize volunteers from around the world, including those from previously warring countries, to work in constructive projects (such as rebuilding Swiss villages destroyed by avalanches or working with Gandhi to rebuild villages in India after the Bihar earthquake of 1934) and the service is now credited as the first example of the pick-and-shovel peace-building projects that would later supersede the notion of peaceful buffer armies as the most practical efforts to help build a more peaceful world.[18]

By the early 1930s American political analyst Walter Lippman had brought the debate back to the fundamental issue of peacekeeping with his essay "The Political Equivalent of War," and Gandhi had demonstrated the value of nonviolent action in the Indian Civil Disobedience movement after his celebrated breaking of the iniquitous salt laws and had talked in Europe about nonviolent defense in the face of invading armies.[19] These forces came together and produced the first and, although unsuccessful, most celebrated example of an unarmed peacekeeping force—Maude Royden's Peace Army.

On 25 February 1932, a now famous letter by Royden (a former suffragist worker for the cause of peace, one of England's first women pastors, and a friend of Gandhi) and her co-signatories, the Reverend H. R. L. Sheppard (a well-known Anglican vicar, church reformer, and, during the last ten years of his life, pacifist and peace activist) and Herbert Gray (a Scottish minister), appeared in the London *Daily Express,* calling for volunteers for a pacifist army that would throw itself between the warring Chinese and Japanese forces in the city of Shanghai.[20]

The force was offered to an unresponsive League of Nations, and eventually the cessation of hostilities in China made it redundant. Although attempts were made over the next eight or so years to resurrect the Peace Army (in slightly less-ambitious incarnations), the idea eventually faded into oblivion.

Pacifist concerns in Britain shifted from the prevention and ending of wars by the interposition of a peaceful buffer force to focus on the Peace Pledge Union organized in 1934 by Sheppard. The union's sponsors included Royden and Bertrand Russell, and its first secretary was the Christian mystic Max Plowman. At its height in 1937, almost 150,000 union members had signed the pledge that stated, "We renounce war and never again will we support or sanction another."[21] Thus, the pacifist movement entered a reactive phase of opposition, and finally, with the rise of Hitler and with a growing suspicion that although Gandhi's methods might be workable against the British, perhaps all nations would not behave like the British, the idea of large-scale nonviolent armies gradually disappeared.

The World Peace Brigade

After the war, a World Pacifist Meeting held in India tentatively suggested the setting up of international "satyagraha units," but it was again the British who publicly resurrected the call for peace armies.[22] With the growing tension in the Middle East, British M. P. Henry Usborne wrote to the *Manchester Guardian* urging that the United Nations recruit a volunteer corps of ten thousand unarmed people to patrol and hold a two kilometer-wide demilitarized zone close to the Egyptian/Israeli border. Usborne suggested that this "peace force" should be "equipped only for passive resistance and designed to ensure that the present border is not violated by force. Its tactics would be essentially those of satyagraha."[23]

Nothing came of the proposal, and a few months later, with the formation of the UNEF, much of the thinking of U.N. protagonists and international dispute settlement theorists turned to the exploration of the possibilities opened by this first major step in practical peacekeeping.

While military strategist Commander Sir Stephen King-Hall was calling, on military grounds, for unilateral nuclear disarmament and the introduction of a system of nonviolent civilian defense for the country,[24] the traditional calls for nonviolent buffer forces, however, managed to continue in Britain.[25]

In 1958 former M.P. Sir Richard Acland reiterated the proposal that Britain discard nuclear weapons and further suggested that the country take the initiative in setting up a world police force that would eventually be adopted by the United Nations. The force, in Acland's proposal, was to be international, consisting of five thousand to fifteen thousand members who could be recruited covertly where national restrictions made such action necessary.[26] It was envisaged that an unarmed component of the force would parachute into trouble spots "without anyone's permission or request. It will be in effect a 'U.N. Observer Corps' with at least four advantages over anything the world has seen as yet. It will be always in instant well-trained readiness; it will be sufficiently numerous to do a thorough job; it will be equipped for mobility and self-maintenance anywhere; lastly (and most important . . .) it will not be under anyone's veto."[27]

The next year the Reverend Ralph Bell advocated an approach to war that he saw as an alternative to the pacifist (do nothing because an agreed practical policy is lacking) position and the militarist (want to fight) position. He called this approach the "Active Non-Violent Resistance Army." The way to build this army, he thought, was to do it gradually by organizing "small groups of pioneers" in active nonviolent resistance until the numbers were such that "a national or international convention might be called to work out the policy which is right and possible with the number of recruits available, and to appoint the leaders of the movement, to whom the members will give their obedience."[28] Bell's central thesis was that merely to say "no" to war was not enough; what was required was an alternative positive approach.[29]

The new experiences with and writings on peacekeeping, coupled with the historical readiness for the emergence of an alternative system of dealing with international conflict—Bell's alternative method to which people could say "yes"—began to yield results.

A model was already in operation. In India the Shanti Sena, or "Peace Army," founded by Gandhi's spiritual heir, Vinoba Bhave, had been active since 1957. The Sena specifically included peacemaking and peacebuilding functions as being of equal importance to the third-party intervention role that had been the main focus of the peacekeeping idea until then. In the West, action committees and antibomb campaigns arose in 1957. In the next few years the growth of nonviolent action moved into the international sphere: for example, in 1958 the voyage of Quaker Albert Bigelow's ship *The Golden Rule* into the U.S. Pacific hydrogen bomb testing areas,[30] in 1959 the Sahara Project, organized by peace groups to protest French nuclear weapons testing,[31] various large European peace marches, and the 1960–61 San Francisco-Moscow Walk for Peace.[32]

Although all these actions were ad hoc, eventually the strands led to the formation of an international nongovernmental organization that would focus, again ad hoc, on "nonviolent intervention on the world scene by way of actions that could 'make a difference', in turn helping to build a world movement based on nonviolence as a political force."[33]

In 1960 Spanish writer, pacifist, former champion of the League of Nations and political critic, Salvador de Madariaga, and Vinoba Bhave's chief lieutenant and former Socialist Party of India leader, Jayaprakash Narayan, wrote to Dag Hammarskjöld to propose setting up a Peace Guard organization.[34] Although they received no reply,[35] the suggestion was later published and again, although largely overlooked (and completely overlooked by the United Nations), rekindled concrete moves to establish an unarmed peacekeeping force.

The Madariaga/Narayan proposal called for the formation of an unarmed international police force that would be an alternative to armed U.N. forces. They argued that, in a world "split into various political camps," such forces operate in a way that "the objectives, prejudices or policy of those who have succeeded in putting the UN machinery in motion will be clearly discerned"[36] and, consequently, conflicts complicated.

The authors of the proposal believed that "the presence of a body of regular 'White Guards' or 'Peace Guards' intervening, with no weapons whatsoever, between two forces in combat or about to fight might have considerable effect. They would not be there as a fanciful improvisation, but as the positive and practical application of a previously negotiated and ratified Charter binding all United Nations members. The Charter should ensure: 1. Inviolability of the White Guards. 2. Their right to go anywhere at any time from the day they are given an assignment by the United Nations. 3. Their right to intervene in any conflict of any nature when asked by one of the parties thereto or by the Secretary-General."[37]

These guards were to be parachutists who "should be able to stop advancing armies by refusing to move from roads, railways or airfields. They would be empowered to act in any capacity their chiefs might think adequate for the situation, though they would never use force. They should be endowed with a complete system for recording and transmitting facts, such as television cameras and broadcasting material."[38]

As could be expected, given the fate of Howard Brinton's overlooked 1932 plan for a peace army[39] and Royden's attempt to set one up, nothing came of the proposal. Hammarskjöld's understanding of the realpolitik of the United Nations precluded him from entertaining the idea of such a force, so the inheritance of this line of peacekeeping came to rest with the nongovernmental world pacifist community. The various strands started coming together at the Triennial Conference of the War Resisters' International (WRI) at Gandhigram, India, in December 1960.[40] Radical pacifists from the United States and from Europe, peace organizations from Europe, Africa, and the United States and the Shanti Sena[41] combined "to set up the machinery necessary for initiating a founding conference for a world peace brigade,"[42] after the initial proposal put forward by Narayan.[43]

The founding conference was held in the town of Brummana, on the outskirts of Beirut in Lebanon, immediately after Christmas 1961. Fifty-five delegates "from all major non-aligned groups and constructive program agencies,"[44] representing thirteen countries, gathered to "establish a World Peace Brigade for Nonviolent Action [WPB], and to plan its initial projects."[45]

Proposals concerning the work to be undertaken by the Brigade started to emerge before the conference convened. JP saw the WPB reflecting the Indian Shanti Sena's work of providing a nonviolent alternative to the police force as well as a nonviolent alternative to the army. He saw the long-term value of such a force as more than it could actually achieve by immediate peacekeeping. For JP the changes in ways of thinking that it could initiate were of equal importance: "The only existing agency for maintaining world peace, the United Nations, is employing nothing but armed forces to achieve peace; and no one sees any contradiction in that. The very idea that it is possible to achieve peace through a non-violent force is absent from the minds of both the peoples and their governments.

The emergence of a World Peace Brigade would give that idea a concrete form. That might become a landmark in the world's quest for peace."[46]

An Indian "Preparatory Conference on the World Peace Brigade," held in Varanasi on October 31 and November 1, concluded that the WPB should not undertake purely relief or service projects such as "sending trained volunteers for work in developing countries,"[47] and War Resisters' International Secretary, Arlo Tatum, stated that the WPB "must become specific if it is to exist in the world"; that already at the founding conference they had to put up "concrete proposals if only for rejection and substitution." He suggested that the international functions of the Brigade should include border patrols in trouble areas, the offer of volunteers to any nation prepared to disarm, the inspection and control of disarmament agreements, fact-finding missions, and development of an information network so that preemptive measures could be taken before crisis situations develop.[48]

At the conference itself participants realized a need to emphasize a program that satisfied the strong feelings of both the cold war actionists and the constructive programmists.[49] It was consequently decided that two projects should be planned: one concerning national liberation in Africa and the other against preparation for war by the superpowers.[50] Some of the fifty-five delegates were concerned lest the actions of the Brigade be negative, shallow, or all protest. The importance of reconciliation and service were stressed.[51] Although by the end of the five-day meeting neither of the initial projects had taken final form,[52] a statement of principles was issued on New Year's Day 1962. Those principles stated that "The World Peace Brigade is constituted to band together those who respond to this call and seek to bring the liberating and transforming power of non-violence to bear more effectively on our world."[53] Besides organizing the Brigade for anti-cold war action, the conference set forth as one of its aims the revolutionizing of "the concept of revolution itself by infusing into the method of resisting injustice the qualities which insure the preservation of human life and dignity and to create the conditions necessary for peace."[54] The idea was to form a disciplined core of people, from many countries, who had already proved themselves in local actions (to discourage the recruitment of those simply seeking adventure),[55] who could be brought together in numbers sufficient to be effective "in situations of potential or actual conflict, internal and international."[56]

The Brigade was constituted in three regions under joint chairpersons Jayaprakash Narayan (Asia), the veteran U.S. peace movement leader A. J. Muste (America), and Scottish clergyman and leader of Britain's antinuclear weapons Committee of 100 Michael Scott (Europe). The regions were to recruit from within their areas "persons experienced in non-violent direct action." Some of these volunteers were to "make up the Emergency Force, ready to drop their affairs and go anywhere in the world on 24 hours' notice. Others held themselves in a Ready Reserve, committed to consider any action call. All Brigade volunteers will undergo training in local units or in the regional training centre."[57]

According to an insider, Indian Shanti Sainik (and later secretary of WRI) Devi Prasad, however, the structural foundations and preparations for the Brigade were not adequately put into place at the beginning.[58] It attempted to operate before it was ready. In its few years of existence the WPB only managed to conduct three projects—the proposed Northern Rhodesia March, the *Everyman III* voyage, and the Delhi to Peking Friendship March—none of them particularly successful.

After the Beirut conference an Indian delegate of the WPB traveled in eastern and central Africa to decide the work of the Brigade and to offer its services to African leaders to help them "keep the pace of revolution going and to keep that revolution non-violent."[59]

At this time a political crisis was brewing in the region with Zambia (Northern Rhodesia) demanding national independence from the white-dominated Federation of Rhodesia and Nyasaland. Prime Minister Sir Roy Welensky was equally adamant in his desire to maintain the status quo. Kenneth Kaunda, leader of the multiracial Zambian United National Independence Party and then still a firm advocate of nonviolence, was planning a general strike because of Britain's lack of action on promised elections for majority rule in Zambia.

The WPB had, meanwhile, established a training centre in Dar es Salaam, Tanganyika, from which they offered to mobilize thousands of marchers, mainly Africans but also others from around the world, in an international Freedom March that would cross the Tanganyikan border into Northern Rhodesia in the face of Federal Rhodesian troops if progress on the independence question was not made.[60]

The aim of the march was many-faceted. It was to dramatize the Zambian political situation to the world, to provide a useful example of the value of nonviolent direct action to militant Africans who were increasingly embracing violence to achieve their desired goals, and to undertake such constructive projects as organizing house construction and sanitation teams to work in the border areas devastated by units under the control of the federal government and to maintain essential services during the threatened general strike.

There was possibly also another aim. The international contingent was to be made up of teams of three people, one of whom was to be a well-known personality if possible, from ten countries. With such volunteers the WPB could not only show the seriousness of the action and generate immediate publicity but also "demonstrate the capacity of the WPB to mobilize volunteers."[61]

The two-pronged plan of the strike and march was never carried out.[62] The massive boycott of the federal elections left Welensky with a hollow victory when only 10 percent of the electorate voted for his party. With Welensky's bargaining power vis à vis London weakened and with the prospect of the involvement in the march of a number of government figures from semicolonial and Commonwealth nations and a prolonged strike, Britain proposed new constitutional provisions that Kaunda accepted.[63]

Here was a success of sorts for the WPB. The impact of the threatened march on the politically favorable outcome for Zambia is widely recognised;[64] however, as Olson notes, to some even this success was something of a failure because the march had not been held and nonviolence had not been demonstrated.[65] Prasad further adds that in any case it would not have been possible to carry out the planned march, citing as evidence the joke about the Brigade that labeled it an "army of generals and not an army of soldiers."[66] A later planned march into South West Africa (Namibia) did not get beyond the discussion stage.[67]

The pressure of other priorities and the shortage of resources[68] meant that after the solution of the Zambian crisis the Brigade faded out of Africa. The Dar es Salaam centre "quietly expired," and the post of teacher of nonviolence in Tanganyika was left unfilled. Perhaps worst of all, although the Brigade was able to influence the pan-African freedom movements of East and Central Africa behind the scenes during its conference, which closely followed the Beirut World Peace Brigade Conference, by the following Pan-African conference there were "no effective voices opposing essentially military solutions for the Portuguese South African problems."[69]

Anton Nelson, an East Africa delegate at the founding conference of the WPB and fund raiser for the Africa action, stated that the WPB action did not achieve the claims made for it and that, in fact, the claims were dishonest because in reality very little was actually done. He claimed that it should be admitted that the project "was an expensive experiment— or failure."[70]

Further, Theodore Olson, the administrative secretary of the North American Regional Council of the WPB at the time, was forced to conclude that "on balance the African experience was a failure. It raised initially high expectations, but was unable to follow through or to adapt to new circumstances. It proved unwilling to make the hard choices that could have put the right people in the right place. Worst of all, it confirmed the African suspicion that non-violence was mainly talk and that in the hard realities of political action, non-violence was largely irrelevant."[71] Prasad added that with the proposed march into Northern Rhodesia the WPB was out of its depth. "It was sheer good luck for the organisers," he claimed, "that the project had to be given up, otherwise it would have proved the greatest flop in the modern history of non-violence."[72]

The other projects were perhaps even less successful. The *Everyman* voyages of 1962 protested against the arms race and nuclear weapons by sailing into the United States Pacific test zones. The first ship, *Everyman I,* was kept in port with a restraining order and the crew was put on trial. *Everyman II* made it to the test area at Johnson Island, but again the crew was arrested. A few days later a new crew took *Everyman I* toward the Christmas Island test zone but were again arrested and tried.[73]

Everyman III was to be centered on the Soviet Union as the Brigade's counterpart of the United States-focused *Everyman I* and *II* projects and as a follow-up to the San Francisco to Moscow peace march. The ship was to sail from London to Leningrad "to speak directly to the people of the Soviet Union and personally hand out . . . 50,000 leaflets printed in Russian."[74] If permission was obtained, the sailing trip was to continue to Moscow by canal and the protesters were to spend four to six weeks in the Soviet Union to "challenge the Soviet people themselves to protest against nuclear weapons testing by all nations including their own."[75] If entry was forbidden, the crew planned to enter the U.S.S.R. "illegally but non-violently."[76]

After the ship arrived in Leningrad on 19 October, the crew was kept waiting for three days and finally, on the day the Cuban missile crisis broke, they were refused permission to go ashore.[77] When they were threatened with being towed out to sea, the crew tried to jump ashore but were restrained by guards. As towing commenced, an attempt was made to scuttle the boat and three crew members tried to swim ashore. They were prevented from doing so by the authorities. The ship was repaired and towed from port to port for eight days until it was towed out into international waters on the day that the Cuban crisis was resolved.[78]

The *Everyman III* voyage was to be supplemented by a WPB–organized goodwill project that aimed to bring Polish and Russian "rank and file workers" to America so that they could present their point of view in the United States and to "meet the public challenge of American audiences as our S.F. to Moscow Peace Walkers met the challenge of Poles and Russians over there last year."[79] Nothing came of this proposed exchange.

Olson notes that the "fuzzy symbolism of the vessel's name . . . was . . . representative of the unclear thinking in WPB" in its involvement "in a rather standard pacifist anti-nuclear protest voyage."[80] Even Walker, a founding member of the WPB, had to admit that instead of "putting the European Council in business" the project, which resulted in heated dispute, "left bitter memories and after-effects."[81]

The Brigade, according to Olson, was losing its vision of being a world force.[82] Prasad added that the *Everyman III* project was undertaken before the Brigade had organized its leadership, an effective mailing list for people interested in becoming members, or even a proper office. Instead of properly establishing the foundations of a functioning World Peace Brigade, Prasad charged, all efforts went into the less than exceptional *Everyman* project.[83] Olson was even more damning. In the United States recruiting literature went out, but respondents were put off with vague notices about future processing and notification. The group seemed content to perpetuate the committee/constituency pattern of United States direct action rather than to take seriously the opportunity to become what had been envisaged at Beirut.[84]

The third and final action of the WPB occurred largely by default. After the Sino-Indian border clash of October 1962, Jayaprakash Narayan wanted to lead a band of Shanti Sainiks personally into the battle area "to offer non-violent resistance to the aggressor and to intervene and appeal, to both sides to stop the fighting."[85] This plan brought out serious divisions and led to heated arguments in the till then seemingly united Gandhian movement in India. Vinoba Bhave appeared to many to be supporting the official "patriotic" view of the war by pushing for energies to be put into "a narrowly-conceived constructive programme."[86]

This less than unequivocal opposition to the war policies of the government caused "keen disappointment among western pacifists" who "have even characterised the peace army [the Shanti Sena] . . . as a non-violent department of the government."[87] Eventually, Narayan "was forced back upon the World Peace Brigade for any attempt at mediation in the border dispute with China."[88]

Ed Lazar, veteran of the San Francisco to Moscow march and crew member of *Everyman I,* wrote a memo proposing a friendship march that would traverse India and China, and the suggestion received a warm reception from Indian Gandhians.[89] At its meeting in December 1962 at Sevagram, the Indian Shanti Sena Mandal resolved that the All-India Shanti Sena "invites the World Peace Brigade to organize a Delhi-Peking Friendship March."[90]

Although JP was not present, the recorded discussion at the joint meeting of the WPB Executive Committee and the European Regional Council, held in London in January 1963, makes it clear that the suggestion for the WPB to organize the march came from JP. The proceedings state that the march "as conceived by the Indian peace movement" was to cover a distance of 4,000–5,000 miles (6,500–8,000 kilometers) at about 10 miles (16 kilometers) a day. There were to be fifteen marchers, five Indians and ten from the WPB. The WPB leadership, in turn, made it clear that if they were to participate then they would insist on their right to speak out against war and armaments and that this included speaking out "against Indian arms and policy in India" because if the marchers were silent on this point "the implication," according to Peace Pledge Union General Secretary Stuart Morris, would be that they were campaigning on the basis that "India was right and China wrong." Muste added that it had to be clear that "this was not a project of the Indian Government."[91] With this understanding the Friendship March was adopted as an official WPB project.

An international team of nineteen marchers, including eleven Indians and five Americans, was gathered and, on 1 March 1963, led by Michael Scott, departed from Rajghat, in New Delhi, where Mahatma Gandhi had been cremated. The trek followed the format of Gandhi's Salt March. It covered an average distance of about fifteen kilometers per day, generally before the onset of the oppressive noonday heat, with lengthy meetings and speeches at stops in towns and villages along the way. Although the march at times met with demonstrations that labeled the exercise traitorous,[92] attracted media criticism for pro-Chinese bias,[93] had unsympathetic questions asked about it by right-wing politicians in both the Uttar Pradesh Legislative Assembly and the Indian Parliament,[94] and was criticized by Vinoba, it attracted large and usually supportive crowds.

Although a lengthy letter was sent to the China Peace Committee soon after the march commenced,[95] Chinese reactions were hostile from the outset, in part at least, because of JP's involvement in the march. The Chinese had labeled JP "a notorious ultra anti-Chinese element" and "a notorious reactionary Indian politician brought up in the lap of U.S. imperialism" because of his vigorous condemnation of the Chinese invasion and takeover of Tibet.[96] Not surprisingly, the marchers were refused permission to enter China, or even Burma, East Pakistan, or Hong Kong. Eventually, this project, too, petered out.

Ultimately, Vinoba Bhave was pressured into withdrawing his outright condemnation of the plan to interpose a force between the combating armies and applying nonviolent resistance to the Indian army if it attempted to prevent such action in the event of renewed hostilities. Hostilities, however, had ceased in November 1962 when the Chinese unilaterally withdrew their forces. Fighting was not renewed, and interpositionary peacekeeping was not put to the test.

Olson, in his assessment during the dying phases of the venture, noted that the march "remained a tiny witness project, unable to break out of the pattern of the past. It absorbs all the meagre resources of the Brigade. It supplies no picture of the dynamic of non-violence."[97]

Lazar, who was with the march until the end, produced a detailed assessment of it for the Assam Friendship March Conference held in January 1964. "Looking back," he wrote, "I feel that this was an Indian project with a few participants from other countries." About two-thirds of the participants were Indian, and the organization and financing remained in the hands of the Sarvodaya movement. He added that although he believed that nonviolent organizations could only be developed through action, he realized that the action had to be within the "limits of reach" of the organization and that, first, there had to be a solid base to work from:

The WPB has no such base of support as yet; at present it is an idea with a letterhead. In order to develop from an idea to a real international shanti sena it seems to me that there first must be developed local, regional and national shanti sena. A very short term project is possible with a top heavy international group but weakness at the base becomes increasingly apparent with the passage of time, which makes sustained international shanti sena at this time extremely difficult if not self defeating. As the idea of shanti sena becomes more real in local situations I feel the international idea and organization will command more respect which is in many ways essential for effectiveness.[98]

War Resisters' International, which called the Beirut conference, characterized the WPB as "an exciting and useful experiment" but also concluded that the experiment was something of a failure:

Serious mistakes have been made and they have sapped confidence and the support which, at one time, were so widespread. The most serious charge that can be levelled against all of us who have participated in this venture is that we have not adhered to the principles and aims which have been agreed upon at the outset. . . . The Brigade attempted to impose an international structure instead of allowing its activities first at local and national level. In consequence adequate support, financial and in terms of volunteers, has not been forthcoming in any of the three regions. Emphasis has been placed on spectacular short term projects, which have achieved little more than temporary publicity, rather than actions over a period of time which would allow for the full application of non-violent methods. Volunteers have been projected into alien situations without adequate preparation. The Brigade has been the responsibility of the few to the exclusion of the many who are only too eager to put their commitment to non-violence at the service of the poor and oppressed for peace and a new and more just social order.[99]

Michael Scott, European regional chairman of the WPB, also felt that the "scope and concept" of the Brigade had proved to be different from his original concept, becoming "only a kind of launching pad for projects involving small teams of people in conflict areas." He was not enthusiastic about the *Everyman* voyage and came to believe that his "early misgivings about the march to China were justified." He concluded, nevertheless, that "There is a future . . . for a kind of international peace force and . . . the UN will stand in need of such a force as time goes on and it may be that this should be organized separately from the UN itself."[100]

After about two years of "operation," without being formally disbanded, the World Peace Brigade simply faded away. Without the stimulus of dramatic action as an immediate prospect it was not possible for the WPB to recruit and train volunteers for further peacekeeping work.[101] Its base had not been expanded to the stage where it could be self-perpetuating, and as the Sino-Indian war produced a crisis among the large Indian contingent, much of the U.S. leadership turned their attention to the civil rights movement back home. Competition for scarce funds became intense, and Narayan claimed that the underestimation of the costs of international organization and the lack of mechanisms to allow ease of consultation at the international level added to the problems the Brigade faced in attempting to become a viable organization.[102]

In October 1965 the New England Committee for Non-Violent Action organized an extended training program in the United States with the intention of taking the first step toward the recreation of a WPB-style international nonviolent peacekeeping corps. The organizers, Robert Swann and Paul Salstrom, envisaged the corps undertaking actions such as the nonviolent "invasion" of South Africa that had earlier been mooted by the Brigade. One of the strategies for organizing the corps was to attract the alumni of the U.S. Peace Corps into a "parallel" nonviolent, nongovernment-controlled organization.[103] The World Peace Brigade, however, was not yet ready for resurrection.

The Cyprus Resettlement Project

In 1967, at the height of the Vietnam War, an English group planned to place a team of nonviolent volunteers in U.S. target areas in North Vietnam to demonstrate "opposition to American aggression and to share the dangers of bombardment with the Vietnamese people."[104] Originally, some of the members of Non-Violent Action in Vietnam (NVAV) saw the aim of such an action as trying to halt the bombing (and, hence, the war) and saw particular significance in the fact that "it would be a serious attempt, for the first time in history, by a sizeable body of people to intervene non-violently on the spot in an actual war occurring thousands of miles away from where they lived. Thus it could put active pacifism—nonviolent resistance—on the map as a potentially viable way of settling major conflicts to a greater extent than ever before."[105]

The group had difficulty raising funds or capturing public attention. Much time was spent debating not only the merit of potential tactics to be employed in the proposed action but often also on heated argument over the strategic aims of the project itself. Although problems were encountered obtaining the required permission from the various governments involved, in January 1968 a team of twenty-six (including the Reverend Michael Scott) left London for Cambodia. They had little prospect of forward passage to Vietnam or even of reaching war-torn areas on the Vietnamese/Cambodian border where U.S. bombing was destroying Cambodian villages.

Revising their goals, the team attempted to gain authorization to undertake constructive village rebuilding work in the most ravaged district of Cambodia. Team members ended up, however, languishing in relative luxury in Phnom Penh at a government facility for almost one month, often squabbling among themselves, with only a brief escorted tour to the border areas, before going their own ways; some engaging in rather standard antiwar protests in Southeast Asia before being deported back to London.

Although NVAV achieved little in terms of its original aims, it did manage to mobilize a team of nonviolent activists and send them toward a war zone. Perhaps it also helped to shift thinking away from emphasizing interpositionary peacekeeping (possibly as a result of a realistic assessment of the likelihood of success for such ventures) to focus on constructive projects in conflict areas, the approach to be taken a few years later by the Cyprus Resettlement Project.

The failure of the World Peace Brigade and NVAV and the nonemergence of Swann and Salstrom's nonviolent peacekeeping corps notwithstanding, the calls for such types of peacekeeping efforts in the world's trouble spots continued. In 1971 the Fellowship of Reconciliation put forward a proposal to "explore the need for, and the feasibility of, a fully trained, disciplined and maintained corps for non-violent action in Northern Ireland."

The aim of the Peace Force was to "attempt to establish its presence at points of violent conflict." The theory behind the proposed action was spelled out: "Simply by observing, interpreting feelings, tending the injured and calming emotions trained people can be of considerable help, whether or not they are fully accepted by the combatants. Their presence can be seen as a symbol of, and a witness to, more humane action." And, further, it included the leap of faith that usually accompanies such calls: "Often the interposition of an unarmed team between violent enemies can be a barrier against an irrational clash. Its existence could encourage others to join in. (Relatively limited numbers, and injuries sustained in such action, will often inhibit violence more than a large or armed intermediary force). On the spot conciliation and other determined intervention can be options for a qualified and respected group."[106]

The proposal was featured prominently in *Peace News* and circulated "as an invitation to others to take interest." The next few issues of the paper carried several rejoinders and critiques. The debate in the main centered on questions about the effectiveness of peacekeeping as generally attempted by the United Nations and advocated by Royden's original "army" idea (that is, without the inclusion of substantial emphasis on peacemaking and peacebuilding), and the choice of action to be taken where the problem was structural. Several replies stated that because the problem resulted from British imperialism, the most efficacious path would be to stay home and work against the British military presence.[107] Another correspondent went further, criticizing the proposal as being "concerned with the point of conflict rather than the source of conflict." The case was made that "the notion of a neutral peacekeeping force should not be taken seriously by pacifists. If the force really has no objective beyond keeping the peace then it is serving the interests of the status quo and is not neutral. If we presume to interfere with the political design and the moral purpose of men bent on vio lence then we must reveal a deep understanding of the predicament and a willingness to suggest alternative means of achieving of their goals which are justifiable."[108]

Such action is slow and unglamorous with none of the emotional and moral impact that would have followed, say, the slaughter of Sheppard, Gray, and Royden's force in Shanghai. The dropping of the proposed World Peace Brigade's Rhodesian march clearly demonstrated how the difficult work of peacemaking seems relatively unenticing when the highly visible peacekeeping or nonviolent direct-action element is removed, yet peacekeeping without peacemaking can end up as little more than a stunt. For the defense, Harding of the Fellowship responded that the critics gave no real answers, stressing that the problem in Northern Ireland was one of security, the lack of which means an increased reliance on armed force. The alternative to a nonviolent peacekeeping force, he maintained, would be communal or civil war.[109]

The plan to introduce a World Peace Brigade-type presence into Northern Ireland continued for half a dozen more years, but nothing came of the project.[110] Instead, the next focus of international pacifist action became strife-torn Cyprus with the main emphasis, this time, directly on peacemaking.

Although the World Peace Brigade had lain dormant for several years, many were still working behind the scenes to keep the idea alive. Narayan Desai, son of Gandhi's late secretary and by this time secretary of the Shanti Sena, Quaker A. Paul Hare of the Haverford College Center for Nonviolent Conflict Resolution in Pennsylvania, and Charles Walker, a long-time Quaker peace activist from the United States and veteran of the Delhi-Peking march, met in India in August 1971 to "work together to try to internationalise the Shanti Sena idea."[111] The Cyprus Resettlement Project (originally Volunteers for Peace) became the first organizational effort to grow out of this meeting.

During October 1971 the International Peace Academy, which had been organizing training sessions for peacekeepers, sent a letter signed by three Nobel Peace Laureates to all United Nations missions, stating that it was ready to "undertake extensive and in-depth training of personnel from all Member States of the United Nations who would then be available to their countries as what might be termed skilled peace contingents for use as appropriate."[112] The memorandum that accompanied the letter stressed the need for conciliation (peacemaking) for the peaceful settlement of disputes and noted that "conciliation has not been widely utilised in and through the United Nations."[113] The memorandum went on to announce that "the time has come when each country would undoubtedly wish to consider creating groups or contingents of persons trained in the techniques of nonviolent action for conciliation and conflict resolution" and, as an example of the use of such contingents, noted that "at the request of the Security Council and with the agreement of the Government of Cyprus, they could perform roles in Cyprus which might eventually reduce the time for which the UN force would be required to stay there."[114]

One month earlier Jayaprakash Narayan had also sent a letter to U.N. Secretary-General U Thant. The United Nations had been unable to play a constructive peacekeeping role during the Bangladesh war,[115] and now the Shanti Sena was suggesting that unarmed contingents could be of value in such crises.[116] The letter suggested "certain radical changes in the peacekeeping machinery" of the United Nations. The Narayan proposal, in brief, was "to have an unarmed peacekeeping volunteers' force as part of the machinery for the solution of international conflicts." JP stressed that a new method of peacekeeping was necessary, one that not only contained violence but also had the ability to "create conditions for better relationships between the conflicting parties." The answer he saw was an international peace brigade under U.N. auspices because "psychologically, it can help in creating the conditions for conciliation by counteracting fear and hatred. Economically it will be less expensive than maintaining an armed force. Politically it may help to prepare the ground for better understanding between nations."[117]

Again nothing came of either of these proposals; however, academy members joined Shanti Sainiks and Quakers to go it on their own and organize a brigade to work in Cyprus.[118] Plans for the brigade were drawn up in discussion with Indarjit Rikhye by former U.S. ambassador to the United Nations Arthur Lall, A. Paul Hare, and Charles Walker. On the work to be done in Cyprus, Lyle Tatum of the American Friends Service Committee and the Shanti Sena's Narayan Desai helped shape the project with advice from Michael Harbottle.[119]

In August 1972 an exploratory team made up of Tatum, Walker, Hare, Desai, and social psychologist Julie Latané arrived in Cyprus to meet the parties involved and "to seek ways in which a group committed to nonviolence might work in conjunction with the mandate of the United Nations to help restore peaceful conditions in Cyprus.[120] Since the "time of troubles" in 1963 (which resulted in civil war in 1964) fifteen to twenty thousand Turkish villagers remained to be resettled from among those who fled their homes.[121] The suggestion of U.N. Special Representative Osorio-

Tafall was followed, and the main thrust of activities became the resettling of approximately seven thousand displaced Turkish Cypriots rather than other areas such as health, education, or welfare, which were also considered.[122] A CRP team surveyed almost one hundred towns and villages, assessing needs and compiling data on who was ready to return.

Negotiations were held with both Greek and Turkish leaders, and it was agreed in March 1973 that a working party, with the CRP acting as third-party facilitator, would be set up. In July another team of five arrived in Cyprus and negotiated an agreement to begin work in four villages. Finally, between November and January, after Turkish authorities had determined who wished to be returned to their homes, an international team of eighteen, from five countries (one-third being Indian Shanti Sainiks), commenced work in the designated villages on getting the resettlement process going: interviewing prospective returnees, developing rebuilding plans, collecting data on needs during resettlement, facilitating negotiations, and finding ways to increase the involvement of the villagers themselves in the process of resettlement. At the height of the project optimism was such that team members considered the possibility of taking up CRP type work on the Israeli/Egyptian border after completing the task that they had set themselves in Cyprus.[123]

In April 1974 a further five-member team arrived to assess progress and prepare for summer activity; however, political developments halted communal negotiations. In July a work camp of Turkish, Greek, and American students had started rebuilding six houses in one village when the mainland Greek military junta staged a coup on the island and installed a hard-line enosist as president. The coup and the ensuing Turkish invasion put an end to the project.

Although the CRP was completely swept away with the new flood of refugees, it had provided valuable lessons on the initiation, organization, and development of peace brigades. Although the scale of the operation was small (or more probably because of it) it was well planned. It was foreseen that incidents, which even the United Nations had difficulty coping with in the past, would be sparked when the Turks returned to their villages. In anticipation the CRP contingent contained riot-control experts recruited from the ranks of the Shanti Sena.[124] It was believed that if conflicts could be kept under "reasonable" control then it "would have signalled a new day in local attitudes, and new possibilities for rapprochement at the national level."[125] Although this experiment never had the chance of a trial, the fact that young Cypriot Turks and Greeks worked together cleaning streets and mosques and rebuilding dwellings achieved the same thing.

The Cypress Resettlement Project also provided a useful lesson in communal politics. Walker reported that once the Project had gained a certain momentum "it became disadvantageous for a party in the conflict to obstruct or circumvent or harass the project." Neither side wanted to lose potential propaganda advantage by appearing to be the ones who blocked the project.[126] Project member Manabendra Mandal added that the CRP proved that "in many cases the presence of a reconciliation group or an international nonviolent third force may help solve the problem through mediation without hampering the work of the judiciary or the government."[127]

Perhaps one of the greatest benefits of the Cyprus experience, however, was that it enabled Walker to draw up a detailed model for a World Peace Guard (WPG) unit that could replace the U.N. forces on the island. Although the invasion made the document obsolete, it provided the basis for further developments of the peace brigade idea.[128]

Charles Walker's World Peace Guard Proposal

In 1981 Walker finally published his small booklet, *A World Peace Guard: An Unarmed Agency for Peacekeeping.* There he noted that "the basic idea of a World Peace Guard is indeed a resilient one, cropping up particularly in times of crisis. It is then left stranded for lack of money, organizational and political support, or impetus from peacekeeping specialists."[129] He was determined to keep the impetus going by calling for the need "to record, analyze and publish case histories and accounts of 'intervention episodes' based on a nonviolent approach" to be met.[130] Further, he was doing all he could to help popularize the idea before the 1981 Canadian consultation on the idea was to commence. In the meantime he urged "those of us who want to work further on this proposal write, talk and meet so that a way opens."[131]

He was proposing an unarmed nonviolent equivalent of the United Nations Article 43 standby force. A World Peace Guard, in Walker's view, would be a peacekeeping agency composed of trained volunteers from many countries. It would be committed to a discipline of nonviolent action, prepared to carry out peace missions between belligerents, whether inter- or intranational, or in situations beyond the control of local authorities. The WPG was to undertake third-party functions and services in dispute control, working in a non-partisan fashion, to fulfil a mandate given to it by the contending parties and/or others involved.[132]

The proposal in itself raises many difficulties and only goes part of the way to avoid duplicating the problems presented by the U.N. model of peacekeeping. Although unarmed, Walker saw the WPG as neither defenseless nor powerless. When it arrived at its place of operation, a legitimizing mandate would presumably already have been conferred on the Guard. This would be based on an agreement between some local authority and an outside agency. The mandate "might flow from" the United Nations, a regional organization, a joint call from two groups on the verge of hostilities, an international conference growing out of an emergency, or, in a politically less nonpartisan approach, through a call from a beleaguered group. Once a Guard was established with a ready reserve and the capability for rapid mobilization, the mandate could come from negotiations between the WPG and any of the above. Walker sees this mandate for use of the WPG as emerging primarily in situations in which military intervention "appears to be impracticable, inappropriate, unlikely or counterproductive."[133]

Legitimacy would be further signified and confirmed by such physical signs as "insignia, movement, paraphernalia, public occasions, unique functions, and the usual incidents and positive interactions."[134] Although the sanctioning power of weapons would be absent, Walker notes that it is generally "organizational power that counts rather than firepower; that is, the power to state what a peacekeeping unit is going to do and then do it."[135]

At times weapons can interfere with the attainment of desirable objectives. Where this means recourse to the ultimate sanction of the WPG, that is, taking casualties (presumably during interposition between belligerents), Walker justifies the sacrifice by noting that, firstly, military commanders have had to face such decisions although their troops were not trained for such an eventuality or even aware that it was a possibility; secondly, it may be an option that the hard facts of the situation require on "prudential grounds"; and, thirdly, "an armed group ordered not to fire may be rendered immobile, but a group *known to be unarmed* still have a chance to take initiative."[136]

During a meeting with the work team of the Cyprus Resettlement Project in 1973, Michael Harbottle suggested that a WPG could take one of three organizational forms: that of an ad hoc project, a specialized agency or of a political agency. An ad hoc group, as with the previous attempts at unarmed peacekeeping, can be formed most easily to meet the challenge of a crisis situation. It would not have the advantage of careful advanced planning, and lack of training would leave it with the problems faced by U.N. soldiers who overnight have to become peacekeepers. Further it would have difficulty in raising funds unless a dramatic situation had already occurred.[137]

A specialized agency would be one that was known to have certain capabilities such as a set of plans and procedures, rosters of available experts, periodic consultation and assessment meetings, established relationships with key individuals and groups in the political arena, and, in addition, the capability to develop a ready reserve.[138] Such an agency would be open to invitations to undertake actions and would be the most appropriate agency to undertake U.N. mandated missions. The "specialized agency" has drawbacks as well, however. It could become "excessively technical" and "nonpolitical" in such a way as to render it incapable of "certain political initiatives that can be critical in a rapidly escalating conflict."[139] Further, if it became excessively costly and reached the point that it had to rely on governments for the necessary funds, it "might run afoul of the same political obstacles endemic in UN operations."[140]

Walker believes that the idea of a political agency could lead to the most optimistic of the possible scenarios for the future shape of the WPG. It would arise "if the forces of nonviolence enter a rapid growth period in several parts of the world."[141] The hope was that there would be a progression in the development of the Guard through three categories: "starting with ad hoc projects, leading onto a specialized agency which would coexist with a later political group and be aided by it."[142] The World Peace Brigade was set up as such a group with the purpose of projecting the idea and practice of nonviolent intervention on the world scene through actions that could "make a difference" and, thus, help build a world movement based on nonviolence as a political force.[143] This political version of the Guard would have "a commitment to combat imperialism, colonialism, oppression of minorities or egregious threats to peace."[144] Somehow such a team would still be "capable of nonpartisan action" and although "tilting emotionally toward one side" would, nevertheless, be capable "of scrupulous fairness in the service of a peacekeeping mission"[145] in the way, Walker writes elsewhere, of "police who may oppose certain demonstrators but nevertheless take risks to protect the right of demonstrators peaceably to assemble."[146] The degree to which this is the rule rather than the exception in police/demonstrator interactions is not clearly demonstrated. One is left with the feeling that even in the case of a WPG such an ideologically sound stance would make practical operations extremely difficult.

Although from the time of the WPB onward the constructive (that is, the peacebuilding) side of operations was stressed, thereby overcoming some of Galtung's reservations about peacekeeping, Walker notes that even in Cyprus, where both sides welcomed the help of the project, a thick U.N. file of proposals for technical and educational aid remained unimplemented because of the political implications: "Mild UN attempts to help one side were severely criticized by the other, as partisan or not exactly comparable."[147]

This envisaged model of the peace army seems to be saddled with contradictions that have not been clearly thought through. In any case, Walker admits that "a World Peace Guard as a political agency could be organized only in a growth period of the forces of nonviolent action."[148] Without this, funds, resources, personnel, and energy for such a project would be lacking,[149] and it is safe to say that, at least for the foreseeable future, this will be the case.

Generally, most of the problems Galtung sees with mainstream peacekeeping efforts apply equally to the unarmed alternative. Whatever the nature of the Guard it would be difficult to see how it could operate where either the Great Powers or their interests were involved. The questions remain of whose peace and what kind of peace is to be kept.

As a solution to this dilemma, Walker claims that the constructive works question may be resolved by parallel action. That is, where the WPG identifies special needs, it can "pave the way quietly for initiative by other groups, national or international," becoming directly involved in such work itself only when the need "encompasses areas in both jurisdictions, where the Peace Guard could facilitate a coordinated effort."[150] A further solution, he believes, would be to compose people's brigades from the region itself to combine "a force from below with dedicated but nonpartisan peacekeepers who enlist for such a cause."[151] And, finally, he replies to his critics that there is a need to "recognise that to some degree the problem is beyond complete resolution, and that every conflict will have to be adjudged in context."[152]

The problems notwithstanding, he claims that such a "force" is needed. Walker notes that, although perhaps valid, the type of criticisms that were leveled at the Fellowship of Reconciliation's Northern Ireland proposal are in a sense not very helpful: "The likelihood that nonviolent forces can fashion some sort of interpositionary group is much greater than the chances they could change national policy, even setting aside the time problems."[153] And as peacekeeping by military forces becomes increasingly unacceptable, particularly in the Third World, Walker ends his plea for a World Peace Guard by asking whether there are "intermediate roles for unarmed peace contingents that are at least preferable to leaving the field to warriors, tyrants, imperialists and adventures?"[154]

Peace Brigades International and the Gulf Peace Team

After the Cyprus project ended, the idea of Peace Guards/Brigades was pursued further. As Walker wrote on the topic and others were actively trying to popularize the idea internationally, still others were equally diligent in their efforts to develop a peace force linked to the United Nations.[155]

One of these attempts got under way in 1978 when Raymond Magee, one of the originators of the Peace Corps concept, helped found the organization Peaceworkers. Peaceworkers tried to convince the United Nations to develop its own peacekeeping/making force on the peace brigade model.[156] The proposed U.N. Volunteer Peaceworkers Service was to send teams of peaceworkers to conflict areas where they would assist with arbitration and mediation, provide unarmed buffer forces if necessary, undertake reconciliation work between communities, and engage in relief work. To press for the resolution of a conflict the teams could organize nonviolent actions in the form of marches, fasts, and civil disobedience.[157]

After several world crises at the end of the 1970s (starting with the taking of American hostages in Iran and the Soviet intervention in Afghanistan) and a call from the aging Vinoba Bhave for a new World Peace Brigade, Magee and Cyprus Resettlement Project veterans came together at an international conference in September 1981 to explore the idea.[158] At the close of the Grindstone Island meeting in Ontario, the founding statement of Peace Brigades International (PBI) was released to the world. Peace Brigades International thus became the latest attempt in the chain leading from the WPB to the present.

PBI took the form of "a specialized agency dedicated to unarmed peacekeeping and peace-making."[159] Although the organization has a centralized international secretariat, it is independent and decentralized, aiming to "promote, support, and coordinate local peace brigades, based in communities, states or provinces, and nations."[160] To acquire authority and gain access to leaders and conflict areas "the brigades would normally operate by arrangement with such international political bodies as the United Nations or the Organization of American States or with one or more national governments."[161]

PBI Secretary Daniel Clark formulated the criteria necessary for inclusion in PBI's short-term response teams and for longer-term team members as well. There was, after the PBI's first action on the Nicaraguan border in 1982, a strong desire to include only suitably qualified persons who had been adequately trained before they were sent into action. Members were to be at least twenty-five years old for long-term teams and at least of legal age for ready response units; have fluency in the appropriate local language for inclusion in a long-term team and at least a working knowledge of the language for short-term units; have a familiarity with the region, including a general knowledge of the social, political, and cultural problems of the area, possibly coupled with previous Third World experience for those working on a long-term assignment in a Third World country; have previous experience with nonviolent action and have an appreciation of, and willingness to work under, a discipline of nonviolence; have the ability and willingness to work in a nonpartisan third-party role; and, finally, have the ability and willingness to work in a team under leadership authority.[162] In this way PBI hoped to overcome some of the organizational problems that have beset U.N. forces.

During the first years of PBI's operation emphasis was placed on planning rather than action. An attempt was being made not to repeat the failures of the WPB, and Peace Brigades International "was convinced that being a small group, one could only start direct projects on a small scale and in a limited number of cases."[163]

The initial, and most concentrated, work of PBI has been centered on Central America.[164] Under the guidance of David Sweet (who was then organizing what was to become Witness for Peace) the Californian Santa Cruz Peace Brigade sent a ten-person unarmed border team into Nicaragua to the Honduran border near the town of Jalapa in 1982. The ready response unit presented an international presence in the area for a time until it fell into leaderless disarray. The Brigade members organized twice-daily vigils in the town plazas of the villages around Jalapa and joined in the coffee picking in a local cooperative. During the presence of the Brigade there were no military incidents, and the regional military commander has been reported as attributing this to the presence of the border team. No response came from the Honduran side to PBI's proposal to place a similar team on their side of the border, and when PBI notified the Contras of their plans, they were informed that "after they defeat the Sandinistas you may have all the peace brigades you want."[165]

Exploratory teams from Switzerland have visited Central America on several occasions and have ended up assisting the Guatemalan team (involving seven "internationals"), which until 1992 was aiding the relatives of the "disappeared" persons in the country and providing nonviolent escorts for human rights activists threatened with death.[166]

Peace Brigades International has also offered to the Contradora group of nations (Mexico, Panama, Colombia, and Venezuela) the placement of a border team between Nicaragua and Costa Rica to help implement the treaty between the two nations negotiated by the Contradora countries. Preparation for this project was undertaken with the technical advice of Harbottle.[167]

Although these actions are qualitatively different from the actions of countless groups of Western volunteers who picked coffee beans in Nicaragua, it is debatable whether they can escape the criticisms that Olson leveled at the WPB. The criticisms of the War Resisters' International, however, have been heeded. As PBI gains confidence in its abilities, its horizons are slowly expanding in a way that reverses the historical processes that left the visionary hopes of the WPB totally unfulfilled. Here the vision was limited, but the field of operations continues to grow: under the direction of PBI council members and the Shanti Sena's Narayan Desai, PBI has been working to support a Forum on Reconciliation in Sri Lanka[168] for assisting in training of persons from South Africa who wish to act as domestic teams in nonviolent interposition and mediation,[169] and in Israel PBI is preparing to work with local nonviolent groups aiming at reconciliation between Arabs and Jews.[170]

The Iraqi invasion and annexation of Kuwait in August 1990 and the resulting buildup of United States-led, United Nations-sanctioned, military forces in neighboring Saudi Arabia resulted in the formation of the Gulf Peace Team (GPT).[171]

As with Royden's and JP's Shanti Sena attempt at interposition, the Gulf Peace Team effort was reactive rather than proactive. This situation ensured that there was no time for adequate planning or organization. With the increasing inevitability of bloody hostility in the Persian Gulf region volunteers and lines of communication were quickly assembled. Although Pat Arrowsmith, one of the main moving forces behind the formation of the GPT, had been a cofounder of NVAV, there appeared to be no time to learn from previous attempts at unarmed interposition, and the project, from the start, seemed somewhat haphazard—a brave but foolhardy witness venture to most observers.[172]

The policy statement put out in October 1990 declared that the GPT was "an international multi-cultural team working for peace and opposing any form of armed aggression, past, present or future, by setting up one or more international peace camps between the opposing armed forces. Our object will be to withstand non-violently any armed aggression by any party to the present Gulf dispute."[173] The proposed line of action was to "interpose between opposing forces, or set up a Peace Camp near the conflict area," and the motivation was stated to be "to stop war in the Gulf."[174] Arrowsmith is reported as vowing that any side making a move in the war would do it "over our dead bodies."[175] Some other GPT members, being more realistic, claimed that the aim of the border camp would be to "serve as a symbol of worldwide opposition to war in the Gulf region."[176]

The organizing committee did not want to appear to be beholden to Iraqi authorities, so they planned to have peace camps "on both sides of the frontier." In a letter to Iraq's ambassador to London the committee sought assurances guaranteeing the "autonomy of the Peace Camp, both in terms of logistics and in terms of internal management" in addition to "open communication with our support group in London" The ambassador was informed that "massive world-wide support" was expected for the project and that the committee was "confident that this initiative can make a significant contribution to the cause of peace."[177]

The Saudi government refused to accept letters from the GPT, and although the original request to Iraqi authorities for an area to be set aside for the camp "near the border between Kuwait and Saudi Arabia, between the Iraqi army and the Saudi border" was originally agreed to, the Iraqis eventually declared the area a prohibited military zone and offered a site, which was accepted, two-thirds of the way along the border toward Jordan, some five hundred kilometers from Kuwait.

A news release of 7 December announced that the Team had been granted permission to establish an international peace camp between the armed forces involved in the dispute. This was to be the only camp of the GPT. And although the news release added that "on 17 December, the 100-strong first wave of the several hundred international volunteers waiting to join the camp will fly to Iraq and proceed to the camp site"[178] altogether only seventy-three GPT members (but, it should be noted, from fifteen different countries) actually made it to the camp.

The existence of the camp and the transit area on Al Aaras Island in Baghdad depended on Iraqi patronage, and no GPT presence was established on the Saudi side of the border. Following the commencement of the bombing of Iraq, GPT members spent ten days in the camp cut off from the rest of the world, engaging in interminable meetings, with food supplies running low until they were removed by Iraqi authorities to Baghdad and thence to Jordan and home.

Despite some nonviolent resistance, the camp was closed by Iraqi officials on 27 January because they had "decided that the continued presence of the camp was a security risk." After a brief period in Baghdad, by the beginning of February all Team members had arrived in Amman in Jordan.

The success of the Gulf Peace Team is difficult to access because the aim of the Team was never completely clear. On 31 December in an open letter to the commanders of the armed forces in the frontier region surrounding the camp it was announced that "we are an international multicultural team working for peace, and we oppose armed aggression. Our aim is to withstand non-violently any form of armed aggression by any party in the present Gulf dispute. . . . We recognise the intense suffering, death and environmental devastation that would occur in the area (and beyond) were the war to escalate, and we consider any non-violent action to prevent such a catastrophe to be of paramount importance."

A volunteer's briefing paper, written two weeks earlier, warned that "it is important that all the volunteers should recognise the very real possibility that they may lose their lives by taking part in this project." It was not explained how the possible loss of life could prevent the foreseen catastrophes or how a camp of seventy-three individuals could oppose armed aggression by more than one million men in uniform apparently committed to fight to the death.

After the close of the GPT's camp in Iraq, discussion among Team members centered on the establishment of further peace camps, in particular on the Israel/Jordan border to guard against an Israeli invasion, and, in consideration of interventionary as well as interpositionary peacekeeping, to the provision of nonviolent escorts for humanitarian convoys of food and medical supplies to affected citizens in Iraq and Kuwait. The ending of the war overtook GPT efforts to set up the new camp; however, fifteen activists did leave Amman as escorts for a truck convoy to Baghdad. Although GPT members were not granted permission to reenter Iraq, the convoy arrived safely in Baghdad, possibly because of the publicized escort operation.

The horrors of war in the former Yugoslavian republic of Bosnia have provided, and continue to provide, the latest impetus to reactive nonviolent interposition. Bosnia is in Europe, making the logistical problem of reaching at least the outskirts of the war zone a smaller obstacle than the one faced by Royden, NVAV, or the Gulf Peace Team. In October 1992 Howard Clark of War Resisters' International announced that "there is no doubt that 1,000 civilians willing to travel to [Bosnia-Hercegovina] and spend some days there could make a significant impact." [179]

Six months after the shelling of the Bosnian capital commenced in April 1992 and after some smaller forays into Sarajevo by peace activists, major interpositionary attempts were again undertaken. Solidarity for Peace in Sarajevo, sponsored by the Italian Catholic peace group Beati i Costruttori di Pace (Blessed are the Peacemakers), brought a convoy of almost five hundred people, mostly Italians, into the besieged city. The aims of the group were to show solidarity with the people of Sarajevo and to demonstrate for human rights and for a peaceful solution to the conflict. The group at least met the first aim. [180]

From the experience of Solidarity for Peace grew We Share One Peace with the aim of setting up three peace camps, one each in areas controlled by Muslims, Serbs, and Croats. Originally, camp members were to be rotated, and they were mainly to work with refugees. The peace activities were to culminate in a mass peace demonstration in Sarajevo in August 1993. The private French relief organization, Equilibre, which had been transporting supplies into Bosnia-Hercegovina for more than one year, had also planned a mass demonstration (they hoped for one hundred thousand participants) in Sarajevo in August. By the end of July, after an increase in fighting around Sarajevo and a rejection of official support for the camps, the original We Share One Peace endeavor collapsed. After negotiations, in August the two groups decided to combine their activities under the name Mir Sada (Peace Now) with the French being responsible for logistics and getting the members of the proposed massive civilian witness to the Bosnian capital.

The action collapsed within days of arrival in the former Yugoslavia. Not only did the main group not reach Sarajevo but, according to one of the participants, what could "have been a big step forward in the discussion about alternatives to military interventions . . . failed almost completely." [181]

From the outset there was competition and lack of coordination between the two parent groups because of cultural and political differences and added tensions because of their vastly different organizational styles: the Italians worked in affinity groups, whereas the French favored hierarchical structures. By the end the organizers and the participants were also seriously divided.

Even before the group of about three thousand left their arrival point, the Croatian port town of Split, some of the organizers were questioning the original plan of proceeding to Sarajevo, suggesting instead that the group go to Mostar, the Hercegovinan capital.[182] When the journey finally began, the marchers only got as far as the first campsite in the countryside. Heated discussions in the morning, after nearby shelling, led to the departure of Equilibre with one-third of the participants, two-thirds of the vehicles, and all the radios. Following much debate, on the next day Beati i Costruttori also withdrew its support for pushing on to Sarajevo, and the majority of the remaining Mir Sada members returned to Split.

The goals of Mir Sada were never clearly articulated, there was no agreement on decision-making processes, and there was no commonality of purpose among the participants. Still, as another participant pointed out, the experience of Mir Sada need not be taken as proof "that pacifists are helpless once a war begins, and that in such a case intervention is better left to the military" because Mir Sada "was too badly prepared to succeed." Mir Sada did prove that nonviolent interposition in a war zone is possible. In this case "3,000 people prepared to risk their lives for peace, not for war."[183] And the sixty-five participants who refused to turn back to Split, after a harrowing journey, made it into Sarajevo. They asserted the right of citizens to free travel, determined to show that the lesson of Mir Sada would not merely be that "it is sufficient to point a few rifles at the peace activists and they will run away."[184]

Conclusion

Galtung noted in 1969 that to obviate the difficulty posed by the noninterference in internal affairs section of the U.N. Charter as well as the veto power and regional hegemony of big powers "many people have been thinking in terms of *world peace brigades* that would mobilize volunteers to penetrate through national borders and intervene in cases of intra-national manifest and/or latent violence." He added that "in order for such operations not to be interpreted as efforts by a third power to use intervention as a pretext to conquest they would probably have to take place under conditions of 1. non-violence and 2. international composition and 3. non-governmental auspices."[185] Being realistic, however, he concluded that "the problems involved in organizing such efforts seem so far almost to be insurmountable."[186]

It seems that regardless of what can only be described as the lack of success of unarmed nonviolent civilian interpositions in war zones the attempts are, and will continue to be, recurrent. For this reason it is important to document these attempts carefully so that previous mistakes are not repeated with each new interpositionary attempt. Dramatic attempts in Bosnia notwithstanding, the difficulties in establishing a Royden- or Acland-style peace army are now generally well appreciated.[187] Most of the current efforts are far less dramatic but probably more practical: work is undertaken at the grass-roots level while efforts are made to interest the United Nations in providing for unarmed peacekeeping forces and a significant international peace corps–style organization. Generally, the continuing emphasis (if not in ad hoc reaction to particular wars) has shifted from large-scale interpositionary peacekeeping to more modest and practical interventionary peacekeeping[188] and especially the less-glamorous peacebuilding and peacemaking dimensions of conflict resolution in line with Ceresole's attempts and Bell's proposals. Although the vision has dimmed, it appears that action, however limited and faltering, is now ongoing.[189]

Questions, nevertheless, remain. Much of the debate at Canada's Grindstone Island "consultation," was concerned with the question of whether the proposed peace brigade should be a nonpartisan peacemaker or a partisan fighter for social justice or whether the approaches could be combined.[190] And even before the commencement of the Beirut conference, which created the World Peace Brigade, doubts about the very validity of the idea had been expressed. Some of those doubts warrant further examination.

When Galtung presented his analysis of the Peace Brigade concept, he pointed out that three possible approaches could be taken:[191] (1) the technical assistance approach, which attempts to prevent an incipient dispute by attacking its causes, (2) the second-party approach, which attempts to fight conflicts by participating nonviolently as a second party, that is, on one side, and (3) the third-party approach, which attempts to end conflicts by participating as a neutral with the aim of reducing violence rather than promoting a particular goal.[192] Galtung sees clear contradictions between the approaches. Although there may be some benefit in combining technical assistance and third-party work, this may compromise both approaches: a technical assistance person may be well known and know the background to the situation, but may not be perceived as impartial as an outside third party. Second-party work is often inconsistent with broadly based technical assistance, and a combination of second-and third-party approaches would probably be even less compatible.

Professor Fred Blum insisted that "there is no place for neutrality in the P.B. To be neutral means ultimately not to care who is winning in a struggle." The brigade, he claimed, must tackle the "central problems" and offer solutions that are better than the solutions offered by the contending parties. In reply to Galtung, Blum declared that "non-violence understood as a struggle to bring about a higher synthesis, to help man to move to a higher level of consciousness cannot be identified within the terms 'second' and 'third' party which are based on traditional Western conceptions of means and ends which are not compatible with non-violence."[193]

Whether Blum's claims for nonviolence overcome Galtung's objections has not clearly been demonstrated in peace brigade actions. Although the theory behind every peace brigade venture, regardless of concerns such as Galtung's, attempted to embrace all three approaches, each action was basically limited to one approach in practice, so the potential contradictions were avoided. Whether nonviolence can bring about the synthesis Blum claims for it can best be sought in India where the Gandhian Shanti Sena has operated intermittently for three decades and, since the death of Gandhi, has provided inspiration for the Western peace brigades.

Bill Sutherland, War Resisters' International council member and later a WPB project leader in Africa, voiced other concerns when, in late 1961, he wrote:

> Although the constructive programme was stressed as an important aspect of the programme, the real question was and is: Can a dedicated highly efficient, mobile world non-violent force act effectively in emergency situations, existent or threatened, in areas of international tension or internal revolution? Now it may be that the nature of satyagraha and non-violence as so far developed is such that the answer is "No." If this turns out to be the case, after the most serious study of experiments and projects tried over the years and a most careful analysis of the principles and practices of satyagraha, *then we should bury this idea of a World Peace Brigade and concentrate on other methods of achieving our objectives.* But we shall take a backward step if the sharp clean emphasis on action in emergency crisis situations as described above is blurred by (1) bringing into the inner organizational structure elements of the Peace movement not primarily concerned or actually opposed to this approach and (2) taking the "easy way out" of concentrating on what Johan Galtung calls the technical assistance approach—which is a most valuable contribution, but which S.C.I. [Service Civil International] and now the National Peace Corps are far better able to develop.[194]

Looking back over the history of unarmed, nonviolent peacekeeping/peacemaking attempts, it would appear that Sutherland's fears of a backward step were generally realized and, perhaps, are doomed to such a fate. Since he wrote this memo, some of the attempts at unarmed nonviolent peacekeeping/making have been limited to the Peace Corps and SCI style of constructive work, and only in the 1990s have peace activists managed to field mobile nonviolent interpositionary world forces and then with only very little success. Perhaps now PBI is beginning to combine technical assistance work with genuine peacekeeping. Experience has shown, however, that until the concept is taken up by the United Nations, because of a lack of resources and finances, unless the most recent planned actions in Bosnia prove otherwise by inspiring the formation of at least a semi-permanent large-scale peace brigade, such peacekeeping actions will remain limited to intervention in disputes rather than interposition between warring parties except in relatively rare circumstances where peace groups manage to assemble ad hoc peace brigades.[195]

But there is another history of unarmed peacekeeping. And the answer to the questions of whether satyagraha, Gandhi's method of nonviolent action, is applicable in "emergency situations . . . in areas of international tension or internal revolution," and the ones raised by Galtung's objections, can best be sought with Gandhi's attempts to set up peace brigades and especially with the Shanti Sena that was finally established by his followers after his death.

3

The Historical Gandhian Background

Because of Gandhi's commitment to the ideology of nonviolence and because of the communal strife that beset India, it was only a matter of time before he turned his attention and applied his philosophy of nonviolent action to ways of peacefully resolving social conflict. Hindu/Muslim clashes were not only alien to the vision of India he held before himself but were used by communal chauvinists to try to thwart that vision from coming into existence. For both moral and political reasons, therefore, Gandhi made several, albeit faltering, attempts to set up peacekeeping brigades.

The Idea of a Shanti Sena

While Gandhi was still in South Africa, his rhetoric already included references to "armies of peace." At a meeting of the British Indian Association, held in Johannesburg on 27 April 1913 to consider action to be taken against a discriminatory immigration bill, Gandhi explained that if the government did not meet their requests, Indians would have to "take up the well-tried weapon of passive resistance" and fight as does an army. But "Theirs was an army of peace. Although they used military terms, they agreed with the soldier only in so far as the latter was a sufferer in his own person. A true passive resister could never be a party to injuring others. His motive power was not vengeance. It was hardly possible to expect the whole community to become soldiers in such an army. But, whether they had five hundred, or fifty, or five, or even one true passive resister on the field, victory was theirs."[1]

After returning to India and establishing himself as a nationalist leader, Gandhi finally took concrete steps toward the organization of a

peace brigade after the riots in Bombay on 17 November 1921 that protested the arrival of the Prince of Wales. The Mahatma went on a fast until
the disturbances subsided and called off the proposed satyagraha campaigns. On the twenty-second he penned a note to his co-workers in which
he laid the framework for a volunteer corps that would maintain peace.

> Workers have lost their lives or limbs, or have suffered brutalities in
> the act of preserving peace, of weaning mad countrymen from their
> wrath. These deaths and injuries show, that in spite of the error of
> many of our countrymen, some of us are prepared to die for the attain-
> ment of our goal. If all of us had imbibed the spirit of non-violence, or
> if some had and others remained passive, no blood need have been spilt.
> But it was not to be. Some must therefore voluntarily give their blood
> in order that a bloodless atmosphere may be created . . . the task before
> workers is to take the blows from the Government and our erring
> countrymen. This is the only way open to us of sterilizing the forces of
> violence. . . . We must secure the full co-operation of the rowdies of
> Bombay. We must know the mill-hands. They must either work for
> the Government or for us, i.e., for violence or against it. . . . Similarly
> we must reach the rowdy elements, befriend them and help them to
> understand the religious character of the struggle. We must neither
> neglect them nor pander to them. We must become their servants.[2]

The next day a meeting in Bombay of the Working Committee of
the All-India Congress Committee requested local congress committees to
organize volunteer corps to quell riots. Every member of the corps was to
take the pledge of nonviolence "in word and deed" and inculcate the spirit
of nonviolence among others.[3]

Not only were the volunteer organizations set up but within one
month Gandhi was complaining that the government was taking active
measures to suppress them. He admitted that the crackdown was partially
a result of the authorities' fear that the corps might not remain nonviolent
but was quick to add: "The other hypothesis . . . is that the Government
dread this non-violence more than an armed revolt. The police-officers are
getting tired and unnerved by being ordered to molest people who do not
retaliate. Some of them confess, 'non-violence is a dreadful foe to meet.
Violence we understand and do not mind. But it makes one feel so small to
beat a man who does not beat you back.' "[4]

During the late 1920s and early 1930s there were further developments. Khan Abdul Ghaffar Khan, the nationalist leader of the warlike
Pathan tribe of the North-West Frontier of British India, initiated the first
extensive application of Gandhi's shanti sena idea. In 1929 the staunchly
Gandhian Khan founded the Khudai Khidmatgar (Servants of God) movement to awaken the nationalist spirit among the Pathans, to work for their

uplift by encouraging education, and especially to help them curb "their anti-social customs, to check their violent outbursts, and to practice good behaviour."[5] Members of the movement were required to take a solemn vow that included the promises to "refrain from violence and from taking revenge," "to forgive those who oppress me or treat me with cruelty," and "to refrain from taking part in feuds and quarrels and from creating enmity." In addition, Khudai Khidmatgars were to lead simple, virtuous, and productive lives that included the devotion of at least two hours daily to social work.[6]

An updated version of the aims of the movement included, inter alia, the additional principles that "a Khudai Khidmatgar will, wherever he is, combat oppression and high-handedness by goodness and wean the opponent from evil by love and affection" and "a Khudai Khidmatgar will not be a party to oppression and will always stand by the oppressed."[7]

In 1930 Khan's "Red Shirts" took part in the Civil Disobedience campaign launched by Gandhi's Salt March and "suffered the most severe of all repressions in the Indian independence movement"[8] while adhering to their pledge. Notwithstanding the banning of the organization shortly thereafter, it continued to increase in popularity and by 1938 boasted some one hundred thousand members.[9] Although originally the main task before the Khudai Khidmatgars was to be nonpolitical constructive work, they were drawn into the independence struggle. Their bravery and unflinching adherence to Gandhi's principles made them a model that Gandhi could hold up for others (and later they became a classic example for use by would-be popularizers of the Shanti Sena idea) while they earned their leader the title of "Frontier Gandhi."[10]

In 1930, as Gandhi neared the Dandi seacoast on his historic Salt March, rumors began circulating that access to the beach (and, consequently, salt) would be prevented by rows of armed soldiers.[11] As it turned out, no military presence awaited the marchers. However, a satirical play foreshadowing the anticipated clash, which was sent to the editors of the *Bombay Chronicle* and *Navajivan*,[12] illustrated popular perceptions of how the Gandhian idea of a peaceful army would operate.

In the imaginary scenario of the play Gandhi's men run onto the bayonets of the soldiers in waves until each soldier has an impaled body in front of him. Rather than kill the Mahatma, the soldiers rebel. The dishonored commanding colonel is talked out of suicide by Gandhi and then, returning to his senses, arrests his men.

The play is melodramatic to the extreme. Gandhi and his followers would never throw themselves onto bayonets—an aggressive, provocative act needlessly sacrificing life and brutalizing the opponents rather than one of persuasive pressure that is the aim of satyagraha. Stripped of its most wildly theatrical elements, however, it is almost a summary of Gandhi's

Geneva speech that seems to have influenced Royden, and events not too far removed from the ones described by the anonymous playwright were acted out by the fences of the salt works near the tiny village of Dharasana some two hundred kilometers north of Bombay.

After Gandhi's arrest, first retired Baroda State High Court judge Abbas Tyabji and then nationalist poetess Sarojini Naidu led the remaining marchers and other volunteers in the nonviolent raids on the salt pans that Gandhi had proposed.[13] The world media were focused on the scene of unarmed raiders being beaten mercilessly as they attempted to gain access to the mounds of forbidden salt.[14] The soldiers, however, did not put down their lathis (canes, often iron tipped, used by police and military personnel in India) in disgust; enraged, they often used them more vigorously. The moral victory that was gained at Dharasana was not achieved through the conversion of the adversary but through the winning of public, including international, support. Gandhi, nevertheless, fondly referred to the Salt Satyagraha as "the high spot of his campaigns"[15] and continued preaching the use of unarmed nonviolent "soldiers" and peacekeepers with increasing conviction.

In 1938, after communal riots in Allahabad during which the police and army had to be called in to quell the disturbances, Gandhi again turned his mind to the formation of shanti dals (peace brigades). Allahabad was the headquarters of Congress, and this indicated to Gandhi that, regardless of the unpleasantness of the "naked truth," the Congress "has not yet become fit to substitute the British authority." He added:

> By this time, i.e., after seventeen years' practice of non-violence, the Congress should be able to put forth a non-violent army of volunteers numbering not a few thousands but lacs [sic] who would be equal to every occasion where the police and military are required. Thus instead of one brave [volunteer] who died in the attempt to secure peace, we should be able to produce hundreds. And a non-violent army acts unlike armed men, as well in times of peace as of disturbances. They would be constantly engaged in constructive activities that make riots impossible. Theirs will be the duty of seeking occasions of bringing warring communities together, carrying on peace propaganda, engaging in activities that would bring and keep them in touch with every single person, male and female, adult and child, in their parish or division. Such an army should be ready to cope with any emergency, and in order to still the frenzy of mobs, should risk their lives in numbers sufficient for the purpose. A few hundred, maybe a few thousand, such spotless deaths will once for all put end to the riots. Surely a few hundred young men and women giving themselves deliberately to mob fury will be any day a cheap and braver method of dealing with such madness than the display and use of the police and the military.[16]

As the struggle for independence intensified so too did tensions between the majority Hindu and minority Muslim communities. Although as a man of peace the Mahatma was hurt by these violent outbreaks, for Gandhi the nationalist leader there was also a more immediate political consideration: communal harmony had to be maintained so that the undivided attention of India's masses could be directed against British imperialism rather than at rival religious groups, and it was difficult to maintain a creditable argument that his country was ready for freedom when only the colonial power could maintain peace among the aspirants to independence. In short, intercommunal peace was necessary for the successful prosecution of the larger battle, and the moral right to independence had to be demonstrated by showing that India could govern itself peacefully.

A few months after Gandhi's admission of Congress's failure he spelled out the qualifications for membership in the contemplated Peace Brigade:

(1) He or she must have a living faith in non-violence. This is impossible without faith in God.[17] A non-violent man can do nothing save by the power and grace of God. Without it he won't have the courage to die without anger, without fear and without retaliation. Such courage comes from the belief that God sits in the hearts of all and that there should be no fear in the presence of God. The knowledge of the omnipresence of God also means respect for the lives of even those who may be called opponents or *goondas* [hooligans]. This contemplated intervention is a process of stilling the fury of man when the brute in him gets the mastery over him.

(2) This messenger of peace must have equal regard for all the principal religions of the earth. Thus, if he is a Hindu, he will respect the other faiths current in India. He must therefore possess a knowledge of the general principles of the different faiths professed in the country.

(3) Generally speaking this work of peace can only be done by local men in their own localities.

(4) The work can be done singly or in groups. Therefore no one need wait for companions. Nevertheless one would naturally seek companions in one's own locality and form a local brigade.

(5) This messenger of peace will cultivate through personal service contacts with the people in his locality or chosen circle, so that when he appears to deal with ugly situations, he does not descend upon the members of a riotous assembly as an utter stranger liable to be looked upon as a suspect or an unwelcome visitor.

(6) Needless to say, a peace-bringer must have a character beyond reproach and must be known for his strict impartiality.

(7) Generally there are previous warnings of coming storms. If these are known, the Peace Brigade will not wait till the conflagration breaks out but will try to handle the situation in anticipation.

(8) Whilst, if the movement spreads, it might be well if there are some whole-time workers, it is not absolutely necessary that there should be. The idea is to have as many good and true men and women as possible. These can be had only if volunteers are drawn from those who are engaged in various walks of life but have leisure enough to cultivate friendly relations with the people living in their circle and otherwise possess the qualifications required of a member of the Peace Brigade.
(9) There should be a distinctive dress worn by the members of the contemplated Brigade so that in course of time they will be recognized without the slightest difficulty.[18]

Although Gandhi had obviously given careful thought to the setting up of the shanti dals and believed in their feasibility, he warned his followers that, because he did not have "the health, energy or time . . . to cope with the tasks I dare not shirk,"[19] he could play no active part in their formation. Without this direct involvement no permanently operating peace brigades were established.

A few years later Gandhi was optimistically suggesting that the brigades would come into being spontaneously if enough people "who will honestly endeavour to observe non-violence"[20] show their ahimsa "when there is rioting or similar disturbance."[21] Through his newspaper columns, however, Gandhi continued to write explaining the workings of shanti dals and encouraging their formation. When a correspondent asked how self-suffering could touch the hearts of outsiders, "the usual perpetrators of violence during riots" who have "no scruples about hurting those whom they have never known before and for whom they can have no regard or consideration," Gandhi responded that would-be peace brigade members had "to come into close touch and cultivate acquaintances with the so-called goonda elements in his vicinity" during peaceful times. The answer was to know and be known by all and to "win the hearts of all" by selfless service, in other words, through the constructive program in the local area.[22]

In May 1941 Gandhi answered the president of the Maharashtra Provincial Congress Committee's question, "Do you desire the starting of peace-brigades?" in the affirmative,[23] and in a discussion with Congress workers at Benares (Varanasi) less than one year later Gandhi complained that although his "suggestion for the formation of peace brigades still held the field," Congress members doubted his seriousness in undertaking the project and "had dismissed it as impracticable without earnestly examining its implications and potentialities."[24] During this period again more immediate events overtook Gandhi and the Congress: Britain was at war (and, consequently, as part of the Empire so was India), India was threatened with Japanese invasion, and Gandhi had launched his "Quit India" campaign against the British.

Gandhi had personally participated in the Boer War and Zulu "Rebellion" in South Africa as the leader of ambulance corps and in the First World War as a recruiting officer for the Allied cause. Initially such actions resulted from patriotic feelings as a citizen of the British Empire and later were justified by arguments containing traces of political pragmatism.[25] His philosophy of nonviolence in these matters firmed as he aged and as his regard for British justice declined (i.e., as he increasingly saw Britain as an exploiting supremacist colonial power rather than as a fair-minded nation that would grant Indians independence as soon as their readiness for it had been demonstrated).

As news of the attempted Nazi genocide of the Jewish people reached him, Gandhi grappled with the ideal way that large-scale evils should be combated. Earlier, speaking of Nazi oppression, he had claimed that if ever there could be "a justifiable war in the name of humanity" then "war against Germany . . . would be completely justified. But I do not believe in any war."[26] And, as the Japanese forces advanced through Burma threatening India with invasion, Gandhi was forced to clarify his ideas on actions to be taken in times of war. He warned against using violence to meet violence even in the case of national defense, "for the defence has to resort to all the damnable things that the enemy does, and then with greater vigour if it has to succeed."[27]

Gandhi's ideal nonviolent society was nonexploitative and aimed to resolve international conflicts by helping its neighbors alleviate their economic problems with the aid of "superior technical knowledge, to develop their local resources to the utmost extent."[28] This ideal society would be disarmed[29] because it would have no one to fear.[30] If either such a hypothetically sharing and nonviolent society or another society deciding to defend itself by peaceful means[31] were, nevertheless, attacked, there would, according to Gandhi, be two ways open for it to cope with the aggressor: firstly, "to yield possession but not co-operate with the aggressor. . . . The second way would be non-violent resistance by the people who have been trained in the non-violent way. They . . . would offer themselves as fodder for the aggressor's cannon . . . the unexpected spectacle of endless rows upon rows of men and women simply dying rather than surrender to the will of an aggressor must ultimately melt him and his soldiery."[32]

Gandhi believed that in this "living wall" approach to self-defense "there will be no greater loss in men than if forcible resistance was offered; there will be no expenditure in armaments and fortifications."[33] This approach would be most effective if undertaken by a community where everyone was a true satyagrahi. In such a case there would be no need to organize elaborate civilian defense programs because the most effective nonviolent measures would occur spontaneously. Although the discipline required for a living wall approach to the defense of borders is more than a little unlikely to be achieved, Gandhi firmly believed that given proper training and proper generalship such nonviolence "can be practiced by masses of mankind."[34]

Mirabehn, Gandhi's English disciple, was dispatched to Orissa, the Indian coastal region facing Burma, to "help prepare the masses for nonviolent non-cooperative resistance to the expected Japanese invasion of the east coast."[35] As preparatory work among the villages commenced so did criticism, often vehement, of Gandhi's national defense policy. Raman, a former follower, for instance, was outraged that while India was threatened with the danger of invasion Gandhi could advocate a completely nonviolent approach.[36] Although the invasion did not materialize, the preparation for it and the answering of critics meant that a clearer picture of Gandhi's attitude to war and nonviolent struggles against war was placed before the public.

N. K. Bose, who was Gandhi's personal secretary for a time after the conclusion of the Second World War, has produced a step-by-step systematization of Gandhian actions and their consequences in cases of the invasion of a nation. According to Bose, in Gandhi's scheme first the shanti sena is sent to confront the aggressors and talk to them if possible, tell them that they are wrong in their actions, "even while they are prepared to be mowed down, yet not lift a finger in order to hurt the 'enemy' in so-called self-defence."[37] If the "enemy," nevertheless, does move on to occupy the land, rather than resorting to a scorched earth policy,[38] the invaders are to be lived with peacefully, but on the satyagrahi's terms and without their submission. The satyagrahis maintain complete noncooperation with the invaders. They refuse to obey orders or to work in the administration, refuse to accept honors from the regime, refuse to pay fines and taxes, boycott the courts, schools, and products manufactured by the oppressor, and engage in strikes and the deliberate breaking of unjust or symbolic laws.[39] The theory goes that if the resisters are firm enough, cling to the truth, and are nonviolent enough (so as not to leave the occupiers afraid or on the defensive) "members of the enemy will start thinking . . . the effects of indoctrination to which they have hitherto been subjected will begin to wear out."[40] Ultimately, the aim of this process is to convert the leadership and soldiers of the opposing army.

Although there is no evidence that invaders can be talked out of an ongoing invasion or halted by a "living wall" before the regime becomes entrenched—it has never been tried—noncooperation with invaders or imperialist rulers has achieved some success in the past.[41] Gandhi, too, had a complete answer for critics who doubted the efficacy of his methods against the likes of Hitler,[42] who knew no pity. "As a believer in non-violence" he could not, he said, "limit its possibilities": "Hitherto he and his likes have built upon their invariable experience that men yield to force. Unarmed

men, women and children offering non-violent resistance without any bitterness in them will be a novel experience for them. Who can dare say that
it is not in their nature to respond to the higher and finer forces? They have
the same soul that I have."[43]

Even though psychological simulation experiments tend strongly to
reject Gandhi's underlying premise, it still would not have worried him.
Gandhi simply continued (and here is the essence of satyagraha, his method
of nonviolence in action): "If Hitler is unaffected by my suffering, it does
not matter. For I have lost nothing worth [preserving]. My honour is the
only thing worth preserving. That is independent of Hitler's pity."[44]

As the war ended and the British prepared to leave India, communal
rioting reached new and tragic heights. This prompted Gandhi, now with
a clearer vision of the role of a satyagrahi army before him, to again set to
work popularizing the shanti sena.

In early 1946 Gandhi's paper carried an article on "Non-Violent Volunteer Corps." There Gandhi alluded to previous attempts at forming
shanti dals and explained that the lesson of those trials was that "the membership . . . of such organizations could not be very large."[45] He was no
longer stressing the spontaneous growth of a vast movement but the need
for sainiks of exceptional character. The emphasis shifted from quantity to
the quality of the membership, and Gandhi noted, "It is difficult to find
many such persons," and explained, "That is why non-violent corps must
be small, if they are to be efficient." In line with the immediate need in the
violence-rent country, Gandhi further adumbrated some rules for corps
that he had "culled from my own experience." In addition to an implicit
faith in God:

(1) A volunteer may not carry any weapons.
(2) The members of a corps must be easily recognizable.
(3) Every volunteer must carry bandages, scissors, needle and thread,
surgical knife etc., for rendering first-aid.
(4) He should know how to carry and remove the wounded.
(5) He should know how to put out fires, how to enter a fire area
without getting burnt, how to climb heights for rescue work and descend safely with or without his charge.
(6) He should be well acquainted with all the residents of his locality.
This is a service in itself.
(7) He should recite Ramanama [the name of God] ceaselessly in his
heart and persuade others who believe in it to do likewise.[46]

After the terrible Calcutta killings of 1947, Gandhi fasted in the city
in a (largely successful) attempt to restore sanity. A Calcuttan shanti sena
was formed at this time and appeared to be having success in restoring

peace[47] and one month later Gandhi was calling for a similar group to be set up in the capital.[48] There is a strong feeling in the speeches that Gandhi's stress that those who had sacrificed their lives for the cause of peace "were the real heroes" was not merely to ensure that the deaths did not further exacerbate communal frenzy but to give meaning to the deaths of peace activists in a far more general sense, one that was applicable for all times and all situations.

Gandhi had personally risked injury or worse by touring riot-torn areas in Calcutta, and when the secretary of the local Shanti Sena called on Gandhi, the Mahatma gave the "soldiers of peace" his blessings and the declaration of encouragement: "My life is my message."[49]

Independence and Gandhi's assassination led to a temporary end of the shanti sena experiments. Although no organized sena persisted into the second half of the century, a large legacy of experience did.

The Contemplation of an International Shanti Sena

Power has pointed out that because much of Gandhi's energy was expended in the battle for Indian national independence "he was in no haste to relinquish his nation's power to a super-state" and, consequently, his few utterances on the League of Nations and the United Nations, although revealing "a modicum of support for these bodies," are "disappointing to proponents of inter-state organizations."[50]

Gandhi's comments on world federalism often omitted any mention of sanctioning or enforcement procedures;[51] however, the Gandhi drafted "Quit India" resolution of August 1942 declared that upon the establishment of a world federation "disarmament would be practicable in all countries, national armies, navy and air forces would no longer be necessary, and a world federal defence force would keep the world peace and prevent aggression."[52] At about the same time, in a letter to a friend, the Polish engineer Maurice Frydman, he conceded, "that there may be a world police to keep order in the absence of universal belief in non-violence."[53] In a statement on the eve of the San Francisco Conference to establish the United Nations Gandhi added the codicil that such an army would be "a concession to human weakness, not . . . an emblem of peace."[54] Earlier he had written that the failure of the League of Nations could partly be blamed on its lack of necessary sanctions. Gandhi continued, suggesting that "the means . . . adopted in India [would] supply the necessary sanction" not only for an organization like the League "but to any voluntary body or association that would take up the great cause of the peace of the world."[55]

A World Pacifist Meeting was planned to be held in India in 1949 "under the guidance of Mahatma Gandhi to find a way out of the present darkness."[56] Despite Gandhi's death and the inability of the majority of foreign guests to arrive by the designated time, a preliminary meeting was held at Sevagram in January of that year, where it was decided, inter alia, "to organize local peace units for allaying conflicts in an effective manner."[57] The full conference, held in Shantiniketan in December and continued in Sevagram in January 1950, decided to undertake "the building up in different countries of small Peace Armies, which the conference decided to call 'Satyagraha Units.' " Although these Units were to develop out of the local background in each country, "a small international group has agreed to keep in close touch with each other and to evolve common plans for training and work."[58]

The delegates at the conference included Vinoba Bhave, A. J. Muste, and the Reverend Michael Scott. The statement on Satyagraha Units or, as they were sometimes called "The Peace Army," penned by Muste, declared:

> We propose that serious and sustained attempts should be made to establish *Satyagraha* units in different countries. These units will be composed of those individuals who have full faith in the superiority of non-violence and moral force over violent methods and who are prepared to discipline their own lives for becoming true *satyagrahis*. . . . Unlike the military forces, the *Satyagraha* units will be fully active during peace time by tackling the roots of violence in social, educational and administrative spheres. Non-violent defence has to lay great emphasis on preventive actions, as illustrated by Mahatma Gandhi's *Constructive Programme*. The *Satyagraha* units will also try to meet crisis situations non-violently in their respective localities or regions. They will not quietly wait for a conflagration to break out, but will, from day to day, try their utmost to create conditions which would nip conflicts in the bud. This could be made more effective if they are able to cultivate intimate personal contacts with people inhabiting those areas. In organising non-violent defence we will have to stress quality rather than quantity, and, unlike military officers, the leaders will be required to be in the front rather than in the rear. There can be no policy of secrecy in such an organization because non-violence and truth are integrally related.

After repeating Gandhi's pronouncement that nonviolent resistance to an invader requires complete noncooperation coupled with maintaining an "attitude of human understanding towards the invading soldier," Muste continues, "The *Satyagraha* units may, when occasions arise, take the 'offensive' in the form of 'Peace or Goodwill Missions' to eradicate misunderstanding and roots of war before it is too late."[59]

The statement concluded with the suggestion "that a preliminary International Liaison Committee be established to coordinate the work of recruiting and training *satyagrahis* on the lines of the scheme indicated above."[60] The committee was set up, but without committed leadership "it soon lapsed into silence and inaction."[61] Action on an international shanti sena had to wait until Vinoba Bhave had firmly established the organization on Indian soil and had demonstrated its effectiveness at peacekeeping over a number of years.

Conclusion

The Gandhian legacy provides a history of the practice of nonviolence on a unparalleled scale. The legacy, however, is more inspirational than organizational and, given the nature of Gandhi's charismatic leadership and of his philosophy of nonviolence, which in many ways is hostile to organization, this may have been inevitable.

The inspiration, nevertheless, was to lead to the creation of an organized Shanti Sena in India. This left Gandhi's followers with the problem of how to develop the Mahatma's ideas without clear guidance, yet in a way that they remained faithful to those ideas. And it was the efforts of these followers that, in turn, inspired those attempting to set up international peace brigades.

All of Gandhi's endeavors to establish a peace brigade were inspired by the need of immediate peacekeeping, but when Gandhi's philosophy of nonviolence is examined closely, it is obvious that peacekeeping for him was aimed at far more than preventing communal strife for political reasons. From his strong emphasis on the uplift of the poor, of getting to the root causes of violence (including structural violence), it is easily demonstrable that his concerns were not merely with narrowly defined peacekeeping. Gandhi was hurt by outbreaks of violence not only because they hampered his political agenda but also because he saw violence as a negation of humanity that blocked the quest for Truth.

Gandhi believed peace to be important as an intrinsic good. He saw nonviolence as an existential necessity—the path to self-realization. This is a corner-stone of Gandhian thought. Although those contemplating the setting up of an international Shanti Sena echoed these broader concerns in a limited way, the fundamental implications of this philosophy are generally misunderstood by Western proponents of Gandhian philosophy in action. To understand the problems associated with applying Gandhi's philosophy, the peace brigade movement generally, and the Shanti Sena in particular, must be placed in the context of this philosophy. This is best achieved through an examination of Gandhian nonviolence, and of some of the concepts already alluded to in the previous discussion.

4

The Philosophical Gandhian Background

Where, during the twentieth century, the impetus for the attempts at unarmed peacekeeping, peacemaking, and peacebuilding (especially when the focus has been on more than mere technical assistance) did not come directly from the Indian Gandhians themselves, the initiators have, nevertheless, tended to look to Mahatma Gandhi or his followers for inspiration. To understand this trend the impact on the international pacifist community of both Gandhi's philosophy of nonviolence and his nonviolent campaigns against the British must be borne in mind. The founding statements that accompanied the setting up of various peace brigades either reflect some of the primary principles of Gandhian satyagraha or assert that the aim is to "internationalize the Shanti Sena idea." Therefore, to understand these Gandhian or Sena-inspired initiatives, the philosophy on which the Sena rests, and hence they also ostensibly rest, needs clarification.

Gandhi's Nonviolence

Gandhi believed in the need for absolutes by which to orient one's life. He explained this toward the end of his life by noting that "a mere mechanical adherence to truth and non-violence is likely to break down at the critical moment. Hence I have said that Truth is God."[1] Truth for him, however, was more than a beacon to keep one on the correct path: Truth (Satya)[2] was the very reason for existence, the search for Truth being a search for God.[3] "Truth is that which you believe to be true at this moment, and that is your God."[4] In fact, Gandhi came "to the conclusion that, for myself, God is Truth. But two years ago, I went a step further and said that Truth is God. You will see the fine distinction between the two statements."[5]

The metaphysical nature of this connection between "Truth" and "God" is explained by Gandhi in a private letter: "In 'God is Truth' *is* certainly does not mean 'equal to' nor does it merely mean, 'is truthful.' He is nothing if he is not That. Truth in Sanskrit means *Sat*. *Sat* means *Is*. Therefore Truth is implied in *Is*. God is, nothing else is. Therefore the more truthful we are, the nearer we are to God. We *are* only to the extent that we are truthful."[6]

Iyer further summarizes Gandhi's position of an individual's relationship to truth in the following paraphrase of various quotations from Gandhi:

> As truth is the substance of morality, man is a moral agent only to the extent that he embraces and seeks truth. By truth is not merely meant the abstention from lies, not just the prudential conviction that honesty is the best policy in the long run, but even more that we must rule our life by this law of Truth at any cost. We must say No when we mean No regardless of consequences. He who ignores this law does not know what it is to speak and to stand for the truth, is like a fake coin, valueless. He has abdicated from his role and status as a moral being. Devotion to truth is the sole reason for human existence, and the truth alone really sustains us at all times. Without truth it would be impossible to observe any principles or rules in life.[7]

For Gandhi there was a distinction between "Truth," that is, Absolute Truth, and "truth," as relative truth. Gandhi was not a monotheist; he did not believe in a personal God. Regardless of the devotional elements in his religious belief he was in essence a monist;[8] for him God was an impersonal all-pervading reality.[9] This reality is the Absolute Truth. Discoveries on the way to the realization of Truth he called relative truth: "As long as I have not realised this Absolute Truth, so long must I hold to the relative truth as I have conceived it. That relative truth must meanwhile be my beacon, my shield, my buckler."[10]

Although Gandhi may have insisted that such a quest for Truth was the foundation of a life worth living, he also issued the obvious warning about the consequences that could flow from such a position. Because, he cautioned, "the human mind works through innumerable media and . . . the evolution of the human mind is not the same for all . . . what may be truth for one may be untruth for another."[11] No one, therefore, "has a right to coerce others to act according to his own view of truth."[12] Thus, the necessity for nonviolence.

Although Truth is the goal, *ahimsa,* or nonviolence, becomes the necessary and only means of realizing it.[13] Because of the conflict that may result from the differing conceptions of truth, nonviolence and, where there is a choice, the voluntary acceptance rather than the infliction of suffering become very important elements in ensuring that coercion does not occur. Gandhi explained this in his testimony before the Disorders Inquiry Committee in 1920.[14] While he admitted that although different individuals had different views about truth and that although even honest striving after truth may differ in every case, he maintained that confusion need not result. "The non–violence part," he insisted, was, therefore, "a necessary corollary. Without that there would be confusion or worse."[15]

But there was also more to nonviolence for Gandhi. Violence arose from ignorance or untruth. Truth, conversely, arose out of nonviolence: "without ahimsa it is not possible to seek and find Truth. Ahimsa and Truth are so intertwined that it is practically impossible to distangle and separate them. They are like two sides of a coin or rather a smooth unstamped metallic disc. Who can say, which is the obverse and which the reverse? Nevertheless, ahimsa is the means, Truth is the end. . . . If we take care of the means we are bound to reach the end sooner or later."[16]

Gandhi, the architect of the dismantling of the mightiest colonial empire ever known by nonviolent means, could not believe in violence as a "cleansing force" that, according to Sartre and Fanon, provided dignity and restored self-respect when the oppressed rose up against their oppressors.[17] Gandhi, too, saw the need for self-respect, going so far as to say that "where there is only a choice between cowardice and violence, I would advise violence."[18] The crux of his message was that these are generally *not* the only two alternatives;[19] there is also nonviolence and "non-violence affords the fullest protection to one's self-respect and sense of honour."[20]

In the Gandhian lexicon ahimsa means far more than what is implied by the negatively focused English word *nonviolence*. Although ahimsa, in the negative, includes refraining from physically harming an opponent, it also embodies a positive concept: it requires doing, not merely abstaining from injury. Ahimsa "is not merely a negative state of harmlessness but it is a positive state of love, of doing good even to the evil-doer. But it does not mean helping the evil-doer to continue the wrong or tolerating it by passive acquiescence. On the contrary, love, the active state of ahimsa requires you to resist the wrong doer."[21]

Ahimsa, then, appears to enjoin positive action in the form of active promotion of good and the active prevention of evil. In other words, it corresponds to Galtung's second-party approach to conflict resolution. But there are also pronounced third-party approach emphases as well. Gandhi noted, "The essence of non-violence technique is that it seeks to liquidate antagonisms but not the antagonists themselves,"[22] and "The satyagrahi's object is to convert, not to coerce, the wrongdoer."[23]

His strong sense of the unity of all life meant that for him the notion of ahimsa was construed widely enough to include not treating another with less dignity than was warranted by a shared humanity. Not only does dehumanization pave the way for violence, but dehumanization *is* violence. Gandhi's writings convey a strong feeling that nonviolence is far more than fighting an enemy without violence. Nonviolence precludes the concept of an enemy, of relating to another as a thing. To borrow Martin Buber's phrases, nonviolence can be characterized as defining even a conflict situation in terms of "I–You" rather than "I–It."[24] "The way of violence works as a monologue," states Ramana Murti, "but the nature of non-violence is a dialogue,"[25] and "there is necessarily a dialogue in nonviolence, because through it you wish to convince the other party and to bring him to discover in you not his adversary, but a man like him."[26]

In other words, intervention in situations of violence is important not only to achieve justice but also to end violence per se because violence does more than maintain structures of oppression, it also prevents the fulfillment of human potential by blocking the honest appreciation of shared humanity that is a prerequisite. Because in the dominant tradition of classical Hinduism "existence is a unity,"[27] suffering and conflict are the result of the introduction of duality into an essentially nondualistic situation. In attempting to end violence satyagrahis are in reality exposing themselves to no more violence than if they allowed violence to proceed unabated. They are, in effect, protecting themselves by ending violence and are assisting the protagonists to achieve their human potential by helping them realize the unity of humankind through personal risk.[28] For satyagrahis, therefore, the intervention in situations of violence, even at the risk of personal loss, is a manifest declaration of the truth of nonduality, which is the essence of Truth.[29]

The connection of violence and the quest for self-realization through the understanding of this nonduality can be summed up in the following formula adapted from Naess:[30]

1. Self-realization presupposes a search for truth.
2. In the last analysis humankind (or even all life) is one.
3. Himsa (violence) against oneself makes complete self-realization impossible.
4. Himsa against another is himsa against the self.
5. Himsa against another makes complete self-realization impossible.

A useful systematization of this argument with "Truth" as the ultimate goal, again produced by Naess, is provided in the figure, "Self-realization and the attainment of truth."[31]

Not long after Gandhi settled in his last ashram at Sevagram, adjacent to Segaon village, he told a European inquirer who had asked whether his aim in taking up village life was "just humanitarian" that he was there to serve no one but himself by finding self-realization through service to the villagers. He added: "Man's ultimate aim is the realization of God, and all

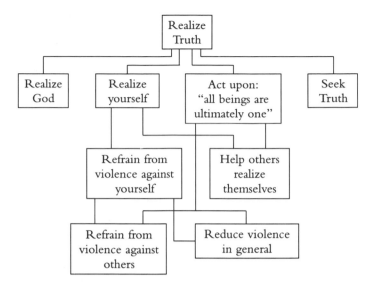

Fig. Self-realization and the attainment of truth.

his activities, political, social and religious, have to be guided by the ultimate aim of the vision of God. The immediate service of all human beings
becomes a necessary part of the endeavour simply because the only way to
find God is to see Him in His creation and be one with it. This can only be
done by service of all."[32]

That some conflicts are vertical (in Galtung's terminology) was clearly
recognized by Gandhi in his moral support for the Poles against the Ger-
mans, the Abyssinians against the Italians, and the Chinese against the
Japanese. Even where conflicts are vertical and the cause is just, however,
Gandhi sees violence as inherently counterproductive in the functional
as well as existential sense ("To answer brutality with brutality is to admit one's moral and intellectual bankruptcy and it can only start a vicious
circle."[33] And "counter violence can only result in further brutalization of human nature"[34]) and, consequently, is another reason why it
should be prevented.

Gandhi's nonviolence included the notion of self-suffering (not violence to the self) as an inescapable element because, as Sharp points out, it
is the price paid for maintaining resistance in a nonviolent way.[35] This
voluntary suffering was also much more, however. Hindu religious philosophy is concerned with suffering in the same way that Christian philosophy
is preoccupied with the problem of evil. Gandhi was the first among the
reformers of Hinduism to regard self-suffering as a way of dealing with the
problem of suffering in the world.[36] In conflict resolution, Gandhi saw

voluntary suffering as a creative process, the role of which was to break a deadlock, to "cut through the rationalized defences of the opponent."[37] Gandhi believed that "reason has to be strengthened by suffering and suffering opens the eyes of understanding"[38] because an "appeal of reason is more to the head but penetration of the heart comes from suffering. It opens up the inner understanding of man."[39]

Here is the reason for Gandhi's calls for the unarmed reenactments of Thermopylae with a "living wall" defense strategy and the basis for some of the peace army proposals. The entire rationale of a method of nonviolent conflict resolution that sees conversion of the opponent as its aim must rest upon the assumption that opponents are open to reason, that they have consciences, that human nature is such that it is bound, or at least likely, "to respond to any noble and friendly action."[40]

Gandhi's analysis of human nature concludes that "Every one of us is a mixture of good and evil. . . . The difference that there is between human beings is the difference of degree."[41] This belief was not merely to be held in the abstract as a generalization for humanity but was to be remembered in times of conflict and applied to opponents in such a way that their dignity as human beings and the respect it commanded was not infringed. For Gandhi the possibility of peace depended on this belief: "Not to believe in the possibility of permanent peace is to disbelieve in the godliness of human nature. Methods hitherto have failed because rock–bottom sincerity on the part of those who have striven has been lacking."[42]

A belief in the rationality of human nature is as important to satyagraha as is the belief in human goodness. Gandhi himself was certain of this; his utterances containing many statements of faith, such as "Every man may know and most of us do know what is a just and an unjust act";[43] "Everyone can think for himself ";[44] and "Unlike the animal man has been given the faculty of reason."[45] This belief, however, need not imply that large areas of nonrationality do not occur in human motivations or behavior. It merely requires, in Bondurant's words, "the assumption that man is endowed with reason, that man can utilize reason to direct his actions, and that a technique for conducting conflict can appeal to the rational in man."[46] A belief in this combination of reason and goodness allows for a faith in the possibility of conversion through acts of creative self-suffering.[47]

Pelton, in his examination of the psychology of nonviolence, claims that the idea that self-suffering "melts the heart" of the opponent is a gross oversimplification, that it may even "elicit a negative reaction towards the victim."[48] Gandhi, however, insisted on retaining a faith in human nature that maintained that such a process does work.[49] Gandhi warned that the suffering or hardship undertaken had to be functional; he "was not in favour of martyrs or suffering not caused by acts conducive to the solution of the present conflict or future conflicts."[50] "Let us all be brave enough to die the death of a martyr," intones Gandhi, while warning in the same breath that no one should "lust for martyrdom."[51]

The opponent must not be encouraged to act against the satyagrahi to bring on self-suffering because "brutalizing the adversary can but make his conversion the more difficult."[52] This brutalization must further be avoided so that the opponent is not compelled to inflict punishment; "the secret of satyagraha" according to Gandhi "lies in not tempting the wrong doer to do wrong."[53]

Self-suffering aims to demonstrate the sincerity of the sufferer as an appeal to the opponent or, in the case of interpositionary actions, opponents, and also aims to purify the sufferer by proving sincerity to the self. Gandhi mentions both these practical and existential benefits of self-suffering (in this case when talking of the extreme position of a nonviolent state involved in a violent international conflict) when he says that "suffering injury in one's own person is . . . of the essence of non–violence and it is the chosen substitute of violence to others. It is not because I value life low that I can countenance with joy thousands voluntarily losing their lives for satyagraha, but because I know that it results in the long run in the least loss of life, and, what is more it ennobles those who lose their lives and morally enriches the world for their sacrifice."[54]

Both the sufferer and the opponent are transformed: the opponents by being forced to confront their own views on the nature of the truth of the given situation and possibly being converted and the sufferer by being morally enriched through not compromising fundamental principles.

Even where self-suffering does not touch the conscience of the opponent it can have objective benefits in a conflict situation, especially in social conflicts. The opponent may be converted indirectly (or coerced by nonviolence?) if the endured suffering moves public opinion to the side of the satyagrahis.[55] Gandhi has on occasion claimed that "the method of reaching the heart is to awaken public opinion" because "public opinion for which one cares is a mightier force than that of gunpowder."[56]

Religious mythology and the Gandhian legend are resplendent with stories of how self-suffering has brought out the good and the reasonable in an opponent, leading to his or her conversion. There are, conversely, just as many stories of failure and disillusionment.[57] In the final analysis the Gandhian technique, to the degree that it is aimed at preventing conflicts rather than achieving self-realization, rests on the belief that opponents can, in fact, be influenced to alter their dispositions and their worldviews. As with religious beliefs, belief in the goodness of human nature and the operation of reason ultimately is the optimist's act of faith in the empirically untestable.

Satyagraha: Nonviolence in Action

The Gandhian technique of nonviolence is known by its Gujarati name of satyagraha, which has variously been interpreted as "passive resistance,"[58] "nonviolent resistance,"[59] "non-violent direct action,"[60] and even as "militant nonviolence."[61] "Satyagraha," Gandhi explained, is "literally holding on to Truth and it means, therefore, Truth-force."[62] The word was coined out of a felt necessity. The technique of nonviolent struggle that Gandhi had evolved in South Africa for the conduct of the Indian indentured laborers' disputes with the government was originally described by the English phrase "passive resistance." Gandhi, however, found that the term "was too narrowly constructed, that it was supposed to be a weapon of the weak, that it could be characterized by hatred, and that it could finally manifest itself as violence."[63]

He decided that a new word had to be coined for the struggle: "But I could not for the life of me find out a new name, and therefore offered a nominal prize through *Indian Opinion* to the reader who made the best suggestion on the subject. As a result Maganlal Gandhi coined the word *Sadagraha* (Sat: truth, Agraha: firmness) and won the prize. But in order to make it clearer I changed the word to *Satyagraha*."[64]

Satyagraha means, in effect, the discovery of truth and working steadily toward it, thus converting the opponent into a friend. In other words, satyagraha is not used against anybody but is done *with* somebody. "It is based on the idea that the moral appeal to the heart or conscience is . . . more effective than an appeal based on threat or bodily pain or violence."[65]

Conflicts and clashes of interests will always occur and, approached with a limited understanding of the psychology of the disputing process, violence often appears to be a superior technique for solving them than nonviolence because it has obvious and tangible strategies and weapons. Nonviolent ways of resolving these conflicts, however, have a far greater chance than other methods of falling within Deutsch's definition of "productive," where the participants "are satisfied with their outcomes and feel that they have gained as a result of the conflict,"[66] rather than "destructive" conflict, where the participants are "dissatisfied with the outcomes and they feel they have lost as a result of the conflict."[67]

Conducting, or attempting to resolve, a conflict in a nonviolent nonthreatening way prevents the opponent "from reacting out of fear in mindless reflex action."[68] Violence in any of its many forms also has the tendency to become self-perpetuating through the cycle of vengeance and counter vengeance. A productive resolution of conflict is more likely to be achieved if it is based on nonviolence (and this is further increased if conversion is successfully carried out) because, in the words of Gregg, it leaves "no aftermath of resentment, bitterness or revenge, no necessity for further threats or force."[69]

The Gandhian technique of satyagraha rests on the belief that the striving for conversion is the most effective method of conducting a struggle or bringing lasting peace to conflicting parties on a pragmatic assessment of the outcome,[70] but more than that Gandhi believed that it is the morally correct way to conduct conflict because only through a dialectical process can Truth be arrived at, or at least approached, and such quest for Truth is, according to him, the aim of human life.

Violence to persons and property has the effect of clouding the real issues involved in the original conflict, whereas noncoercive, nonviolent action invites the parties to a dialogue about the issues themselves.[71] Bondurant points out that "the objective is not to assert propositions, but to create possibilities. In opening up new choices and in confronting an opponent with the demand that he make a choice, the satyagrahi involves himself in acts of 'ethical existence.' The process forces a continuing examination of one's own motives, an examination undertaken within the context of relationships as they are changed towards a new, restructured, and reintegrated pattern."[72]

This dialectical process is essentially creative and inherently constructive.[73] Its immediate object is "a restructuring of the opposing elements to achieve a situation which is satisfactory to both the original opposing antagonists but in such a way as to present an entirely new total circumstance . . . through the operation of non-violent action the truth as judged by the fulfillment of human needs will emerge in the form of a mutually satisfactory and agreed-upon solution."[74]

In conflict situations, then, satyagraha merely means that the satyagrahi follows no other plan than the adherence to nonviolence and has no other goal than to reach the Truth, the Truth being the end of the process, nonviolence the means to achieve it. Because, for Gandhi, good ends can never grow out of bad means the opponent is not forced to expose him or herself to loss. There is no threat, coercion, or punishment. The person offering the satyagraha instead undergoes self-suffering with the optimistic belief that opponents can be converted to see the truth of their claims by touching the opponents' consciences, or that a clearer vision of truth will grow out of the dialectical process for both parties. While the satyagrahis try to convert, they must also remain open to persuasion.

Techniques of conflict resolution based on moral appeals are often seen as politically absurd. This is because the nature of such appeals entails the call for a response, which can either be given or withheld. By contrast, the idea behind the use of coercion is that the opponent *must* respond.[75] Gandhi, moreover, believed that nobody was entirely out of reach of such appeals "especially if one's good will is made sufficiently manifest and one's willingness to suffer for the truth is clearly demonstrated." [76]

Satyagraha in its pure sense aims not so much at changing the behavior of the opponent (or opponents) as at bringing about a change in values *so that* a change in behavior will result. Changed behavior without changed attitudes can only be maintained through coercion, which is fundamentally opposed by the philosophy of satyagraha. Satyagraha, in short, goes beyond redressing merely the immediate grievance that has surfaced as conflict and aims to resolve the distrust and friction that may be the underlying sources of the conflict. And with its ultimate achievement of realizing the unity of all, such distrust and friction is by definition extinguished.

The basic precepts and rules of an action that purports to be based on Gandhian satyagraha can be systematized in ten points:[77]

1. Violence is invited from opponents if they are humiliated or provoked.[78]

2. Violent attitudes are less likely on the part of would-be satyagrahis if they have made clear to themselves the essential elements of their case and the purpose of the struggle.[79]

3. Opponents are less likely to use violent means, the better they understand the satyagrahi's case and conduct.[80]

4. The essential interests that the opponents have in common should be clearly formulated and cooperation established on that basis.[81]

5. Opponents should not be judged harder than the self.[82]

6. Opponents should be trusted.[83]

7. An unwillingness to compromise on nonessentials decreases the likelihood of converting the opponent.[84]

8. The conversion of an opponent is furthered by personal sincerity.[85]

9. The best way of convincing an opponent of the sincerity of the satyagrahi is to make sacrifices for the given cause.[86]

10. A position of weakness in an opponent should not be exploited.[87]

The success of a campaign based on satyagraha in the resolution of any conflict rests upon three basic assumptions. They are:[88]

1. That there can always be found some elements of interest common to all the contending parties.

2. That the parties are, or at least might be, amenable to an "appeal to the heart and mind."

3. That those in a position to commence satyagraha are also in a position to carry it through to the end.

If these prerequisites are fulfilled the scene is set for the process aimed at the required conversion to be initiated. This can involve several steps: firstly, reasoning with the opponent; secondly persuasion through self-suffering "wherein the satyagrahi attempts to dramatise the issues at stake and to get through to the opponent's unprejudiced judgement so that he may willingly come again onto a level where he may be persuaded through natural argument."[89] This process of moral appeal through self-suffering in lieu of violence or coercion Gregg has aptly termed "moral jiu-jitsu."[90] A moral choice is demanded of opponents, which they otherwise may not even have contemplated. Gregg summarizes the dynamics of this position by explaining that the attacker loses moral balance: "He suddenly and unexpectedly loses the moral support which the usual violent resistance of most victims would render him. He plunges forward, as it were, into a new world of values. He feels insecure because of the novelty of the situation and his ignorance of how to handle it. He loses his poise and self-confidence. The victim not only lets the attacker come, but, as it were, pulls him forward by kindness, generosity and voluntary suffering, so that the attacker loses his moral balance."[91]

Gandhi has provided an analogous summary of this process: "I seek entirely to blunt the edge of the tyrant's sword, not by putting up against it a sharper edged weapon but by disappointing his expectation that I would be offering physical resistance. The resistance of the soul that I should offer instead would elude him. It would at first dazzle him and at last compel recognition from him which recognition would not humiliate him but uplift him."[92]

Because coercion rarely leads to conversion and because it does not encourage the dialectical process of finding truth, Gandhi cautions against its use.[93] Although it was plain for Gandhi that coercion vitiated the spirit of satyagraha, it is also plain that moral and nonviolent coercion is preferable to physical coercion.[94] It can galvanize public support and has a greater chance of leading eventually to conversion than does physical coercion.[95] It is also generally more indicative of sincerity than a mere reliance on strength would be.

The Constructive Program

Something similar to what has often been termed the *technical assistance* approach to the broader aspects of the quest for peace (especially as peace-building) has also played a significant part in the Gandhian vision. Gandhi held before himself, and attempted to place before the masses, a picture of an ideal society that was to be the goal of collective endeavor as the approach toward truth was to be goal for the individual. This vision was summed up in the word *Ramrajya*, the "Kingdom of God," where there were equal rights for princes and paupers,[96] where even the lowliest person could get swift justice without elaborate and costly procedures,[97] where inequalities that allowed some to roll in riches while the masses did not have enough to eat were abolished,[98] and where sovereignty of the people was based on pure moral authority rather than power.[99]

To achieve this end a new movement was needed. The day before his death on 30 January 1948, Gandhi wrote, in what was to become known as his "last will and testament," that the Indian National Congress[100] in its present form had outlived its use. The Congress had been set up to achieve political independence; and that goal accomplished the emphasis had to shift to the social, moral, and economic independence of the rural masses. With this in mind Gandhi proposed that the Congress organization be disbanded to allow Lok Seva Sanghs, organizations for the service of the people, to grow in its place.[101]

But even earlier in his career Gandhi had championed the idea of Peace Corps-style activities. His early attempt to establish a Shanti Sena in 1921–22 included the idea that the organization was to get its authority from community service rendered by the volunteers. Ten years later the concept was expanded to include the prospect of an international service corps when Gandhi encouraged Ceresole's Civilian Service operation in India.[102]

Gandhi firmly believed that all forms of exploitation and oppression rest to a large degree on the acquiescence of the victims. With this in mind he noted that "exploitation of the poor can be extinguished not by effecting the destruction of a few millionaires, but by removing the ignorance of the poor and teaching them to non-cooperate with the exploiters."[103] It was partly for the educative purpose of pointing this out to the oppressed that Gandhi instituted what he called the "Constructive Program." This Constructive Program was originally part of the struggle to obtain India's independence. It involved future leaders in the struggle and put them in contact with the masses (it is not enough, Gregg points out, to work *for* people, they must be worked *with*[104]), helping to bring about the society Gandhi envisaged in a free India. In fact, Gandhi claimed that the wholesale fulfillment of the Constructive Program "*is* complete Independence" because if the nation was involved in the very process of rebuilding itself in the image of its dreams "from the very bottom upwards," it would by definition be free.[105]

The program, in its original context, dealt mainly with the problems of communal unity, the removal of untouchability, the reestablishment of rural industries, village sanitation, prohibition, basic education for all, the promotion of a national language, education in health and hygiene, and work toward economic equality.[106] This approach aimed to produce "something beneficial to the community, especially to the poor and unemployed" and provided "the kind of work which the poor and unemployed can themselves do and thus self-respectingly help themselves."[107]

For Gandhi this constructive work offered replacement for what the nationalists were opposing at the very time they were opposing it.[108] Without it, civil disobedience, if it succeeded in overthrowing the imperialist rulers, would merely exchange one group of leaders for another, resulting in "English rule without the Englishmen . . . the tiger's nature, but not the tiger."[109]

In situations of social conflict and mass campaigns of civil disobedience Gandhi made it a point to couple constructive work to civil disobedience, sometimes seeming to say that constructive work was an aid to the civil disobedience campaign[110] and at other times putting the formula around the other way.[111] Civil disobedience, he claimed, was capable of use as a technique for the redressing of local wrongs or to rouse local consciousness or conscience; alone, however, it could never be used in a general cause such as, for example, a struggle for independence. For a civil disobedience campaign to be effective "the issue must be definite and capable of being clearly understood and within the power of the opponent to yield."[112] It could, however, be used to assist a "constructive effort" in such a case. Where a campaign is focused on local issues, or on the winning of specific concessions, no elaborate constructive program is necessary, but where the issue revolves around structural problems, civil disobedience without it becomes "mere bravado and worse than useless."[113] Constructive work, in other words, becomes a key weapon in the undertaking of large and general nonviolent campaigns, and perhaps such campaigns are not fully nonviolent unless accompanied by some kind of constructive activity.[114]

There is, however, more to constructive work than the objectively "socially useful and brotherly"[115] aspects of technical assistance. It also has a subjective side: furnishing a discipline for nonviolence. Gandhi made the point that "the best preparation for, and even the expression of, nonviolence lies, in the determined pursuit of the Constructive Programme. Anyone who believes that, without the backing of the constructive programme he will show non-violent strength when the testing time comes, will fail miserably."[116]

After Gandhi settled on the terminology for his form of nonviolent resistance, he took pains to distinguish satyagraha from passive resistance which he saw as inaction, often stemming from weakness.[117] He explained that the nonviolence of his conception actively sought to prevent violence and right wrongs. Constructive work provided the discipline as well as a method for tackling major problems of structural violence that require the long-term approach of peacebuilding.

Gandhi knew that political freedom was easier to achieve than economic, social, and moral freedom because the work for the latter, being constructive, was "less exciting and not spectacular."[118] As Gandhi was setting off for London for talks with the British, after the political turmoil of the Salt Satyagraha, he stated that "the work of social reform or self-purification . . . is a hundred times dearer to me than what is called purely political work."[119] During the Second World War, a time when many

wanted to push ahead with civil disobedience, Gandhi stated that "those
. . . who wish to see India realize her destiny through non-violence should
devote every ounce of their energy towards the fulfillment of the constructive programme in right earnest without any thought of civil disobedience"[120] and soon thereafer confessed that "in placing civil disobedience
before constructive work I was wrong. I feared that I should estrange co-
workers and so carried on with imperfect Ahimsa."[121]

In later Shanti Sena experiments care was taken to ensure an equal, or
even primary role, for constructive work. In particular Vinoba Bhave was
to stress this peacebuilding aspect of Gandhi's philosophy in action.

Conclusion

It is clear from the previous discussion that Gandhi's philosophy is
explicitly and simultaneously concerned with peacekeeping, peacemaking,
and peacebuilding. Peace, and even more broadly a nonviolence-based way
of life, is important because self-realization, which comes through a recognition of the synthesis of the self and other, is blocked by violence. It is also
largely blocked if the other is prevented from realizing the self. This high-
lights the need for peacebuilding so that the possibility of spiritual growth
is not hindered through structural violence.

Given the nature of Gandhi's philosophy, it is inevitable that to at
least some degree the viability of an alternative peacekeeping model based
on this philosophy will rest on subjective ideological definitions of the
notion of success. Whether the philosophy of nonviolence can provide a
viable and more immediately objectively recognizable and practical basis
for unarmed peacekeeping ventures than the desire for self-realization
should be discoverable by examining the history of the Shanti Sena.

5

A History of the Shanti Sena

In January 1948 Gandhi had decided to call together those engaged in constructive work to plan for future activities. The conference was scheduled for early February 1948, but a few days before he was to leave for Sevagram, the venue, he was assassinated. A meeting was, nevertheless, held in mid-March "to review the general and political situation in the country after the martyrdom of Mahatma Gandhi."[1] Five hundred people, including luminaries such as Jawaharlal Nehru, Vinoba Bhave, Jayaprakash Narayan, Kakasaheb Kalelkar, Shankarrao Deo, and J. B. Kripalani, attended the conference, which was presided over by Congress President Rajendra Prasad. In his summary of the proceedings Prasad observed:

> Gandhiji had for a long time been considering the desirability and feasibility of raising a band of workers who would devote themselves more or less exclusively to the maintenance of peace among people. He had on more than one occasion suggested the organization of a "Shanti Sena." But, for some reason or other, this could not be accomplished during his lifetime. If the communal tension [is] to be removed, some organization of this sort would be of immense help. It was, therefore, decided at the Conference that efforts should be made to organize "Shanti Seva Dals." It should be understood clearly that the Shanti Seva Dal is nothing like a police force or a body of volunteers whose function may be to suppress riots and disturbances. The function of the "Shanti Dal" will be, by constant work among the people, to create an atmosphere of peace and goodwill so that communal riots and disturbances may not occur at all and, if they unfortunately do occur, to throw itself between the fighting forces and thus prevent or at any rate reduce the intensity of the clashes. The Seva Dal being without any arms, and thoroughly non-violent, will be able to achieve this.[2]

One of the five resolutions passed at the conference called for the organization of the people of the country, especially the youth, "without any communal distinction on the basis of truth, non-violence and good conduct" to fight communalism. The vehicle for this was to be the Shanti Seva Dal, "which should strive to create an atmosphere of harmony in the country, give relief to riot sufferers, help refugees and organize singing parties in both towns and villages."[3]

Soon after the conference Gandhian workers Kakasaheb Kalelkar, G. Ramachandran, and Shriman Narayan "took certain steps to form a unit of Shanti Seva Dal in Wardha."[4] There is no evidence, however, that the unit actually engaged in any practical work.

The next step came about two years later when seventy-five constructive workers of the national institutions of Wardha/Sevagram met in March 1950 under Vinoba's presidency to discuss the setting up of a Shanti Sena. The meeting resolved to set up two Shanti Sena units in Wardha and one in Sevagram.

A constitution was drawn up, and the aim of the Sena was spelled out as organizing collective nonviolence to check violence in different spheres of life. Membership was to be open to all: men and women, young and old (initially, however, restricted to those more than eighteen years of age), who believed in truth and nonviolence and were "prepared to make the supreme sacrifice without malice in facing violence." Training was to encompass the physical (drill, productive labor), the intellectual (a study of Gandhi's thought, the history of the Indian nonviolence movement and modern economic and political ideologies through books, study circles, and lectures) and the practical spheres (including study of first aid, methods of conducting and controlling meetings to ensure that they remain peaceful, and training for emergencies). The program of the Sena was to include constructive work of all kinds, spinning, the prevention of corruption, and an attempt "to try to remove economic inequality." The organization itself was to remain aloof from political parties, was to eschew secrecy, and was to be based on quality rather than quantity of the recruits. It was to have a decentralized command structure and was to be perfectly disciplined.[5]

Although Vinoba was unable to attend, at the second annual Sarvodaya[6] *sammelan* (conference), held in April at Angul in Orissa, it was decided that experiments with Shanti Senas should be conducted in several places.[7]

Vinoba endorsed the scheme and the name, spelled out the qualifications for membership and pointed out that any uniform had to be made of khadi (handspun, handwoven cloth).[8] As Gandhi's experience had previously demonstrated, however, by not doing more he also ensured that, at this stage at least, the Sena would be doomed to nonactualization. Vinoba also pointed out that although the idea of a Shanti Sena had appealed to many, the units had to be formed localy without an India-wide central organization. Each locality, he declared, should have its own Shanti Sena. In answering the question about how to commence the work Vinoba responded:

> The work gets done once it is begun. . . . Make a very natural beginning. Take a day off in a week and go out as if for an excursion. Go to a village alone, or with friends and members of your family five or six kilometres away. Take your food with you for the day. . . . Mix with the people there, make friends with them. Interest yourself in their joys and sorrows. In this way make your acquaintance with a few villages in the neighbourhood one after another, and then repeat the cycle. The time would soon arrive when the village folk will learn to look on you as their friend who does not make any demand on them other than that of love and cooperation. Moving among the people is the initial stage of the programme before Shanti Sena. . . . The rest will follow automatically.[9]

On 13 July 1950 the newly formed umbrella grouping of most of the major Gandhian associations, the Sarva Seva Sangh,[10] decided at its Wardha meeting that the time for a nationwide Shanti Sena organization was not yet ripe and that efforts should be concentrated at the local level. Shriman Narayan was entrusted with the task of being the link between these local efforts.[11]

Not surprisingly, nothing came of Vinoba's vague call, and apparently nothing came of the three proposed Wardha/Sevagram units either.[12] The actual establishment of the Shanti Sena had to wait another half-dozen years until Vinoba's celebrated "land-gift" Bhoodan campaign was astonishing the world with its novel Gandhian approach to the pressing problem of landlessness among India's rural poor.

The Establishment of the Shanti Sena

In the early 1940s Vinoba had spent considerable time in prison as Gandhi's principal satyagrahi soldier. While in Nagpur gaol he conceived the outlines for the principles of a nonviolent political order. The booklet spelling out these ideas, *Swaraj Sastra,* when it finally appeared, proclaimed that "in an ideal non-violent order there will be no police but only a band of public spirited workers."[13] It appears that this vision was constantly before him, and, although his advice to potential sainiks may not have inspired them to form local senas, Vinoba did follow his own advice.

When Vinoba set out from his ashram at Paunar, near Wardha, for the third annual conference of Sarvodaya workers at Shivarampalli near Hyderabad, almost five hundred kilometers distant, he resolved to do so on foot. He had already decided to make the return journey by way of Telengana, a Communist-dominated district where the wealthy were being driven from the land, which, in turn, was redistributed to the landless. As the military sought to reestablish control, the hapless peasants were caught in the middle of a deadly power struggle and a cycle of retribution and counter retribution.

At the conference a letter from Shriman Narayan, suggesting that Shanti Sena work be entrusted to a competent person who could give it full-time attention, was read. By resolution it was decided that a search for such a person should be made and that Gandhian organizations and institutions should be advised that in their daily curricula and camps the subject of the Shanti Sena should be included.[14]

After the conference, on 15 April 1951, when Vinoba commenced his walking tour of the district, he explained that "I wanted to tour Telengana as a soldier of *Shanti Sena* in order to propagate the message of peace."[15] As he noted later: "It was the Bhoodan-Yagna movement which came out of that journey; but my intention was to go as a Shanti Sainik to see the conditions and to help in whatever way might prove possible. The thought of Shanti Sena, in fact, has thus been constantly in my mind."[16]

At the following Sarva Seva Sangh meeting, held at Wardha less than three months later, Kakasaheb Kalelkar was deputed to draw up a scheme for an all-India Shanti Sena.[17] Three days after leaving Shivarampalli, however, Vinoba arrived at the village of Pochampalli where a landowner offered to donate some land to the landless, and the "land-gift" movement was born.[18] The next twelve years Vinoba, "the walking saint," spent "continuously on the march throughout the length and breadth of India." He covered tens of thousands of kilometers[19] and received pledges for more than four million acres of land (of which one and one-quarter million were found suitable and were redistributed)[20] and again, at least until 1957, the formation of a Shanti Sena was relegated to the background.

Bhoodan was relatively successful for six years although only a fraction of the targeted fifty million acres had been collected by the 1957 deadline. At this stage Vinoba, in a utopian move,[21] shifted emphasis from Bhoodan to "village-gift" Gramdan. In Gramdan "the whole or a major part of a village was to be 'donated' by not less than seventy-five per cent of the villagers who were required to relinquish their right of ownership over lands in favour of the village, with power to equitably redistribute the total land among its families with a proviso for revision after some interval."[22]

Vinoba realized that if Gramdan proved to be a success he had to consider the next step in the creation of a nonviolent social order—the step that he had foreshadowed fifteen years before in *Swaraj Sastra*.

During his padayatra (foot march) through the state of Kerala, Vinoba fell ill, and, during the four-day interruption to the walk schedule, the idea of the Shanti Sena again suggested itself to him.[23] At Kozhikode (Calicut), on 11 July, Vinoba revealed his plans during the evening prayer meeting:

> What I have thought during my recent illness has led me to the conclusion that we have to establish a mighty force called *Shanti Sena* in our country. This will be an army of workers who would ceaselessly render constructive service to the people, produce moral effect upon them and allow no quarter to violence to come in the forefront.
>
> These workers must be trained properly. They must understand the implications of Sarvodaya. They must know that theirs is to abolish the institution of State power. So long as there is this power, there can be no peace. Our workers must, therefore, be free from commitment to any party or any narrow group or sect. India must have a *Shanti Sena* of this type.[24]

Vinoba continued to spell out his idea of the Sena at his various prayer meetings and called for seventy thousand volunteers, at least one sainik for every five thousand people.[25] Finally, at Manjeshwaram on 23 August, the last day of Vinoba's march through Kerala, eight volunteers came forward and took the Shanti Sena pledge, and the establishment of the Sena was publicly announced.[26]

In the address after that historic meeting Vinoba declared that Kerala had achieved a special privilege in being the place where the Shanti Sena was initiated. He continued:

> You have heard just now a description of what this Shanti Sena will be, and here today eight people have taken the pledge. What is the meaning of this Shanti Sena? It is, that they offer their lives for the service of the people. In this service they will recognize no distinctions. They will endeavour to walk always in non-violence and truth and to lead the people along the same path.
>
> The eyes of the whole world will turn to Kerala now, and to India, because Shanti Sena has been started here. The Lord has laid upon these workers a heavy burden of responsibility, and they have accepted it in faith. I have no wish that a large number of people should take this pledge. I do not want a mere show but a strong foundation. This foundation has been laid today by eight people, and day by day the work will go on growing. First we shall need hundreds of Lok Sevaks [lit. "servants of the people"], and out of their number Shanti Sainiks will be recruited.[27]

Vinoba had realized that if anything was to become of his now cherished peace brigade he would have to take positive organizational steps. In late September, at a camp for leading full-time Bhoodan workers held at

Mysore, he announced: "I think we must have a network of *Shanti Sena* all over the country. That requires a Supreme Command. Who else but God can take that Command? Nevertheless I feel I would have to shoulder the responsibility of the All India Shanti Sena and I have prepared my-self accordingly."[28]

Shanti Sainiks were required to take and fulfil the five-fold pledge of the Lok Sevak with the additional requirement of being willing to go where sent by the Sena, and if need be give their lives in the service of peace.[29]

Vinoba Bhave also finally addressed himself to the question of the support of Shanti Sainiks in a way that would bypass the need for a central-ized organization. He decided that it was up to the people served by the sainiks to support them by voluntary contributions. The system to be used for this purpose was to be the Sarvodaya Patra,[30] a small earthen vessel in the home of the supporter into which the youngest child would place a daily handful of grain or the smallest coin for the upkeep of Sarvodaya workers generally and Shanti Sainiks in particular. The idea behind the scheme was that such giving would remind families of those less fortunate than themselves. It would bring the peace worker, who depended on the locally collected grain, into intimate contact with his "constituency," and the daily observance of the vow of giving would impress on the mind of the family's youngest "an individual's debt to the society as a whole and the individual's duty to repay it in various ways."[31] The significance of the Sarvodaya Patra, in other words, was not merely to provide material sup-port but also to provide "a spiritual fellowship of friends."[32] Vinoba had calculated that each Bhoodan worker or Shanti Sainik could be supported by five hundred Sarvodaya Patras, and, in turn, the number of patras would serve as an indication of the spread of the Sarvodaya ideology, which was a prerequisite for the raising of a national army of Shanti Sainiks.[33]

During the 1960s, leading Gujarati Sarvodaya worker Ravishankar Maharaj established fifty thousand Sarvodaya Patras in Ahmedabad,[34] and by 1967 there were forty-five thousand patras in Madras State and twenty thousand in Madras city managed by full-time women workers.[35] The greatest success, however, came in Andhra Pradesh where between sixty and seventy Shanti Sainiks were maintained on the grain collected in the patras.[36] In a well-organized area of the state patras were installed in forty thousand homes and reportedly became "one of the most potent means of establishing mass contact and spreading the message of Sarvodaya." Women workers collected grain from the patras weekly while doing propa-ganda work for the Gandhian movement. In eight years the paddy from the Andhra patras yielded an income of more than Rs. 500,000.[37]

Because the care of children precluded them from being sent on peacekeeping missions in the far corners of the country, women workers in Bombay had pointed out to Vinoba the need for a Sena-style organization that they could join to serve their local community and to which, in an emergency, they could give their lives. Vinoba promptly suggested the formation of the Shanti Sahayaks (assistants). The sahayaks were to do work similar to that of the sainiks, serving localities of five thousand, but they were not to be seen as alternatives to the sainiks for, as Vinoba pointed out, "non-violence would be a poor weapon if . . . we were not able to send help from outside. There is a disturbed atmosphere throughout the country today, and no one can say when or where violence may break out. We therefore need Shanti Sainiks in large numbers."[38]

The first committee for the Shanti Sena was formed in May 1958. Because Vinoba believed that peace work was especially suitable for women, the committee was composed entirely of females, with long-time Gandhi supporter Quaker Marjorie Sykes as convener.[39] The committee organized a camp of about forty sainiks and sympathizers to make a detailed study of the philosophy and organization of the Sena at Sevagram in October,[40] and gradually, as Vinoba took up the points raised, a comprehensive plan for the Sena emerged.

The eleventh Sarvodaya conference was held in the Rajasthani city of Ajmer on the last days of February 1959. It attracted about seven thousand workers and was presided over by K. Kelappan, the chief of the first Shanti Sena unit formed in Kerala one and one-half years before. Following the conference, on 2 March, Shanti Sainiks from all over India rallied on the Ajmer-Jaipur road. Eight hundred and fifty volunteers (accompanied by Martin Luther King, Jr.) marched fifteen kilometers to Gagwana, where the inauguration of the first Peace Army took place.[41] Vinoba declared that he had expected five hundred sainiks to attend the rally and considering those who were not present because they could not leave their posts, he reckoned "that there are now about a thousand Shanti Sainiks, that is double the number that I had expected."[42]

The Shanti Sena was now in operation; however, the commander, although in control, felt the need for assistance. Vinoba had already mentally sketched the loose organizational structure that would encompass the largely decentralized sena:

> Suppose I were to be asked to make a plan for the whole of India, I would choose an all India group of fifteen to twenty persons who have complete faith in the power of peace, who apply this faith in their own lives, who practice daily self-examination and constant self-correction, and who have a measure of purity of mind.
>
> Our imagined All-India Peace Committee would not issue any orders, but it would give advice to those who sought it. It would also occasionally give advice without being asked. Its second task would be to send Shanti Sainiks to any part of the country where rioting takes place or any disturbance of the peace.

Then, there should be a State Committee for the Shanti Sena which would do the work in its own villages and see that Sarvodaya literature reaches every home. It would have a publications committee which would make sure that not one house was left out. . . . Its second work will be to supply any Shanti Sainik or Lok Sevak at once with any information they may need.

Then there must be a unit in each district. Shanti Sainiks are needed in numbers proportionate to the number of the population, and thousands of sevaks are needed to help them. For this, Sarvodaya Patras have to be placed in every home. This is what I envisage as regards the district organization of the Shanti Sena. No one will give any orders to the district committee from above. Sainiks will keep in close touch with one another and regard the practice of love as their religious duty.[43]

The sainik, then, was to be more than a person who goes where he or she is directed. The peace soldier was seen as a completely self-sufficient person independent in carrying out "service" in his or her locality. After initial training and assessment as being suitable for sena work the sainik was to serve in one of seventy thousand decentralized areas, "using his own independent initiative" with "complete freedom to take responsibility for himself, for his principles, and for the community which he serves."[44] If no occasion presented itself for peacekeeping or peacemaking work, then the Shanti Sena was to "turn itself into a Seva Sena,"[45] or army of service, in other words, to devote its time to the task of peacebuilding. There was, however, the possibility of one command that a sainik was bound to obey, a command consisting of only two words: "Go there." In the event of major trouble a sainik could be sent anywhere in India, but once at the appointed place "there will be no further command" and, again, individual initiative was to be the guide.[46]

At Pathankot on 24 September 1959, Vinoba finally declared the formation of the Akhil Bharat (all-India) Shanti Sena Mandal (assembly) with Ashadevi Aryanayakam[47] as convener. The Mandal, comprising thirteen members (nine men and four women), was, in the words of Suresh Ram, to "act as a referee for the people" and to give guidance to sainiks.[48] The task placed before it in sharing Vinoba's burden of leadership closely resembled the duties Vinoba had envisaged as being the lot of the All-India Peace Committee.[49] With the formation of the Mandal, Vinoba foresaw that "people throughout the country would feel that the Shanti Sena . . . has really been established."[50]

By 1960 the Sena was an active organization with work going on in several areas, including the troubled Maharashtra/Karnataka border,[51] Assam,[52] and the Chambal valley. The need for training was being given serious consideration; organization of rural units was being discussed, and even the importance of Shanti Sena work in the international field was being mooted.[53] A review of the first four years of the Sena's operation, while noting many successes, makes the point that to a large extent those successes depended on the personality of influential sainiks and that the "Shanti Sena has not yet become very popular among the people and is not a force to reckon with."[54] By 1962 peace work was going on in Aligarh after communal disturbances, and the need for the enrollment of additional Muslim sainiks had been realized.[55] There were almost twenty-five hundred enrolled Shanti Sainiks,[56] the majority of whom were volunteers in the Bhoodan movement.[57]

Reorganization and the First Crisis

The Shanti Sena Mandal had been operating only as an advisory body. It was realized that efficiency would be improved if it was granted executive powers, a proposition with which Vinoba agreed.[58] But other changes were also needed. The riots that followed the reorganization of states along linguistic lines were mainly confined to the major cities where the Bhoodan working Lok Sevak/Shanti Sainiks were fewest. At the Patna Prabhand Samiti meeting of the Sarva Seva Sangh, held on 7 April 1962, Ashadevi tabled a paper detailing her discussions with Vinoba about widening the scope of the Shanti Sena and making the organization more effective, and at the full Sangh session two days later the following resolution was passed: "The Shanti Sena should not be limited as it is today, to Loksevaks only, but should be open to all citizens who are prepared to lay down their lives non-violently during times of disturbance. Such citizens should be encouraged to join the non-violent force, meet regularly together, and undertake some form of service for peace. With this view the present Shanti Sena Mandal may be reorganised and the basis of the membership be changed."[59]

Discussion on the reorganization of the movement commenced, and the pledge of the Shanti Sainik was liberalized to attract more members.[60] Until this point membership was open only to those who could work full-time. Others had to be content with being Shanti Sahayaks, and this "gave them a rather secondary role and did not help to mobilise effectively their efforts."[61] The distinctions were removed to give the sahayaks "a fuller sense of participation and responsibility and thus help to draw out their talents."[62]

It was realized that making the clause requiring readiness to do peace work in distant areas optional could lead to a shortage of sainiks ready to serve in emergency situations. The names of those who did not opt out of nationwide service were to be included on the reserve force list of the Tatpar (ever-ready) Shanti Sena.[63] Although by the end of the decade nearly five hundred Shanti Sainiks had consented to having their name on its roll,[64] and some had been sent to Assam and the Northeast Frontier Agency (NEFA, later to become the Union Territory of Arunachal Pradesh) in 1962, the Tatpar Shanti Sena never really managed to operate effectively as a quick response unit that could intervene in riot situations.[65]

Debate also took place at Patna about whether, given the felt need to broaden and energize the Shanti Sena, membership should be thrown open to those involved in party politics. No unanimous decision could be reached, and the proposal was dropped.[66]

After discussions with Vinoba, Ashadevi, JP, and Sarva Seva Sangh president Nabhakrushna Choudhuri were deputed to produce a list of names for a reorganized Shanti Sena Mandal. Two months later, again at Patna, they presented the Prabhand Samiti with a provisional list of names, designating Jayaprakash Narayan as chairperson.[67]

Although he had been a member of the executive committee of the Shanti Sena, JP had been openly critical of its organization. Eventually, after pressure from Narayan Desai and others, he agreed to take on the position of chair on the condition that some young person, such as Desai, assisted him.

Desai had been asked to leave Bhoodan work in Gujarat by Vinoba and to work at the headquarters of the Sarva Seva Sangh at Rajghat in Varanasi. He accepted the invitation on the conditions that he hold no position of power within the Sangh and that he could lead a normal family life rather than taking a vow of celibacy. He wanted to be a teacher rather than an organizer and took up the position of principal of the newly established Shanti Vidyalaya (School for Peace). Because he had convinced JP to accept the chairmanship, Desai felt that he had little choice but to change his own mind about holding a position of power and agreed to work with JP.[68] On 23 July 1962 Choudhuri announced the names of the new All-India Shanti Sena Mandal with JP as chair and Narayan Desai as secretary. Soon, however, the Sena was involved in controversy, and its two leading lights engaged in the type of struggle that was to characterize much of their future relationship.[69]

In 1958, at a speech before the United Nations Association of Coleford in Wales, JP was already indicating that in the Sena he saw the eventuality of the type of unarmed peacekeeping force that would be ready to operate in the international arena (as his later proposal for an international Peace Guard also contemplated, and the World Peace Brigade he inspired attempted):

> Vinoba has been saying for the last few years that India should unilaterally adopt a policy of disarmament, irrespective of what Pakistan may be doing, or of what our powerful neighbour China is doing . . . we ourselves should adopt this policy of disarmament . . . [but] the peo-

ple's minds are not *ready*. They do not see any alternative to arms. Well, Vinoba is trying to create that alternative. He is proposing to the people that it is possible to defend ourselves, without arms, and that any nation can defend itself without arms.

Well, if it is possible to fight for freedom without arms why cannot we defend that freedom without arms?

Vinoba says that before we presume to ask the government of India to start on this policy of disarmament, we should demonstrate that at least for our internal security, it is possible to do without the militia.[70]

Further, at about the time he took over chairmanship of the Mandal, JP was saying that although "it has not much to show by way of achievement. (It has to be shamefully admitted that in relation to the Goa incident[71] it failed entirely . . .)," he still saw the Shanti Sena as a positive approach toward a nonviolent alternative to the army.[72]

Vinoba Bhave, by contrast, concentrated his energies on the villages of India, and even his utterances on the question of war and defense were concerned primarily with the building of a peaceful social structure rather than on armies and peacekeeping. For example, in answer to the question "What would happen if some other country were to attack us?" Vinoba answered:

> That question is not really apposite at present. It is only when one has reached the top of the mountain that one can contemplate the view from the top, not when one is still down below. We can only know the power of Shanti Sena to save the country when strength has been built to deal with the country's internal affairs. Now-a-days we have to call on the police and the army to protect us from internal disorders and they have to resort to firing in order to do so. If the Shanti Sena were to make the army unnecessary for the protection of society at home, the nation's confidence in it would grow. As a result the size of our armed forces could be reduced.[73]

And in answer to a further question, "What will the Shanti Sena do when confronted by an armed force in time of war?" Vinoba's answer again evaded any reference to Gandhi's "living wall" approach to national civilian defense and neglected JP Narayan's concern with interpositionary international peacekeeping. Vinoba noted that wars are relatively rare and, consequently, it was more important to set up an "army of service" to "benefit the nation." The duty of this sena was to bring the plight of the poor to the notice of the rich (to win their sympathy so that they would voluntarily want to do something to alleviate it), to give personal service to the sick, to try to increase productivity in the village, and to arrange for education. In other words, the Shanti Sena's task was to destroy the root causes of unrest—the gulf between the haves and the have-nots, cruelty, the pride of ownership, the insistence on mine and thine, on high and low, on caste distinctions, on religious differences and disputes. These are all causes of unrest, some economic, some social, and some religious. And now-a-days, in addition, party politics has entered into it. The Shanti Sena will, therefore, be a whole-time service army. . . . The result will be a cleansing of the national mind and the growth of mutual goodwill. When that takes place the government will not have to spend so much on the army, the moral strength of the nation will be increased and it will be able to make its influence felt in the international field. . . . World opinion is alert, now-a-days, and so no country can invade another without warning. In the court of world opinion, a nation's moral authority will be greatly increased if it has a Shanti Sena and, therefore, enjoys internal peace.[74]

The two views were to clash when the question of how the Gandhian movement ought to respond to the Chinese invasion required urgent answer.[75] When news of the incursion reached Vinoba on 22 October 1962, he admitted that he suspected that China was the aggressor and quickly claimed that the best "defence measure" was Gramdan.[76] At a rally of Shanti Sainiks held in Bihar on 2 November, without denouncing the Indian war effort or suggesting any peacekeeping action by the Sena, he issued a statement on the situation claiming first that as a soldier of peace he renounced war, and then he attacked Chinese expansionism, adding that "it is a matter of great pride for India that it has never been guilty of territorial expansionism. . . . Therefore, my sympathy goes out to India."[77] He advised sainiks to demonstrate the raison d'être of the Sena by consolidating it and spreading the Gramdan message while advising the Indian Government "not to flinch from its commendable attitude of 'firmness without hatred' against China."[78] Vinoba, in expressing dissatisfaction with the work of the Sena to date, made his stand clear: "I hope that all the Shanti Sainiks will recognise their true function at this juncture and make their full contribution towards the maintenance of internal peace. This will be our special responsibility the fulfilment of which will lead towards nonviolence and make the nation strong."[79]

When asked whether the Shanti Sainiks should go to the front to meet the Chinese aggression, Vinoba replied that "it would be foolish to do so. Those who have committed aggression are not individuals, but part of a machine. They have been sent here by their masters and the soldiers have to carry out the orders. Sarvodaya workers going to the front would embarrass the Government of India too. Moreover, *Shanti sena* should concentrate for the time being on the maintenance of internal unity. How can it succeed in the international field without gaining sufficient experience within the country?"[80]

Further, to dispel "the false impression that he was against the use of the Army for meeting Chinese aggression on Indian soil"[81] Vinoba added that "when India maintains an army, it has to be used to repel an armed attack."[82]

A section of the Shanti Sena pledge denouncing war as a crime was softened to read, "I believe that war blocks all human progress and is a denial of a non-violent way of life" so as not to cause offence to an embattled government. Some Gandhians believed that the original wording could be seen as an accusation of criminal activity leveled against the government as it organized armed resistance to the invading Chinese. One explained that "I cannot call Nehru a criminal."[83]

Other Gandhian activists, including JP Narayan, were accused of obstructionism when they refused to sanction India's war effort or unambiguously condemn China. JP wanted to lead a contingent of Shanti Sainiks into the battle areas to offer nonviolent resistance to the Chinese troops while intervening in the battles and appealing to both sides to stop the fighting.[84] At the Vedchhi Sarva Seva Sangh Conference, held in November 1962, JP, enthusiastic for action, thought that the majority would be behind him.[85] The statement issued at the conference, however, endorsed Vinoba's stand and rejected the idea of the major experiment in peacekeeping that JP had envisaged. Vinoba's dominant role in the formulation of the document can clearly be seen. It reiterated Vinoba's contention that China was the aggressor, while maintaining that India had been "working consistently for a peaceful solution of the border question."[86] Although proclaiming that it was the duty of a Shanti Sainik to "do his utmost to end the war as soon as possible," the document continued:

> The thought of non-violent resistance immediately brings to the mind the idea of going to the front and facing aggression. It is a matter for joy and congratulation that many *Shanti Sainiks* have expressed their eagerness to offer their lives for such a programme. However, in present conditions a programme of this nature could be undertaken only after serious consideration.
>
> One of our important programmes in the present circumstances must be to awaken the capacity for non-violent resistance among the people of the border areas. Wherever the atmosphere is favorable the *Shanti Sainik* should visit the villages in such areas and try to inspire the people to adopt a programme of self reliance and non-cooperation with the aggressor. He must be prepared to lay down his life in this effort, if necessary, and exhort the people to do like-wise.[87]

Although the Chinese may have disliked JP for his forceful criticism of their annexation of Tibet, JP was unsure that right lay completely with India. According to his biographers, the Scarfes who were with JP at this time, he believed that Vinoba, in supporting Nehru's position so uncritically, "was playing Gandhi false."[88] JP, however, was unwilling to criticize Vinoba, and this left him in an untenable position. He went as far as tendering his resignation as chair of the Shanti Sena[89] and eventually was forced to rely on the World Peace Brigade to initiate a diluted form of nonviolent action, the Delhi to Peking Friendship March.[90]

Some JP supporters, led by Professor Thakurdas Bang, decided to act on their own initiative if hostilities resumed following the Chinese withdrawal. They approached JP, informing him that in such circumstances they would be compelled to resign from the Sarvodaya movement because they did not want to breach the organization's code of discipline.[91] JP informed them that their contemplated action had not been barred, but it may as well have been. In August JP visited Vinoba to discuss the issue of nonviolent resistance. Vinoba responded by saying that "there was nothing immoral" about going to the disputed Kashmir border but added that such action was "crude and unnecessary."[92] He went on to write: "Our fellow-workers feel that the experiment of the Friendship March is something better than what Baba [Vinoba] is doing, and to go and take up positions between the two forces on the front would still be better. It appears to them that it would be the best programme. . . . To me the idea seems to be crude with nothing scientific about it. What should predominate in satyagraha—spiritual power or physical power?"[93]

The "militants" including, besides Professor Bang, such active Sarvodaya leaders as Jagannathan, Harivallabh Parekh, and G. Ramachandra Rao ("Gora"), after the discussion of their concerns with JP at the Vedchhi conference, took preliminary steps to organize a new body that would specifically tackle the task of confronting the problem of war resistance, a move not favored by Vinoba.[94] JP, however, took Vinoba's lack of outright condemnation as a surprisingly "rather kindly view" and informed Bang that he could now "seek Vinoba's advice and guidance,"[95] although it had been reported that when discussing the planned initiative, Vinoba had quipped that "those with no head may go ahead!"[96]

Bang convened a conference of those with views similar to his own in Bombay. Although JP presided over the meeting and agreed with the resolution that they should go to the border to offer nonviolent resistance,[97] "on account of the short notice"[98] and "in the absence of any public encouragement from Vinoba,"[99] the attendance was poor, and, consequently, the proposed new body proved abortive.[100] In any case, by then the hostilities had ended.

These maneuverings showed, in short, the degree to which the Chinese invasion and its ideological aftermath had revealed divisions in the Gandhian movement. Many of the senior politically active Gandhians sided with Vinoba in his "moderate" philosophy. Gandhian patriarch Kakasaheb

Kalelkar, for instance, was of the opinion that until a country had a fully functioning peace brigade it was the duty of the government to use the armed forces to defend the nation and that such a move should not be opposed. He argued, rather tortuously, that it would be cowardice to refuse to join the armed forces of a government to which taxes were paid and from which benefits were derived. Kalelkar suggested that a satyagrahi should join the defense forces but refuse to kill. The nonviolent soldier could either march in the front of the army without weapons or engage in other "perilous" noncombatant tasks. In such a way, his reasoning went, "it would be possible to propagate non-violence and to discover some day the method of non-violent resistance through the government."[101]

Rajendra Prasad, former president of the Congress and of India, supported the government's policy on the grounds that "non-violent resistance was simply infeasible,"[102] and Dhirendra Mazumdar, who became president of the All-India Spinners' Association upon Gandhi's death, felt that direct intervention would not only not advance the cause of nonviolence but could "have even an adverse reaction."[103] Ostergaard and Currel, authors of a major study on the Sarvodaya movement, claim that these arguments were made using carefully selected quotations from Gandhi to show that preparations for war were sanctionable.[104] Vinoba, too, had objections on "practical" grounds. He believed that because there were not enough sainiks to constitute a division, they could not "demand of the government to allot them some specific front for their exclusive action."[105]

Vishwanath Tandon, a scholar of the Sarvodaya movement and of Sarvodaya philosophy, strongly supports the position taken by the "moderates" in this debate and dwells at length on the views of Vinoba, Kalelkar, and other, as he calls them, "senior Sarvodaya leaders." The "militants," those favoring interpositionary action, he characterizes as "junior thinkers and workers." Strangely, he invited one of these juniors so-called, Jayaprakash Narayan, to write the foreword to his study when it appeared in book form. JP, while noting that he wished Tandon "had been more critical of his material," added that in places the Sarvodaya philosophy was weak and contained gaps, that in several spheres "it is still in the stage of generalities, even slogans."[106]

One of the main gaps in this philosophy, particularly when considering the role of the Shanti Sena, was the permissibility of resistance to the policies of the government when that government has been popularly elected—a problem that the old guard did not have to face as they battled the imperialist British. After India's independence many of the Gandhians' comrades from the nationalist movement held the reins of power in the newly established republic.[107]

Although the JP-supporting "militants" were by no means all young (for example Shankarrao Deo, the former general-secretary of the All-India

Congress Committee, notable Sarvodaya worker and a leader of the Delhi to Peking Friendship March, was born in 1895) most of them had not played as prominent roles in the independence movement and, consequently, did not have quite the emotional attachment to Nehru and other leading politicians as had the "moderates." This, and the situation in which extremely strong and gifted personalities with different worldviews are in positions of leadership in the one organization, only partially explains the divisions in the till then seemingly united Sarvodaya movement. The differences were also, in part, based on the conflict Galtung sees as inherent in a program that tried to encompass both the JP-favored peacekeeping and the Vinoba-approved peacebuilding functions.

The field work for Ostergaard and Currel's study of the Sarvodaya leadership, conducted in 1965, showed that the respondents were almost evenly divided between the two approaches. In response to the statement, "If China renews her aggression, the Shanti Sena should be asked to go to the battle areas to offer non-violent resistance," 51 percent of the respondents agreed with the assertion.[108] In their profile the "average Sarvodaya leader" saw the Shanti Sena as a nonviolent police force rather than as a national defense force. "But," they concluded, "he is half-inclined to agree with those who urge that, if China renews her aggression on the Northern borders, the Shanti Sena should be sent there to offer non-violent resistance."[109]

These mixed feelings were further reflected in the Nargolkars' account of their peace mission to the North East Frontier Agency. Sarvodaya worker and Vinoba biographer Vasant Nargolkar had pleaded for some form of direct nonviolent action at the Vedchhi conference and expressed a desire to enlist in any peace brigade that would be sent to the border area.[110] While the unilateral Chinese withdrawal took the urgency out of the situation, Vinoba's attitude must have proved a disappointment. With their belief that "if we did not make an honest effort to establish peace or to experiment in non-violent solutions, it would amount to a failure on our part to preserve the great legacy that Gandhiji left us,"[111] they took it upon themselves to do the work of sainiks in the troubled areas. Kusum Nargolkar, in detailing their experiences, refused to speak negatively about Vinoba's stance; instead in somewhat of a gloss, she notes that: "Vinobaji thinks that even the idea of a Shanti-sena would not take root in the country, unless a proper atmosphere is created by inducing people to declare their villages *gramdan*. That is why he lays more stress on *gramdan* than on any other programme. But he would certainly give his blessings to any worker who felt inspired to rush to a spot troubled by communal riots or to the Indo-Chinese border for demonstrating, or experimenting in, the efficacy of the non-violent approach."[112]

Consolidation

After the border clash, liberalized membership requirements ensured that the numbers of volunteers joining the Sena accelerated greatly, and increasingly they came from outside the ranks of Bhoodan workers. Veteran Gujarati Gandhian worker, Jugatram Dave, with Vinoba's consent, issued an appeal to all idle citizens, male or female, to dedicate a year to Shanti Sena work. Under this scheme youths would be given an opportunity for "service and sacrifice." They were to receive two months training and do ten months active work without renumeration; their basic needs to be met from a wider program of Sarvodaya Patras.[113] Although Vinoba's personal appeals during his padayatra were more successful than such ambitious but vague ideas, by the end of 1963 the ranks of the Sena had swelled to more than five thousand,[114] and by mid-1964 there were in excess of eight thousand sainiks, more than three thousand of them coming from Bihar, JP's home state.[115]

JP was quick to note that without a proper organizational framework the Sena could not function efficiently. He recalled how Vinoba had called for the recruitment of a large number of Shanti Sevaks, pledged only to peace not to the higher nonviolence, who could work for peace when they had the spare time. Almost two hundred were enrolled in Calcutta yet only two months later the city erupted in its worst riots in a decade. Vinoba called his effort a 100 percent failure. The reason was, JP pointed out, that the sevaks were merely isolated individuals in a large city without a support structure.[116]

Vinoba, however, had also provided the blueprint for the necessary structure. That, of course, revolved around the success of the Sarvodaya Patra. The patra should have located the sevaks within a circle of citizens committed to peace and given them the necessary popular sanction. This network, in turn, was to be surrounded by the circle of Sarvodaya mitras (friends): those who, although not devotees of nonviolence, showed their sympathy with the aims of Sarvodaya by paying a yearly Re.1 as a contribution to the movement.[117] "This Programme of the Shanti Sena," JP explained, "can be described as made up of concentric circles, with the Shanti sainik in the centre, the Shanti sevaks forming the next outer circle, the Sarvodaya patras the next, and the Sarvodaya mitras the last. While the Shanti Sena by itself cannot be a very large body, the whole Shanti Sena programme can indeed become a mass movement."[118]

To many, however, the scheme seemed impractical because the patra lacked appeal.[119] Except in a few isolated places, the Sarvodaya Patra as a system of financing the Sena and of linking it to the wider community did not catch on. For all the early publicity, patras were generally confined to a symbolic role in institutions where only weekly contributions were made. The need for a more organized structure became necessary.

At its meeting in Varanasi in May 1960, the Shanti Sena Mandal decided that Shanti Sainiks of each province should select a few from among their ranks to form provincial (state) Shanti Sena mandals, which would be autonomous but would work in close collaboration with provincial Sarvodaya mandals. As far as possible, training of Shanti Sainik was to be undertaken in the provinces, and where that was not possible, the central Shanti Sena Mandal in Varanasi would undertake the task.[120]

With the rapid increase in numbers, provincial Shanti Sena committees, with their own conveners, were set up. Within one year fourteen of the eighteen states were able to boast of having state-level Shanti Sena organizations.[121] The new Mandal began its task of reorganization by attempting to establish shanti kendras (centers) as the primary units of the Shanti Sena[122] while centralizing overall control of the Sena in the Akhil Bharat Shanti Sena Mandal. By 1969 there were 632 kendras in country.[123]

A kendra was to be composed of at least two, and never more than twenty-five, members. It was to provide the basis for disciplined communal interaction and to ensure that sainiks would be available for peace work at short notice. The kendra was to meet regularly (generally weekly), plan daily programs, compile reports on the week's activities, discuss incidents of potential tension, plan for the following week, undertake service activities and collective study, share a monthly meal, and send monthly reports to the Mandal.[124]

In 1963 Narayan Desai produced a *Handbook for Shanti Sainiks* based in part on Charles Walker's pamphlet, *Organizing for Non-Violent Direct Action*.[125] In his introduction Desai noted that the Indo-Chinese conflict "brought home the realization that the organization of Shanti Sena must be undertaken urgently on a large-scale and should form an important and integral part of the movement for Sarvodaya." He added that events had proved not only the need for better organization but also for the more intensive training of volunteers.[126]

Nirmala Deshpande, a member of the earlier Shanti Sena Mandal, had organized training camps at Kasturbagram in Indore and training courses for recruits and summer camps for its newly formed youth section were conducted at the Varanasi headquarters of the Sarva Seva Sangh.[127] In 1961 the Akhil Bharat Sarva Seva Sangh established its Shanti Vidyalaya to provide training in the correct attitude for Shanti Sainiks, to provide fieldwork experience in the urban setting and to give the students a theoretical grounding for their future vocation.[128] Varanasi became the training center for men, and, until it eventually faded into oblivion, Indore maintained responsibility for women. Varanasi was chosen as the site for the training center not only because it was where the Sarva Seva Sangh had its headquarters but also because, as one of the world's oldest cities and one of India's foremost places of pilgrimage, it was also quite cosmopolitan and thereby was able to serve "as a good practising ground for the trainees." [129] It became one of the world's first training centers for peace volunteers.

The Vidyalaya set out, in its daily three hours of fieldwork, to study the causes of tension in society: "forming groups of four or five, the trainees select particular types of various problems, such as alcoholism, student indiscipline, child-labor. They visit a certain locality regularly trying to understand the various problems of different classes of society. Some amount of service is rendered to the society by the trainees doing sanitation and adult education work etc." [130]

After the completion of two four-month-long Varanasi-based training courses, it was decided that the training process should commence with short training camps for sainiks held in various parts of the country. Suitable volunteers from these camps were then selected to attend the Shanti Vidyalaya course. [131]

The increase in numbers and advances in training did not, however, mean that the Sena had even approached the vision of its organizers. At the April 1966 Sarvodaya Conference held in Balia, Desai was still saying that the Shanti Sena *could* play a crucial role in dealing with the problem of violence but that it was as yet in an infantile stage with negligible strength. The organization was described not as a mere peacekeeping force but as an emerging "instrument of social change and reconstruction," one, however, that was still without a training institute that could "provide comprehensive training and ideological orientation to shanti sainiks." Desai observed that although sainiks were still primarily Sarvodaya workers doing constructive work, "such workers often have no clear idea of the nature and magnitude of the problem of violence in our body-politic nor do they possess the necessary skills to face a crisis situation. The result is that whenever there is a crisis, the shanti sainiks find themselves helpless spectators in spite of their noble intentions. There have been several violent incidents in various parts of the country but nowhere was the shanti sena in evidence during the crises; it has of course done some rehabilitative work after the storms have blown over." [132]

Other training programs also commenced. Jugatram Dave's ashram, in operation since the Bardoli Satyagraha campaign of 1928, was situated near the village of Vedchhi among the tribal people of southern Gujarat. As the ashram grew, it launched its own higher education program, and in 1967 the Gandhi Vidyapith (college) was founded. In 1969, in addition to schools of sociology and education, an off-campus Shanti Sena Vidyalaya was established to foster nonviolence. The Vidyalaya was situated at Karadi, where Gandhi was arrested after the Salt March, under the directorship of Sombhai Patel, a sainik since 1960 who had spent two years doing peace work in the Garhwal border area after the war with China. The training program of the institution was to equip sainiks with the skills required during emergencies, whether natural or human–made. Patel and leading Gujarati Shanti Sainik Indrasingh Rawat[133] produced a training guidebook[134] to assist in the work at their training camps. The book, while using Desai's writings, deals in the main with practical matters such as drill, first aid, lifesaving, fire extinguishing, signaling, physical exercises, and so on, rather than more ideological matters that Desai saw as increasingly important. The institution ran many training camps of varying duration and organized relief work in flooded areas, during riots, on the Bangladesh border, worked in prisons attempting to resocialize ex–Chambal valley dacoits, and constructed leper colonies.

After the War Resisters' International conference in Gandhigram, another training course, this time integrated into the curriculum of what was to become the Gandhigram Rural University near Madurai in Tamilnadu, was also established. Under the guidance of veteran Gandhian G. Ramachandran the institute made the Shanti Sena central to its educational and constructive activities. All those involved with Gandhigram, students, teachers, and workers alike, took (and still do take) the pledge of the Shanti Sainik. This has helped to spread the idea of the Sena and the ideals of Sarvodaya in the surrounding district.[135]

After the border crisis, talk of the Shanti Sena intervening in international hostilities ceased. The leaders had to admit that they had no clear idea of how nonviolent resistance to foreign invasion could be carried out by the Sena.[136] Instead they saw their task as the boosting of morale in the border areas so as to encourage nonviolent resistance if the situation warranted it. The role of the Shanti Sena in the border areas was redefined as serving the injured and homeless in time of war[137] and encouraging nonviolent attitudes by doing constructive work in times of peace.[138]

Because news of disturbances frequently reached the Sena late, by the time sainiks could be dispatched to the affected areas the trouble had often subsided. To counteract this problem it was decided to institute a system of peace correspondents "who would take the responsibility of informing the Shanti Sena whenever tension arises or violence breaks out."[139]

An attempt was also made to increase the effectiveness of the Shanti Sena by upgrading the calibre of the Shanti Sainiks through a process of screening and pledge renewal: "We are organizing camps in every state to come into personal contact with all the Shanti Sainiks and to find out what everyone is doing in order to fit into the general plan of the Shanti Sena. If there are some who have signed the pledge without proper understanding of its implications, or who are at present unable to do the work of the Shanti Sena, their names may be deleted from the general register."[140]

As the Gandhi birth centenary year approached, Narayan Desai was able to announce that the number of Shanti Sainiks had exceeded fifteen thousand and that there were Shanti Samitis in all regions.[141] He counseled that more attention had to be paid to attracting youth into the movement and that a goal of five sainiks in each village, and five hundred thousand altogether, should be aimed at for the centenary.[142]

The goals were wildly optimistic.

During the twentieth anniversary of the commencement of Vinoba's Bhoodan/Gramdan crusade, Professor Bang produced a "for Private Circulation Only" pamphlet reflecting his dismay at the state of the Gandhian movement. He called for added efforts to be put into the formation and training of village Shanti Senas, warning that "otherwise the whole organization is likely to remain on paper"[143] and asked for greater attention to be paid to the recruitment and training of Tarun (youth) Shanti Sainiks.[144]

At the Nasik Sarva Seva Sangh session in May 1971 it was noted that during the communal disturbances in Aligarh, Varanasi, Moradabad and Allahabad "our Shanti Sainiks could visit these places only after riots had taken their toll of many human beings." On the positive side, it was noted that students leaving colleges for a year or resolving to join the Tarun Shanti Sena for a year when they completed their studies "is a novel feature in our movement and is full of rich possibilities."[145] One year later, at the Nakodar conference it was noted that there was a need "to make some special efforts in every state to bring the various wings of the Shanti Sena into some concrete organization." Two years later Sangh members were noting that because it lacked a clear program for sainiks the Sena was not active and because for the previous four or five years the Shanti Sena Mandal had concentrated so much of its work on the Tarun Shanti Sena other work had not progressed.[146]

The Nakodar meeting had decided that a committee should be constituted to reevaluate the work of the Shanti Sena to date from all points of view and then suggest measures for future work. It was also decided that activities should be concentrated in a few select areas and the Sena to be sent to other areas when there was an immediate necessity.

The Tarun Shanti Sena

With the reorganization of the Shanti Sena it was decided to incorporate disaffected students, and youth generally, into the expanded Sena that Jayaprakash Narayan and Narayan Desai hoped to create. In 1962 the Kishore Shanti Dal (Teenagers' Peace Corps) was organized in the basic education high schools of Gujarat, Desai's home state. Youth, of either sex, who were prepared to give one day a month for the service of their village, were enrolled.[147] For one year the Dal served as the youth wing of the Sena, doing constructive work in rural Gujarat.

In 1963 the idea was taken up by the Akhil Bharat Shanti Sena Mandal and camps were organized on a yearly all-India basis during the summer vacation. Camp "graduates" formed small units in schools and colleges and the number of camps grew with the demand. (In 1967 more than one thousand young people attended seventeen camps organized by the Mandal.)[148]

The Bihar famine of 1966–67, and the volunteer work done by foreigners, brought to light the general indifference of Bihari students to the plight of their less-fortunate fellow citizens.[149] Although warned about the disruptive intention of students who had been drawn into left violence,[150] students' famine service camps were organized, and, in JP's words, this demonstrated that the students were "sound at heart," needing "leadership and guidance and a sustained program to channelise constructively their exuberant energy."[151]

Even though Kishore Dals had been founded in fourteen states it was decided to widen the scope of the organization to take in others beside adolescents and to link it with "some permanent nation-building activity." The idea of students' national reconstruction camps, that grew out of the famine relief camps, was grafted onto the Dals. At its meeting in Pathankot, on 19–20 June 1968, the Akhil Bharat Shanti Sena Mandal resolved to focus its activities on youth. It was decided that thirty-two full-time instructors would be appointed to propagate the idea of the youth peace corps, recruit members, and organize them by conducting camps.[152] The result was the establishment of the Bharatiya Tarun Shanti Sena in 1969 by Narayan Desai. The aim of this youth peace corps was to provide youth with constructive opportunities to "find self-expression and to seek training in responsibility," to channel their energies towards peace, to instill "healthy attitudes" and provide "programmes of self-help and community effort," as well as to "organise youth for active participation in constructive tasks of national reconstruction."[153]

Membership in the Tarun Shanti Sena was open to youth, aged between fourteen and twenty-two, of either sex, who had faith in democracy, secularism, and national integration, who were willing to set aside a month every year for constructive work and who signed a simple pledge to work for a peaceful society.[154] The Tarun Sainiks were to dress in the distinctive uniform of "white shirt and white half-pant for boys and white skirt and blouse, salwar kurta or saree for girls. A saffron-coloured Khadi band to be tied around the waist and a scarf of the same colour around the neck, for both boys and girls. A small medal of the Tarun Shanti Sena be pinned on the chest."[155]

By 1973, according to records at the central office in Varanasi, the Tarun Shanti Sena had 1,900 members in 280 centers in thirteen states[156] and, in his *Towards a Non-Violent Revolution,* Narayan Desai was able to write that the Tarun Shanti Sena was "growing so fast that the reader may find a completely new chapter if a second edition of this book is published."[157] His optimism was misplaced, however. As was to be the case with the entire Sarva Seva Sangh, the Tarun Shanti Sena was to self-destruct in the turbulence of the mid-1970s.

Although the Tarun Shanti Sena was a completely independent movement of Indian youth, free from allegiance to all political parties and even from the Shanti Sena itself,[158] it could always rely upon the support of the Shanti Sena, and most members had a strong personal loyalty to JP.

In 1973 Narayan Desai relinquished coordinatorship of the organization in favor of the youthful political science M.A. graduate Ashok Bhargava. At this stage about fifteen young people had decided to dedicate at least one year of their lives to the youth peace corps. Most were working in Bihar and Maharashtra. A further 150–200 were committing their vacations and spare time to Tarun Shanti Sena work on a regular basis. With the advent of the Bihar movement most of this hard core group were strongly attracted and became deeply involved.[159]

Thousands of youths were being swept up in the JP movement. The context of the Tarun Shanti Sena was not satisfactory to most, who, in any case, were not wedded to its ideals. A mass organization was needed, which could grow out of the movement rather than out of a commitment to Sarvodaya philosophy. In January 1975 JP established his new Chhatra Yuva Sangharsh Vahini (Student and Youth Struggle Force) to operate as the youth wing of his "Total Revolution."[160] The aims of the Vahini were stated as "Total Revolution" through "peaceful and pure means" in a way that was "non-party" and "free from power politics". The activities of the Vahini were to be based on the four-fold program of the Total Revolution, namely: "People's Education, Organization, Construction and Confrontation."[161] JP disbanded the Bihar section of the Tarun Shanti Sena, and most of the members had no difficulty finding their places in the Sangharsh Vahini.

Outside Bihar the Tarun Shanti Sena continued to operate as a parallel organization. Eventually it was felt that this situation was causing confusion, and both JP and the leading figures in the Sangharsh Vahini wished to expand the Vahini outside the confines of Bihar. The amalgamation of all nonpolitical youth organizations into the Vahini was mooted frequently and finally became inevitable. Because many young people belonged to both groups and considered themselves as followers of JP, this caused no problem.

Some of the leaders of the Tarun Shanti Sena, including Ashok Bhargava and Ashok Bang, however, resisted this move. Although JP was the inspiration and guide, and even though he had set up the organization, he was not officially the leader of the Tarun Shanti Sena. In the Vahini JP was the supreme commander who had to be obeyed. Some felt that the circumstances of the Total Revolution required such rigid discipline, whereas others believed that the idea of a supreme commander with dictatorial powers (even if JP himself never behaved like a dictator) was against the teachings of both Sarvodaya and JP himself. Because of ideological convictions focused around a firm belief in democracy and autonomy,[162] and, perhaps, because they did not want to lose their own positions of power,[163] the leaders of the Tarun Shanti Sena held out against enforced regimentation. Long debates were held with leading Sangharsh Vahini members (many of whom had previously been Tarun Shanti Sena colleagues) and finally, at the May 1977 Bombay Sarvodaya conference, almost one-half year after the lifting of the Emergency, it was decided that, rather than disband the Tarun Shanti Sena or merge it with the Chhatra Yuva Sangharsh Vahini, it would be frozen.

Although its remaining members continued their social work activities, the Tarun Shanti Sena had disappeared from the political agenda of the Gandhian movement. The Sena was not taking in new members, and many old ones left to do their own work at the grass-roots level. There was no longer anyone doing the work of central organization. It was realized that the Tarun Shanti Sena could not run effectively on the strength of the ten to fifteen old guard members who remained.[164] The leadership decided that it was more pragmatic and more convenient to the Vahini if the Sena was dissolved.[165]

At the Patna meeting of the Prabhand Samiti of the Sarva Seva Sangh in March 1978, the question of merger was again debated. The different backgrounds and aims of the two groups was discussed, and although there was a general feeling that there was no need for two Gandhian youth organizations, one of the main arguments against a merger was the undiscipline demonstrated by many Vahini members.[166] Instead of agreeing to a merger the Tarun Shanti Sena voluntarily decided to disband itself.

The Kerala unit of the Tarun Shanti Sena continued for a further eight months. Without support at the national level, however, its members, too, saw the impracticality of pressing on and finally dissolved this last group.[167]

The Demise of the Shanti Sena and New Beginnings

In October 1969, after a majority of the people in the majority of Bihar villages had signed the Gramdan pledge, Bihardan was announced. Although this should have been the high point of almost two decades of effort in the work of Gandhian social revolution, it was, in fact, the beginning of the end for an organized and united Gandhian movement.[168]

Sarvodaya workers were tired, and the Bhoodan/Gramdan drive began to lose momentum. The expectations that accompanied the quest for

Bihardan remained unfulfilled, and the revolutionary violence that Bhoodan was originally designed to replace was again reasserting itself. Furthermore, Vinoba Bhave retired from active leadership of the Sarvodaya movement, and traveling the country in its cause, for a more introspective and religious life.

As Vinoba withdrew to his Paunar ashram in mid-1970, JP ensconced himself in the villages of Musahari, in north Bihar, to devote his full energy to Gramdan work.[169] JP's Musahari experience had two major consequences. First, it signaled JP's emergence from Vinoba's shadow and, secondly, JP realized that many of the recorded Gramdan pledges were bogus and consequently, that the results of the Gramdan work did not justify the effort.[170]

During the Bhopal Sarva Seva Sangh meeting in October 1971 differences over the future strategy to be adopted by the Gandhian movement emerged. JP suggested that later tactics adopted by Vinoba in the push for Gramdan may have been a mistake. One of the senior Sarvodaya thinkers, Dada Dharmadhikari, started a heated debate when, with JP's endorsement, he attacked the Vinoban line of consensus at all costs and the insistence on absolute nonviolence while suggesting that fear of class war should not prevent the Sangh from organizing the landless and poor farmers in nonviolent confrontation with exploiting landowners.

In 1971 Prime Minister Indira Gandhi's increasingly authoritarian approach to politics was beginning to alarm JP, and by the middle of the following year he had taken the political initiative by writing articles and organizing conferences on national issues, and by taking action to broaden the scope of the Sarvodaya movement and making it more effective by resorting to satyagraha if necessary. Many of Vinoba's close followers saw JP's move into confrontational politics as contrary to their master's teaching and a betrayal of the essential Sarvodaya philosophy of avoiding conflict and being willing to work with everyone, including the government.[171]

As the decline in the Indian economy during 1973 led to civil unrest, some of the more militant Sarva Seva Sangh leaders were calling for the "politicization of the movement" while Vinoba supporters were insisting that the movement stood for the "spiritualization of politics." JP, meanwhile, was issuing an appeal to the youth to take an active part in politics by becoming engaged in a major voter education campaign to ensure the health of Indian democracy. As JP came to occupy the position of Mrs. Gandhi's chief critic, Vinoba, at least tacitly, appeared to be lending her his influential support.

During March 1974 a student agitation against mismanagement and corruption in the Congress-dominated Bihar State Assembly led to rioting and a swift and brutal government crackdown. On 19 March the ailing seventy-year-old Narayan accepted the students' request to direct and guide their movement on the condition that the students were to remain nonviolent and nonpartisan in the party political sense and that he had the final say on major decisions.

The agitation that followed, commonly called the "Bihar (or JP) Movement," had mass support from the people of Bihar and severely shook the State Assembly; however, it became increasingly obvious that the state government was not free to yield. The realization that the political situation in the state was being controlled by New Delhi led JP to make Mrs. Gandhi the chief target of his criticism.

On 5 June at a mass meeting in Patna, the capital of Bihar, JP issued his call for "Total Revolution," the restructuring of society along the lines of Sarvodaya philosophy by harnessing people's power and launching direct attacks against all systems fostering oppression and injustice on all fronts at once rather than continuing with lifeless Sarvodaya "charity work."[172] Vinoba refused to lend his support and gradually moved to outright opposition.[173] To JP followers the call was a reenergization of the movement, an emulation of the Mahatma's satyagrahas against the government. To the Vinobans it was a resort to "negative satyagraha" that had no place in an independent country. The battle lines, both inside the Gandhian fraternity and without were now clearly drawn.

The July Sarva Seva Sangh session held at Wardha was dominated by the growing rift. Sangh meetings had previously always come to consensus decisions, but this time the meeting ended in shouting and confusion. The vast majority of the delegates supported JP and the Bihar movement but the minority was not prepared to concede the issue. Most of the JP-supporting Prabhand Samiti members, including the president and secretary, resigned their positions. With the Sangh on the verge of collapse the issue was taken to Vinoba, who proposed a compromise: all Sangh members should do what they felt was correct, they could go to Bihar if that was what their consciences dictated, the only conditions were that they observe truth, nonviolence, and self-restraint.[174]

The solution was only temporary, however. Both sides saw Vinoba's compromise statement as endorsing their own view, and within days the Vinoba faction, led by Nirmala Deshpande, the most vocal critic of the politicization of the Sarvodaya movement, stated publicly that Vinoba had not only not blessed the Bihar agitation but believed that it would achieve nothing. The air of rapprochement soon vanished.

Mrs. Gandhi started using these utterances apparently to divide the Sarvodaya movement and challenged JP to demonstrate the accuracy of his statements that his movement represented public opinion in the next Bihar election. The confrontations with the police turned increasingly violent, Sarvodaya workers were banned from the state, many youth were becoming disillusioned with the lack of visible results, and the government stood firm. JP announced the cessation of mass actions and, on 18 November, accepted Mrs. Gandhi's challenge. Although JP claimed that the foray into party politics was not going against Sarvodaya philosophy because it was not a quest for political power by Sarvodaya workers but merely a referendum on the question of whether the state government represented the people of Bihar, many did not see his move in the same light.

Again the Sangh was in turmoil, and this time there would be no compromise. Vinoba stated that he would disassociate himself from the Sangh if it involved itself in elections, yet the JP followers, still the overwhelming majority in the Sangh, felt that they could not resign and turn the organization over to the Vinoba faction. While the idea of "freezing" the Sarva Seva Sangh was being mooted, Vinoba announced that he was commencing a year of silence.

The Sangh conference at Paunar in mid-March 1975 heralded the end of the organization as an active united body. Vinoba asked JP directly, in the name of the Indian people, to give up his opposition to the government. JP refused, and amid heated argument and a flurry of resignations the few remaining members of the polarized Sangh temporarily "froze" the organization.[175] This state was to continue at least until the end of the year when Vinoba was to end his period of silence. The "freezing" of the Sangh encompassed the "freezing" of its constituent parts, bringing the operations of the Shanti Sena to an end. Sainiks remained, but the Sena and Sena pati (leader) were no more.

Although the Sangh decided to resume its activities after Vinoba's period of self-imposed silence ended, the continuing political turmoil in the country, the "Emergency," and the ensuing imprisonment of senior JP-line Sarva Seva Sangh members left the Gandhian movement broken and dazed for years to come and the Shanti Sena dormant.

One year after the immobilization of the Sangh, Vinoba announced that "though the deliberations go on, the Sangh is not doing anything. So the experienced persons suggested to dissolve it. We may keep on meeting once or twice every year as gentlemen but the organization as a Sangh or Committee is dissolved."[176] With the Emergency ended, and the Janata government in power, Vinoba's directive was not heeded. The Sangh was again able to conduct large meetings; however, the divisions had not evaporated.

One year after the installment of the Janata government the Sarva Seva Sangh's Prabhand Samiti again took up the question of the Shanti Sena. At the Patna meeting on 8–9 March 1978 Professor Bang stated that the Shanti Sena was created out of national emergency to prevent riots and tackle the problem of refugee relief work and that in the present circumstances the importance of the Sena was greater than before. Narayan Desai added that he had undertaken discussions with Shanti Sainiks and that they were in favor of continuing the Shanti Sena. Desai thought that the work of the Sena should encompass (1) the establishment of peace, (2) work for community change, (3) service and, thus, the prevention of violence, (4) work in the border areas, (5) investigation of the reasons for violence, in order to pinpoint its causes and discover remedies, and (6) establishment of connections to facilitate peace work in the international sphere.

The view was, however, not unanimous. Some members were of the opinion that ad hoc committees could be formed to take care of immediate problems and that, consequently, there was no need to continue with an organized Shanti Sena. Both Manmohan Choudhuri and Vasant Nargolkar believed that the Sena should be reactivated, and Sangh president Siddharaj Dhadda added that although there was a need for trained people, ordinarily every Lok Sevak should be a Shanti Sainik and that a Tatpar Shanti Sena should be reestablished. He continued by stressing that trained sainiks should go on working in the border areas and that international peace work should be the province of the Sarva Seva Sangh and not of the Shanti Sena. Senior Sangh member Acharya Ramamurti made a point that was to become his war cry in later years: to save democracy people should be ready to lay down their lives, and for this they should be sainiks. After lengthy discussions, it was decided that the Shanti Sena should be continued on the same basis as before as a branch of the Sarva Seva Sangh.

Narayan Desai asked to be relieved of the task of convening the Sena, and Amarnathbhai (Amarnath Mishra) was appointed in his place.[177] That the reorganization of the Shanti Sena did not receive a high priority, however, can be seen by the meager budget of Rs.25,000 allocated for this work by the Prabhand Samiti.[178]

In mid-1979 Amarnathbhai produced a report of the activities of the Shanti Sena for the previous year. He reported that little had been achieved. Two hundred and fifty sainiks had taken the pledge and ten kendras had been established, but state conveners remained inactive and a strong need was felt for a youth organization. In his report on organization he concluded: "On the whole it pains me to say that the Shanti Sena has been greatly neglected within the framework of the Total Revolution while other wings have prospered. If in the present situation we admit that the Shanti Sena is indeed important, then we shall have to give the matter solemn thought."[179]

The Sena had no visible program aimed at fighting injustices, but, Amarnathbhai noted, it had undertaken flood relief work in severely affected areas of the United Provinces and riot-disturbed areas of Varanasi, Aligarh, and Jamshedpur. The valuable work in the border areas had to be discontinued during the Emergency but was slowly being recommenced under the guidance of Narayan Desai.

After the tabling of the report, discussion reflected some confusion about the definition of the sainik. Some speakers (e.g., Kamala Patibhai, Pultan Azad, and Dineshbhai) insisted that all Lok Sevaks should be included in the list of Shanti Sainiks and that only then could an accurate number of sainiks be determined. Surendranath Dwivedi pointed out the confusion about the distinction between the two groups and that it had to be clarified. Since the liberalization of Sena membership in the early 1960s, the Lok Sevak pledge had been more restrictive than the Shanti Sena pledge, so it could be assumed that Lok Sevaks were also sainiks. After the dormant period of the mid-1970s, however, the membership qualifications and distinctions had to be sorted out anew.

In September 1979 Amarnathbhai took up the issue by noting that the claim that all sevaks were automatically sainiks should not be made until Lok Sevaks were consulted and their agreement obtained. He also emphasized that efforts had to be concentrated on setting up state units of the Sena with offices and separate budgets and that a Tatpar Shanti Sena had to be set up immediately. These fledgling efforts by the Sangh to breath new life into the Shanti Sena were again to prove abortive, again because of the actions of Vinoba Bhave.

When the Emergency ended and the Sarva Seva Sangh had recommenced its meetings, Vinoba asked that a no-voting clause be included in the pledge taken by Shanti Sainiks.[180] He wanted to ensure that the Sangh would become depoliticized. This was not acceptable to the Sangh.[181]

Vinoba firmly believed that the world's peacemakers had to work for the disarmament of military forces. The ballot, he claimed, "smelled of bullets," and political parties were the representatives of violence. The only party that deserved a vote was one that stood for disarmament, for all others a military sanction was the final prop and a vote for such a party was a vote in support of the military.[182] He had long called upon the United Nations to raise a peace army,[183] and less than three months after JP's death, at the World Women's Conference held at Paunar in December 1979, he repeated his assurance that India would provide one hundred thousand of his proposed seven hundred thousand world sainiks.[184] To bring this about[185] and ensure that politics was removed from the Sena, in January Vinoba announced the formation of his Bharatiya Shanti Sena.

This was done without consulting the Sarva Seva Sangh. A new pledge, containing a clause prohibiting participation in party politics and voting, was issued by the new sena. The old sainik leaders did not see the pledge until it was made public, and they refused to sign it.[186] Some sainiks, however, did fill in the form and sent it to Paunar without informing the Shanti Sena Mandal, thereby bypassing the Sangh.[187]

The Sangh's leaders were upset at the setting up of a parallel sena just as they were attempting to breathe life into the old Shanti Sena. Some saw the move as one that denied even common courtesy[188] while others were even more forthright in their criticisms. Manmohan Choudhuri, for example, called Vinoba's action a "gross violation of public morality."[189] Whatever the feelings among Sangh members, Vinoba had presented them with a fait accompli.

Amarnathbhai and Narayan Desai held separate meetings with Vinoba as soon as he announced the formation of the new sena. Vinoba wanted the clause relating to the resistance of injustice, exploitation, and corruption removed and one prohibiting voting included in the pledge. Shanti Sena Mandal and Sarva Seva Sangh executive committee members held further lengthy meetings with Vinoba but still no agreement was reached.[190] Vinoba officially designated Paunar as the headquarters of the new sena and appointed Paunar ashramite Achyut Deshpande as convener.

At the Sangh's Khadagpur conference in June 1980 the situation was deliberated. Reporting on the recently held discussions, Amarnathbhai announced that Vinoba was adamant on the issue that sainiks could not vote. The incongruity of the Gandhian movement fielding two peace armies because no agreement could be reached by the factions, especially when Vinoba had just called on the world to unite and inaugurate an international Shanti Sena, was not lost on the delegates.

In a question and answer session Vinoba was quite clear on the essence of the dispute. It was put to him that "some colleagues have been of the view that the right of franchise is a sacred right. It is a step to wean citizens away from the path of violence and to induce them to adopt nonviolence. Hence it would be an unprincipled action to prohibit Shanti Sainiks from exercising their fundamental right of franchise. It does not mean that they must vote; but to prohibit them from doing so would be improper. Rules can, however, be laid down regarding the types of candidates for whom they may vote, and for whom they must not." Vinoba answered saying that Shanti Sainiks should not vote for any party.[191] He added that "if a party declares his [sic] support to (full) disarmament, it may be voted for. But it is extremely doubtful if there would be any such party."[192] The delegates echoed these concerns with the sentiment on one side that to protect the democratic system democratic norms such as voting had to be protected and voting was necessary to produce responsible nonparty "people's candidates" and, on the other, that not voting was symbolic of a nonpartisan attitude and that Vinoba had turned his back on the prevailing situation to create a new and better situation.

Most Sangh leaders had trouble accepting the Bharatiya Shanti Sena, but they could not openly defy Vinoba. After the debate, it was decided that Vinoba was the supreme commander and rather than have a separate group the Sangh should dissolve its Shanti Sena Mandal and work in harmony with Vinoba while reopening dialogue with him on the voting issue.[193] When the matter was again discussed with Vinoba, his attitude on the issue remained inflexible and at the Nadiad meeting of the Prabhand

Samiti later in the year talk about the revival of the Sangh's Shanti Sena was again commenced.[194]

At the Sangh's next conference, at Shrimangeshi in Goa, it was thought that choice of state conveners by the Bharatiya Shanti Sena was biased against Sarva Seva Sangh workers who had been engaged in the struggle against dictatorship and the choice of Deshpande as overall convener was causing resentment. The increase in violence, it was agreed, necessitated a strong Shanti Sena, yet Vinoba's no-voting stipulation was still causing confusion in the sainik ranks. The assembly felt that it would be impossible to maintain the status quo, and, therefore, the Sangh should again create its own sena. Bang, however, counseled patience. He requested those who were friendly with both sides to bring about a reconciliation while Sangh members continued to assist with peace work where it was required.[195]

By the time of the All-India Shanti Sena Conference at Paunar in October 1981 three thousand sainiks had been enrolled in the Bharatiya Shanti Sena,[196] and Vinoba had decided not to form a separate Tarun Shanti Sena.[197] The new sena had been instituted as a body independent from all others with the main organization at state level. The function of the central organization was to "keep record of the number of Shanti Sainiks statewise, to provide them necessary help, to coordinate the work of different units and to undertake any special project if the activity demands it."[198]

The activities of the organization for the previous year were listed as work during riots in Moradabad, Aligarh, and Allahabad as well as in Gujarat on the contentious reservation issue and, providing a taste of things to come, "satyagraha . . . in Maharashtra for ban on cow slaughter."[199] The conference decided to step up its efforts to prevent cow slaughter and asked Vinoba for guidance. He encouraged the Sena to take up the task.[200]

In early 1982 under Vinoba's guidance a mass satyagraha for cow protection was to commence at Bombay's Deonar slaughter yards. Vinoba entrusted this work to Achyut Deshpande and it quickly became the sole function of the Bharatiya Shanti Sena. On 15 November the ailing Vinoba died at Paunar.

One month after the Paunar conference the Sarva Seva Sangh was again in session. Amarnathbhai outlined the position of the Sangh when he reminded the audience that at Khadagpur they discussed the freezing of the Shanti Sena while continuing with peace work. He noted that their hopes that the Bharatiya Shanti Sena could meet the threat of violence in the country had not been fulfilled and, consequently, some members had started sena work in their own areas while the nationwide immobilization continued. He placed three options before the delegates: (1) restarting the Sangh's Shanti Sena, (2) maintaining the freeze, and (3) changing the name and continuing the work.

Heated debate again broke out on the voting issue, and one delegate demanded to know how it was possible that many people belonged to both senas. The difference between the two groups was then again carefully explained by Amarnathbhai, and he asked for a committee to be appointed to investigate the structure around which the Sangh's Shanti Sena should be reorganized.[201] It was decided that at a national level the Sena should remain dormant but that it should be reactivated at the state and village level on the basis of its previous organizational system and pledge. In order to avoid confusion it was further decided not to work where the Bharatiya Shanti Sena was active.[202]

Violence had escalated to epidemic proportions in Bihar where Rama-murti's Khadigram Ashram was situated. The Bharatiya Shanti Sena was inactive and Ramamurti believed that only a strong peace brigade could tackle the problem. After a weeklong camp at Khadigram for Bihar con-structive workers in 1983, he started enrolling sainiks on a large scale.[203] About four thousand were recruited and in some areas proved very effective in reducing violence. Although the Bharatiya Shanti Sena boasted large numbers at its 1981 conference, most members were active on paper only and the rest were fully occupied at Deonar.[204] Consequently, after congratu-lations to Ramamurti for his efforts in Bihar, the idea of a Sarva Seva Sangh-controlled sena was again on the agenda at the Sevagram Prabhand Samiti meeting in August 1984. Ramamurti was asked to prepare a report on the question.[205]

One year later at the Prabhand Samiti meeting in Varanasi, Rama-murti presented his report with the recommendation that the Sangh should start organizing and training its Shanti Sena at the all-India level. Badripra-sad Swami, however, was of the view that there should be only one na-tional Shanti Sena, and, consequently, Deshpande should be contacted, and, after discussions, a concise, simple pledge for sainiks formulated. While some counseled caution, others thought that the program outlined by Ramamurti should be implemented without delay. Eventually, it was decided unanimously that village and state Shanti Sena work should con-tinue with Amarnathbhai as coordinator but that they should not go ahead on a national level.

Talks between representatives of the Sangh and Achyut Deshpande and Balbhai of the Bharatiya Shanti Sena eventually led to a compromise. Although Deshpande was not willing to give way on the voting issue because it had been Vinoba's firm decision, he conceded that others could do Shanti Sena work as long as they did not call the organization by the name Vinoba had given to his new sena. The Bharatiya Shanti Sena would restrict itself to cow protection work. Balbhai added that sena work was so important that it should be made more comprehensive and to secure an extension of the work the nonvoting clause should not be insisted upon.[206]

Finally, at Alindi in Pune during November 1985, the Sangh revoked its suspension resolution taken at the Khadagpur meeting and decided to formally revive its Shanti Sena along previous lines. The question of voting was left for each sainik to decide in light of his or her own conscience. The importance of the Sena in the proposed restructuring of India on a Gramswaraj (village government) basis by the turn of the century was spelled out: "there would be Gramswaraj Sabhas [assemblies], Voters Councils and Shanti Sena in the villages. The villages would be free from dependence on the police and the courts."[207]

At the Sarva Seva Sangh meeting in Ranipatra, Bihar, a lengthy discussion on the ideas concerning the detailed organization of a national Shanti Sena was conducted. The perceived role of the sainiks was an expanded one that resembled that of the old Lok Sevaks. Ramamurti's influence was clearly visible when the deliberations on the duties of the Shanti Sainiks included the tasks of bringing electoral rolls up to date and influencing legislative procedure.[208]

The program for the Sena, as seen by Ramamurti, was ambitious. The revitalized Shanti Sena was to be a vast India-wide organization that played a key role in the administration of a nonviolent society:

> A trained and disciplined army of about a million shanti sainiks should be able to take preventive peace action against much of the violence that is corroding the life of the country today. It is only in very difficult situations involving hardened criminals that intervention by armed forces may be necessary. The Shanti Sena will have its units of ten (a dusta) in the villages and mohallas of the cities throughout the country. It will be organized from the village up to the national level. As such it will be an effective instrument of social control and discipline, progressively it will induce among people self-control and self-discipline as well.[209]

In mid-1987 state Shanti Sena conveners and state Sarvodaya leaders met at Ramamurti's ashram in Bihar. This meeting was immediately followed by one of the Sangh's leadership. The outcome of the discussions was that the newly organized sena was to be named the Akhil Bharat Shanti Sena, that Ramamurti would serve as the national convener, and that a national conveners' committee, comprising state conveners and those, selected by the Sangh's president and the national convener, who had taken an interest in the work of the Shanti Sena, should be formed.[210]

One and one-half months later the newly established Conveners' Committee met for the first time in the Gujarat city of Baroda. Decisions were taken about the scarf, banner, and pledge of the Sena.[211] A training camp for Shanti Sena trainers was planned, and it was decided that at the forthcoming Sarva Seva Sangh conference at Bombay a Shanti Sena rally was to be organized.

Ramamurti continued the reorganization of the Sena in Bihar. As he moved ever increasingly into anti–Rajiv Gandhi politics,[212] however, his involvements at the national level remained limited, and at the Bombay conference, at the end of 1987, he announced his resignation as convener to take effect in three months.[213] At that time, at the Sangh's executive committee meeting in Sevagram, a committee was set up to oversee the Shanti Sena and Sarva Seva Sangh training. The committee included all state Shanti Sena conveners and such important ex-Sena leaders as Narayan Desai and Amarnathbhai as well. Gangaprasad Agarwal became the new committee's convener.[214]

It soon became evident that such an organizational structure was not working, and, consequently, in December 1988 at Trivandrum the functions of training and responsibility for the Sena were again separated with Amarnathbhai becoming convener of the training committee and, after Agarwal's resignation, Badriprasad Swami taking responsibility for the Shanti Sena.[215]

Swami had joined JP when the latter left the Socialist Party to dedicate his life to the cause of Sarvodaya. He set up people's courts in villages until 1957 when, after Vinoba's tour of Rajasthan, he was appointed state Shanti Sena convener.[216]

On 18 April 1989, the anniversary of the first "land gift," a major discussion on the Shanti Sena was to be held at the scheduled Shivarampalli Sarvodaya sammelan. All leading Shanti Sainiks of the country were asked to attend so that a program and financing structure for the organization could be worked out.[217] For various reasons (possibly political—the Congress-controlled state government put major obstacles in the way of the gathering by claiming logistical and resource difficulties after a devastating hurricane) the gathering was postponed for a year.[218] In May 1990 at a seminar held at Sevagram it was finally decided again to try to revitalize the Shanti Sena and to set up peace centers in all towns experiencing communal disharmony as part of a so-called Challenge of Gandhi campaign.[219] At the postponed sammelan, which had finally been convened one month earlier in April 1990 at Melkote, Karnataka, discussion on the Shanti Sena does not appear to have played a major part outside general discussions on strategy for the campaign.[220]

In short, besides the organization of an Akhil Bharat Shanti Sena camp at Vedchhi in October/November 1987, during the late 1980s and since, the Sarva Seva Sangh achieved relatively little in bringing the Sena back to anything resembling its heyday in the late 1960s and early 1970s.

During the prime ministership of Rajiv Gandhi the Gandhian movement again faced tensions between those who wanted to support the opposition parties in order to remove the Congress government before, as they saw it, it destroyed the country and those to whom, because of a firm belief in a partyless democracy, such actions were seen as a contradiction. Questions about whether these differences had the potential to reopen the rift that accompanied the JP movement, and whether this time a newly emerging Shanti Sena could survive if it did, became irrelevant with the defeat of Rajiv Gandhi at the polls.

Conclusion

In Vinoba's conception, as reflected in the earliest history of the Shanti Sena, before it was formally constituted, the Sena was to be a decentralized network of dedicated peacebuilders spreading Gandhi's message in the villages through personal example. The hope, however, that a spontaneous Sena would spring up remained nothing more than a hope. A significant degree of organization was found to be necessary to get the Sena actually off the ground. Further, JP wanted to involve youth, to get them to dedicate a limited part of their lives to full-time peace work to undertake specific nonviolent "revolutionary" projects. This experience has been reflected in the various peace brigade attempts.

For any understanding of unarmed peacekeeping the history of the Shanti Sena is important. As this history clearly illustrates, however, vast differences developed between Vinoba and JP about the direction that should be taken by the Sena. Whether these differences, which centered on varying interpretations of satyagraha, peacekeeping compared to peacebuilding, and the political organization of society generally, resulted from personality differences between the two or because the philosophical legacy on which they founded the Sena readily lends itself to differing interpretations will be discussed in chapters 7 and 8.

Given that the institutional history of the Shanti Sena reflects serious conflicts, the question of its viability as a model for other nonviolent nonstate peace brigades is raised. Before examining this issue, however, it is appropriate to consider the history of the Sena from another perspective, namely, its achievements in peacekeeping. Although the peacebuilding work favored by Vinoba is difficult to record, the peacekeeping efforts of the Sena that were championed by JP can readily be chronicled. And it is these activities that have generally been held up as examples by the advocates of internationalizing the Shanti Sena idea.

6

Peacekeeping and the Shanti Sena

After its first crisis and subsequent reorganization, the Sena experienced a period that was full of promise for an effective and lengthy future. Until the near demise of the Shanti Sena in the mid-1970s, the organization boasted several campaigns that demonstrated its philosophy in action in ways more obvious than day-to-day grass-roots peacebuilding. These actions were, in the main, concerned with restoring peace in communal disturbances, working with refugees (after the war in Bangladesh and in the international sphere in Cyprus), doing peace work in India's sensitive border areas, and establishing training camps to instill the ethos of service and nonviolence in the youth of India. Since the early 1980s, much of the effort of what has remained of the Shanti Sena, rather than concentrating on peacekeeping activities, has been directed toward cow protection.

As an organization the Shanti Sena is committed in principle to grass-roots action. Nevertheless, the most celebrated Shanti Sena campaigns, the Nagaland Peace Mission and peace work among the dacoits (bandits) of the Chambal valley, were in reality campaigns of the charismatic leaders of the Sena.

The Nagaland Peace Mission

Although the much-publicized peace mission to Nagaland was not, strictly speaking, a Shanti Sena action, it is often talked about as if it were.[1] Ostergaard and Currel, in their study of Sarvodaya leaders, noted that of those questioned many mentioned the promotion of peace as one of the most important achievements of the Sarvodaya movement since Indian independence, and in this regard the Nagaland mission was often highlighted.[2]

British contact with the Nagas of northeast India started in 1832, and by 1881 the Naga Hills district, under British rule, had been established.[3] In 1918 the Naga Club was formed, and in 1929 it informed the Simon Commission, set up to examine the options for increasing self-government, that the Nagas should be excluded from reforms for India. In 1946, President of the Indian National Congress and Prime Minister elect Jawaharlal Nehru expressed his views on the subject to the Naga National Council when he wrote that "it is obvious that the Naga territory in eastern Assam is much too small to stand by itself, politically or economically. When India is independent, it will not be possible for the British Government to hold on to Naga territory or any part of it. Inevitably, therefore, this Naga territory must form part of India."[4]

As independence approached, in 1947 Naga leaders wrote to Governor-General Lord Mountbatten that after Britain's withdrawal India might act as guardian power for ten years, after which time the Christian Nagas should be free to determine their own political future. No understanding was reached between the Naga Nationalists and the Indian Government, so on 14 August 1947, the eve of Indian independence, the Nagas declared themselves independent. "Thus," as Aram, a member of the Delhi-Peking march, secretary of the Asian Regional Council of the WPB, and later a peace observer in Nagaland and then convener of the Nagaland Peace Center, remarked "a unique situation had arisen. India which had just become independent was confronted with the Nagas who wanted to be independent."[5]

Meanwhile, Naga independence advocate A. Z. Phizo, who had fought with the Japanese against the British during the war and had escaped to London in the late 1950s, had by 1960 gained the support of the WPB's Reverend Michael Scott who, in turn, had asked his colleague JP Narayan to undertake mediatory work between India and the Nagas.[6]

The 1950s and early 1960s were a time of police operations, violence, and counterviolence. After the India-China war, the government moved to extend its administration more firmly into the strategically important border tribal areas, including Nagaland. The Nagas resisted the intrusion, and the army was called in to restore order.[7] As a response to Naga political demands and, according to some, the influence on Nehru of JP's arguments that India appeared an "unjust bully,"[8] in December 1963 Nagaland was inaugurated as the sixteenth state of the Indian Union. Rather than solving the conflict this action merely added a new dimension to it. From 1947 the protagonists were the Naga underground and the government of India; the conflict became triangular with the addition of the Naga State Government. The Nagas' case was that their territory had never been conquered by the Indian Army or ruled by the Indian government and that although the British had forcibly annexed their land, as the case was put to JP, "before the British came . . . we were free; after they had left we should also be free."[9] From the Indian point of view Nagaland formed an integral part of British India, and after the transfer of power Nagaland became a part of India in the same way as all the other Indian States.

Other important political considerations were involved, however. Even JP, who was to play a leading role in the peacemaking efforts and had some sympathy with the Naga cause, realized that "for India, mindful of its past divisions and wounded deeply by partition, territorial integrity is a matter of life and death. . . . Had Nagaland been the only area involved India might have taken the risk. . . , [but] what happens in Nagaland would affect the entire northeast border of the country. That is a risk no nation should be asked to run."[10] JP reiterated this sentiment at a speech in the Nagan capital, Kohima, on 12 August 1966 when he told his audience bluntly that their "leaders must understand that India *cannot* agree to anything that might start the process of disintegration of its territory."[11] He had the further concern that an independent Nagaland could follow Tibet and be swallowed by China.[12]

In 1964 the Naga Baptist Church Council appealed for a cease-fire and invited Narayan to establish a peace mission for the troubled area.[13] JP had the prestige to undertake the task, and his sympathy for the Nagas and political distance from Nehru, coupled with his Gandhian nonviolence and intense nationalism, made him acceptable to all sides. The second member of the Mission was to be Scott. Although initially the government objected to the inclusion of a foreigner, the insistence of the Naga Baptist Church leaders eventually ensured his acceptance, albeit reluctantly.[14] The third member of the Mission was B. P. Chaliha, the chief minister of Assam. Sarvodaya leader Shankarrao Deo was to be the final member; however, owing to ill health, he declined the invitation.[15]

By shuttling between federal, state, and underground leaders, within six months the Peace Mission had secured a cease-fire and paved the way for a conference of the various parties. Although the violence had stopped and talks continued, a political solution seemed as distant as ever. JP proposed a formula by which the Nagas would be granted self-determination after which they would voluntarily join the Indian Union. The Union government begged the question by insisting that peace could only be achieved by Nagaland *continuing* to remain within the Union. This position swung the Nagas to the opposite extreme.[16]

The Nagas wanted to "internationalize" their cause and used the acceptance by India of Scott's involvement in the Peace Mission as a lever. They were, thus, attempting to maintain a case that they were a sovereign nation. India, for similar tactical reasons, could not be seen as allowing foreigners to "meddle" in the internal affairs of the country. The insistence that the Nagaland question was entirely a domestic matter was consistently maintained.[17] India further charged that the foreigner, Scott, was helping to sustain Naga resistance to the national will.[18]

A pro-war "crush the Nagas" hysteria within India[19] and the accusations against Scott further hampered the achievement of settlement as did Naga demands that the security forces (occupation forces to many) had to be withdrawn as a first step toward permanent peace and the government counterinsistence that such a withdrawal could only come about after a satisfactory political settlement had been reached.[20]

But the cease-fire held, and progress was made. The All-India Shanti Sena Mandal set up a peace center in Kohima in 1965 to promote a climate of peace by establishing favorable public opinion.[21] The main attempts at conflict resolution, however, were through the use of a nonaligned third party in the role of peacemaker. In the early days of the cease-fire Scott examined reported violations, made recommendations, and informed the parties,[22] and at one stage JP proposed that "if the peace talks failed the members of the Peace Mission should undertake a token fast for a limited period, or a fast unto death, or alternatively they should risk their lives by a padayatra into the interior of Nagaland without escort."[23] The main task, however, was mediation.

In February 1965, feeling that press misreporting of certain of his comments had lost him Naga support, JP resigned from the Peace Mission. By May, Scott had been forced out of India[24] and, after an extremist bombing, Chaliha, too, had resigned, ending the Peace Mission.[25] The third-party role, however, was continued by the Kohima Peace Center[26] and the Peace Observers Team, a JP-inspired offspring of the mission that was composed of representatives of the government, the underground and, notably, such Gandhian workers as Marjorie Sykes, former Chief Minister of Orissa Nabakrushna Choudhuri, and Aram.[27]

The Team worked to supervise the cease-fire and acted as a liaison between conflicting parties. It successfully put forward proposals for the continuance of the cease-fire and convened joint conferences to ensure its continuation. When the inevitable violent incidents did occur, the team visited the site of the disturbance to ascertain the facts and made "recommendations for remedial action," thus helping "to localize the incident and prevent further escalation of tension."[28] Further peace centers were opened, in 1970 a Tarun Shanti Sena unit was formed, and in 1971 a women's peace training camp was conducted.[29]

The failure of progress in the peace talks led to a resumption of hostilities on the part of some of the rebel Nagas, who apparently were receiving Chinese arms.[30] In 1972, after open attacks on government institutions, the government ended its ritual monthly extension of the cease-fire, and, consequently, the Peace Observers Team was terminated. Sarvodaya and peace work, however, continued.

In 1974 a Peace Council, headed by Naga Baptist church leaders and Sarvodaya workers such as Aram, was set up. The following year a major breakthrough occurred in the form of the Shillong Peace Accord. Under the accord the underground organizations agreed to accept the Indian Constitution and to hand in their arms. In return, "It was agreed that the representatives of the underground organizations should have reasonable time to formulate other issues for discussion for a final settlement." Early in 1976 a majority of the underground deposited their arms with the Peace Council and moved into peace camps while the government released all political prisoners. That some Nagas have held out, that no peace had been made with Phizo, that sporadic conflict continues, and that some commentators have claimed that the accord is generally an irrelevance[31] cannot alter the fact that it did succeed in leaving an atmosphere largely devoid of conflict tensions. Aram maintains that there "has been a qualitative transformation of the social situation" and that this has resulted from the sustained third party work of the Sarvodaya movement and the Baptist church.[32]

The Chambal Valley Peace Missions

Gandhian constructive work among so-called criminal tribes has a long history. Since the early 1920s, Ravishankar Maharaj dedicated much of his long life to the rehabilitation of coastal central Gujarat's Baraiya and Patanvadiya castes (designated "criminal tribes" by the British).[33] In 1960 Vinoba Bhave, and again in 1972 JP Narayan, continued this tradition with the help of Shanti Sainiks.

The Chambal valley, between the towns of Agra and Gwalior, where the states of Uttar Pradesh, Madhya Pradesh, and Rajasthan meet, had a long history of violence and lawlessness. Banditry had become a practical and, at times, necessary way of life for many, and kidnapping and subsequent ransom requests by the dacoit gangs was commonplace.[34]

The emergence of the Bhoodan movement as a possible answer to the social ills caused by landlessness had caught public imagination. Suggestions were made that the technique Vinoba had developed could be applied in the Chambal valley. In July 1953 the editor of the Ujjain Hindi monthly *Vikram* wrote in his paper: "The Governments of Madhya Barat, Uttar Pradesh and Rajasthan have not been able to solve the dacoit problem of the Chambal ravines through methods of force and violence. . . . It would, therefore, be advisable for these governments to request Acharya Vinoba Bhave to undertake an experiment in applying the technique of non-violence to the situation in the Chambal valley. In order that it should be possible for him and his followers to establish contacts with the absconding dacoits, all facilities should be made available to him."[35]

No heed was paid to the suggestion.

In 1959 Gandhian workers of the area visited Vinoba, requesting his help, and the dacoit Tehsildar Singh, while awaiting execution, wrote a lengthy letter to the Acharya, repeating the plea of the *Vikram* editorial.[36] Vinoba sent Major General Yadunath Singh to talk with the condemned man. On hearing again the appeal for the use of nonviolence to assist those who through circumstances had taken to banditry in the ravines, he decided to act.

In May 1960 Vinoba commenced a month-long padayatra at Agra. He and his party walked an average of sixteen kilometers per day and camped at twenty-six ravine villages, which had association with dacoits or their relatives, before ending the tour at Gwalior. The sainiks appealed to the dacoits, often by face-to-face contact, to repent, change their lives, and surrender to the authorities. In turn, the authorities supported the novel experiment. As a result of Vinoba's efforts, twenty dacoits surrendered.[37]

After leaving the valley, at the Akhil Bharat Shanti Sena Mandal meeting at Indore in mid-June, Vinoba called Shanti Sainiks to "keep the lamp of peace and goodwill aflame in the Chambal valley," adding that "the problem is still alive there. It is a virgin field for all sorts of constructive work. As we have lighted the lamp of peace and goodwill in that area, we must keep it burning and should strive to spread its light to larger and larger areas."[38]

Some years later, JP, in his assessment of Vinoba's peace mission, noted that "the enlightenment produced by Vinoba's work was short-lived, and though the small band of his followers struggled on, it soon became patent that there had been no radical change in the thinking of the powers that be, some of them going so far, later on, as to express their displeasure of Vinoba's 'meddling.' "[39]

In fact, some highly placed Madhya Pradesh government officials strongly criticized Vinoba's approach as being soft on criminals and not putting an end to the problem (the twenty who turned themselves in were only a small percentage of the estimated three to four hundred dacoits active in the area). Consequently, the "Chambalghati Peace Mission," formed at Vinoba's insistence by the Sarva Seva Sangh from the members of the Shanti Sena, "stopped further attempts at contacting dacoits in the ravines and forests, and persuading them to surrender voluntarily."[40] The Mission members, nevertheless, continued to organize legal aid for the trials of those who had surrendered, started village industries to train the families of those convicted and incarcerated, and collected funds to reclaim waste land in the ravines.[41] Unfortunately, Yadunath Singh, the mainstay of the work in the valley, died of a heart attack in August 1960, and gradually the efforts petered out.

Some Peace Mission workers, notably Hemdev Sharma and Mahavir

Singh,[42] remained in the valley, providing continuity between the peace mission conducted by Vinoba and the one undertaken by JP. Vinoba's mission had popularized the surrender idea, and in the mid-1960s Madho Singh, the most prominent and feared dacoit gang leader, had started flirting with the idea—possibly as a result of continued contact with the Peace Mission and because of increased police terror against the gangs and their families.[43] By the late 1960s, however, the police operations had ended in total failure with the gangs emerging stronger than ever and with a sense of cohesion that had not previously existed.[44]

The early 1970s became a boom time for the gangs, and the police came under increasing pressure to produce results. In late-1971, at the time that surrender initiatives surfaced afresh, the police again initiated a major antigang campaign. A report by the Gandhian Institute of Studies concluded, however, that this renewed pressure "was not so frightening as to infer, as has been done by many, that the dacoits were hard-pressed to surrender."[45] Madho Singh was still toying with the idea of leaving the dacoit life behind. He had almost withdrawn from the leadership of his gang and had even procured a passport.[46]

In late September 1971, after sending an emissary to Paunar to see Vinoba, Madho Singh was informed that because Vinoba was old and had confined himself to his ashram, he should seek the assistance of JP. Narayan's initial reaction was against becoming involved because of his many other ongoing Sarvodaya activities, including Gramdan follow-up work and his preoccupation with the Bangladesh issue and because "he doubted the chances of success."[47] Vinoba's earlier work had been limited and only partially successful, and the "attitude of the State government leaders had entirely spoiled the goodwill that Vinoba had generated."[48]

Madho Singh went to JP in disguise, pretending he was his own envoy. When he disclosed his identity, JP was impressed with his sincerity and the risk he had taken (Singh had a reward of Rs.150,000 on his head, dead or alive). He assured JP that he was in touch with other gang leaders and that "they were all inclined to surrender provided that an 'honourable' way could be found."[49] This assurance provided the possibility for an end to the terror in the Chambal valley by a mass surrender of all the gangs.

Madho Singh announced that as far as he was concerned he had already surrendered to JP at their meeting on the first of October and that he was prepared to face the consequences. It was, however, decided that his formal surrender would have to wait because he had a role to play in persuading the other gang members to lay down their arms. He was to return to the Chambal valley and help the sainiks to contact the other gangs if JP decided to undertake the task of coordinating a new surrender initiative.

Madho Singh stayed at JP's ashram in Bihar while the Sarvodaya leader consulted other colleagues who were familiar with the dacoit problems of the Chambal area and those who had been involved in Vinoba's mission before giving his final word to the gang leader.

JP received a note from Singh highlighting the terror under which people in the valley lived because of the violence from both the dacoits and the police, how the dacoity eradication programs of the authorities were exacerbating the situation, and how the millions spent on these operations could far better be used for the development of the area by removing the root causes of the problem.

JP, believing crime to be socially conditioned and that no individual was beyond redemption, saw that once gang warfare was eliminated the available resources could be devoted to removing the causative factors and, thus, provide a permanent solution to the problem. He decided to take on the task.

JP started by approaching the central as well as the three state governments concerned "to assess their reactions to the surrender proposal and also to get their opinion on the tentative conditions put forth on behalf of the gangs."[50] He also undertook a survey of the problem to clarify the appropriate strategy, to assess the likelihood of success, and to prepare his brief for the negotiations. He then assembled Sarvodaya workers from the Chambal area, especially those who had been involved in the 1960 mission, and commenced to establish contact with dacoits, or their family members who were expected to have some influence over them.

The personal appeals by JP were carried to the gangs by Shanti Sainiks. Often the sainiks, at presumably considerable personal risk, stayed with undecided gang leaders for several days and even weeks while trying to persuade them of the benefits of surrender. They took on the task of acting as intermediaries between, on the one hand, gang leaders and, on the other, their enemies, the authorities and the families of alleged kidnap victims. Finally, they escorted the dacoits to the Pagara Peace Camp for the informal surrender ceremonies with Gandhian workers on 11 and 13 April.[51]

JP did not personally meet any of the dacoits until they arrived at Pagara immediately before the formal surrender ceremony. Almost none of the dacoits returned to the ravines from the camp although they still possessed their weapons and the option was still open to them; by then the decision to surrender had become a commitment.

The state governments were at first equivocal in their support for JP's peace mission, and then their resistance looked as if it was going to abort the process. "The tactical support given by the top government leadership, including the Prime Minister, and the strong voice raised by some prominent opposition leaders" against the state government leadership about an "entirely good-intentioned effort, saved the situation."[52] Once the promise that none of the dacoits would be hanged was secured, the surrender process could commence.

Political considerations, however, continued to dog the operation. To gang members the notion of honor was extremely important, and the process of surrender was almost derailed when they were made to feel that their voluntary decision to surrender was being belittled by governments wanting to imply that they were surrendering under pressure.

Besides the peace workers, some of the dacoits who had surrendered in 1960 and had served their sentences, played a crucial role in the campaign. They joined with the sainiks and "served as the living example that there is promise of 'normal life' after surrender."[53] The formal surrenders took place on 14 and 16 April 1972 at the Jaura ashram of veteran Sarvodaya worker S. N. Subba Rao.[54] Between 14 April and the end of May a total of about 450 dacoits surrendered.

The surrender formula was detailed and attempted to tackle the root causes of the dacoity problem. After the surrender, a rehabilitation program was to include the provision of viable agricultural holdings and the necessary inputs (e.g., bullocks and starting capital) to the families of the dacoits and educational facilities for their children. The peace mission was to see that the promises were fulfilled by the state governments.[55]

Men often joined gangs after feuds with neighbors or after an interfamily quarrel. Membership in a gang provided security for family members from reprisals by enemies. A major consideration during the surrender negotiations was the future safety of family members if the dacoits gave themselves up, thereby depriving them of gang protection. Dacoits wanted arms confiscated from their enemies before they surrendered. Peace workers were asked to draw up lists of "enemies" and of the alleged arms in their possession. The police provided assurances that family members would be protected and in the case of enemies of high-ranking dacoits went as far as confiscating weapons. The peace workers had the task of ensuring that police harassment of the dacoits' families ceased and that police, in fact, did provide the necessary protection for families and, where possible, also attempted to heal the social breaches between the families and enemies.

The rehabilitation scheme was based on the demands of the surrendering dacoits as mediated by the Gandhian workers as part of the total deal for their surrender. In addition, the dacoits were to receive legal aid to defend the charges against them.

In turn, to prove their bona fides, the dacoits (or *baghis:* rebels, as they were always called by the sainiks) were to release all kidnapped persons immediately, cease collecting their punitive taxes from the villages in their areas of operation, and refrain from committing further dacoities during the negotiations. By and large the gangs conformed to the conditions.[56]

Although some dacoits tried to make peace with their enemies before the surrender, after the event reconciliation became the most important task for the Gandhians. Vinoba's Peace Mission was revamped under JP's chairmanship to carry out this task.

In prison dacoits were housed separately from other prisoners, given special facilities, and eventually put in especially established open jails. Peace Mission workers were allowed to run educational activities among them, and in the years 1973, 1974, and 1975 Shanti Sainiks from the Gujarat Shanti Sena Vidyalaya conducted training camps within the prisons to aid the socialization process of the dacoits.

By the end of 1974 Madhya Pradesh had completed and commissioned the open jail Navajivan Shivir (New-life Center) at Mungawali. Part of the surrender deal was that trials would be expedited through the system (while prisoners remained in normal jails), and within two years most proceedings had been completed. All dacoits, even those from Uttar Pradesh and Rajasthan, were then transferred to Mungawali.

The prison had no outer walls and was enclosed solely by barbed wire fencing. The complex included dormitories, a library, a Sarvodaya contact center, and guesthouse, which provided self-contained quarters for visiting dacoit family members who were permitted to stay for a fortnight. The rooms were all lit by fluorescent tubes and contained electric fans, the toilet-block boasted flush toilets, and the prison incorporated sporting facilities. The inmates were not required to wear prison uniforms. Dormitories were not locked, and security arrangements were deliberately kept quite informal.[57]

The new rehabilitative regime, however, did not secure universal praise. The prison was conceived as an agriculture-based institution, but that aspect had not materialized even years after opening, leading to criticism that the prisoners were "sumptuously fed without any work whatsoever."[58] Further, the fact that gangs were imprisoned en masse ensured that gang hierarchies remained intact, and, thus, the ideal of instilling "self-confidence, self-reliance and self-discipline" was defeated.[59] The involvement of inmates in the management of the prison meant that gang leaders remained spokesmen, and gang rivalries were able to continue. In effect, therefore, regardless of the reformist aims of the Mungawali experiment, the prison perpetuated the hierarchy and authoritarian structure of the gangs rather than providing an alternative model.[60]

The moral education program, conducted by the Gandhian workers, also had equivocal results. The program was based on the celebration of Hindu festivals, folk songs, and dances (which proved very popular according to the only detailed study of the achievements of the Peace Mission), and the celebration of the anniversaries of important leaders as well as the occasional lecture by eminent Sarvodaya and social workers, "which do not evoke much interest, and most importantly a daily prayer meeting —attended by only about one-quarter of inmates."[61]

The idea behind the surrender strategy was a Gandhian "change of heart"; however, the Gandhian Institute of Studies report notes that because the surrender came after at least six months of negotiations, it could not be seen as a change of heart in the true sense of the term.[62] It has been suggested that the leading gang bosses had amassed substantial amounts of money (e.g., Madho Singh had acquired land and a petrol pump in addition to a modest fortune) and wanted to leave the ravines and enjoy a secure and reasonably prosperous life.[63] Further, given the structure of the gangs, there was little choice *but* to surrender if the gang leader had decided to do so.[64]

The report claims that the educational potential provided by the situation was not sufficiently exploited: "The Peace Mission as an organ of the Gandhian movement could not play the role that it was intended to play, as part of the peace campaign. In the beginning some ad hoc arrangements were made. Some Sarvodaya workers kept regular contact with them. In this the main emphasis was on furnishing religious and moral inputs only. There was hardly any opportunity given for self-analysis and of analysis of the socio-economic issues relating to dacoity as a more institutionalised form of crime in the regional society and its consequences at social and individual levels."[65]

The report concedes, however, that most of the dacoits "imbibed significant changes in their orientation and attitudes" and that most of them had rejected their criminal pasts "at the personal level."[66] Nargolkar maintains that to a large degree the "change of heart" was genuine and that the continuing contact by the Sarvodaya workers helped to forestall the frustration and resignation that can come as a result of the psychological effect of a loss of freedom.[67]

In other words, this celebrated Shanti Sena action did achieve a measure of success. And from the States', rather than the Gandhian, point of view the success was substantial. The surrender ended the existence of organized gangs in the Chambal valley. New gangs formed after the surrender but were unable to build organizational strength to oppose the authorities, and because gang membership was small, police resources could easily be directed against embryonic gangs and readily eliminated them. Juyal's report cautions in its conclusion that "the infrastructure of dacoity is largely intact, and the potential of the Peace campaign was not explored beyond the surrender of the dacoits. Yet, in the new situation it is going to be much easier for the law and order approach to succeed within its limited confines and with all its vagaries."[68]

JP had caused considerable controversy by openly embracing the dacoits, and many police officers resented the concessions to the dacoits and perceived interference in their job of mercilessly eradicating the criminals. That the peace education work of the Mission remained incomplete, however, in part at least, can be blamed on factors outside its control. The deterioration of the relationship between the Gandhian movement and the ruling Congress Party, at the level of both the State and Center immediately following the surrender, and the complete breach that occurred during JP's Bihar movement and the ensuing Emergency, ensured that the effectiveness of the Chambalghati Peace Mission would be greatly reduced and that the cooperation of the authorities would cease. As official support declined, on the one hand, the charges that the dacoits in Mungawali lived in luxury became more loudly voiced and, as in 1960, the charges that Sarvodaya workers were glorifying the dacoits flourished. On the other hand, the Gandhian establishment protested that the governments were not discharging their responsibilities under the terms of the surrender.[69]

Maladministration and the inequities of the rural power structure had driven many into the ravines. However, the Mission's suggestion of the creation of a vigilance mechanism to curb the situation was not heeded. And, as Juyal reported, it was "impossible for a voluntary organization like the peace mission to do these things on its own."[70]

Although the Chambalghati Peace Mission did demonstrate the employment of the Shanti Sena philosophy of nonviolence, conversion, and conciliation in action, the experiment did not have either the number of dedicated workers or institutional support to make it a complete success.

Shanti Sena Work in Communal Disturbances

Gandhi's initial decision to recommend the founding of peace brigades was as a response to Hindu/Muslim communal disturbances. And it has been during riot situations that the Shanti Sena has done its most significant work. Most Shanti Sainiks see Gandhi as the archetypical sainik and his "walking tour" of Noakhali, in late 1946 and early 1947, as the quintessence of Shanti Sena work. After mass killings in Bengal Presidency, where tensions over the separation of India along (broadly) religious lines before independence was high, Gandhi went personally from village to village preaching peace and attempting (with a fair amount of success)[71] to reestablish harmony or at least tolerance among the warring communities.

Although for brief moments the idea of the Shanti Sena as a nonviolent army had held favor in some circles, for much of the time the theoretical purpose of the Sena was to provide the means by which the nonviolent revolution that bypassed central governments and power (as opposed to people's) politics could be achieved. In reality, however, the Shanti Sena generally functioned as the nonviolent police force equivalent or relief agency that Gandhi had originally foreseen.

In the context of quelling violence through nonviolent means the task of the Shanti Sena can be divided into three phases: (1) the removal of tensions that have led to the unrest without resort to police or courts after a careful investigation of the background to the situation; (2) intervention in the disturbance (even at the risk of death); and (3) relief work among the victims after a riot has subsided.[72]

In 1970 Narayan Desai went to some lengths to spell out the sequence of steps to be taken by sainiks in the event violence broke out.[73] He noted that generally there are warnings provided by signs of tension that violence is imminent and, therefore, it is the task of the Shanti Sainik "to remove tensions in order to prevent riots." Where this was impossible, he advised them to meet and discuss the situation and immediately draw up a program of action, notify the convener of the State Shanti Sena Mandal of the proposals, and, if necessary, request him to send contingents of Shanti Sainiks from other areas. After that, leading citizens of the city were to be contacted and informed of the situation so that an appeal for peace could be issued under their signatures. If possible, the appeal was to be published in the newspapers and broadcast on the radio. Steps were then to be taken to contact the leaders and followers of parties to the dispute.

As soon as reports of a violent incident reached a member of the Shanti Sena, efforts were to be made to reach the site of the disturbance to get an unbiased first-hand picture that could be shared with other Shanti Sainiks in preparation for a decision on an immediate program of action. The sainiks are reminded of the connection between rumors and violence and are enjoined to counteract them by disseminating the truth. Where applicable this was to be done by the publication of pamphlets. Duties were to be assigned to sainiks in such a way that those Shanti Sainiks, "who are already well-known to the area for their service, are able to discuss matters dispassionately and intelligently and make on-the-spot decisions as the situation demands."[74] Sainiks were to undertake rescue work at the location of violence as long as the violence continued. If the situation permitted, a peace procession, which included citizens of the locality, was to be organized. Immediately after the subsidence of violent outbreaks, the task for Shanti Sainiks included taking the injured to a hospital and contacting their families followed by relief work and reconstruction efforts.

A few years later, based on his years of experience and, in particular, the pattern of action that had emerged during the Baroda riots,[75] Shanti Sena leader Desai went further in outlining the work of sainiks in riot situations by classifying the six areas in which action was necessary and implying that in a properly organized Sena action the functions would ideally be performed by six different groups of Shanti Sainiks. Although it is doubtful that any Shanti Sena action had the number of sainiks available to allow such efficient organization, the plan does provide a summary of an ideal Sena action.

Desai envisages one group of Shanti Sainiks meeting the leaders of the conflicting parties and attempting to convince them that violence would harm not just their opponents but the whole community. They would then try to enlist their support to keep the conflict from turning violent.

Another group was to counteract rumors by reassuring the community through personal contact and by providing factual accounts of events through bulletins and the mass media. Meanwhile, a third group, comprising most of the sainiks, was to fight fear by physically intervening in violent situations. A fourth group was to reconstruct damaged dwellings, distribute clothing and blankets, and so on, and visit hospitals. Although these actions proved often to be no more than symbolic in major disturbances, Desai noted that, nevertheless, they can "go a long way in creating a situation of reconciliation."[76]

A fifth group was to deal with the educated people of the area and "at the proper psychological moment" conduct educative seminars to discuss the issues underlying the eruption of violence. To the final group fell the task of contacting people, listening to their stories, attempting to evaluate the kind of image each community has of the other, collecting and disseminating objective information, attempting to organize a joint meeting of the conflicting sides, and, after the violence has been brought under control or burned itself out, encouraging acts of repentance such as helping to rebuild the homes of victims, and, finally, attempting to normalize the atmosphere by celebrating joint festivals.[77]

There are many instances of intervention in areas of tension or riots by the Shanti Sena that illustrate the use of the guidelines mapped out above. Early in the history of the Sena, for example, after the 1960 disturbances in the Belgaum district of Mysore that resulted from the drawing of new linguistic boundaries, a joint camp of sainiks from Maharashtra and Karnataka was held with ten sainiks from each province. After discussing the problem, the camp participants decided to try to "restore mutual goodwill and friendly relations among the two linguistic groups and the people should be advised to conduct the agitation, if at all necessary, in a peaceful manner."[78] It was to be emphasized that the border problem was less significant than the fact that both provinces were part of India. The Shanti Sainiks formed into groups of four, with two members from each province in every group, and set about the daily task of cleaning the locality in which the disturbances had occurred. The Gandhian press reported that "this joint effort at constructive service succeeded in easing the tension to a considerable extent."[79]

"Language riots" also occurred in Gujarat in 1965. Violence broke out both in the then capital, Ahmedabad, and the second largest city, the cultural center of Baroda. The Sena, in a pragmatic move, decided that Ahmedabad was too large a city for them to have a significant impact, so the work of Shanti Sainiks was concentrated in Baroda where a batch of volunteers was already active. At the time, a city-to-city padayatra was in the town attempting to spread Sarvodaya ideals. It contained ten sainiks in its ranks. Baroda was also the center from where the Bhoodan periodical *Bhoomiputra* was published and it was hoped that this would ensure that efforts of the Sena would elicit cooperation or, at least, sympathy. Within a few days a further twelve Gujarati sainiks arrived. The thirty-two sainiks, including five women, were divided into three teams. Two members, with reputations for service and impartiality, were responsible for contacting the police chief and leaders of public opinion. Four members had the task of fighting rumors, and the remaining twenty-six, once those contacting the leaders had secured permission to operate in areas under curfew, undertook patrols in the affected areas. Daily meetings of the sainiks were organized to make important strategic decisions. Those fighting rumors issued a daily bulletin enjoining the populace not to believe the politically motivated casualty figures and highlighting incidents of bravery and nonviolence among the populace. After three days of concentrated work, the Shanti Sena group was able to organize a peace procession in the city. According to Desai, "As the situation started getting normalised, some Shanti Sainiks wanted to go to other places where violence had spread. But they were requested both by the police officer as well as the political leaders to continue to operate in Baroda, because they found, their service to be useful in the maintenance of peace in the city."[80]

A similar example from the period after the reorganization of the Sena provides a further illustration of the Shanti Sena's peace work. The town of Panoor, in the Cannanore district of Kerala, had been enveloped in an atmosphere of hatred and conflict for several years owing to party political quarrels that had left the "common man . . . living in a state of fear and uncertainty" and the region lagging in development. In April 1964 after panchayat elections, the situation deteriorated even further and the Kerala Sarvodaya Mandal decided to set up a Shanti Sena camp in the area to restore peace and security. Twenty Shanti Sainiks toured the town with the message of peace and cooperation, and eventually the padayatra program intensified to cover an area of more than 150 square kilometers in a month. House-to-house visits were conducted, group discussions and Gandhi study circles were organized, Sarvodaya literature was sold and Mahila (women's) Mandals were set up. Through the efforts of the camp administrators, a conference of the leaders of the different political parties was organized. Members of the feuding parties met on a common platform for the first time in many years "and pledged full support for the cause of peace." The paper *Bhoodan* concluded that the camp "on the whole, has made a significant contribution to peace in Panoor. It has built firm foundations."[81]

In October 1968 Agra found itself gripped with tension when angry student leaders insisted that the whole city should observe a hartal (strike) in sympathy with their demands. A large procession organized by them sporadically erupted in violence. At a crossroad the demonstrators and the police found themselves in a face-off that threatened to end in a bloody clash. Then the Shanti Sainiks intervened. Braving stoning, the sainiks, under the leadership of Shri Chimanlal, "averted the crisis with tact and patience." That evening eight Shanti Sainiks toured various trouble spots in vehicles and addressed thirty-five small meetings. They advised the students to use only peaceful means to seek redress for their just grievances, to contact parliamentarians and place their demands before them. Although some students tried to disrupt the meetings, by evening the sainiks had managed to arrange a meeting between students, district authorities, and a local MP. The meeting, according to a report in a Gandhian newsletter, "was helpful in restoring peace." The activities of the Shanti Sena continued for several days until "complete peace prevailed." [82]

During the early 1980s the town of Porbandar, Gandhi's birthplace, experienced severe intracommunity tension that resulted in regular killings. The fishing community of the town was divided along an invisible yet almost impenetrable barrier. Veteran Gandhian worker Vimala Thakkar decided to initiate a reconciliation attempt. Fifty students, both male and female, who were undertaking courses at the Karadi Shanti Sena Vidyalaya, accompanied Indrasingh Rawat and Sombhai Patel to Porbandar. After discussions it was decided to set up two kindergartens, one in the neighborhood of each faction, for three-to five-year-old children. The kindergartens, with about two hundred children in each, were conducted for more than two weeks as the workers gradually became familiar with some of the parents and earned their trust. Slowly, they hinted to the parents that they wanted to take a procession of the children across the line. Initially, they were informed that such a venture would be impossible, but gradually they gained the confidence of the adults and a march was organized. Children with brightly colored flags and slogans of peace from one of the centers walked in formation toward the other center. As they neared the "line," tension and excitement grew, but no one was willing to abuse or stone the children. Large groups of onlookers gathered and the rooftops were crowded with the curious. Often spectators would recognize youthful relatives whom they had not seen for years and call out to them in affectionate greeting. The column reached the other kindergarten, was joined by the other group of children, and a combined procession made its way back to the commencement point for a feast. The next day the leaders of both communities met with the sainiks, and the normalization of relations commenced. [83]

In spite of actions such as that at Porbandar, the *de facto* demise of the Sena in the mid-1970s meant that there was no longer any Gandhian organization able to provide effective peacekeeping forces in the face of massive communal disturbances that occurred in the more recent past. Although several Gandhian workers rushed to Assam after the massacres in 1982–83 and worked at restoring communal harmony and providing relief to victims and their families, their impact on the situation was insignificant.[84] Similarly, Shanti Sainiks have been able to do little in the continuing bloody situation in the Punjab. Since 1982, several peace padayatras have been organized. The marchers (or, in some instances, more accurately, processions because some of the peace missions were conducted by vehicle) were well received by both Hindus and Sikhs, but they were not able to contact the terrorists.[85] The padayatras remained little more than fact-finding missions, their greatest achievement being, perhaps, that none of the yatris was attacked by insurrectionists.

To gain a clearer appreciation of the work of the Shanti Sena in riot situations it would be instructive to examine two instances, where sainiks were effective, in greater detail. The communal riots in the industrial Orissan town of Rourkela, after the killing of Hindus in East Bengal in 1964, provided the worst death figures since the mass slaughters at the time of partition; and the communal riots in the Gujarat city of Ahmedabad in 1969 claimed more than two thousand lives and left large areas of the city burned out and looted.

The Rourkela Riots

In February there had been a riot in which Hindus were the main victims, in Jessore, East Pakistan. This confrontation was followed by a retaliatory anti-Muslim riot in Calcutta.[86] Communal tension was already high in eastern India when the transportation of train loads of Hindu refugees from the Jessore disturbances began from Calcutta to the Raipur area of Madya Pradesh. Since 6 March, the refugee trains had stopped at the new Orissan steel town of Rourkela to pick up rations. Large crowds came to the railway station with gifts of food. Stories of atrocities and rumors were readily spread by the inciting language used by some of those helping in the feeding program. Although Rourkela had a majority population of Sanskritized Adivasis (tribals) and only relatively few Muslims, the rumor that the Muslims were hoarding arms in mosques and coming into town to attack Hindus was widely believed.[87]

Even some Muslims helped in the relief efforts; however, when, on the 14th, one refugee vomited after taking bread from an alleged Muslim, the news that Muslims were trying to poison the Hindus swept the town. Although there was no truth in the popularly accepted version of the incident (it was medically verified that the bread contained no poison, and the bread giver turned out to be a Hindu), even one month later the facts were not widely known among the population; however, at the time the rumor received coverage in the Oriya press.[88] After this incident, some Muslims were beaten up and Muslim relief efforts ceased, causing further alienation between the communities.

As tension increased, the government discontinued the halting of trains at the town on 17 March, but the police force of seventy-two officers, for a population of more than one hundred thousand spread over eighty-three square kilometers, was not strengthened.

Between 15 and 19 March approximately five thousand Muslims and almost as many Hindus left Rourkela. Because the rumors had created a strong fear that they would be attacked by the Muslims, Hindu workers began manufacturing weapons out of iron bars inside the steel plant. Muslims, in turn, started sending telegrams to Bhubaneshwar, the state capital, expressing their feelings of insecurity and requesting protection.

Kshetrabasi Pati, the Shanti Sainik in charge of the Rourkela Sarvodaya Center, telegraphed the chief minister, district magistrate and the state Sarvodaya Mandal in Cuttack on the 18th that a riot was imminent.[89] Although the chief minister received the warning, no official steps were taken to ease the tense situation, and lower-ranking police actively sympathized with the Hindu communalists.

Some Muslims played Pakistan radio news publicly in a busy market square, and Hindus demanded that the authorities search the mosque for weapons. The refusal to carry out this action was taken as confirmation that the building was being used as an arms dump. On the evening of the 18th the fatal stabbing of a milk vendor near the railway station finally released the floodgates of violence, and an unimaginable slaughter of Muslims continued for several days. The Gandhians who worked in Rourkela during the immediate aftermath of the riot estimated that two thousand to three thousand were killed.[90]

On 20 March the military was requested to restore order, and the first units reached Rourkela early on the following morning. The military presence was beginning to have some effect by the 22d, but by then the rioting had spread to the countryside, and riots continued until the 24th when the entire responsibility for law and order was handed over to the military authorities.

Although called a riot, the Rourkela incident was in reality a systematic slaughter of an unarmed population. There were almost no attempts at counterattack or even defence by the Muslims.[91]

At roughly the same time, and as a result of the same tensions, riots also broke out in the Bihari industrial city of Jamshedpur, 150 kilometers away. There, too, the tribal population slaughtered the Muslim minority. Although Bihar had the largest number of Shanti Sainiks in India at this time, there were none in Jamshedpur. One hundred and thirty-nine arrived soon after the disturbances had subsided and divided themselves into fifteen batches: nine to work in the city and six to go to the affected villages. In Jamshedpur they buried the dead, extinguished fires, undertook sanitation work, and tried to restore an atmosphere of calm.[92] The presence of JP in Jamshedpur did much to reestablish the confidence of the minority community. JP made speeches in the city on 5 and 12 April, and what he said there applied equally well to the situation in Rourkela:

> The credulous aboriginals were misled; they were told that the Muslims were preparing to kill them, that they were collecting arms in their mosques. It was a well planned scheme for massacre on a large scale; it cannot be brushed aside as a mere reaction to what happened elsewhere [i.e., in East Pakistan]. I had a talk with local Government officers who bear testimony to the fact that not a single Muslim in [the district around Jamshedpur] was guilty of the murder of any Hindu. A stray case of death that had taken place was the result of the police or military firing. The Hindus are in an overwhelming majority over the Muslims here. The Adivasis form a still greater majority. And yet rumors were spread that the Muslims were converging for an attack on them. Tales were also current here and in Sundergarh [the district containing the town of Rourkela] that war was on between India and Pakistan and that the Government had issued orders to massacre the Muslims in India, and the simple Adivasis believed them to be true and resorted to large scale murders. When arrests were made in this connection, those accused of the charges of murder stated, "We only obeyed the Government orders. Why are we being taken into custody?"[93]

Nabhakrushna Choudhuri arrived in Rourkela on the 22d, Sarva Seva Sangh President Manmohan Choudhuri on the 23d, and the well-respected Gandhian worker (and, incidentally, Narayan Desai's mother-in-law) Malati Devi Choudhury, a few days later. The first Sena arrivals, along with Pati, obtained curfew passes and tried to assess the situation while helping the authorities organize relief camps. Malati Devi and others, including former MP Dhananjoy Mohanty toured the villages in an attempt to restore normality. Still others, led by veteran Maharashtran Sarvodaya worker Apasaheb Patwardhan, undertook padayatras in the town and conducted daily prayer meetings. Shanti Sena centers were opened "to help change the attitudes of the villagers and rehabilitate the Muslims."[94]

Eventually, twenty sainiks arrived in Rourkela. Although their numbers were small, they were able to mobilize local volunteers, especially college students, who later joined a Shanti Sena organized peace procession. To fight rumors the sainiks organized large public meetings. They were told that all Muslims were Pakistani spies, who deserved to be killed or at least expelled from the country. The sainiks replied that although it might be true that spies were everywhere, surely an Indian spy in Pakistan would dress as a Muslim and not wear a topknot or sacred thread. Why should Pakistani spies want to be so much more conspicuous? And why would spies be tea-stall owners and rickshaw wallahs rather than employees in the Secretariat? These meetings and the antirumor pamphlets produced by the sainiks and distributed at factory gates at shift changes seemed to have a calming effect.[95] The work of the Shanti Sainiks continued for about two weeks.

Much of the killing occurred in the villages surrounding the town, and there, under Malati Devi's direction one of the Sena's most often-mentioned successes occurred. According to Desai and Manmohan Choudhuri, the tribal villagers were gradually persuaded to "realize their mistake" and to pledge not to resort to violence in the future. The Adivasis were persuaded to return goods they had looted from Muslim homes and some even to assist in the reconstruction of Muslim houses they had destroyed only a few days before.[96] This reversal, in part, may have been aided by the fact that, unlike the case with the Hindus, there had traditionally been no animosity between the Adivasis and the Muslims.

In his assessment of the 1964 riots Narayan Desai claimed that although the function of the Shanti Sena is to channel the feelings of the populace into "peaceful ways of living," and prevent the outbreak of violence or neutralize it, by facing it "coldly and calmly," its success should not only be measured by the number of sainiks facing angry mobs but also "by the amount of potential violence which it could prevent, and by the number of sympathisers of violence it could neutralize."[97] By this measure, he claims, the achievements of the Shanti Sena in the riots "have been significant though not spectacular."

The Ahmedabad Riots

The riots in the city of Ahmedabad during 1969 occurred after a combination of compounding circumstances. The Indo-Pakistan war on Gujarat's borders in 1965 and the accidental death of the state's chief minister at the time had increased anti-Muslim sentiments in the city. The organization of a statewide movement for the prohibition of cow slaughter by a right-wing Hindu party and a right-wing Muslim procession protesting against damage caused to the Al Aksa mosque in Palestine further exacerbated the situation.[98] Then a police jeep hit a paper hawker, causing a copy of the Koran to fall to the ground, and later a Muslim officer, breaking up a prohibited Hindu festival, allegedly trampled upon a copy of the Ramayana that was being recited from. The final straw seems to have been the minor scuffles that broke out when Hindu priests herded some temple cows through a Muslim crowd gathered to celebrate the Urs festival and an alleged retaliatory stoning of the Jagannath temple by Muslims. The "attack" upon the temple appears to have been minor: there were no deaths or serious injuries. In fact, the only confirmed indication of damage was some broken panes of glass on one of the temple's outside gates. Next day some leading Ahmedabad Muslims apologized for the incident, but by then the riots had broken out.[99]

As with the Rourkela riot, rumors played an important part in the events leading up to the disturbance and continued to fan the violence once rioting had erupted.[100] According to expanding rumors, the attack on the temple was a deliberate attempt to dishonor the Hindu community; then they intimated that temple cows had been killed, then that priests had been killed, and, finally, that sacred images had been destroyed. During the initial stages of the violent outbreak Hindu communalists "went around the city on foot, on scooters, in jeeps and in private cars,"[101] spreading rumors of the molestation of women and killings by Muslims in distant parts of the city. Propaganda pamphlets were printed and newspapers published baseless inflammatory stories as fact.[102]

Looting and arson broke out; Muslim sections of the city were attacked on a mass scale. Eventually, the military was called in to restore order, and the violence gradually subsided to a verbal rather than physical level.

A Gujarat Sena leader maintains that if the sainiks had been able to maintain monthly contact with the fifty thousand families that had adopted Sarvodaya patras following the pioneering work in this area by Ravishankar Maharaj, the violence would not have been possible.[103] The Sena, however, had not been equal to the task. When violence did break out, the relative weakness of the organization was revealed. The city did not have a well-organized Shanti Sena, so the early efforts of individual sainiks were haphazard. Although Shanti Sainiks were able to save a few individuals from mob violence, initially their work was overshadowed by the savagery of the disorder. After two days of rioting, sainiks from around the state began to pour into the city and by the fourth day the Sena finally began to function in an organized manner.

First the saffron-scarfed sainiks visited affected areas to become acquainted with the situation. The response to their presence was mixed. Feelings of relief and appreciation were intermingled with resentment and ridicule.[104] The sainiks soon discovered that the majority of those affected were poor slum dwellers, often not wanted back by landlords; that many in the majority Hindu community, rather than displaying repentance, were rejoicing in the misfortunes of the minority Muslims; that mutual hostility had grown among the youth of both groups; and that political leaders were in a state of political paralysis, more concerned with the forthcoming election and blaming opponents than with taking positive action.[105]

The Shanti Sena called for assistance from Gandhian ashrams, and the students and their teachers went as volunteers to the riot-affected areas to remove debris and clean the streets. The primary task of the sainiks was to convince people to return to their homes from the refugee camps. To succeed they had to persuade the majority to welcome the minority back, persuade the minority to have the courage to do so with forgiveness, and, finally, to help the government reconstruct destroyed dwellings.[106] This task required the establishment of a favorable atmosphere. To achieve it Shanti Sainiks undertook house-to-house contacts, organized group discussions and street-corner meetings, and addressed crowds in mosques and temples. Further, the Sena published a biweekly journal, *Insan,* answering the types of questions that were regularly put to sainiks. The Sena also undertook the distribution of medicines and the collection and reallocation of blankets and cooking utensils.

The relief and rehabilitation work continued from October to December. In that time the Shanti Sena distributed blankets to twenty-five hundred families, utensils to one hundred families, treated twelve hundred patients and "was instrumental in rehabilitating about five hundred families to their new tenements."[107] Follow-up work commenced in January. A "Peace Week" was announced and almost five hundred volunteers, recruited from various teacher training institutions, moved from house to house with the message of peace. About twenty thousand homes were reached in this way. Almost one thousand signed a peace pledge, enrolling themselves as peace volunteers[108]—the proposed membership of the future Ahmedabad Shanti Sena.

The thirtieth of January (the anniversary of Gandhi's assassination in the Mahatma's birth centenary year) was observed as world Peace Day with six hymn-singing, placard-carrying processions converging on the city. Hindus and Muslims "in thousands" walked together for the first time since the riot. In the city the strands came together for a mass prayer meeting presided over by Ravishankar Maharaj.[109]

The longer-term programs of the Shanti Sena included forming a committee of women who undertook to arrange the resettlement of widows and the economic rehabilitation of petty traders who had lost their implements of trade. The Sena arranged bank loans for the traders and guaranteed repayment. The scheme, however, remained limited owing to a lack of funds.[110] The Sena also organized weekend camps for the youth of the city, focusing on the communal problem.

The lack of preparedness of the Shanti Sena, despite the groundwork of Maharaj, and its lack of numbers relative to the size of the problems facing it would also hamper future peace efforts.

In 1981 students at a leading Ahmedabad medical college started agitating because they felt that they were being denied places in specialist courses because of a scheme that reserved seats for Scheduled Caste students. Between January and March riots broke out. Harijan areas were attacked and more than fifty people, mostly Harijans, were killed.[111] In February peace work commenced and took on an organized form when aging Gujarati Gandhian leader Babalbhai Mehta and sainiks of both sexes conducted padayatras in the city. Although the police did not grant permission for a procession, the Shanti Sainiks were issued permits that enabled them to move about during curfew hours. Narayan Desai and the Bombay Sarvodaya leader Govind Rao Deshpande managed to bring the various groups together for discussions in late February. Although the Ahmedabad dailies called the move a "breakthrough," the agitationists refused to take part in a proposed three-month moratorium on further disruption. Although the Sena played a leading part in the peace efforts, neither it nor local committees or other Gandhian institutions could bring a lasting easing of tensions. In March Dada Dharmadhikari organized a further conference of the parties, and additional recruits joined the Shanti Sena. The conference of the "all party leaders committee" convened for more than two weeks but was eventually disbanded owing to a lack of "unity of purpose" among its members.[112]

In 1985 Ahmedabad again erupted into violence over opposition to the positive discrimination "reservation policy" of the government. The policy provided for the preferential treatment of Harijans, tribal people, and "Other Backward Classes" by providing them with positions in legislatures, educational institutions, and government employment by way of quota. Several hundred died in the city, and the damage from arson was enormous.[113]

During the first stage of rioting, between March and August, some volunteers, again under the directorship of Babalbhai Mehta, went from house to house talking to the people, while others, including Desai and Deshpande, talked to caste leaders. Despite the peace-pledge signatures obtained in 1969, the collapse of the Sena during the Emergency ensured that the number of sainiks who could be fielded remained pitifully small. Eventually, a round-table conference was organized and may have helped to reduce tensions. The end of the violence among the riot-weary populace, however, was probably as much attributable to "a combination of conciliatory and coercive measures"[114] employed by the newly appointed chief minister of the state as it was to the actions of the Shanti Sena. When violence flared again in July–August of the following year, it had become a Hindu/Muslim conflict and the Gandhian organizations could do little. Dhirubhai Patel, a Bharatiya Shanti Sena leader living at the Harijan Ashram, was almost the sole representative of the Sena during a period of turmoil that claimed many more lives.

Relief Work and the Shanti Sena

Often Shanti Sainiks arrive at the scene of disturbances after the violent outbursts have subsided. Their work, then, becomes that of providing assistance to the victims. One of the largest relief efforts engaged in by the Shanti Sena was the one following the liberation struggle in Bangladesh, resulting in literally millions of refugees fleeing to the safety of India. Along with the members of many other voluntary agencies, hundreds of sainiks converged on the Tripura, Meghalaya, and West Bengal areas surrounding East Pakistan/Bangladesh where the displaced persons were crammed into more than nine hundred "camps," some with populations in excess of one hundred thousand.[115] Malnutrition and disease were endemic in the camps, and the problems were exacerbated by unusually heavy rains.

In April 1971 Narayan Desai toured the Tripura border area, and shortly thereafter JP Narayan toured the West Bengal border area. A meeting of Sarvodaya workers, which chalked out a plan of action, followed. The first Sena activity was a sanitation camp organized by the Tarun Shanti Sena. More than one hundred youth from several universities paid their own fares to the refugee camp at Bongaon, one hundred kilometers northeast of Calcutta.[116]

A major relief project was financed by Oxfam, and the Sena was requested to provide the labor. The work of the sainiks commenced with burying the dead (fuel wood was too scarce to permit cremations), and then centered around sanitation work (constructing latrines, digging of drainage ditches, sweeping, disposing of garbage, and spraying disinfectants), and teaching an appreciation for the need of cleanliness (by recruiting volunteers from among the refugees, by conducting placard-carrying and slogan-shouting processions, and by conducting adult education classes that placed a heavy emphasis on sanitation).[117]

Young sainiks (many from Jugatram Dave's Gandhi Vidyapith in Gujarat) worked as volunteer nurses and attendants side by side with volunteer doctors; they organized milk centers for children and distributed food and clothing. By mid-1972 Narayan Desai was able to report to the Sarva Seva Sangh that Shanti Sainiks were working in about thirty centers with a total population of 200,000–300,000 refugees.[118]

Some of the leading sainiks also conducted training courses for Bangladeshi youth "to give them some political orientation and practical skills of community life," including talks on "unarmed civilian struggle against tyrannies."[119]

The Sarva Seva Sangh also had more ambitious peace endeavors. The Sangh's Bangladesh Assistance Committee mooted the idea of a peace march in which thousands of refugees were to march back to their homeland in a nonviolent procession. The idea lapsed owing to lack of support from the Bangladeshi government, who believed that the move would not only be premature but would also divert some of the attention from the armed struggle in which their liberation forces were engaged, and the reluctance of the refugees themselves, who did not want to go against the wishes of their government.[120]

The Shanti Sena, however, did organize a "March to Awaken the Conscience of the World." Thirty-six volunteers, half of them from various districts of Bangladesh and half of them from India, were to walk from the Shantiniketan ashram of Bengali poet the late Rabindranath Tagore to New Delhi. By the time that the marchers had reached Varanasi, India had gone to war with Pakistan and had recognized the independence of Bangladesh. The marchers proceeded by train to the Uttar Pradesh state capital of Lucknow, where the march was abandoned because Bangladesh had been liberated.[121]

Experiments with Nonviolent Defense

After the 1962 clash with China, Narayan Desai and JP became the first leading figures to visit the border area. They had long been concerned with nonviolent approaches to invasion, and they realized that here was the chance for experimental work in this field. Because JP's energies were increasingly being taken up with the Nagaland question and other national issues, he instructed Desai to oversee peace work in NEFA.[122]

The ultimate aim of Shanti Sena work in NEFA was twofold: to bring about reconciliation between the two neighbors and to prepare the region for nonviolent defense in case of aggression.[123] The first step lay in winning the confidence of the border tribal population. After decisions taken at the Vedchhi Sarva Seva Sangh meeting in mid-December, 1962 in collaboration with several other Gandhian organizations, the Shanti Sena established peace centers in the sensitive border areas.

The objectives of the Shanti Sena were eventually spelled out as (1) creating a spirit of fraternity between the local people and those of the rest of the country, (2) rendering constructive service to the hitherto completely neglected tribal population, (3) creating a spirit of nonviolent resistance among the people in case of aggression, and (4) establishing "goodwill missions" in the areas in the hope that eventually they would be able to spread the message of friendship even across the border. The program was visualized as occurring in three phases: (1) getting to know the people, their customs, language, and so on, (2) providing service, especially in the fields of agriculture, local industries, khadi, education, and health, and (3) building up nonviolent strength by enrolling Shanti Sainiks and, thus, laying the foundation for a defense strategy for the area based on noncooperation.[124]

After commencing work in NEFA and after familiarizing themselves with the local dialect, the sainiks set about teaching all three of the official languages of the area—Assamese, Hindi, and English—in a nonpartisan way (which language should predominate is a contentious issue). Where sainiks were not familiar with all the languages, the problem was overcome by a judicious selection of those staffing the centers.[125] The isolation of the valleys in the region coupled with anti-Indian Chinese propaganda made the task of getting a tribal member "to comprehend that his village is part of a vast country that is India" difficult.[126] Desai notes the very act of selfless provision of service by the sainiks is a large step in the process of integration: "When the tribal finds that some of his 'friends' or 'brothers', Shanti Sainiks, come from distant Kerala, Mysore, Gujarat or Uttarkhand, they naturally feel that they are part of the same brotherhood of man."[127]

The sainiks realized that the distribution of aid can lead to demoralization through dependence. This had been the outcome of much of the government's welfare activities, and the Sena had to take care to ensure that their work did not suffer from the same defect. The Muri Shanti Kendra, for example, turned the villagers' demand for a local school into a self-help project where the school buildings, the students' hostels, and the teachers' quarters were built by indigenous labor and where the rations for the hostel were contributed by the villagers instead of being provided by the government.[128]

Apparently, although the sainiks were faced with problems stemming from geographical isolation, corrupt local officials, cross-border smuggling, and even "maladjustment among themselves,"[129] the Shanti Sena has done some valuable constructive work and run several educative camps and seminars in the border areas. Desai, however, had to admit at the 1973 Sarva Seva Sangh Prabhand Samiti meeting at Kurukshetra that it was difficult to make any assessment of the Sena's achievement in the area of nonviolent resistance or contribution toward world peace, and soon thereafter the experiment was forced to end.

Shanti Sainiks worked with the tribal population of the area until the clamping down of the Emergency led to the closure of ten Shanti Sena centers and the ejection of thirty sainiks. When the Janata Party came to power, Desai visited Assam with Prime Minister Moraji Desai. In Jorhat he met with the chief administrator of NEFA, who requested the return of the Sena. The official explained that the expulsion was a move that was politically dictated at the time. Desai, nevertheless, decided not to make the same potential mistake of continuing the national integration work under the leadership of outsiders. He helped, instead, to set up the locally staffed Arunachal Seva Sangh (now Himalaya Seva Sangh) with only the vice president, Ravindra Upadhyay, being an outsider.[130]

Shanti Sena Work in the International Sphere

Speaking of the Cyprus Resettlement Project, Project member Shanti Sainik Manabendranath Mandal, a young Calcuttan activist who had worked among the Bangladesh refugees, informed the readers of the Sarva Seva Sangh's journal, *People's Action,* that "the presence of the nonviolent group has definitely created a climate for the displaced persons to return to their old homes. The Indian members with their experience of work in villages were able not only to persuade the DPs to return but also to take up reconstruction programmes on their own initiative. They also experimented with a walking tour programme which continued for four days, but the Turkish leadership did not like this sort of mission of meeting people. The foremost thing in their minds was a final settlement of the dispute without which, they asserted, no progress could be made."[131]

Not all the other sainiks involved in the CRP were quite as positive in their assessments. The active leading members of the Shanti Sena had gained much experience in the most effective form of peace work in communal riot situations. They had practical knowledge of reconciliation work (visiting trouble spots during riots, fighting rumors, contacting leaders of the opposing factions, and taking victims to relief camps) and in rehabilitation and relief work. In Cyprus, too, the situation was one of communal tension and the need was for the type of work in which the sainiks had specialized. In the words of Charles Walker the sainiks were "some of India's best riots specialists recruited from the Gandhian movement."[132]

Narayan Desai, like his mentor JP, had long wanted to demonstrate the efficacy of a Shanti Sena-type organization in the international field. Now, as one of the cofounders of the CRP, he had the chance to involve the Sena directly. Desai, in discussions with Walker and Hare, decided on an Indian contingent of half a dozen members. Besides Mandal, former convener of the Gujarat Shanti Sena, Jagdishbhai Lakhia, instructor of the Akhil Bharat Shanti Sena Mandal, Amarnath Mishra, leading Gujarati Gramdan and Shanti Sena worker, Arunbhai Bhatt, and member of the national committee of the Tarun Shanti Sena, Desai's son Nachiketa, were selected.

The Cyprus Resettlement Project worked at two levels. The central secretariat, consisting of the Project leaders, including Desai, were involved with negotiations at the highest levels. The task of the teams working at the grass-roots level was to locate Turkish refugees who wanted to return to their erstwhile villages. Turkish social workers interviewed Turkish refugees and produced an official list of villagers who wished to return while Project members encouraged them to do so[133] and attempted to get their Greek neighbors to show willingness to accept them. In short, their role was one of third-party mediation.

The experience of the Sena in Cyprus, in ideal circumstances, may have been able to provide some indication as to whether the Shanti Sena philosophy in action, given its "Gandhianness," is still relevant in a different social/philosophical setting. Unfortunately, the experiment did not last long enough to provide even a preliminary answer to the question.

Different sainiks had different experiences. Nachiketa Desai was a Tarun Shanti Sena organizer who, besides having worked with Bangladesh refugees, had been engaged in youth work in Baroda. He was only twenty-one years old at the time, and this, coupled with his relatively cosmopolitan family background and experience with youth, enabled him to work at bringing this least-conservative element of the two communities together. The language barrier meant, however, that his activities were largely confined to those who were educated and could speak English.

He went to cafes and played chess with the young men. Rather than moralize he let them ask the questions. As the curious asked about his background he talked about the Indian communal problem as a way of broaching the situation in Cyprus. Eventually, he was able to organize reconciliation camps for the youth, but he readily admits that his actions had no impact among the diehard nationalists on either side. [134]

The senior Shanti Sainiks had riot control skills and experience in Gandhian constructive work. In Cyprus there were no riots while they were there, and their activities did not extend long enough for an effective constructive program to be devised. None of the sainiks could speak Turkish or Greek, and Jagdishbhai's command of English was faltering, while Arunbhai could not speak English at all. These two "traditional" teetotaler Gandhians, who wore only khadi, ate only strictly vegetarian food, and preferred to undertake padayatras to traveling in motor cars, were culturally the most removed from the Cypriot community, yet paradoxically, it appears that they were the most acceptable to the community.

From his experiences in the Project, Nachiketa Desai concluded that attempts at doing third-party work outside of one's own culture is doomed to be of limited value. The three months that the sainiks worked in Cyprus were not enough to have any real impact. They were, perhaps, just starting to make some headway when the contingent was withdrawn. Desai believed that the slow-moving Gandhian approach of the two leading Gujarati sainiks, given time, would have been instinctively understood by the people. Because they did not speak English adequately, their activities were not confined to a certain class; and undertaking padayatras, rather than moving about in cars, put them in direct contact with the common people. This approach, however, is more applicable to a sainik's home region, where he or she has already gained the trust of the population and where the time scale is unimportant.

Because most Cypriots did not speak English, the impact of the Project was greatest at the level of the central secretariat rather than at the grass roots. The fieldwork was as much a learning experience for the sainiks as it was of direct benefit to resolving the refugee problem. [135] The secretariat met weekly with the Project members who were working in the villages, however, some felt that this was inadequate. The youthful Desai believed that a system of rotation that enabled field staff to work in Nicosia and the negotiators to visit the villages so that they could remain in touch with grass-roots feelings would have been useful. [136]

Although the three-day orientation course was inadequate to prepare the sainiks for the task at hand, ironically perhaps, communication problems, even at another unexpected level, were as great between Project members themselves as between members and the local village population. For those who had never left India before the greatest cultural shock was provided by Western members of the CRP whose sexual attitudes were completely alien to the celibate sainiks.[137]

Toward the end of the sainiks' tour of duty, Arunbhai and Jagdishbhai undertook a week-long padayatra through the villages. Although the concept of the padayatra is foreign to Cypriot culture and the appearance of an unarmed stranger in a village asking to be put up is almost unknown, the problems this may have caused were outweighed by the curiosity value that gave the sainiks a forum.[138] Arunbhai felt that because of India's reputation, stemming from reverence for Gandhi and the admirable behavior of Indian troops in Cyprus during the Second World War, and because of their obvious impartiality, they were well received and that was an adequate starting point.

Because of the language difficulty, the sainiks could not judge the effectiveness of the tours. Nevertheless, Arunbhai, an ideologically totally dedicated sainik in the Vinoban mould, maintains that a firm belief in ahimsa can overcome the problems of culture.[139] He provides two illustrative examples.

When they entered a village, while waiting for a person of authority to arrive, they would distribute a pamphlet in English, Turkish, and Greek to the inevitably large crowd that they readily attracted. On one occasion two small children were among the curious. A small boy held a bunch of uninflated balloons; near him was an empty-handed little girl who was making it quite obvious that she wanted one. The boy was refusing to part with any of his treasures. Arunbhai approached the boy and, in Gujarati, asked him why he would not share his balloons with the girl. The girl, immediately realizing that he was endorsing her point of view, left her mother's side and the tussling with the boy to stand next to him. The crowd quickly responded by putting pressure on the boy to part with at least one balloon. Eventually, he was forced to yield. The girl, however, was unable to blow up the balloon and so gave it to her mother to try. She was also unsuccessful. The girl then retrieved the balloon and gave it to Arunbhai who blew it up. The mother then invited the Shanti Sainik home and fed him while they waited for someone who could read and explain the pamphlet. Arunbhai believes that the winning of the confidence of the local people is half the work, and this he had managed to accomplish during this small episode.

At another time when Arunbhai was taking a walk in the countryside, he saw two young shepherds on a small hill ahead of him. They laughed at his unusual dress, and he thought that because they saw him as an object of fun he should make contact with them. The shepherds, who were scarcely more than ten years old, were frightened by his approach and ran away. When Arunbhai reached the summit, the boys returned and confronted him with air guns. He smiled and greeted them. They saw that he was no threat and dropped their guns. As he walked past them, he patted each of them on the back. When he returned the same way an hour later, they were waiting for him with a bowl of fruit.

Arunbhai concluded that the resettlement work was valuable, but it was not enough to fulfil the purpose of the Shanti Sena. Any Red Cross-type of group could have done the survey work. The main reason why the Sena should be involved in such work, he maintains, is that it is an effective way of meeting the people. He saw the resettlement process as having three components. Firstly, the construction of houses, which could most effectively be undertaken by the government; secondly, social reconstruction, which had to be undertaken by the people themselves; and thirdly, the welcoming of the refugees into the *hearts* of the rest of the community. He saw the fundamental role of the Shanti Sena as the bringing about of this change of heart. Why this was not achieved in Cyprus was not because of the language barrier but because of the limited time available to them and because other Project members did not see this as the primary objective.[140]

Another CRP sainik, Amarnath Mishra, expressed similar views. Amarnathbhai firmly believes that for a nonviolent army to be of any real use it must have a deep contact with the local people based on faith, trust, and love that can only come from lengthy service in the area. Without such contact, work is difficult and results will be superficial. In normal times the Shanti Sena must operate as a service sena and in Cyprus this background was lacking. If there had been a Cypriot Shanti Sena in operation that had invited them to the troubled area, *then* something positive could have been achieved. He noted that whereas intimacy was a hindrance for a violent army, it was an essential for an effective nonviolent army.[141]

Some of the Shanti Sainiks, in short, were engaged in an enterprise different from that of other members of the Cyprus Resettlement Project. The experience of the Shanti Sainiks in Cyprus, therefore, could prove little. Narayan Desai, the leader of the team, however, believes that the culture shock suffered by at least some of the sainiks made them ineffective in the work that the Project leaders had seen as important and achievable. Because of this, in the work assigned, the most-experienced sainik proved to be the least effective while the least-experienced sainik was most effective.[142] This observation may support Amarnathbhai's conclusion or merely point to divergent ideological interpretations about what the role of the Project was, or that of the Shanti Sena should be.

The Training Role of the Shanti Sena

Given that the main aim of the Gandhian movement was to create a nonviolent revolution to bring about a new nonexploiting, decentralized society based on the Gandhian ideals of truth and nonviolence and that the Shanti Sena was to be one of the primary mediums in achieving this, it is, perhaps, not surprising that Narayan Desai, in the first line of the introduction to his *A Hand Book for Shanti Sena Instructors,* announces that "The entire activity of Shanti Sena consists of a continuous process of education." [143]

The primary method of accomplishing this was by running various camps, and this became one of the main ongoing activities of the Shanti Sena. The first major meeting of sainiks, in October 1958, occurred within the framework of a camp. [144] The experiment of that initial camp, which was planned in consultation with Vinoba, provided a model for future camps. [145] At various times in the history of the Sena, prospective sainiks, in addition to signing the Shanti Sena pledge, had to take part in a training camp before they could become Shanti Sainiks, and Tarun Shanti Sainiks were expected to set aside a period of at least thirty days in a year for camping activities. [146]

Shanti Sena instructors were advised that, through these camps, they were to recruit new Shanti Sainiks, Shanti Sevaks, and Tarun Shanti Sevaks. Further, the camps were to be aids to the organization of the Shanti Sena movement, help new sainiks and sevaks in their initial training, and help build up a new leadership in the Shanti Sena movement. [147]

The camps for Tarun Shanti Sainiks, and after mid-1968 much of the Sena's training activity was directed toward youth, were specifically designated as "work-cum-study camps" where "work projects will be undertaken which may range from sanitation or harvesting to road building or well digging depending on the season and work available in the area. Part of the time in the camp will be utilised for studies which will include an understanding of the project undertaken, an analytical study of the national situation and appreciation of the cultural heritage of the country." [148]

The training camps conducted by the Sena were generally either weekend camps or camps of one week duration. The shorter camps were specifically designed as recruiting or contact-making exercises on behalf of the Sena. Because of the Sena's emphasis on national integration and communal harmony, care was taken to ensure that the camps were not sectarian. The typical daily program included prayer and meditation times (to "evolve a common spirit of brotherhood and service, and to search for a higher common truth"), time for contacting local people (to give novices a sample of what they could expect from the people, to give the experienced "an index of the people's enthusiasm for the movement," and to provide "an excellent opportunity to study the local problems"), time for free discussions, collective study, games, and drill (that encouraged a collective and cooperative effort rather than competition), and a cultural program. Notwithstanding this general format, care was taken to allow the participants a direct input into formulating the program.[149]

Besides the recruitment potential, the objectives of the longer camps were listed as providing initial "training to a homogeneous set of people e.g. students, villagers etc.," an opportunity "to give some idea of community living," and as providing the participants with a short course in a specific topic.[150] Where campers hailed from different backgrounds, efforts were taken to ensure a mixed allocation to shared rooms to "provide an extra occasion for integrated living."[151]

Because of its practical aspects, its enforcement of humility, and the transgression of caste barriers, in true Gandhian fashion, attention was "paid to every detail of sanitation." And here the instructors themselves were reminded that they, too, had to pull their weight: "It is easy to preach about sanitation, and easier still to accept that theoretically. But it is a different thing to demonstrate it by your own example. Besides the science of sanitation, a sense of sanitation is also needed to go into the details of the whole sanitation programme, which can only be demonstrated by actual practice."[152]

Camps for villagers especially emphasized communal living as a way of removing caste or religious barriers and providing experience of latrine cleaning. They featured a thorough canvassing of the problems of tension in the rural areas, provided instruction in the ideology of the Sena in "a simple language and style," and employed the local techniques of folk songs and dances in their cultural programs.

Camps for youth, by contrast, were designed to be more adventurous, had a greater emphasis on games, sports, and drill. They provided a greater opportunity for integrated living (e.g., acquainting participants with different foods, customs, and languages). The camps allowed detailed discussion of the problems faced by youth, including educational problems and those causing tensions. Finally, the camps featured programs that engaged the participants in constructive tasks such as work among refugees or relief work following riots or natural calamities.[153]

For the intelligentsia the focus of the week-long camps was different again. Particular emphasis was placed on manual labor where the participants undertook most of the camp activities themselves (while, the instructor's handbook notes, "care should be taken not to make the life too difficult for the beginners"). The theoretical aspects of the Shanti Sena were stressed and discussions were focused on tensions at the national and international levels.[154]

In addition to producing manuals for Shanti Sena instructors, Narayan Desai has also provided descriptions of the activities of various camps. Ten-day-long annual camps had been conducted in NEFA since the border war. The objective of the fourth camp, held at Along in December 1966, was to give "the Shanti Sainiks working in NEFA a chance to compare notes, discuss their problems and plan for the next year" and to give "the tribal people some idea about the working of the Shanti Sena" as well. The syllabus was prepared to represent the agricultural, industrial, educational, and health activities of the Sena in the region. There were sixty-four participants, including twenty-nine sainiks (eighteen of whom were working in NEFA) and thirty-five tribals from various NEFA regions, but generally from villages where the Sena "has been working for some time."[155]

While the four main Sena activities were stressed by practical plantation work, instruction in various crafts, especially the production of khadi, the organization of a kindergarten, sanitation work, and so on, the camp's underlying focus was governed by the special needs of NEFA that were highlighted by the Chinese invasion. The national integration program was started by acquainting members from different tribes with each other and continued with the participants preparing a relief map of India and storytelling sessions that attempted to provide the tribal people with a knowledge of India's history and an acquaintance with some of her great men.[156]

Desai also published the details of a two-week Tarun Shanti Sena camp held near Belgaum, in what was then still Mysore State, in May 1972. The 149 participants represented thirteen Indian states and territories as well as Bangladesh. The camp, with a rising time of 4.45 A.M. emphasized lectures and discussions, community living, and practical work.

Experts lectured on the issues of education, land, revolution, and nonviolence. The lectures were followed by group discussions and the writing of reports. The community-living aspects of the camp, such as manual work, games, sports, discussions, cultural programs, and so forth, were managed by the participants themselves. The practical work of the camp, with the exception of cooking, was, again, done by the participants themselves. This work included helping in the kitchen, cleaning, drawing water, looking after guests, guarding the camp, organizing classes, and caring for the ill.[157]

After the camp, fourteen youth, including some females, decided to dedicate a year of their lives to the Tarun Shanti Sena. Forty decided "to renounce their right over their ancestral property as a step towards revolution in their individual lives," and all "decided that they would not allow their parents to draw any dowry for their marriages." The five Bangladeshi participants "decided to start some youth organizations based on the positive values of the Youth Peace Corps."[158]

Conclusion

Although most of the examples of the Shanti Sena philosophy in action are in the JP/Narayan Desai mould, they do more than provide a useful blueprint of the modus operandi to be employed in situations of communal disturbance by unarmed peacekeeping ventures.

The Nagaland experience illustrates the way that peacemaking work can be carried out, whereas the national integration efforts in the border areas demonstrate how this can be complemented by peacebuilding. The participation of sainiks in the Cyprus Resettlement Project further demonstrates the combination of the two approaches in the international sphere. Similarly, the experiences in the ravines of the Chambal clearly show that with government assistance, or at least acquiescence, a nongovernmental organization can successfully combine the approaches. The Chambal Valley Peace Mission also shows the difficulty of obtaining governmental support for such endeavors and the problems inherent in the maintenance of unglamorous peacebuilding work for sufficient time to arrive at long-term solutions to the conflict at hand.

Some of these examples show that it is possible to combine at least some of the elements that Blum saw as integral to Gandhian based peacekeeping. And it is this limited combination that appears to be the "Shanti Sena idea" that some of the champions of the model want to emulate. Others take it to be the peacekeeping work undertaken by sainiks during riots or the proposed interposition during the border war with China. These projections, however, do little to answer the question of what the Shanti Sena idea really is.

The Cyprus project experience confirmed for some of the leading sainiks that Vinoba was right in his belief that truly effective peacebuilding cannot be achieved by teams imported from outside the conflict area as peacekeepers or peacemakers and also demonstrates that even among Shanti Sainiks there is no unanimity about the relative weighting to be given to tasks of medium-term peacemaking or to long-term peacebuilding. Consequently, before any conclusion can be drawn about the viability of a Gandhian model for unarmed peacekeepers from the lessons of peace actions by the Shanti Sena, the notion of the Shanti Sena idea must be examined more thoroughly.

7

The Ideological Basis of the Shanti Sena

The conclusions that the history of the Shanti Sena should provide about the validity of the unarmed peacekeeping model as a whole are difficult to draw. To a large degree this is because Gandhi's disciples, the leading figures in the Sena, interpreted his philosophy so differently.

As already seen in chapter 3, Mahatma Gandhi's reasons for recommending and then attempting to set up his Shanti Dals during periods of rioting and communal disturbance were primarily to do with peacekeeping. Although Gandhi had also alluded to the possibility of a peace army as the defense force of a disarmed and neutral India, the suggestion was quickly relegated to the realm of obscure fantasy when the leadership of the newly independent country considered its defense policy.

Along with exhortations about the use of unarmed civilian defense in the face of international aggression, Gandhi had also made vague suggestions about a world police force. The working through of these propositions and the determination of the role to be played by a Shanti Sena in the restructuring of independent India and its contribution to world peace depended however, on the way that Vinoba and JP interpreted and built upon his philosophy.

After independence, Gandhi had desired that his followers work for the poor and downtrodden rather than enter the realm of power politics. It is quite reasonable to assume that, had the Mahatma lived longer, his energies would have been directed at attempting to bring about the nonviolent revolution in the country that would ultimately herald in the society that he termed *Ramrajya*. Whether Gandhi would have considered the type of satyagraha that had been used against the British as applicable to bring this about in a democratic society is a moot point. In the development of his ideal decentralized society, however, a Shanti Sena would still have been needed to secure peace, and, presumably, increasingly its focus would have shifted from the realm of peacekeeping, through peacemaking, to peace-building in order to established a Sarvodaya social order.

Not long after Gandhi's passing, and before the advent of the Bhoo-dan movement, the Sarva Seva Sangh produced its Principles of Sarvodaya Plan. The 1950 plan was enlarged and updated five years later. Although in its chapter on defense the ideal of unilateral disarmament was spelled out, it was realized that this would not come about without the spreading of a "deep-rooted faith in the feasibility, efficacy and superiority of non-violent defence."[1] To do this the Gandhians realized that they had to achieve a situation in which the police no longer had to be relied upon in situations of crime and disorder and that they had to form a Shanti Sena to deal "with the violent situations that may arise within their locality." During the year that this revised plan was made public Vinoba established the Shanti Sena, and, given Vinoba's world view and unrivaled influence within the Sangh, these aims became somewhat modified in practice.

After the founding of the Sena, many called for the "internationalizing of the Shanti Sena idea." Generally, these calls concentrated on the Sena as a peacekeeping force, and, until the differences over the question of what the role of the Shanti Sena should be had clearly emerged, they presupposed the existence of a fixed unambiguous ideological foundation on which the Shanti Sena was based. That assumption is unsustainable on closer examination. The ideological differences between Vinoba and JP, reflecting their visions concerning the shape of the Sena and a proposed international shanti sena as well, were clearly evident from the time of their earliest writings and utterances on the subject.

Further, to comprehend the basis (or bases) on which the Indian Shanti Sena, the accepted model for unarmed peace brigade attempts, was founded, it is important to understand the differing philosophies of the two leading lights in the established Sena and to examine the philosophical shifts that have occurred since their passing. In this way the degree to which the callers are in reality campaigning for the adoption of *their* idea of the Shanti Sena idea can be discerned.

The Position of Vinoba Bhave

Vinoba's View of Satyagraha

In early 1958 Vinoba laid down what he saw as the four principles of satyagraha: satyagraha is positive not negative; it should proceed from gentle to gentler to gentlest; there should be happiness on the mere hearing of the word *satyagraha;* and, finally, that there should be no insistence on the part of the satyagrahi, insistence should come from truth itself.[2] Here he was being completely consistent with Gandhi's view of ideal satyagraha. Like his mentor, Vinoba placed high importance on *swaraj,* or "self-rule," a concept both of them defined in terms that encompassed far more than the mere political. Vinoba remarked that the term meant ruling the self, and that was impossible if one was under some other person's command: "It is one mark of swaraj not to allow any outside power in the world to exercise control over oneself. And the second mark of swaraj is not to exercise power over any other. These two things together make swaraj— no submission and no exploitation."[3]

In the maintenance of consistency this meant that satyagraha had to remain noncoercive and had to respect the sovereignty of the opponent by relying solely on conversion.[4]

To achieve this satyagraha had to be spiritualized by conforming to the precepts laid down by Vinoba. Gandhi had to practice the "science of satyagraha" in an atmosphere of foreign domination, whereas in an atmosphere of democracy Vinoba was under much less pressure to compromise on the ideals.[5]

Vinoba also apparently believed that until the Sarvodaya movement had gained the strength and public acceptance to launch effective "pure" satyagraha campaigns, it should refrain from employing satyagraha.[6] Tandon points out that the experience of the Bihar Movement (which ultimately had to rely on political parties, which, in turn, exploited the movement for their own purposes and quickly forgot the cause of JP's Total Revolution when they gained political power) seems to justify this stricture.[7]

There was also another factor according to Vinoba. He explained that with the progress of science and the creation of nuclear weapons humanity faced ultimate destruction. To neutralize this force of violence and to arouse the world's conscience Gandhi's nonviolence had to take on "more subtle and finer forms." Satyagraha could no longer afford to "create agitation or tension in the minds of the opponent," it had to avoid a "collision of minds and seek harmony in thought."[8] Until change was brought about through understanding and acceptance, rather than through imposition, "the seeds of violence, imperialism and world wars would not be rooted out."[9]

Satyagraha had to progress as the political situation progressed (from imperialist domination to "democracy" in India) and as science progressed. Consequently, Vinoba declared that Jesus's concept of "resist not evil" and Gandhi's "nonviolent resistance" were no longer adequate, and what now had to take their place was "nonviolent assistance" in right thinking.[10] Without this all that could be achieved was legislative reform, and that could never lead to total revolution. Vinoba was determined not to end up where the Mahatma had found himself at the end of his life. He would never have to admit to the mistake of placing civil disobedience before the slower, surer path to more lasting and real reform through constructive work.

Vinoba's View of Society

Although the British had gone, according to Vinoba the strength of village India was being sapped by a centralized authority that was slowly creating a welfare state (Vinoba quipped that perhaps 15 August should be called "Dependence" rather than Independence Day).[11] Vinoba talked of the burden of governments and called government the "one disease from which the entire world suffers."[12] What he wanted was a move away from the current forms of government, "the rule by one" and "the rule by more than one," to a form where "all the people may combine and equally share in the responsibility of carrying on their own administration," in other words, "rule by all."[13] The way to achieve this was to arouse people's power and create a system of self-sufficient village republics free from the coercive power of the state.[14]

In line with his views on government Vinoba saw the use of political structures as a method of solving problems as doomed to failure: "When one problem appears to be nearing a solution, ten others crop up," and when a solution appears to have been achieved "soon it raises its head again."[15] In his analysis of the Bihar Movement, Shah maintains that Vinoba was anxious to discover a new technique because of the traps of the false assumption that once an opposing leader is removed all will be well and the "impassioned tensions" of political movements that distract people from their original objectives.[16] And that technique was his "positive" satyagraha.

Bhoodan, an example of nonviolent assistance, was a stepping stone on the way to this rule by all ideal, which it was hoped would be ushered in by the Gramdan movement. In the realized state of gram swaraj the village collectively owned the land and an assembly consisting of all adult village members, through a process of consensual grass-roots democracy, governed the village without outside interference.

This transformation was to be accomplished without directly challenging the legitimacy of the state, for, after all, in a democratic system power had been entrusted to the state by the people. It could not, however, be achieved through the ballot, which Vinoba saw as either a farce that left real power in the hands of the few[17] or as a formula for disruption.[18]

Vinoba's aim was to create conditions that would "do away with the need to use even the power of the State."[19] The achievement of this anarchist polity was to come about gradually (he was not antistate); he hoped to bypass the structures on which the state rested (including the police and military) and, thus, allow it to wither away.

Vinoba was fond of saying that politics disintegrates and spirituality unites.[20] He made it clear that for him there could be no outward revolution without a corresponding internal one, without a change in mental attitude: "All revolutions which take place, whether they are social or economic, have their roots in spiritual ideas. At first there is a change in spiritual values and later on social, political and economic values undergo change."[21]

In the early days of the ostensibly land-redistributing Bhoodan movement, Vinoba claimed that his aim was to bring about a threefold revolution. First, he wanted to change people's hearts, second, to bring about a change in their lives, and third, to change the social structure.[22] Vinoba went so far as to say *this* was the important aspect of Gramdan, the solving of the land problem being "a very minor matter."[23] The Shanti Sena was itself to be a part of the educative program designed to achieve the threefold revolution.

Vinoba's View of Peacekeeping

As already noted, for Vinoba the Shanti Sainik was primarily to be a dedicated local village Sarvodaya worker, and the Shanti Sena was the "advance column" of Sarvodaya.[24] To be effective the sainik "should have complete knowledge of the area under his jurisdiction. Otherwise Shanti Sainiks would have to be sent from other areas, a procedure which would not answer the purpose" because ultimately "real peace" is the responsibility of those in the town or village and the responsibility of the Shanti Sainik is only as "a resident of that town or village."[25] In his early thinking on the organization of the Shanti Sena, before JP reorganized it, Vinoba stressed the decentralization of the Sena and the complete autonomy of the sainik: "Each volunteer will be fully responsible for his work of service in the community and for putting his principles into practice. Only when he is completely free will he be able to meet every situation as it arises. If another at a central place is responsible for directing the work, the Shanti Sainik . . . will have to refer to him for everything, and he not having lived in the community concerned will not be able to answer correctly."[26]

While maintaining that the purpose of the Shanti Sena is to eliminate the causes that generate disorder (disorder being a sign that the Sena has not done its constructive tasks well enough),[27] Vinoba does discuss the peacekeeping function of the Shanti Sena in the circumstances in which disorder nevertheless occurs. On these occasions he talks of self-sacrifice on the part of the sainiks with love in their hearts, and a readiness to lay down their lives if necessary.[28] Further, Vinoba concedes that on special occasions the local cadre may be supplemented by sainiks from the outside. Although in these instances Vinoba is emphasizing the peacekeeping function of the

Sena, most of his attention is focused on peacebuilding through spiritual awakening with the Shanti Sena being one of the chief instruments to bring this about.

Rather than discuss the idea of sainiks forming a nonviolent army to defend the country's borders, Vinoba would repeat his well-known dictum that "Gramdan was the best defence measure." After the establishment of the Sena, but well before his 1962–63 clashes with JP on this point, Vinoba was already thinking along such lines: "As a first step we should create such conditions in the country that the police or the army became unnecessary for internal peace. If we can achieve this, the next step of the extension of non-violence to external defence, would become apparent."[29]

This line of thinking was also carried over to his thoughts concerning the international situation. Vinoba knew that state power rested on military support (and, consequently, believed that "the citizens of a country which maintains an army have no right to conduct satyagraha in another country")[30] and that wars would only cease when a world government came into existence. There were two alternate ways to bring this about. Firstly, the United Nations had to be strengthened so that it could boast an army bigger than that of either the United States or the USSR[31] or, more practically, raise a large peace army to function in the way that Maude Royden envisaged.[32] This idea was the basis of his offer to raise one hundred thousand Indian volunteers. Secondly, the causes of war had to be removed by bringing about mutual goodwill between people through a spiritual revolution that would ultimately make the coercive apparatus of the state, and eventually the state itself, redundant.

Vinoba admitted that one of the most significant questions that could be asked is whether a situation can be achieved where satyagrahis can "go to the theatre of war and, facing bullets, offer nonviolent resistance."[33] Rather than pushing for the creation of an international shanti sena force, however, Vinoba would have preferred that "fellow-pilgrims the world over" create model units of the Shanti Sena in their own countries.[34] But for even these units his counsel is novel. He notes that individuals and small communities, and on an even larger scale the whole of India, have undertaken such noncooperation but that, given the present state of war technology, a new situation requiring new answers has presented itself. He implies that the previous attempts are no longer applicable and calls for an inner cleansing rather than outward activity, echoing the Mahatma's dictum that one perfect satyagrahi can end the sufferings of the world.[35] The task, therefore, is to "concentrate on purifying ourselves": "If we become too immersed in outward activity we shall not be able to develop that subtle power in us which alone can solve the problems that confront us. Therefore, we should not be obsessed with action, we should free our minds of the burden of doing and give ourselves to reflection constantly perfecting the theory of non-violence. We shall then be able to carry out Gandhiji's teaching a step further."[36]

In other words, his calls for world peace armies were secondary in his overall strategy of generating nonviolent revolution through the spiritual uplift of the self and then the masses. The basis, even here, was that peace without depends on peace within.

The Position of Jayaprakash Narayan

JP's View of Satyagraha

Before coming to national and world prominence with the inauguration of the Bhoodan movement, Vinoba had spent much of his life as a semirecluse in the quest of spiritual fulfillment and the study of sacred texts. By way of contrast, Jayaprakash Narayan had spent most of his life as a major actor on the political stage. During the 1920s, while his young wife stayed with Gandhi at the Sabarmati Ashram, JP undertook seven years of higher education in the United States where he studied Marx and completed a highly praised master's degree, analyzing societal changes from a Marxist perspective. On his return to India he worked closely with Nehru and became a spokesman for the socialist members of the Indian National Congress. During the war years JP was imprisoned, escaped, and spent one year "underground" as a progressively more notorious (and in popular circles, celebrated) revolutionary.

After independence, JP became one of the founders of the Socialist Party and a severe critic of the ruling Congress Party. Soon, however, he began to have doubts about the efficacy of power politics. Increasingly, he looked to Gandhi's philosophy as a way of bringing about the social revolution he had so long struggled to achieve. He took part in Vinoba's Bhoodan movement, retired from party politics, and, on 18 April 1954, at the Bodh Gaya Sarvodaya Conference, took a vow of *jivandan* (life-gift)—a pledge to devote the remainder of his life to Sarvodaya and Bhoodan work. For many years he remained in Vinoba's shadow, and his speeches reflected Vinoba's worldview. After his experiences at Musahari, however, which culminated in the realization that there had been a lack of genuine progress toward a Sarvodaya social order, their paths were to diverge.

Given his background, it is not surprising that at the time of this intellectual reassessment JP's analysis of the political situation and his understanding of satyagraha would mature into something substantially different from Vinoba's, that unlike Vinoba he would embrace the position of Gandhi the politician over Gandhi the saint.

While still very much in the shadow of Vinoba, JP saw Bhoodan, bringing about "changes of the heart," as the vehicle for the establishment of a Sarvodaya social order. If this failed in the first instance, he looked to the experience of Gandhi to provide a path for further action. Subsequent steps were to include an attempt to educate the public about the evil that was being opposed followed by the launching of movements to place moral pressure on the "wrongdoer" or "mistaken party" and, finally, by resorting to noncooperation on the assumption that injustice was only possible with the cooperation of the wronged party. Nevertheless, JP concluded by stating, "I believe that if we work with faith and confidence and in the proper spirit, the need for Satyagraha will not arise."[37]

For a long time JP echoed Vinoba's views on satyagraha and, following Vinoba, even defined his constructive activities in terms of satyagraha:

> There is always talk about satyagraha and it is argued that Gandhiji used to resort to satyagraha and Vinobaji does not do so. That is why his movement has no impact on society. . . . What do these people think? Do they think that Vinobaji does not understand Gandhiji? . . . Will Sarvodaya materialize by just resorting to satyagraha here and there? . . . I do not think that it is possible to start any countrywide satyagraha movement in the present circumstances. . . . I have taken up the work of consolidating gramdans in the Musahari block (in Bihar). I consider this work of mine as satyagraha itself. This is my stand on satyagraha. In this respect, my point of view is just identical with that of Vinobaji.[38]

Around the time of his Musahari experiences, becoming somewhat disillusioned with Vinoba's interpretation of Gandhian activism in terms confined to constructive work, JP started defining satyagraha as something different from persuasion and conversion. It now became a "powerful weapon" to be used when those methods failed.[39] His assessment of the progress of the Bhoodan/Gramdan campaigns after his work at the grass roots saw him commenting that "conditions seem to be ripening in the context of our present programme that may necessitate larger-scale satyagrahas."[40] Like Gandhi before him, he was now ready to place civil disobedience before constructive work.

In the diary that he wrote while in prison during Mrs. Gandhi's Emergency, JP noted that although Vinoba seemed to hold that "systematic change in the political order could be brought about without a struggle, even a peaceful struggle," after twenty years of effort success had not been achieved anywhere.[41] He continued, pointing out that one of the reasons for this was a lack of *atmosphere* of struggle: "It seems to me that in such an atmosphere psychological forces are created that attract men and drive them to accept challenges and to change themselves and others." While conced-

ing that during the Bhoodan movement through "spiritual and moral appeals, the saintly influence of Vinobaji, did bring about some remarkable
moral changes in some individuals," he concluded that these could "never
become a social or psychological force"[42] that would be effective in securing a more just society.

He added: "There are fields—such as social and economic repression
—in which not civil disobedience proper but satyagraha may become necessary. Social workers may be involved, or maybe Opposition groups. Such
satyagraha may turn into civil disobedience against the government, when
the latter comes heavily on the side of the oppressors. This has happened
again and again in parts of India where the Congress has been in power.
The Opposition can never promise to keep out of such satyagraha."[43]

During the Bihar Movement JP had often talked of "offering" satyagraha, in the form of picketing, at the gates of the State Assembly as a way
of compelling the dissolution of the Assembly because it was "quite obvious that the State Legislators in Bihar have forfeited the confidence of the
people."[44] Vinoba would certainly not have understood the distinctions
between civil disobedience and satyagraha that JP was now making, and he
saw neither the objective sought nor the methods employed during the
Bihar Movement as "satyagraha." Seizing on a statement of Gandhi's,[45] JP
made his understanding clear: "Gandhiji had declared in 1930 that if he
remained alive after Independence he would have to wage against the people of the country struggles of the same kind as the struggle for Independence." He added, "I hope my critics will allow me the liberty of following
in the footsteps of this greatest innovator of the twentieth century."[46]

JP made the telling point that although he had renounced power politics to join Vinoba, he "did not rule out the possibility of a non-violent,
non-cooperation movement or satyagraha on the lines of civil disobedience
if the bhoodan movement did not attain its targets."[47] While Vinoba strove
for perfect nonviolence, JP spoke of social change through a mass movement of peaceful people's power.[48] Not surprisingly, as their respective
definitions of satyagraha became so divergent, problems were bound to
arise for the Gandhian movement that they dominated.

JP's View of Society

JP's primary concern was the achievement of real democracy and a
society devoid of inequalities where all lived in a state of freedom.[49] His
concerns, like Vinoba's, were centered on the problems of the human condition—freedom of the human personality, of the mind, and of the spirit—
but his quest was a political, not a spiritual one.[50] He was searching for the
form of social organization that would provide the masses with the maximum freedom and the most appropriate way of bringing it about.

JP shared Vinoba's view of a village society and the way that it should be organized. In an open letter to his Praja Socialist comrades, when he finally announced his resignation from the party in 1957, JP made the point that although he had withdrawn from politics, Sarvodaya also had its politics—a politics of a different kind.[51] Unlike the politics of party and power, Sarvodaya politics rested on *lokniti* as opposed to *rajniti*. He added that Sarvodaya politics could have "no party and no concern with power." Its aim was to abolish all centers of power and to achieve a withering away of the state. As this "new politics grew," JP saw a corresponding diminution of the "old politics."[52]

During the same year, however, JP demonstrated that he had not completely managed to turn his back on his party political past. In a press statement, "An Appeal to Voters," he explained: "The election is as much an expression of the people's will as the bhoodan revolution. The two cannot and should not be kept separate either in the thoughts of the people or in their acts. Just as the people are making bhoodan, gramdan, gramsamkalpa,[53] so too they must cast their votes for those candidates who stand for these ideas and who pledge to advocate them in legislatures."[54]

In his analysis of the relationship of the Gandhian movement to politics at the Thirteenth All-India Sarvodaya Conference at Unguturu in 1961 JP noted that, as Gandhians, they did not belong in political parties and should not "take part, directly or indirectly, in any political contest for position and power." He added, however, that this did not mean that they should be unconcerned with how democracy was working in the political field. He asked rhetorically whether, if democracy were in peril or if there were danger of political chaos or dictatorship, they should "sit back smugly and twiddle our thumbs on the ground that we have nothing to do with politics?"[55]

JP was for a partyless democracy, but he saw that there was no alternative to parties in the short term, not until a lengthy process of mass political education had managed to eradicate the distinctions of class and caste.[56] Rather than merely allowing the state to wither away he saw danger for the future if antidemocratic tendencies in power politics were not tackled. During the Bihar Movement he reiterated the partyless ideal while he organized a party to oppose Mrs. Gandhi.[57] In his prison diary, in direct contrast to the position of Vinoba, JP wrote: "No one, at least no one who has no party affiliation and therefore no motivation to exploit every situation for partisan ends, and who is still anxious to start a peaceful revolutionary movement, i.e. a movement to bring about basic changes in society and in social attitudes, can ever, in the conditions of our country, avoid a confrontation with the kind of government we have."[58]

His rejection of Vinoba's "positive" satyagraha came from his realization that it was inadequate to produce the psychological climate necessary to bring about the social revolution he desired. And to the charge that his change of direction was politicizing the Sarvodaya movement he answered that such politicization "should give it immense strength and make it more relevant to contemporary society."[59]

JP's View of Peacekeeping

Eight years after the border war with China, Vinoba was still adamant that if the country was attacked Shanti Sainiks should stay away rather than interfere in the work of the army. If sainiks wanted to oppose something, it should be the existence of the army itself, and this could be achieved by securing internal peace so that the army was no longer required for that function.[60]

Whereas for Vinoba the peacekeeping role of the Shanti Sena was a secondary one, on reading some of JP's pronouncements on the issue it seems that it was almost the only role. After the border clash with China, JP felt the need to demonstrate a unity of purpose with Vinoba by pointing out that the aims of the Sena, and the Sarvodaya movement as a whole, were not merely to demobilize the army but also to demobilize the internal police forces. "As a matter of fact," he continued, "only to the extent to which the Shanti Sena and the forces of nonviolence . . . succeed . . . in the maintenance and preservation of internal peace" will the movement succeed in the external field.[61]

Nevertheless, the differing attitudes of the two Gandhian leaders were clearly illustrated during the war and in JP's questioning of Vinoba's stand that sainiks should not practice satyagraha in the international field, that they had no business becoming involved in Goa or the border dispute "as long as there is the sanction of the people behind the army." JP saw the injunction to challenge the very existence of the army as "very frustrating," adding that he did not know "how long it would take for the nonviolent movement in India to be strong enough to persuade the Government to disarm." As a way out of the dilemma, JP, the champion of unarmed peacekeeping, proposed the formula that saw him becoming one of the prime movers of the World Peace Brigade: "It might be different . . . if Indian volunteers went to another part of the world, which was not in dispute with India itself."[62]

While JP was envisaging the formation of an international Shanti Sena to operate as the shock troops of peace (that may even require paratroop training),[63] Vinoba was emphasizing the organic growth of nonviolence through the spearhead of constructive work. Vinoba's vision of a world peace brigade mirrored the one he held for the Shanti Sena. It focused on the establishment of a spiritual relationship among different peace groups to "protest" whenever special problems relating to world peace arose, to select a particular area in which to build up a society or community free from state control followed by an attempt to create world interest in the issues involved.[64]

Narayan Desai's interpretation of the way that the Shanti Sena grew out of the Gramdan movement fits with the peacekeeping model that he and JP favored. According to Desai, in 1957 Vinoba was concerned about the riots that followed the reorganization of the Indian states. Some riots occurred near Gramdan villages and, if they spread, could threaten "the whole purpose of Gramdan." Whereas Gramdan aimed to replace the system of centralized government and offer the possibility of social and economic justice, the Shanti Sena aimed to replace the police and army with a nonviolent volunteer force. In addition to preserving law and order, the Sena was to create nonviolent strength and provide a constructive channel for the stresses and strains that would exist even under gram swaraj. This was to be achieved by the peaceful solving of intracommunity conflicts, providing village security, organizing constructive projects, and training village youth.[65]

In both the contending models Gramdan and the Shanti Sena were inextricably linked. In the vision of JP and Desai, however, rather than being spiritual, the objects of the Sena were to prevent outbreaks of violence, to bring these under control where they did occur, and to create such an atmosphere of nonviolent strength in the country that it would strengthen the spirit of cooperation in the international field.[66] In 1968 JP repeated this peacekeeping-emphasizing definition of the sainiks' role: "The Shanti Sena . . . is a corps of volunteers whose job it is to jump into a fray, into the midst of violence, and try to curb it, to restore peace and to create good will between the warring sections to prevent a recrudescence of trouble. But here too, we found that peacekeeping operations cannot be restricted to reconciliation efforts. To be effective, they have to be continuous and they must have a social content."[67]

A Summary of the Debate

Both Vinoba and JP knew that the nonviolent revolution they desired would only be achieved through the efforts of the people themselves. The differences centered around the means that would be employed by the people to bring this revolution about. Ostergaard makes the point that whereas Western anarchism is "immediatist," Indian anarchism is "gradualist."[68] JP was more anarchistic in the Western sense, reverting to active struggle and "negative" satyagraha. Unlike Vinoba, he was also antistate, pitting people's power *against* that of the state.[69] Vinoba, by contrast, was a gradualist, far more concerned with the purity of the means than with any immediate ends that might be achieved. In this he was following the Gandhian dictum that the ends grew out of the means employed and echoing Gandhi's statement that even if a Hitler's heart was not "melted" by the efforts of the pure satyagrahi, it did not matter because intrinsic values were as important as any instrumental considerations. Vinoba states that "Fire merely burns; it does not worry whether anyone puts a pot on it, fills it with water and puts rice in it to make a meal. Fire burns and does its duty. It is for others to do theirs."[70]

One of the major consequences of this difference was the heated debate within the Gandhian movement over the position that should be taken on voting by Shanti Sainiks. Badshah Khan had warned that the government was also a power and should not be ignored and that efforts had to be taken to ensure that "self-less, honest and desire-less persons have access to governmental power."[71] Vinoba was clearly of the opinion that there could be no shortcuts in this process; it had to be built on public education and village organization. And this, in turn, could only be successfully achieved after Gramdan had been accomplished and people's candidates under the control of village councils had been selected.[72]

For Vinoba, JP's involvement with power politics was a shift away from ethics that would enhance the strength of parties rather than of the people.[73] He asked his workers to take up intensive work in selected areas to ensure that nonparty candidates were chosen to represent the whole area rather than sectional interests. As this program spread, the state would no longer have anything to do.[74]

JP's experience in intensive local work convinced him that villages were too divided to secure genuine people's candidates in the short term and that threats to democracy would stifle any progress toward a more equitable nonviolent society. Vinoba wanted people's candidates but did not want sainiks to vote even for them. JP, while working for a partyless future, believed that it was important for members of the Gandhian movement to ensure the election of the best possible candidates and that it was their duty to help shore up the democratic tradition by exercising the democratic duty of casting votes even for party members.

Some critics have claimed that the Sarvodaya stance of not participating in electoral politics had weakened the movement because people to whom it directed its message saw it as irrelevant.[75] Yet when the movement became directly involved in power politics as a de facto opposition, it was torn apart. Since the mid-1980s the Sarva Seva Sangh has experimented with putting up so-called people's candidates, and, after that experience, the charges of irrelevance need to be taken seriously. The candidates secured so few votes that they lost their deposits.[76] The question is not only one of how far the movement needs to be involved in politics in order to push on with its revolutionary program but also how far it can do this and still ensure that the program remains Gandhian.[77]

For the Shanti Sainik the position is spelled out coherently by members of Vinoba's Bharatiya Shanti Sena. If a Shanti Sainik votes, even
though ballots are secret, people continually try to guess the preferred party
and label the sainik. They will watch the sainik's friends, see who he has
dealings with, attribute political motives to his activities, and treat him
accordingly. The reasons for not voting, therefore, are practical ones: if
there is a dispute in the village, people can turn to the sainik with confidence, knowing he or she is impartial.[78]

Vinoba was even against political activity short of voting on the part
of sainiks. One leading sainik remembers Narayan Desai asking Vinoba if,
perhaps, his insistence on eschewing all political involvement was not too
strict. Elections are held only every five years, and, perhaps, for a few days
before the casting of ballots sainiks could inform the people of the best
candidates. That, too, Desai reportedly suggested, could be seen as constructive. Vinoba answered with the question, "If you spend ten years
building a house and then set fire to it, is that constructive?"[79]

On another level Achyut Deshpande points out that even the
peacekeeping work stressed by JP is hampered when sainiks engage in party
politics, even if this means only casting votes. It is not possible to work in
riot-torn areas without a government curfew pass. To receive such passes,
sainiks must establish a rapport with the government. This comes about
through the establishment of a credible position of neutrality. He notes that
to preserve credibility a sainik should not work for the opposition or against
the government but may oppose the latter on *issues*.[80] Since the JP Movement, Gandhians have been viewed as opposition forces and so obstacles
are continually placed in their path. Sainiks had no problem securing curfew
passes during the 1969 Ahmedabad riots but were not granted any during
later episodes of violence.[81]

The point is further illustrated by the reputation gained by the Shanti
Sena after the 1967 Ranchi riots.[82] Sainiks moved from relief camp to relief
camp, undertaking sanitation and food distribution work and gradually
gaining the confidence of the Muslim refugees. They worked to build
goodwill among the Hindu communities from which the Muslims had fled,
and owing in part to these efforts, the situation greatly improved. When
Indira Gandhi visited one of the camps, it is alleged that crying women
informed the prime minister that, given the conditions, they would have
died had it not been for the efforts of the Shanti Sainiks. Mrs. Gandhi saw
the saffron scarfed volunteers and noted their activities. She asked the district magistrate who they were. Until then she had known nothing of the
Shanti Sena program of the Sarva Seva Sangh. Upon her return to Delhi
she asked a still-friendly JP how she could aid the work of the Sena.[83] Any
possibility of such government cooperation vanished as the Sena became
embroiled in party politics.

The issue of the status of the Shanti Sena as a peacekeeping force is also dependent on the personal convictions and, perhaps, even more on the differences in personality between Vinoba and JP. Vinoba, stressing spiritual values, placed primary consideration on the conversion of the individual so that these individuals could bring about the hoped for changes in society. For him changes in the social structure would not come about without adequate moral development.[84] JP, unsurprisingly, given his lengthy association with Marxism, saw it as more practical and perhaps more logical that people would change once the environment had been changed.[85]

While the saintly Vinoba was planning and attempting to bring about a Gandhian revolution in India through the peacebuilding work of Bhoodan and Gramdan, JP, the more cosmopolitan of the two by far, was as much concerned with the question of what Gandhians had to contribute, in the short term, to the prevention of wars generally, that is, to peacekeeping. Although the early rhetoric of both leaders included the two perspectives of peacekeeping and peacebuilding equally, during the India/China border conflict the differing emphases became quite clear. Vinoba's plan, to succeed, required a concerted effort at grass-roots work by the Sarvodaya movement, an effort to which major distractions could prove fatal. Further, Vinoba's program depended on government support, or at least noninterference, for its success, whereas JP's had to be seen as totally impartial to maintain any credibility.

Vinoba knew that with the numbers available any proposed intervention between the opposing forces would not prove effective, could not be supported by the government, and "attempts to organize non-violent resistance by the Shanti Sena would arouse public hostility and react on the movement's other activities."[86] The JPites, however, felt that "unless the movement is prepared to risk offending the government and the chauvinists, it will be discredited as the vanguard of the non-violent revolution."[87] At a Sarvodaya conference in Tamilnadu in May 1963, after the Chinese withdrawal without any peace effort by the Shanti Sainiks, JP added that "the tragedy of the situation is that India is just adopting the same method against which we have been advising others."[88]

Gandhi set up Shanti Dals to function as nonviolent police forces, that is, to act purely as "peacekeepers" maintaining communal harmony in the struggle against the British. Vinoba also saw the Shanti Sena in instrumental terms but in a greatly expanded role and in a far longer time frame. The job of the Sena is to lead in the building up of the ideal nonviolent society of the future—a position Gandhi would undoubtedly have come to in independent India. JP did not see Vinoba's grand scheme in quite the same way. He took Vinoba's political, but not spiritual, view and overlaid it with his internationalist sympathies, something to which Vinoba paid only lip service.

During its most notable period of operation, under the guidance of JP and Narayan Desai, the Shanti Sena did work that resembled the tasks that Gandhi had envisaged it would be engaged in. This is not because JP's vision was more correct or insightful than Vinoba's but because it was *more limited,* and for practical reasons that was all the Sena was capable of.

The Current Ideological Basis of the Shanti

By the time Vinoba and JP had died not only was the Gandhian movement hopelessly split but two rival Shanti Senas were in operation. The experiences of the turbulent 1970s and the passing of the strong-willed and charismatic leaders had led to the tempering of some of the more extreme positions in both camps. The ideological bases of the Senas were partially remolded to confront new political realities. Yet the Akhil Bharat Shanti Sena of the Sarva Seva Sangh still cleaved to the line adopted by JP on many fundamental issues, and the Bharatiya Shanti Sena looked to the philosophical stance of Vinoba.

The Position of the Sarva Seva Sangh

The Sarva Seva Sangh sees no current threat of external aggression. Danger to the existence of the country comes from internal forces, and these, it believes, are such that the need for a Shanti Sena is greater than ever before. The Sena is needed to keep the peace and to help the government to do so, but the main role will be the creation of conditions that will eliminate breaches of the peace.[89] Until the early 1990s, the process for achieving this seems largely to have centered around the removal of Rajiv Gandhi's Congress (I) government from power.

During a high-level meeting of the Sangh's leadership at Siminthala on 14 July 1988 three views on this role were expressed: (1) The work of the Sena should be one of education and mass organization. It should make the masses aware that a simple change in government will not of itself ensure permanent peace. (2) Currently there is an emergency allowing no time for mass education. In the interests of the country it is necessary to change the government, and if need be, this may entail collaboration with political parties. (3) This is political work, and as a Gandhian organization, the Sangh should restrict itself to constructive work. Given this lack of agreement, it was suggested that a working paper on future directions be produced.[90] At the Trivandrum meeting of the Prabhand Samiti support was given to cow protection work, marches were planned to celebrate the Vinoba birth centenary and Gandhi's 120th birth anniversary, but still no consensus could be reached on the direction to be taken by the Sena. It was decided that members could follow their consciences and that the matter was again to be raised at the aborted Sarva Seva Sangh/Shanti Sena meeting at Shivarampalli in April 1989. Finally, at a 1990 Sevagram seminar it was decided to concentrate on gram swaraj and to seize the opportunity that this provides for the repopularization of the Shanti Sena.[91]

The lessons of the history of the Gandhian movement have not been lost on its leadership. Acharya Ramamurti, the most important theoretician of the post-Emergency Shanti Sena, sees the efforts of the Bhoodan and Gramdan movements as a "tragedy of good intentions self-defeated."[92] The movements were the brainchild of Vinoba. Only he, the guru, had the vision; all the others, including JP, were mere workers; disciples not colleagues. When Gandhi was the leader, people knew what he wanted. Vinoba's intentions, however, according to Ramamurti, remained a mystery to the bulk of his followers. The Sangh was, thus, trained to follow, not lead, and consequently, when the leaders departed, Gandhian workers became moral orphans, an army without a general.[93] Because of the failure of JP's Bihar Movement, many have seen political action as a mistake, and he believes that because of this there is a tendency to steer clear of political involvement. This, in turn, has meant that the Sarvodaya movement has lost its dynamism, that it has become little more than the welfare arm of the state.[94]

Ramamurti believes that there is widespread insecurity in the country and that this results from the government's failure to protect life and property. He reiterates Vinoba's point that the Shanti Sena must also be a kranti (revolution) sena and agrees that the role of the Sena must not be limited to that of Red Cross work or work as a "fire brigade," that it must fight against injustice and struggle for a new social order.[95] Nevertheless, for him the first job of the Shanti Sena appears to be the provision of basic security and a strengthening of grass-roots democracy; revolutionary nation building has become secondary.

Ramamurti believes that a moral society must be preceded by a democratic one and that the structures that cause violence must be changed rather than individuals. Once democracy has been quashed, all hope of peaceful change is lost. He sees the need for building people's power, noting that without it history will merely repeat itself and claims this is the primary task of the Gandhian movement. He adds, however, that it is insufficient to depend on this because the consequences will be a perpetual conflict between state power and people's power. It is also necessary to build up a responsive government,[96] and for this to occur the Shanti Sena has a key task in ensuring that voters lists are kept up-to-date.[97]

As he increasingly perceived democracy as threatened by the Congress Party/Nehru family monopoly, its removal became his first priority. He asked rhetorically how a social order can be rebuilt by keeping out of politics. Had Bhoodan been even partially successful then this step may not have become necessary and a new way might have been available. Because this is not the case, politics remains the only available mechanism whereby the masses can be mobilized for moral ends. This, moral action in the political field, is his definition of satyagraha. And he sees action in the political field as the only way of bringing young people with moral values into the Gandhian movement to provide for its revitalization.[98]

Although he concedes that Gandhians should not stand for elected office, he strongly disagrees with the proposition that they should remain totally outside the realm of power politics. As the removal of the Rajiv Gandhi government became "the need of the hour" his energies were directed to the political sphere and to some extent the Shanti Sena was again relegated to the background.[99]

Many other senior Sangh thinkers echoed the theme of the state as the root cause of violence and, therefore, declared that it was imperative to directly confront it.[100] This approach will undoubtedly alienate the party in power and will, for example, make the obtaining of curfew passes less probable. Sarva Seva Sangh secretary Chunibhai Vaidya, however, makes the point that it was not only the lack of such passes that hampered Sena activities in recent riot situations but also that many of the riots were politically motivated in the first place and even financed by politicians.[101] By implication, to stop violence it is not enough to cooperate with the government but one must confront the system of government itself.

Narayan Desai believes that the avoidance of political struggles was a mistake. He now sees the state and political opportunism as the root causes of much of the current climate of violence and believes that these, and not merely the symptoms, must be fought. This means that the task of voter education must be undertaken seriously.

He believes that the basic ideas upon which the Shanti Sena was founded are still sound but has realized the need for more grass-roots work and less centralization. A decentralized Sena should be the aim and not merely a consequence of a lack of leaders of the stature of Vinoba and JP who could provide effective central control. Desai sees Vinoba as having had so much power that for years he could direct the Sena's activities away from questions that should have been addressed. Perhaps there is room for a body that could coordinate the activities of a tatpar sena, but, essentially, the Sena must learn to work in small loosely linked groups (as Vinoba saw it doing before he formerly inaugurated it), and for this, although it never operated as planned, the kendra is the ideal unit.[102]

Ramamurti sees the Sena as operating at varying levels from the village (with the *dusta* of ten members as the primary unit) to the national, generally with the leaders of one tier forming the members of the next[103] and, unlike Desai, envisages a detailed chain of command with the Sarva Seva Sangh president as supreme commander.[104] The Sangh in general, however, favors a decentralized Shanti Sena over a nationally centralized one, allowing for some coordination at the top for matters such as the efficient deployment of a tatpar sena.[105]

At the Ranipatra meeting of the Sarva Seva Sangh's Prabhand Samiti in early 1986 the Sangh explicitly distanced itself from Vinoba's "gentle" satyagraha by endorsing active and, where necessary, aggressive nonviolent action to fight exploitation, injustice, and oppression. Ramamurti sees satyagraha as being the proper response in cases where attempts are made to defeat a constructive effort and notes that where the government infringes the rights of the people, it is the responsibility of the Shanti Sainik to work to regain them.[106]

Notwithstanding the Sangh's total disagreement with Vinoba's views on the inapplicability of "negative" satyagraha and involvement in the party political process, it is close to his position on the role of the Shanti Sena in many other key respects.

Again, the sainiks are to be more than peacekeepers; they are to actively undertake peacebuilding activities. Along with Ramamurti other Sangh leaders see the Sena as the instrument for developing a feeling of swaraj in the villages, for ensuring liberation from police and courts in all except the most serious cases of crime, for organizing constructive village activities, and, eventually, for evolving a social order based on truth and nonviolence.[107] A realization has dawned that peacekeeping work will never produce a peaceful society. Peacekeeping will become more applicable when exploitation and structural violence have ceased. Until then efforts must be directed at the system itself, which contains the source of violence.[108]

The failure of a piecemeal approach to nonviolent revolution has also been accepted. A concerted attempt to maintain (or bring back) prohibition, to ensure cow protection, or to promote a particular village industry is seen as being as insufficient as was the securing of countless paper Gramdans. Integrated development is necessary, and the way to achieve this is not through a general propaganda effort but through intense efforts in small pockets. The mistakes of Vinoba in spreading resources too thinly and being satisfied with only superficial results have been understood by senior Sangh thinkers. Badriprasad Swami, the current convener of the Shanti Sena, believes that a few successful areas of consolidated "village republics," with their own senas and courts, will enable the Sarvodaya ideal to catch on and spread.[109]

On the question of nonviolent defense the present position of the Sangh resembles that of Vinoba more closely than that of JP. Talk of sainiks facing invaders has almost completely ceased. In the early 1970s the movement noted that the "maintenance of an armed force is not compatible with a non-exploitative and non-violent order" and claimed that the ultimate disappearance of the armed forces was an "explicitly held goal." The way to achieve this was to "arouse and organise" the people so that they no longer relied on the army for their defense either in terms of internal security or in terms of dealing with invasion.[110]

The Sangh leaders realize that in the event of another border clash sainiks could not even approach the front without government assistance in the form of airplane and helicopter transport, which in any event they would never receive. And if they could get to a battle zone, they would probably cause confusion rather than do good.[111] Unless the state has disarmed, their role should be limited to constructive work in border areas (echoing Vinoba's dictum about Gramdan and defense), and until the Sena has proven itself in the internal setting, it would be foolish to expect it to achieve anything on the international front. In this respect the sainiks from both camps agree.[112]

Under JP's guidance the forging of international links with other peace organizations became part of the official program of the Shanti Sena.[113] In its current thinking about the relevance of the Shanti Sena in the international sphere, again the Sangh leadership has approached Vinoba's concept of peacekeeping (minus the unrealistic offer of one hundred thousand sainiks for an unarmed United Nations force). It is accepted that the primary function of the Sena is to work for basic change in the local community and only incidentally for world peace. There is still the feeling that contact between heads of government will not fundamentally change the world order, that people-to-people contact is necessary and possibly offers a role for peace brigade efforts such as that of the World Peace Brigade.[114] The Sangh, however, is no longer discussing this as any priority for the Shanti Sena. Rather, it talks of the networking of small local revolutionary peace groups.

The Position of the Bharatiya Shanti Sena

During the later years of his life Vinoba did make an exception to his injunction against "aggressive" satyagraha in his involvement with the movement to prevent the slaughter of cows. His disciples in the Bharatiya Shanti Sena continue this work. While many see the campaign as an exercise in futility (after all, even though Vinoba had undertaken a lengthy fast to safeguard cattle, the killing has not stopped), his supporters claim that the critics "fail to see [the cow] as a 'symbol' for animal life. Vinoba was for the protection of all life, but chose the cow because of the importance given to it in the cultural and religious heritage of India."[115] But should this be the task of the Shanti Sena?

Even some leading Bharatiya Shanti Sena members are questioning an approach that places inordinate emphasis on cow protection. They argue that although cow protection work is important, the welfare of people should be placed before that of animals. In short, a Shanti Sena should do more or rename itself as a cow protection league.[116] The Gujarati Bharatiya Shanti Sena, for example, takes part in the work but does not devote itself to it exclusively. Members believe that without gramswaraj the task is, in fact, hopeless and the cow cannot be saved.[117]

Arunbhai Bhatt, however, declares that cow protection work was taken up by the Bharatiya Shanti Sena as part of its peacekeeping program. According to him, intercommunal violence and growing rural poverty are the largest threats to the country, and so cow protection is peacekeeping in the real sense. Instead of tackling small projects, it is in this work that the Sena is confronting the fundamental causes of tensions and future problems. The other major issue of concern is the achievement of world peace. Consequently, the other main aim of the Sena should be working toward the provision of Vinoba's dreamed of world unarmed army. Work in the middle ground only leads to confusion.[118]

At Vinoba's Shanti Sena conference in October 1981, it was decided that the Bharatiya Shanti Sena should make an effort to prevent cow slaughter by organizing five hundred thousand people to undertake a two-day fast to bring attention to the issue. Vinoba obviously agreed that cow protection work should be taken up by the Sena, but he was not impressed by the idea of the mass fast, declaring that it "would not lead to any result for the government would say that it would lead to better health in those persons."[119] Achyut Deshpande made it clear that the fasts were intended for the education of the people and not to "influence the government." Given those assurances, Vinoba endorsed the action.[120]

For more than ten years now the Bharatiya Shanti Sena has made cow protection its sole area of operation. More than three hundred thousand have offered satyagraha in the cause of the cow, and demonstrations have attracted thousands of participants, but at low points only about twenty permanent hard-core activists remain. The usual scenario outside the gates of Bombay's Deonar slaughter yards (the largest in Asia with a capacity of handling eleven thousand animals per day) is that a small group of ten or so sainiks staff a continual protest camp. Daily at 8:00 A.M., and again at 3:00 P.M., they nonviolently block the way between the holding yards and the abattoir proper. They are arrested by police, held until the animals have passed and then released—to repeat the performance at the next movement of animals. The satyagrahis see their action as a lamp that must remain alight until a new phase of the struggle presents itself.

In 1987 Deshpande threatened to fast to the death to resolve the deadlock. He was dissuaded from doing so by his followers. Now even prominent Bharatiya Shanti Sainiks are saying that they are fighting the symptoms rather than the causes. The years without progress in stopping the slaughter has led them to think that perhaps the time for a tactical change has come, but they see this as something only Gandhi or Vinoba were capable of.[121] Perhaps if propaganda work were done in the villages where the bullocks are needed, farmers could be persuaded not to sell their animals. Deshpande, however, having received his instructions from his leader, follows them inflexibly.

But Achyut Deshpande also has answers for his critics. While admitting that the Bharatiya Shanti Sena may in a sense be tackling symptoms, he notes that they cannot stop the process at the village end because the farmers are being paid too much for the animals, because they cannot compete with the corruption and bribery involved, and because they cannot stop a system that dooms thousands of cattle to slaughter by protesting in a few villages.[122]

Deshpande sees cow protection work as work for the needy. In a poor, predominantly agricultural country with an already high rate of unemployment and underemployment, where the soil is degraded and fuel is short a strong economic and purely secular argument can be made to back this view. He further believes that it will aid communal harmony because the economic consequences of the removal of cattle from the countryside will affect Hindus and Muslims equally. At the moment he sees this as the only action program that the Sena should have.

Article 48 of the Indian Constitution requires "the State" to "take steps for preserving and improving breeds, and prohibiting slaughter, of cows and calves and other milch and draught animals." Enforcement is in state hands, and in any case the guidelines laid down in the Constitution can be easily circumvented by issuing false age certificates, a practice the sainiks claim is carried out by a team of veterinarians who routinely make out such certificates for all animals. The battle, therefore, is not only being waged at the entrance to slaughter yards but also in the courts.[123]

If cow slaughter is stopped by law, then the Bharatiya Shanti Sainiks will go to the villages to help educate the peasants about the long-term need for cattle to ensure their survival[124] and to promote a Sarvodaya social order that is not centered on expensive agricultural machinery in the hands of the few. If this also were guaranteed, then the Sena might again turn to other work and again perhaps find itself in conflict with the Sarva Seva Sangh's Shanti Sena. Because not only Shanti Sainiks are involved, a commitment to refrain from voting is not considered a prerequisite for cow protection work. Nevertheless, Deshpande is still firmly behind Vinoba's instruction that sainiks, whatever work they are engaged in, must not vote.

Conclusion

The fact that Vinoba and JP differed in their views on active nonviolence, social organization, and peacekeeping so radically does not augur well for those wanting to use the Shanti Sena as a model for unarmed peacekeeping. Did one of the Sena's leaders misunderstand Gandhi's philosophy, or did they both take relatively extreme positions that removed them from the more central position that the Mahatma himself had occupied? That the positions of the Sarva Seva Sangh and the Bharatiya Shanti Sena appear to have converged somewhat during recent times seems to indicate either that one of the above propositions is true or that the experiences of the movement have encouraged convergence. A more detailed examination of Gandhi's thought in light of the interpretation of his two principal followers should allow a further conclusion to be drawn on the first point. It should also clarify whether Gandhian philosophy can provide the type of foundation for unarmed peacekeeping that the champions of the model insist it can or whether they, too, must make the best they can of an imperfectly worked out philosophy in light of their own experiences.

8

Lessons from the Shanti Sena

The Gandhian movement split over fundamental philosophical issues, and this was reflected in the history of the Shanti Sena. For purposes here, however, the importance of the Sena experience is not that it provides a manageable microcosm for investigating the history of the Sarvodaya movement as a whole but that it provides the only vehicle for a long-term case study of unarmed peacekeeping. As with all such nonviolent attempts, occasionally the approach taken in various circumstances was not thought through adequately. Sometimes the hard light of practice showed theory to be inadequate for the situation or incapable of fulfillment by the majority of the individuals involved. Nevertheless, the three decades of practical experience and debate about strategy and tactics provides a wealth of experience for others and possibly some clues as to the viability of the model itself.

Whether the Shanti Sena should be actively engaged in power politics or completely divorced from it, (which, in part, depends on whether it is believed that the individual or society should be changed first), whether sainiks should vote or not, whether the Sena should be a peacekeeping force because of the growing violence in India or a peacebuilding force working steadily toward a total revolution, whether it has a role in international affairs greater than ad hoc contacts with other peace groups, whether sainiks can be effective outside their usual area of constructive work, whether they should defy their government if it goes to war, and whether the Sena should be centralized or totally decentralized are some of the questions that troubled the organization during its active years.

It will be argued that some of these questions do not have any one appropriate answer because of the contradiction within the very philosophy upon which the Sena was based. The answer to several others depends on the ideology of individual sainiks, whether their world view has been colored more by Vinoba Bhave or Jayaprakash Narayan and whether they believe that the political situation is deteriorating so rapidly that the "need of the hour" forces them to compromise on ideals (if not their fundamental principles) in the way that Gandhi often did. I, nevertheless, analyze these issues in turn to determine whether the problems Galtung and others have claimed are inherent in a Gandhian philosophy-based unarmed peacekeeping/making/building force have proved to be spurious given the Shanti Sena's experience.

The Shanti Sena in India

In the next four sections I examine the position of the Shanti Sena in India in light of the lessons of its history. What leading sainiks are now thinking should provide some clarification of tactics for those attempting to embark on the path that the sainiks have long traveled. In the first two sections I survey current thinking in the Sena on key issues. In the third I examine future prospects for the Indian Shanti Sena, particularly as an unarmed nonviolent peacekeeping force. In the final section I discuss the optimism of leading Shanti Sainiks about the future prospects for Gandhian peace work.

Back to the Basics

For the Shanti Sainik, helping the poor and oppressed was to be the matrix within which daily life was conducted. In times of emergency, however, as the basic step, direct violence had to be eliminated in order to come to grips with structural violence in a way that did not alienate the rich or aggressors or both. In keeping with Gandhi's doctrine that oppression, not the oppressors themselves, had to be eliminated, the process was to include both resistance and assistance simultaneously.[1] Oppressors were to be won over and helped to understand the nature of their actions (and one way of doing this was by helping the rich if they had problems).[2] At the visible level this strategy is necessary because an all-out second-party approach, which leads to class conflict and agitation, does little to usher in a peaceful society.[3] Resistance without assistance converts the oppressor into an enemy.[4] Although the duty of the sainik was to side with the poor and oppressed, this response was not to be at the cost of nonviolence broadly defined.[5] Because both the decreasing of manifest violence while maintaining social injustice *and* the decreasing of social injustice while maintaining manifest violence are unacceptable, a balancing act is required[6]—one that the sainiks feel is possible with an adherence to Gandhian nonviolence.

During interviews many sainiks pointed out that rather than see contradictions between the values of neutrality and championing the oppressed they believed that one of the major problems with Western peace movements is that they do not take an holistic enough approach to their peace work. They see non-Gandhian pacifists as tending to spend most of their time in continual opposition to the government or oppressors and note that this can prove demoralizing and unproductive. Sainiks see their role as primarily one of technical assistance/constructive work with opposition to the government only becoming necessary if it gets in the way of their constructive efforts.[7]

For Shanti Sainiks the strength to continue working comes from steady constructive activities rather than from short bursts of intense opposition. The task of working for a nonviolent society is a slow and continuing process that occasionally, when the call comes, can be interrupted for peacekeeping[8] or, perhaps, direct "negative" satyagraha. This has been missed in the West, and Harris argues that even in India all too often the means of satyagraha has been confused with the goal of Sarvodaya.[9]

During episodes of outright opposition, constructive work provides a tangible function for satyagrahis while the "proper channels" are being exhausted; it is "able to compensate for the apparent lack of headway towards the specific objectives of the struggle."[10] Besides the positive aspects of influencing public opinion, it aids morale by giving the sainiks something positive to do rather than merely leaving them to suffer the negative aspects of frustration while waiting for something to happen. Gregg explains that without a program of practical action "many pacifists cannot maintain their belief" because the "moral and psychological need for deeds is compelling," and without something concrete to do "pacifism seems and feels too negative."[11] It is for these reasons, he suggests, that such former distinguished pacifists as Albert Einstein and Bertrand Russell abandoned their faith in pacifism.[12] Horsburgh adds that constructive work as a "requirement of satyagraha has been much neglected in recent years, especially in the West"[13] and suggests that Martin Luther King's "gradual loss of influence within the American civil rights movement was largely due to this oversight."[14]

Although this appears to be true, it is also true that for the majority of sainiks, steeped in Gandhi's transcendent worldview, the reasons are functional in a far more fundamental sense. A life of continual work with and for one's neighbors is the only appropriate mode of behavior where self-realization comes from the realization of the unity of humankind.[15] Those who do not share a belief in this doctrine may experience greater difficulty in exchanging confrontational short-term goal-oriented activities for the adoption of the life style that is basic to the operation of the Shanti Sena.

While Western peace activists have called for the internationalizing of the Shanti Sena idea, a flow of influence in the reverse direction has also occurred. The strong influence of Western, and particularly U.S. peace movements has gone into the shaping of the Sena. Devi Prasad has pointed out that at the 1949 and 1960 international peace conferences held in India a great impact was made by the U.S. movement with its antiwar preoccupation and the championing of the ideal of Gandhi's Shanti Sena by Western pacifists. From this interaction came the inspiration for the World Peace Brigade, which, in turn, with its major objectives of tackling the immediate concern about war, substantially influenced the Shanti Sena, especially through the personalities of JP and Narayan Desai.[16] This led to a focus on peacekeeping at least partially so that the Sena could play a leading role in the international antiwar movement.[17]

Given the failure of outright opposition to the government during the 1970s and the relative lack of success of joint international peacekeeping ventures, it is not surprising that the majority in the Gandhian movement is again talking about grass-roots work in the villages. After the Janata debacle, even JP seemed to admit that political action was probably not the correct approach when he claimed that "our main attention should have been focussed on national reconstruction. Political activities, however, did not allow us to do so."[18] The Sena ostensibly was always working for social change and was deeply concerned with the problems of structural violence. In reality however, during its heyday, emphasis was placed on its role as a peacekeeping force operating during the overt disturbances of communal and caste violence.[19]

Prasad notes that the idea of nonviolence can be very attractive, especially to those who are economically and socially well placed and, consequently, threatened by disruptions. A nonviolent solution to social conflicts helps to preserve the status quo, that is, the position of power holders, and so they readily accepted the Shanti Sena. There is danger that the oppressed are left out in these situations, and, understandably, they view organizations that talk of human rights with suspicion. While the Shanti Sena was concentrating its activities on peacekeeping, and the contributions it could make to world peace, there was a danger that it could have been included in this category. This forms another reason for concentrating on the basics of working closely with the people at a local level, helping them with their day-to-day problems rather than just in emergencies.[20] And perhaps the logical outcome of this is the realization that this is the task of Sarvodaya workers in general; the only real role for a Shanti Sena is to supply a tatpar force made up of other dedicated Sarvodaya workers when called by a local worker.[21]

Peacekeeping or Peacebuilding?

Vinoba saw the Shanti Sena as a service sena except in extraordinary circumstances when, out of necessity, it became a peacekeeping force. In contrast to police and the constabulary, the ideal, as spelled out by Sen in his *Gandhian Way and the Bhoodan Movement,* rested on building local feelings of trust: "Without the requisite moral sanction that flows from selfless service of the locality, of the people at large, programmes of action operated by unknown, unfriendly faces on a landless or rowdy elements are bound to be abortive or only very temporarily effective. A person or persons noted for service can exercise a natural command, born of love and affection, on the local people and is a fit, [sic] instrument to deal with frayed tempers by a moral technique."[22]

At about the time that this was written, increasing communal and linguistic tensions and the ideological bent of the new leadership saw JP and Desai reorienting the Shanti Sena toward, and even beyond, the peacekeeping role originally envisaged by Gandhi. This was very much in keeping with the views of the peace movements in the West; and these views were reflected to a far greater degree in the approach of JP and Desai than that of Vinoba. The Madariaga / Narayan proposal and the founding conference of the World Peace Brigade were to a large degree about the setting up of an international tatpar shanti sena.[23] The Shanti Sena experience, however, does not prove the overwhelming effectiveness of this approach.

As noted in chapter 6, some of the Shanti Sainiks stationed in Cyprus suffered a degree of culture shock, which, according to Narayan Desai, reduced their effectiveness. Although they produced a corresponding culture shock among their hosts, enabling the sainiks to capture local imagination, the Cyprus experience may still provide some concrete evidence for the belief, strongly held by Vinoba and his followers and now endorsed by the Sarva Seva Sangh leadership, that for Shanti Sena-type work to be effective the sainik must be a local worker. It may suggest that international nonviolent ready-response teams may prove to be a waste of time if there is no local nonviolent network already in place which the outsiders would merely supplement. Without this it can be argued that peacekeeping operations are best undertaken by a force provided by the internationally known and respected United Nations.[24]

Leading Vinoba-following sainik, Dilkhushbhai Divanji, for example, firmly believes that the Shanti Sainiks must be village workers who have gained the respect of the villagers through their work. A commander at a higher level can only be one who has gained wider prestige through selfless action. The effectiveness of a peacekeeping Sena must be proved in the villages and then in India before it can be suggested for deployment elsewhere.[25] And this has not yet happened. Indrasingh Rawat emphasizes this point by claiming that the peace army concept cannot work unless its members have given extensive service to their constituents in constructive areas. The general feeling among sainiks of both camps is that an effective nonviolent peace force can only be formed through a networking of peace centers around the world. If a local peace center feels the need it may then call on workers from other centers. The outsiders would then assist and obey the directions of the locals.[26]

A closely related question concerns the degree of centralization required for a Shanti Sena-type of organization. Vinoba originally saw sainiks as village Sarvodaya workers operating totally independently at the grassroots level. One of the main tasks of the reorganization under JP and Desai was the establishment of a hierarchically structured and centrally controlled Shanti Sena.

Desai, the chief architect of the changes, saw this move as necessary to provide an adequate response to violent outbreaks and to coordinate peacekeeping efforts around the country. He, however, has since reconsidered the desirability of this approach somewhat but for political rather than organizational reasons. Desai believes that the centralized structure of the Shanti Sena allowed Vinoba, the commander in chief, to force the organization into paths disagreeable to many. A largely decentralized structure (with possibly some coordinating body to issue a call to sainiks if there were major disturbances) would overcome the potential for problems that could arise with the "capturing" of the organization. For him the basic ideas behind the Sena are still sound. Too much was attempted in overly large groups and the kendra, the ideal unit of operation, rarely worked as envisaged.[27]

The amount of centralization that is most desirable depends on one's view of the primary role of a peace brigade. For effective peacekeeping a highly trained, mobile, and disciplined force is necessary. Peacebuilding, however, is most effectively carried out by dedicated local workers. For those who argue that a slow organic approach to peacebuilding is the only effective method of producing lasting peace, who see peacekeeping, and even possibly peacemaking, by outsiders as essentially futile (and this now is the predominant view among Gandhians), decentralization is the only viable strategy.

This conclusion does not augur well for those calling for the internationalizing of the Shanti Sena idea. Nevertheless, the peacekeeping experiences of the Sena in its heyday can provide the blueprint of an organizational structure for those who retain faith in the efficacy of peacekeeping as a way of buying time for peacemaking/building.[28] And it could be argued that the relative disappointment felt by Gandhians in the model results largely from a lack of finances and logistical support that hampered the effective operation of the model—problems that could be overcome if the unarmed peacekeeping idea were taken up by a body such as the United Nations[29] (and somehow it could be ensured that the quality of dedication among peacekeepers could be maintained).

Given the admitted failures of the previous approach to usher in the nonviolent revolution, a reevaluation and change of tack is to be expected. That efforts in India are again being concentrated on local peacebuilding, which is a far longer-term project, seems to reflect a return to Gandhian basics enabled by the stubborn optimism of the Gandhian fraternity. Perhaps this can be coupled with the simple fact that this approach embodies a more realistic interpretation of the current political circumstances prevailing in the country.

With the passing of the old guard of Gandhian politicians and the alienation of the weakened Gandhian movement from the central authorities, there is very little scope for the toleration of a highly organized group that aims to make the state redundant by usurping the functions of its enforcement apparatus, the police and military. And, by analogy, this may apply in other countries and at the international level. (Countries are most reluctant to allow the training of their citizens in techniques that could used against the power elite).

The Marginalization of the Gandhian Movement

In his landmark work, *Asian Drama,* published in 1968, Swedish economist Gunnar Myrdal provided an analysis of the social and economic factors affecting India's rate and level of development. There, Myrdal designated the country a "soft state," that is, one where governmental decision making shies away from placing obligations on the populace, and if policies are framed in legislative terms at all, often they are not enforced.[30]

The Indian State bureaucracy did not have the ability to reach into every village, and this, coupled with the Gandhian legacy, including that of resistance to governmental coercion and a philosophical commitment to the proposition "that democratic planning requires the people's participation and initiative . . . in the course of creating the new institutions for self-government and cooperation"[31] ensured that a large part would be played by Sarvodaya workers in the country's path to development. Myrdal believed that "rapid development will be exceedingly difficult to engender without an increase in social discipline in all strata and even in the villages."[32] And here he means state-imposed discipline. In other words, for effective "development" a "strong" or "hard" state was a necessity; the Gandhians, however, by very definition, were the champions of an even further "softening" of the state.

Much has happened since the words of Myrdal were written. During his inaugural address at the half-yearly conference of the Sarva Seva Sangh, held at Ernakulam toward the end of 1972, Siddharaj Dhadda stated:

The aim of the Sarvodaya movement is to make the people conscious about the reality of the present situation, to diminish their reliance on

government, to help them organise their strength and take the management of their affairs in their own hands. We want the establishment of
a real participatory democracy in the place of the present representative
one. Representative democracy may have been good in the past when
science and technology had not advanced to the extent as to enable the
representatives to obtain a stranglehold on the lives of the people
through state machinery. The exercise of the power of the Government
in the old context was confined to performing its legitimate function of
a peacekeeping and coordinating agency . . . the people were masters
of their own lives and destiny, without let or hindrance from outside
forces. But the phenomenal advance of science has created a strange
paradox. It has made possible and has actually led to an ever increasing
concentration of power, political, economic, military, into the hands of
an ever diminishing number of people—a smaller and smaller coterie.[33]

In short, India was rapidly losing its status as a "soft state."

With the passing of Nehru and the estrangement between the Gandhian movement and his daughter after JP's call for "Total Revolution,"
the Sarvodaya establishment lost government support for, and was even
actively obstructed in, carrying out its voluntary social work activities. As
the nation increasingly took on the trappings of a "hard state," particularly
under the regime of Rajiv Gandhi, the Gandhian movement (along with
other voluntary agencies) was pushed further to the periphery in terms of
the inputs it could provide to shape social organization and development.[34]
This trend has been exacerbated by the ever-declining appeal of Gandhian
philosophy to the youth of the country with a rapidly swelling middle class
desiring an increase in consumer goods and the absence of a charismatic
leader among Gandhians that could counter it.

Perhaps a Shanti Sena, as it worked in the 1960s and early 1970s,
cannot be tolerated by a state where the political leadership no longer has a
philosophical commitment to the values of the "Father of the Nation,"
where Gandhian ideas about societal organization are often derided as being
utopian and irrelevant as the country moves toward the twenty-first century, and where the organization itself is the self-declared vanguard of a
revolution aimed at a destruction of the Indian polity as it has evolved in
the years since independence. Further, perhaps Shanti Sena-type organizations can only be tolerated where bureaucracy does not permeate all levels
of society, where the state does not have the resources to provide rapid and
adequate intervention in times of social turmoil. As states "harden," the
operation of such groups becomes incompatible with a government that
seeks to establish its position as legitimate and sole sovereign.[35]

In 1964 Narayan Desai was already lamenting that the Shanti Sena
faced two problems that prevented it from being as "effective as it should
be." He pointed to a lack of means of quick communication and an extreme
lack of finances.[36] The situation for the voluntary sector has deteriorated

since. At a time when the ability of the state to move its own functionaries around the country has been aided by the increasing mobility of its armed forces, Gandhian institutions, ever further removed in history from Gandhi himself, are increasingly feeling the economic pinch. And, as the government moves inexorably into areas that were once the domain of Gandhian institutions, people are less willing to donate money to groups that are increasingly seen as costly and amateur parallel organizations. [37]

Erica Linton, an observer of the Sarvodaya movement at the height of the power of the Shanti Sena, made a telling point in this regard. Touring Gandhian pilgrimage sites in Pune with a non-Gandhian chauffeur, at the samadhi of the Mahatma's late secretary Mahadev Desai in the Agha Khan's palace, she turned to her escort and remarked, " 'You know, I suppose, that Mahadev's son Narayan is the secretary of the Shanti Sena?' 'Oh, you mean the American Peace Corps,' explained the driver. What a sorry state of affairs," she commented, "when foreign volunteers make a greater impact on the community than their own young men."[38] It was this realization that led to the setting up of the Tarun Shanti Sena after the Bihar famine. The attempts at Gandhian peace and constructive work, however, never reached the critical mass necessary to make the ignorance of Linton's driver anything other than the norm. And with the decline in and marginalization of the Gandhian movement in the years since there is little evidence for any optimism by the Gandhian establishment in the foreseeable future.

Optimism

Despite the objective reality of their present position, the Gandhians *are* generally optimistic about their future as a force to be reckoned with. And this is particularly true of the Vinoba supporters. They see that their message is one for the ages. They realize that the process will be slow, that there will be setbacks, but they are convinced that it will eventually win through, that with a continuation of grass-roots work success is assured. By organic means Gandhi's message will triumph. They firmly believe that all signs point to this outcome: the increasing number of people's movements around the world now employing Gandhian methods and the approach of environmental collapse is forcing a reevaluation of the hegemony of Western life style and consumption patterns in a way that indicates a shift toward a Gandhian outlook. Although others may see them as anachronistic, they believe that the march of history is now coming the full circle and that they are merely ahead of the times. For life on the planet to continue a simple life is necessary, and in order to survive the rest of the world will catch up eventually. This self-assured belief in being on the right path leaves no room for pessimism.

Those who have thrown their lot with direct political action as the vehicle of change exhibit a far lower level of optimism. They see a long-term view and strategy as inadequate in a rapidly deteriorating world; the "need of the hour" compels immediate action.[39] This approach, however, also means many short-term defeats. Without a charismatic leader they are unable to capture the imagination of the populace, their message is considered irrelevant in the light of a growing consumerist ethic, and people's candidates fail in elections that are dominated by personalities rather than issues. As the state takes on an increasing number of the functions that were previously the domain of the voluntary sector, and the Gandhians are categorized (or were during the Indira Gandhi government) as a de facto opposition party, the Sarvodaya movement has become increasingly marginalized. They, too, have the long-term vision of the Vinobans, but the lack of direct short-term victories dampens their feelings of optimism. Although the vision of a peacekeeping Shanti Sena of old remains current for a few, generally it has been relegated to the background.

In line with Vinoba's original concept, both groups now tend to see the Shanti Sainik as a constructive worker who at times will be engaged in rescue work. The peacekeeping vision of JP no longer exists. The Vinoba supporters have occupied the two extreme ends of the Sarvodaya philosophy continuum: at the local level cow protection work and in the international sphere (at least in theory) support for a world peace army. Whether their faith-based optimism or their belief in the intrinsic good regardless of the apparent instrumental applications of a philosophy in action are enough to convince outsiders, especially bodies such as the United Nations, to adopt the idea of this world Shanti Sena is to a large degree irrelevant. They carry on as they do because they must.

The JP followers occupy the middle ground. They want to change the shape of the Indian polity to allow a chance for Gandhian ideas to spread before it is too late. But even they no longer talk about international peacekeeping except in the most general terms.

The Contradiction Inherent in the Gandhian Underpinning of the Shanti Sena

Although the generally presented reasons for the disintegration of the Gandhian movement since Gandhi's death show substantial depth in analysis, they, nevertheless, overlook one essential aspect. They focus on issues such as whether a movement that was effective against a specific enemy, for example, the British, can continue when the focus of the movement has been removed (and that, in this case, amounts to whether a movement can maintain its popular momentum when it moves from the realm of an easily identifiable instrumental good, the removal of a foreign overlord, to a less easily definable intrinsic good, the building of a spiritual society) and whether such a movement that stresses self-sacrifice can survive in an emerging consumerist and "democratic" society, whether it is really anachronistic and inapplicable as we move toward the twenty-first century. Or, perhaps, the movement was not able to survive the passing of a charismatic leader, especially when that leader's philosophy was adopted by the populace as a policy because of its instrumental value rather than as a creed and that leader was determined not to set up a sect of the chosen faithful around himself.

The Shanti Sena is an excellent microcosm of the (post-Mahatma) Gandhian movement as a whole. It reflects the problems in the larger movement completely while providing a manageable framework within which to examine its decline. A study of the leadership of the Sena points to the possibility that the seeds of the organization's demise are imbedded in its ideological foundations.

Although Gandhi preached nonviolent resistance, Reinhold Niebuhr claimed, more than sixty years ago, that at times Gandhi confused this with nonresistance. Niebuhr notes that this "is a pardonable confusion in the soul of a man who is trying to harmonise the insights of a saint with the necessities of statecraft, a very difficult achievement."[40]

On careful examination it appears that Gandhi's philosophy did suffer from a fundamental contradiction that was papered over by the towering personality of the Mahatma. When he died and the mantle of leadership fell to Gandhi's so called "heirs," this contradiction became obvious and its underlying incompatibility surfaced.

Part of the reason that this has not adequately been realized is that the "heir" question has been obscured by the confusion inherent in the accepted division that has Vinoba as the Mahatma's "spiritual heir" and Jawaharlal Nehru as his "political heir." For Vinoba this classification is correct,[41] but for Nehru it is not. Anyone who knows anything about the political and economic philosophies of Gandhi and Nehru must have wondered how this designation could have been possible: their thought in these areas is almost diametrically opposed, and Nehru's actions in office soon dispel any notion of heirdom in anything but name.

The explanation is that the relationship was based on something far deeper and less tangible than philosophical consistency. A thorough reading of their correspondence reveals that the bond was one of, for lack of a better word, love. The relationship was a filial/paternal one that transcended their vast differences. It may be true that there was no person with Nehru's authority who could have carried Gandhi's policies into government, but the reality is that the Gandhian scheme was to operate outside the organized political framework. At the time of the Mahatma's death there was no political heir, and there was no colonial exploiter against whom to direct mass political action. Nehru was inserted into this seeming vacuum, but that insertion takes on a diversionary character.

Philosophically, Gandhi had strong anarchist tendencies. He distrusted centralized state power. His political work was to be carried on by selfless Sarvodaya workers who labored for the uplift of the people outside the framework of government in a way that aimed, ultimately, at bringing about a state of "people's power" in a system of interconnected village republics where political self-government was synonymous with individual self-government.[42] Gandhi's true political heir, the one who was to employ the techniques that had characterized Gandhi's satyagraha campaigns, emerged in the person of the post-jivandan (or, perhaps even more accurately, the post-Musahari) Jayaprakash Narayan.[43]

It has been argued that in Vinoba's hands Gandhi's revolutionary ideology was spiritualized to the point where it "was rendered pro-status quo," whereas JP's actions were decidedly anti-status quo and secular. Analyst Devdutt, however, further noted that in JP's hands Gandhism "was shorn of one of its highly ineffable quality [sic] which has something to do with metaphysics, spiritual, and creative quality of Gandhi's original ideas and activities."[44] To the degree that these observations are right, and to a substantial degree they are, it would appear that neither Vinoba nor JP understood the totality of satyagraha as expounded by Gandhi (and if, given their backgrounds, they could not understand it, probably nobody can), or, more probably, that the concept of satyagraha suffers from an inherent contradiction that surfaced after the all-consuming independence struggle was over and the towering personality of the Mahatma had passed from the scene. If either of these two propositions is correct, those who advocate a philosophically Gandhian model for international peace brigades, who see the Indian Shanti Sena as a prototype, may have to rethink some of their assumptions.

Verma quite rightly maintains that the "soul force" of satyagraha, for Gandhi, ceased "to be merely a political technique to overcome injustice: it also implies a metaphysical position."[45] This, however, led to inconsistencies in the Mahatma's actions resulting from an inherent contradiction in his philosophy that can be uncovered when it is pushed to its logical conclusion. There is, as Verma points out, an essentially other worldly underpinning to Gandhi's philosophy, and it was the quest for this spiritual ideal that, for him, gave meaning to life. Often, however, the *need of the hour* (a term frequently used by those Gandhians who favor JP's, as opposed to Vinoba's, approach to acting in the world) meant that Gandhi employed the techniques of satyagraha in a given battle in a form that deviated from the stated ideal.[46]

Gene Sharp has produced a detailed typology of the many varying types of nonviolence, one of which is the Gandhian technique of satyagraha.[47] Sharp is correct when he notes that one characteristic that differentiates satyagraha from other types of nonviolence is the supplementing of the approach by a positive "constructive program." He also notes, however, that there seems to be some ambiguity in satyagraha over whether while attempting conversion it is permissible to couple nonviolent resistance with direct action that may force a policy change on opponents even though their attitudes may not have been changed first (see table 1).

Table 1

Methods of Satyagraha

Mechanisms of Social Change	Sharp's	Gandhi's	Vinoba's	JP's
Persuasion/conversion leading to social change	yes	yes	yes	yes
NVR-DA* to create climate for rethinking attitudes, thus policy change	yes	yes	yes	yes
Attempting persuasion, NVR-DA to force policy change without changed attitudes	unclear	unclear	no	yes
No attempted persuasion, NVR-DA to force policy change	no	no	no	no

* Nonviolent resistance and direct action.

Sharp fails to see the reason for this ambiguity because he has categorized satyagraha as being completely "this worldly" as opposed to "other worldly."[48] Satyagraha in its ideal *does* have a very pronounced "other worldly" underpinning (see table 2), and in its ideal operation employs no coercive tactics.

Table 2

Aspects of Satyagraha

Attitudes to Self and Society	Sharp's	Gandhi's	Vinoba's	JP's
Other worldly	no	yes	yes	no
This worldly	yes	yes	maybe*	yes
Concern with own purity	yes	yes	yes	yes
Supports status quo in society	no	no	no	no
Desire to effect particular social change only	no	no	no	no
Desire to effect social reforms, not basic changes	no	no	no	no
Desire to effect social revolution (basic changes)	yes	yes	yes	yes

* In the sense of permissible, rather than denoting uncertainty.

Generally, as interpreted, the term *other worldly* contains an element of world-renunciation or, in its extreme form, a preoccupation with the world to come. It may imply ignoring evil as much as possible and suffering without resisting evil, even by nonviolent means, as part of religious duty.[49] The concern is generally with consistency of beliefs and individual integrity rather than with social reconstruction.[50] Galtung is correct when he notes that generally the "mundane Kingdom" and the "transcendental Kingdom" are "two separate components in an ideological space," yet in Gandhi's "kingdom" the components are combined.[51] A question remains whether this is an artificial construct that entails an unresolvable contradiction.[52]

Although the avowed aim of Vinoba's life was to bring about a nonviolent revolution, including a social one, this revolution was to be social reconstruction *through* individual integrity rather than the other way around. Vinoba supporters may take unkindly to the suggestion that their master's attitudes to the self and society were other worldly, and although there is ground for a semantic debate on this point, it is reasonably clear that his critics would not be far off the mark in claiming that, intentions aside, the objective reality of Vinoba's philosophy was decidedly other worldly.

A leading interpreter of Sarvodaya philosophy, Indu Tikekar, makes the point that "man on earth is the central theme of Sarvodaya thought. It is not interested in the hereafter."[53] Although this is undoubtedly true, Sarvodaya philosophy is concerned with self-realization and spiritual matters rather than merely with the material world. For the Mahatma "human actions should serve a new social order *and* also be instrumental to a self-realization that ultimately would be transcendental."[54] Nonviolence and self-reliance, although important, are subordinate to and instrumental in achieving self-realization.[55] Sarvodaya, in short, can be defined as humanism with a "unifying spiritual reality [that] brings holiness to human life."[56]

For Gandhi and Vinoba[57] (the issue does not appear to have greatly concerned JP),[58] the ultimate aim of life was *moksha* (liberation), and that meant the extinction of the ego. The achievement of moksha is by way of realizing the oneness of the universe and especially of the whole of humankind. Or, to again quote Tikekar, "In the language of Sarvodaya metaphysics the realization of the fundamental spiritual unity of life is the final consummation of human life."[59] The method for achieving this liberation is the selfless service of humanity and an eschewing of methods, such as violence (broadly defined) and coercion, which reinforced the illusion of duality. The philosophy, therefore, can be seen as being "this worldly" while the reason for this "action in the world" is essentially because of "other-worldly" considerations.[60]

The point, however, is that the noncoercive ideal that was to pave the way for liberation was preached by Gandhi, but what he practiced was often a more-coercive form of nonviolent direct action that did not always seem to take cognizance of the oneness of humanity but aimed at achieving a desired short-term worldly goal.

Being objective, one would be hard-pressed to find in the annals of satyagraha a campaign or action that was completely noncoercive and achieved the conversion of the opponent. At times Gandhi himself realized that his actions were contrary to his ideals,[61] and he admitted his failures by referring to "Himalayan blunders" or at least acknowledging the impurity of his actions. In criticizing those who claimed to be his followers, Gandhi insists that it is "enough that I should be my own follower" and adds that "I know what an inadequate follower I am of myself, for I cannot live up to the convictions I stand for."[62] On other occasions, with his celebrated fasts, for example, although generally he did not admit to an inconsistency with his own ideals, the inconsistency is evident to the impartial observer.

Many of Gandhi's fasts, for example, his last in January 1948 for communal peace, had no selfish motive but did have a coercive element. The leaders of the warring religious communities gave assurances of peace on Gandhi's terms because they did not want the death of the Mahatma on their hands. In some of his other fasts the element of coercion was even more blatant. The 1918 fast during the Ahmedabad textile mill workers' strike upheld the strikers' resolve and pressured the owners to give in to their demands. The two fasts in Yeravda prison during 1932 saw the government give in on the question of separate electorates for Harijans and the prison officials alter their policy concerning the type of work prisoners could do. In 1939 a fast against the civil liberties record of the ruler of Rajkot forced government intervention, not the conversion of the ruler.[63]

Deciding what constitutes coercion is a difficult task. It can be defined as the use of force, including moral force, to compel opponents to act in ways that are contrary to either their will or judgment. Despite his insistence on a principle of noncoercion, and, on a broad definition of the term (see chap. 4), at times Gandhi himself was guilty of coercion. Some of his interpreters, for example, Bondurant, claim that as a method satyagraha itself contains a positive element of coercion. She points out that the tools of noncooperation, boycott and strike, which can be used in satyagraha, do involve elements of compulsion that may effect a change in opponents that was originally against their will.[64] Case, meanwhile, asserts that satyagraha is "explicitly *non-violent* and implicitly *coercive*,"[65] and Shridharani, similarly claims that satyagraha does contain an aspect of coercion albeit in a modified form,[66] which he prefers to call the *compelling* element.[67] These distinctions are difficult to make, and the answer to the question of just where the line can be drawn so that an action remains within the spirit of satyagraha is unclear from a reading of Gandhi.

Naess states that although satyagraha is incompatible with coerced changes of opinion or attitude, some forms of coercion are acceptable. He gives an example where subjects are carried, against their will, into a street where a riot is under way and where, as a consequence of something they witness, they change some of their attitudes and opinions. Naess says that the changed attitudes and opinions were not coerced but that the subjects were coerced into seeing something that caused the change.[68] In other words, direct action can be used to bring about the creation of a climate that allows conversion. This begs the question of whether, if the subjects are not converted, such action amounts, ex post facto, to coercion?

Gandhi himself talks, in a similar vein, of putting pressure on an opponent through the engineering of hostile social opinion: "A Satyagrahi . . . must first mobilise public opinion against the evil which he is out to eradicate, by means of a wide and intensive agitation. When public opinion is sufficiently roused against a social abuse even the tallest will not dare to practice or openly to lend support to it. An awakened and intelligent public opinion is the most potent weapon of a Satyagrahi. When a person supports a social evil in total disregard of unanimous public opinion, it indicates a clear justification for his social ostracism."[69]

This leaves open the question of whether, as long as persuasion has been attempted first, nonviolent direct action (by way of total noncooperation, for instance) may be employed to bring about the desired changes even though attitudes and opinions had not first been changed.[70] With some justification, therefore, Gandhi's followers have differed in their interpretation of this matter. Ideally, satyagraha is free from all coercion, yet Gandhi used coercive fasts and other measures and called them satyagraha. In short, when Gandhi's techniques proved politically successful, they were, in fact, often failures of his spiritual ideology. The reasons for this may be that satyagraha, in its ideal form, does not work or that it works on a level far removed from the political.

Most Gandhian scholarship stops with Gandhi. Although there has been some analysis of the "JP Movement," very little attention has been paid to the life and thought of Vinoba Bhave, especially by Western scholars. It is, however, these two, Vinoba and JP, in which the two contrasting elements—the spiritual and the political—that were embodied in Gandhi, were distilled out after his death. Whereas JP is the follower of Gandhi's techniques, which proved politically successful, Vinoba is the follower of Gandhi's ideals.

Had the contrasting streams of Gandhian thought not manifested themselves in such a convenient form, their presence would have been more difficult to perceive and, hence, even more difficult to come to grips with. The Gandhians did not have to confront the problems inherent in this dichotomy while Gandhi was alive holding them together, and did not successfully grapple with them on his passing.[71]

Vinoba's gentle/gentler/gentlest form of nonviolent action is the only one that is completely consistent with Gandhi's spiritual ideal. This method did not satisfy those who wanted to act on a more political and immediate plane. They were worried that the Vinoban approach in some respects did not apply to problems in the "real" world.[72] And it is possible that this approach is doomed to being seen as an objective failure, while subjectively being a complete success (as it would be if it is accepted that nonviolence is a way to the Truth of nonduality and the process is taken as the process of creating the self). The assertion that subjective success is the same as objective success, because of the underlying unity of all, is not satisfactory to many. For them it is either only partially true or is only true in a long time-frame, and the world is moving so fast that perhaps ideals must undergo some subordination to the "need of the hour." Gandhi, given his emphasis on means over ends, would not agree in principle, but this is *exactly* what he did in practice time and again. And here, in this unresolved contradiction, lies one of the main reasons for the demise of the Shanti Sena and the still not completely healed split in the Gandhian movement.

The walls of almost every Gandhian home or institution are adorned with pictures of Gandhi (the tenuously held together whole), and the pictures of both JP and Vinoba (the manifestation of the separate and inherently antagonistic parts). It is possible to see Vinoba's gradualist approach as being ultimately correct in a deep Gandhian sense while still maintaining a desire for tangible results. The path of ignoring the government, of working outside its structures and letting it wither away ("worldly" success), can only be achieved if enough people follow it through, not merely the odd saint. The result-oriented confrontational approach has a far better chance of mobilizing the masses and seems to have a better chance of at least limited success and a greater chance of ultimate failure. Its success cannot make government wither away or achieve the "other worldly" ideals inherent in "pure" satyagraha, it can only replace the political structure with a less-oppressive one.

Confronting the power structure head-on, however, means that the government cannot ignore its antagonist and ensures that all the forces at its disposal will be directed at crushing any direct opposition. Some opted for the political approach of JP hoping that it could succeed, while maintaining the nagging feeling that in the long run it could not provide the ushering in of the Gandhian ideal.[73] Since the failure of the Total Revolution, the conundrum involved in the "this worldly" compared to the "other worldly" manifestations of satyagraha is still being worked through. It must also be considered by those calling for an adoption of "Gandhian" nonviolent peacekeeping.

Unarmed Peacekeeping and the Lessons from the Shanti Sena Experiment

What, then, are the lessons for unarmed peacekeeping from the Shanti Sena experience? Are any answers provided to the problems raised by Galtung and others (discussed in chaps. 1 and 2) that beset peacekeeping ventures in general, and their unarmed nonviolent variant in particular?

Is the Combination of Technical Assistance, Second and Third Party Roles a Contradiction?

The Nagaland Peace Mission ostensibly operated as a third party to the conflict between the Nagas and the government. First, it attempted to bring about a cessation of the hostilities and then ensure a maintenance of peace. To achieve the latter goal, constructive work in the areas of education, health, economic development, and social welfare was initiated in the affected regions. It appears that in this instance the combination of these two approaches worked to achieve the desired goal: "an atmosphere of tranquillity and normalcy, as also a craving for permanent peace, was generated at the base among the masses of the population. This atmosphere acted as a positive sanction strengthening the hands of the Third Force, and also as a deterrent to any attempt on the part of the conflicting parties to break the peace talks and to resort to violent methods."[74]

Sainiks, although adhering to no single "party line," generally do not see the contradictions pointed to by Galtung in the combined approach to the solution of conflicts. There are some semantic differences: for example, sainiks must remain impartial to be effective, but they are not neutral when it comes to oppression.[75] The general view, however, seems to be that if sainiks work long enough and fairly enough in a given area, then their impartiality will be accepted and constructive work will not get in the way of third-party conflict resolution work.[76]

Narayan Desai sees the work of the Shanti Sainik as both an art and a science. While conceding that scientifically Galtung may be correct, he notes that the situation dictates how the art of peace work is practiced, and often, regardless of the science, the application of the art proves to work.[77]

Although this is not a scientific refutation of Galtung's position or verification of Blum's (and at this stage, on the evidence available, neither is possible), it is not the only way of looking at the situation. Others have provided strong reasons for favoring Blum's view.

In a review of these issues and the implications of the Shanti Sena experience for other peace brigades, Narayan Desai has written that "the main function of the Shanti Sena . . . was within the country where the Shanti Sainiks served as volunteers for peacebuilding in normal days, and as peacekeeping volunteers intervening in riot situations. In normal days most of the Shanti Sainiks were engaged in the land-gift mission or in some other 'constructive work.' When carrying out a Third party role in a conflict, there may be occasions when the sympathies of those in a peace brigade would be with the oppressed people in the conflict. It would nevertheless function as a Third party in resolving the conflict."[78]

There is anecdotal evidence from many leading sainiks of this having been successfully achieved. No systematic studies have been undertaken, however, that could either back up or refute the assertion that this could be the expected outcome. A study by Nakhre seems to point to a somewhat less-optimistic expectation. In his survey of satyagrahi attitudes during three successful satyagraha campaigns, two during Gandhi's time (Bardoli and Rajkot) and one since his passing (Pardi), he found that a far greater number of satyagrahis believed that the opponents were "coerced" (47 percent in the Gandhi sample, 4 percent in the Pardi sample) or "persuaded" (29 percent and 77 percent) than "converted" (21 percent and 2 percent).[79] The relatively high figures for coercion and low figures for conversion are not indicative of a creation of harmony or a successful third-party effort. It should be pointed out, however, that sainiks working in one area over a lengthy period may expect better outcomes in "pure" Gandhian terms than activists who engage in a "one off" action in a given location.

The work of peacebuilding provides the strength for fighting oppression or engaging in peacekeeping. Sainiks are quick to point out that the constructive element in their work means that they do not suffer the same problems with frustration that Western peace activists face when their "negative satyagraha" suffers setbacks because they are always doing positive work.[80] In short, not only are the approaches not contradictory but they are mutually dependent—peacebuilding (technical assistance work) provides the strength for third-party peacekeeping and peacemaking, which, in turn, is necessary to allow the all-important work of peacebuilding to continue.

Is Nonviolent Peacekeeping Applicable in Vertical as well as Horizontal Conflicts?

Even in situations of vertical violence the position of Shanti Sainiks as peacekeepers was quite often far removed from the status quo-endorsing position feared by Galtung. A great deal of the vertical violence in India does not occur as a result of the oppressed fighting to rid themselves of the oppressors. Generally, rather than the poor violently resisting the oppressor, when they complain about their oppression violence is directed against *them*. And "riots" are often little more than systematic campaigns against minority groups. In short, from the Shanti Sena experience there can be important and non–status quo–ist applications for peacekeeping in situations other than horizontal conflicts. However, this situation may not hold true for all other social settings.

Elsewhere Galtung makes the express point that the majority of Gandhi's experience was in situations where "conflict is vertical and . . . violence is structural." While admitting that Gandhi did have some experience in situations where sudden conflict between "equally autonomous actors using direct violence against each other" broke out, he concludes that Gandhian techniques are more suitable to dealing with structural conflict than with situations that call for peacekeeping in horizontal conflicts.[81] In other words, even he does not see problems with the use of Gandhian techniques as depending on whether the given conflict is vertical or horizontal and implies that peacebuilding rather than peacekeeping is the natural manifestation of the philosophy in action. Given the well-documented and, at least relatively, successful peacekeeping operations of the Shanti Sena, it would seem that he answers in the negative his own query about whether there is a necessary contradiction in combining the approaches in the aims of a peace brigade (while leaving the question of whether the approaches can be combined in a given campaign, open).

Galtung also seems to resolve his own difficulty with attempted combinations of second–and third–party roles by peacekeepers, at least if they cleave closely to Gandhian ideals. The central dilemma is that sainiks pledge to fight against both injustice *and* violence. As Galtung points out, this causes little problem in cases of structural violence (where sainiks side with the victims and their actions are directed against the structure) or where a direct conflict can be identified as a structure of dominance (where although sainiks will identify "with man everywhere" their loyalty will again be to the victims). If, however, the conflict is purely horizontal, then a neutral third-party model is employed: "The satyagrahi becomes a live bridge of communication, to the point of sacrificing himself for the sake of preventing violence between the groups. He becomes an embodiment of the unity-of-man doctrine acting symmetrically between the groups, or with the amount of asymmetry that tendencies towards dominance should warrant."[82]

Other Issues

As already stated, Galtung has noted that peacekeeping is "possible but not very effective," whereas peacemaking and peacebuilding are "very effective, but not very possible." This realization has permeated some of the currently operating unarmed "peacekeeping" organizations. Peace Brigades International, for example, seems to have reduced its aims from the all-encompassing (as attempted by World Peace Brigade, at least in theory) to a more modest and perhaps realistic level. PBI letterhead proclaims that the organization is concerned with "Unarmed Peacekeeping and Peacemaking." Gone is any reference to peacebuilding; this, however, is the very basis of the Gandhian approach and the approach again being concentrated on by the Shanti Sena.

In discussing the difficulty of combining the possible approaches to conflict, Galtung notes that under some conditions "it might be possible to combine the peacekeeping function of the UN soldier, the peacemaking function of the mediator, e.g. of the Quaker type,[83] and the peacebuilding function of the peace corps volunteer." This he sees as a "very rich role combination" that "might even be highly effective," and the example he gives is Gandhi's nonviolent satyagraha brigades.[84]

This is a vote of confidence of sorts from the person who raised the most coherent objections to the model. However even if the absence of coercion in the Gandhian technique is an illusion, if satyagraha minus coercion does not work and has never worked, if the best it could achieve is indirect coercion through public pressure, or if these questions are less than crucial because the worldview based on complete nonviolence as the path to a transcendent reality is absent, then rather than carry on with an idealized view of Gandhian techniques, either a more realistic approach should be articulated or the goals should be clarified and adjusted accordingly. This choice has immediate and practical consequences for nonviolent peacekeeping/making/building operations. Although the likelihood of existential gain in unity-of-humankind terms is possibly diminished, a hope of conversion, that may never eventuate and however indirectly achieved, remains. Further, a "practical" weapon that mobilizes public opinion against injustice and violence through self-suffering emerges.

Peacekeeping is often characterized as a short-term measure, whereas peacebuilding operates in the long term by concentrating on the underlying causes of conflict or, in Gandhian terminology, on means rather than on ends. Ramamurti believes that international peace brigades are neutral; they do not create conditions of peace. As Galtung pointed out, their role is limited to "buying" time for other processes to take effect. This, however, is not to devalue the role of peacekeeping as something inferior to peacebuilding. It can also operate at another, symbolic, level, which can have great importance.

Ramamurti, and Gandhians generally, firmly believe that those who lay down their lives as martyrs to quell an outburst of violence (the correct means) can have a profound impact in shaping consciousness[85] and, thus, have an effect upon the general level of violence (the end that is not in their hands).

If viewed in this way, the efforts of the World Peace Brigade and the *Everyman* voyages no longer seem to be such failures. Although nuclear tests were not stopped, a great deal of public awareness was generated, which could amount to the same form of indirect pressure as the Gandhian technique of appealing to public opinion where conversion has failed.

Conclusion

A conclusion on the practicality of various peacekeeping techniques, broadly defined, will generally revolve around the question of whether humanitarian (nonviolent) third-party intervention results in more effective settlement of violent disputes than does an authoritarian (violent) third-party intervention. Schonborn conducted research during the racially troubled 1960s in the United States aimed at testing this hypothesis by measuring "effectiveness" in terms of the quality of the conflict outcome (varying from the most positive, viz., integration, through compromise, to the least positive, viz., domination), the duration of the conflict intervention (the amount of time peacekeepers spent intervening), permanence of the conflict outcome (how many repeat interventions were necessary), and the casualties of the conflict intervention (the number of deaths and injuries among first, second, third, and fourth [innocent bystander] parties during the intervention).[86]

The results supported the effectiveness hypothesis by pointing to a higher quality of conflict outcome[87] and better outcomes in terms of duration[88] and the level of casualties[89] in nonviolent third-party interventions. It was only on the permanence subhypothesis that his results were equivocal.[90]

A second hypothesis that interested Schonborn was the proposition that nonviolent third-party intervention is decreasingly effective in increasingly large conflicts because "person-to-person interaction and flexibility—the mainstay of non-violent intervention—becomes more and more difficult."[91] The results were, however, inconclusive on this consideration.[92]

The result of such studies will undoubtedly have major bearing on the likelihood of the adoption of nonviolent approaches to dispute settlement and conflict resolution. If the question is about the practicality of Gandhian techniques, however, then these are not the only, and perhaps not even the primary, questions that need to be asked.

Gordon Zahn once noted that people tend to judge actions and ideals almost entirely in narrowly defined pragmatic terms with questions such as "How practical is it?" or "What are the real chances of affecting events or changing attitudes?" He adds that where one does take note of things such as "the subject's personal intentions or spiritual satisfactions," it is only to determine into which of the currently popular psychological or psycho-pathological categories the actions should be slotted.[93] Yet these "spiritual satisfactions" are precisely the values that are given the highest consideration in the Gandhian scheme of things.

To those holding a view that categorizes means as ends-in-the-making the notion of "success" is not a relevant one. The intrinsic and the instrumental value of their actions are inseparable.

Along with Huxley, who asserted that "good ends . . . can only be achieved by the employment of appropriate means," and that "the end cannot justify the means, for the simple reason that the means employed determine the nature of the ends produced,"[94] Gandhi maintained that "the means may be likened to a seed, the end to a tree: and there is just the same inviolable connection between the means and the end as there is between the seed and the tree."[95] He added, "They say 'Means are after all means.' I would say, 'means are after all everything.' As the means so the ends. There is no wall of separation between means and ends."[96] And, "if one takes care of the means, the end will take care of itself."[97]

If, in Gandhian cosmology, Truth is God and nonviolence is the means of realizing this Truth, then the spiritual interpretation (the "other worldly" element of satyagraha) is correct. Or, if there is a strong belief in "existence as unity" then a life devoted to peacebuilding work or endeavors in peacekeeping, even in the face of extreme personal danger, makes sense. If however, the religious tradition is different (e.g., Christian or Muslim, where duality is taken for granted rather than being seen as an illusion), perhaps such self-sacrifice does not make quite as much sense.[98] And whether it is enough to give popularly acceptable meaning to the sacrifice of life in interpositionary actions has not been demonstrated. All that can be said is that it is probably more likely in a culture where belief in reincarnation is the prevailing norm and where the self and the other are intimately and directly connected (rather than through a superior god).[99] And it also means that the questions concerning "success" will be answered quite differently from the distinct standpoints.

Gandhi's belief in the interrelationship of means and ends was not merely a reflection of the Hindu belief in *karma*. The cosmic law of reaping what one sows applies as much in this life as in future lives: "There is a law of nature that a thing can be retained by the same means by which it has been acquired. A thing acquired by violence can be retained by violence alone."[100] However, an understanding of, and belief in, the karmic law that operates over innumerable lives and the acceptance of the principles of karma yoga[101] help to put the ideal of Gandhian action in the world and the ideal on which Vinoba founded the Shanti Sena, into a more understandable context.

Gandhi claimed that a person's "highest duty in life is to serve mankind and take his share in bettering its condition,"[102] and because of the interconnectedness of humanity this could not be done unless one understands and respects the self.[103] A person, therefore, "does some good deed . . . not . . . to win applause, but he does it because he must": it is the purpose for existence.[104] Nonviolence as the key to the quest for the self is "the only permanent thing in life, . . . [and] is the only thing that counts . . . [therefore] whatever effort you bestow on mastering it is well spent."[105]

Instrumental nonviolence is that which can be pursued as a policy of convenience, whereas a belief in the intrinsic value of nonviolence means that it will be practiced as a creed.[106] As already noted, generally for most sainiks the question of whether actions are engaged in because they are right or because they are effective is meaningless. For them, any narrow cost/benefit analysis indicates a concern primarily about symptoms rather than the fundamental existential issues involved with the entire concept of violence.[107] By contrast some point out that the objectively instrumental aspect of nonviolence must be developed so that it can be made acceptable to international organizations and those who do not accept nonviolence as a creed.[108]

The point is that a life of continual peacebuilding, coupled with peacemaking during times of tension and peacekeeping during emergencies, is a natural corollary to a belief in a Gandhian cosmology in its ideal[109] (and probably would prove quite difficult without it). A more individual-centered worldview, which is concerned with the survival of the person (and where individual salvation occurs apart from "the other"), will operate in a shorter time frame and with a different, more concrete result-oriented emphasis—the stopping of wars and manifest conflicts that threaten individual life. It is from this latter standpoint that the calls for the internationalizing of the peacekeeping function of the Shanti Sena come and from this standpoint that attempts were made to comprehend (and to some degree managed to influence) the Shanti Sena during its heyday.

Although the use of Gandhian techniques in their ideal may, if the philosophical underpinning is accepted, pave the way for spiritual fulfillment or even self-realization, given the experiences of Vinoba and JP, it appears that they are not capable of generating the psychological conditions necessary to mobilize the masses for large-scale action even in a cultural milieu where the philosophical foundation is quite acceptable. Although the emphasis on stopping wars means that the periodic calls for unarmed interpositionary peacekeeping will continue in the West, the Indian experience indicates that there should not be too much optimism for the successful employment of such forces in cultures where this philosophical underpinning is absent. Possibly this goes toward explaining why Royden et al. had such difficulty in recruiting volunteers for, and interesting others in, their projects.

The basis of Shanti Sena work is peacebuilding, and this is far less glamorous than the dangerous (to paraphrase James) moral alternative to war provided by peacekeeping. Although unarmed nonviolent interpositionary peacekeeping is demonstrably different from other forms of peacekeeping, without accepting Gandhi's philosophical position it is difficult to conceive of a peacebuilding project that can generate the long-term commitment required for effective action or any characteristic that would distinguish it from Peace Corps work. Yet, in what may most accurately be categorized as the *current* Shanti Sena idea, it is this life of peacebuilding that provides the background from which occasional peacekeeping ventures emerge.

During the Gandhi centenary additional material was added to the published version of the BBC's historical broadcast detailing reminiscences of Gandhi. One of the newly added pieces was an interview with N. Krishnaswamy. Krishnaswamy was (then) not a close follower or associate of the Mahatma's as were so many of the others.[110] His can be taken as the voice of the sympathetic Westernized post-Gandhi youth. He talked of the irony of the body of the slain Mahatma being transported on a gun carriage and of free India wanting the trappings of sovereign status. His most important points, for the purposes of this study, however, have to do with peacekeeping. He noted that in late 1955 approximately fifteen thousand satyagrahis were about to illegally enter the then still Portuguese territory of Goa when the Indian government stopped them. The Portuguese had badly beaten up smaller earlier contingents (three thousand "invaded" Goa in mid-August and suffered several casualties)[111] but it was thought unlikely that they would fire on such a large unarmed, nonviolent crowd. If they had, he continues:

> There would have been a tremendous upsurge of public opinion at international level, and I think that would have meant adding a new dimension to international politics—an unarmed people resisting a power that was fully armed. That was the first case where I felt that we bungled it. The second case was the Chinese attack, which was a crucial test for the Gandhians. I am afraid they did not rise to the occasion. If in October 1962, when the Chinese attacked, a few thousand Indians committed to non-violence had marched to the front and said, Well, it doesn't matter, let the Indian soldiers shoot us down or the Chinese soldiers shoot us down, we are going to stand here and try to separate these two armies, it would have looked a little foolhardy, but I think it would have caught the imagination of people all over the world and it would probably have made a large number of people in different parts of the world, the young at least, say, well, we are going to India now to join this international brigade for peace.[112]

It is difficult not to agree. Although such acts would have been tangential to the operation of the Shanti Sena in the Vinoban ideal,[113] they would have provided the model that those calling for the internationalizing of the Sena seem so intent on finding in the actions of the Gandhian community. Being realistic, with the back-to-basics philosophy of the weakened Sarvodaya establishment and the continual "hardening" of the Indian state, one must assume that the opportunity for such actions will not present itself in the foreseeable future. In any case, to be valid, the lessons of the Shanti Sena experiment should be drawn from its achievements within the given framework of its basic philosophy rather than from the perspective of an imposed framework.[114]

This need not mean that the experience of the Sena is not directly relevant in the area of unarmed peacekeeping generally. Without focusing on the long-term strategy of the Sena ("the Shanti Sena idea"), a great many valuable tactical guidelines can be found in the techniques developed by the Shanti Sena during its "peacekeeping years" under Jayaprakash Narayan and Narayan Desai. It is, however, doubtful whether independent interpositionary peacekeeping ventures would very often be able to command the economic and logistical resources required and, more importantly, raise enough volunteers to achieve a critical mass that would make a difference in preventing or stopping hostilities (rather than merely raising consciousness about nonviolent alternatives). It would appear that the most appropriate tasks for those advocating the establishment of an international Shanti Sena are in the realms of peacekeeping limited to escort duties and the like (that is interventionary rather than interpositionary peacekeeping), and especially peacemaking and peacebuilding, while continuing in their efforts to encourage the establishment of local peace brigades and to interest the United Nations in the creation of a truly nonviolent and unarmed peacekeeping force.

The Establishment of United Nations Peacekeeping Forces

After the Second World War many attributed the League of Nations' failure to preserve world peace to its lack of "teeth" in effective enforcement.[1] When the delegates of fifty nations met in San Francisco in mid-1945 to draft a charter for the "general international organization"[2] that was to replace the League, they were determined to rectify this fault. The aim of the United Nations, established on 24 October 1945, was, inter alia, "to save succeeding generations from the scourge of war, which twice in our lifetime has brought untold sorrow to mankind." The signatories to the charter resolved to combine their efforts in ways that included uniting "our strength to maintain international peace and security" and ensuring "by the acceptance of principles and the institution of methods, that armed forces shall not be used, save in the common interest."[3]

Membership in the United Nations was to be open to all "peace-loving states" that accepted and were able and willing to carry out the obligations of the charter. The United Nations was to consist of a General Assembly made up of all the member nations, each with one equal vote. The Assembly was to have power to consider any question related to peace and security and to the promotion of world prosperity and justice with the exception of matters that were being acted upon by the Security Council and the internal affairs of member nations. The Security Council was made up of eleven members,[4] five of them—China, France, the United Kingdom, the United States, and the Soviet Union—permanent members, the others elected by the General Assembly for two years.

The chief administrative officer of the United Nations was to be the secretary-general who had the privilege of approaching the council to place before it matters he considered threatening to peace.

Some of the early protagonists in the move to establish the United Nations, such as U.S. president F. D. Roosevelt, saw the "Big Four" (the United States, Soviet Union, United Kingdom, and France) as the world's "four policemen."

Eventually, the charter that emerged, reflecting this position, gave the Security Council "the means to mobilise forces that the League never had, and gave it the authority to order mandatory use of the resources."[5]

It was hoped that an international force would be established concurrently with the United Nations to help play a major role in the preservation of peace. Such a permanent force, drawn from the armies of the four large powers and under the authority of the Security Council, was considered the only effective way to deter or prevent breaches of the peace. This proposal, called by Frye "unquestionably mankind's most far-reaching blueprint for world collective security,"[6] ran into problems from the outset. Like the United Nations itself, the force was to be founded on great power unity; unity that was soon to dissolve.

Article 47 provided for a Military Staff Committee to be established. The committee, consisting of the chiefs of staff of the permanent members of the Security Council or their representatives, was to "advise and assist" the council and provide over-all "strategic direction" of the force.

On 16 February 1946 the Security Council directed the committee to "examine from the military point of view the provisions contained in Article 43 of the Charter,[7] and to submit the results of the Study and any recommendations to the Council in due course." A little more than six months later the undertaking had ended in total failure. The proposal foundered on disagreements over the size of the force and the proportions and sizes of contributions to be made by Security Council members.[8] The commencement of the cold war ended any hope for the use of great power police. The powers came to regard each other as lawbreakers "rather than as coguarantors of a stable world peace,"[9] dooming the force to nonrealization.[10] Even if the force had been set up, the veto power of the permanent council members (Art. 27[3]) would have left it fatally hamstrung. The veto ensured that charter procedures could not be used against "Great Powers." This provision, Brierly pointed out at the time, made no sense if the only purpose was to deal with small powers when they misbehave because small-power aggression could not be a problem to world peace "if the Great Powers are agreed among themselves, and if they are not, then this machinery cannot be used."[11]

Trygve Lie, the first U.N. Secretary-General, summed up the situation when he remarked that the delegates at San Francisco had created "as strong an organization as all of them could agree upon and as, in their judgement could, in practice, be effective at this stage in the history of the world."[12]

The United Nations was able to raise a force to fight in the Korean War only because of an accident that made the veto power temporarily irrelevant. On 25 June 1950, as the North Koreans crossed the 38th parallel on their push south, the Soviet Union was boycotting the Security Council. The parties could, therefore, be unanimous in their decision. With the failure of the Military Staff Committee not only had no Article 43 forces been assembled but procedures for the creation of such a force in the future had also been destroyed. Nevertheless, a resolution called for member countries to assist the United Nations in the crisis and to refrain from assisting the North Koreans. Two days later (with the Soviets still not present) a second resolution "recommending" that member states assist the South in repelling the attack was passed. Ten hours before this second resolution the United States had already commenced sending its troops to Korea. A third resolution established a unified command and asked member states to provide military forces pursuant to the two earlier resolutions and to "make such forces and other assistance available to the unified command under the United States."[13]

Article 27[3] provided that on matters more than merely procedural not only was the required majority vote essential but that it had to include "the concurring votes of the permanent members." Whether the Korean intervention was legal under this provision is debatable.[14] That question aside, Article 39 appeared to be broad enough to enable the council to recommend such action.[15]

Because under normal circumstances the Korean action could not have taken place,[16] this was an inadequate precedent for international peacekeeping operations. Better arrangements for dealing with future aggression were plainly needed.

On 3 November the United States, the dominant force in the United Nations, saw its "Uniting for Peace" proposal passed.[17] The five opposition votes were from communist states. The resolution sought, in the event force was used, to ensure that it was done in such a way that permanent Security Council members would be excluded from membership in United Nations forces and also to deprive them of their power to control such forces by delegating sweeping authority to the General Assembly. The resolution laid down that if any aggression occurs and a resolution to deal with it fails in the Security Council because of the veto, an emergency session of the General Assembly may be called on twenty-four hours notice by *any* seven members of the council.

The resolution derived its authority from Article 10, which enabled the Assembly to discuss any questions or matters within the scope of the charter, and Article 11, which gave the General Assembly power to "consider the general principles of cooperation in the maintenance of international peace and security" (Art. 11[1]) and the power to "discuss any questions relating to the maintenance of international peace and security" (Art. 11[2]).

The proposal also called for member states to earmark troops for use in U.N. forces.[18] Such forces were to go into action in cases where the contributing country consented and there was a call by the Security Council or, in case of a veto, by the General Assembly. Although it was supported by a majority of states, the scheme foundered on the resistance of national sovereignty, and Article 12, which gave the Security Council precedence over the General Assembly, was not amended to take cognizance of the resolution. Most states (including the United States) placed their faith in regional alliances rather than universal collective security. Neutral states suspected that earmarking troops in the cold war atmosphere could become an exercise in taking sides (only Denmark, Norway, Greece, and Thailand unequivocally offered forces), and there was generally an unwillingness to fight the wars of others and a lack of confidence in the General Assembly.[19]

Various other propositions to organize a permanent U.N. force, for example, the Guard and Legion proposals by Trygve Lie, were mooted in the late 1940s and early 1950s, but by 1952 these efforts had also come to a final dead end.[20] It was not until the advent of another crisis, six years after the Korean intervention, that the United Nations took renewed action on this issue. The 1956 Suez conflict, through the lobbying of the leader of the Canadian delegation to the General Assembly, Lester Pearson, and then concerted effort by Secretary-General Dag Hammarskjöld, led to the emergence of a completely different method of coping with international breaches of the peace[21]—the UNEF, the prototype of United Nations peacekeeping forces.

This did not mean that calls for a standing U.N. army ceased. In 1958 Clark and Sohn, in their *World Peace Through World Law,* proposed a plan for limited world government in the form of a revised version of the U.N. Charter. The proposal included provision for a world police force that would ensure complete disarmament by all nations and deter or suppress any attempted international violence. To them such a force was to be "the only *military* force permitted anywhere in the world after the process of national disarmament has been completed."[22] The force, ultimately to be under the control of the U.N. General Assembly, was to be composed of two components: a standing army and a Peace Force Reserve, composed of individually recruited volunteers. The army's strength was to be 200,000–600,000 men; (their proposals were revised downward in the third edition of their book)[23] and was to be recruited from smaller nations. The reserve force was to be approximately twice the size of the army and was to consist of partly trained individuals, not in organized units but subject to calls to service with the standing army if needed. It was proposed that this world police force be supplied with the most modern equipment and weapons, including nuclear weapons in extraordinary circumstances.

In his *International Military Forces,* published in 1964 (and revised in 1971 as *The Power to Keep Peace*), Lincoln Bloomfield proposed a standby force of twenty-five thousand to be trained at a facility made available by a neutral country. Like Clark and Sohn, Bloomfield stated that an effective international force, that is, a world army, could only come about after general national disarmament and more than likely not before the setting up of a world government.[24] Like the previous authors, he noted that such a force would need ground, sea, air, and space elements and five hundred thousand men, recruited individually and wearing an international uniform. Nuclear monopoly would have to be in the hands of the central authority, and the force would have to be equipped with 50–100 nuclear-tipped land and sea launch ballistic missiles. The fact that the force Bloomfield proposed was only a fraction of this possible ideal demonstrated a shift in thinking brought about by the realization of the ideological consequences of such a world force and the practical and political problems of ever bringing it into existence.

Some people foreshadowed this new thinking quite early in the discussions on U.N. peacekeeping. In 1957 the Carnegie Endowment for International Peace, after the creation of the UNEF, sponsored Frye to write *A UN Peace Force*. Frye put forward the possibility of a small, permanent U.N. force of about seven thousand soldiers, with troops from interested member states serving for periods of six months to two years, stationed in a U.N. base or engaging in peacekeeping operations. Frye was forced to conclude that it would be impractical to keep even such a modest force on a standby basis. Such a force (in 1957 terms) would cost a minimum of U.S.$5,000,000 a year, which was half the entire U.N. budget.[25] The larger "ideal" force proposals would have cost thirty times the entire U.N. budget.

There were additional problems also: Where would such a force be based? Who would provide support? And who would command it?[26] (Hammarskjöld had been given wide discretion in directing the UNEF because of personal confidence in him and because the emergency demanded unusual measures,[27] but such factors could not be permanently guaranteed.) How would U.N. and military field command lines be organized? Could a state support an international force and an alliance such as NATO or the Warsaw Pact at the same time when that could potentially mean viewing an ally as more dangerous than the common enemy?[28] What was to prevent a permanent standby force from becoming an instrument of the status quo, one that was opposed by the middle powers, who could not hope to control it yet desired to move up in the political hierarchy,[29] or opposed by the lesser powers (the most likely peacekeepers) who viewed such a force as a limit on their freedom imposed by the great powers?[30]

Hoffman summed up the two major sets of obstacles that confronted the establishment of a standby permanent force by stating that "the larger powers, because they have a preponderance of military strength, are unlikely to erect any institution capable of interfering with their own conflicting attempts at shaping the world they want. The smaller states, because they do not have enough power to shape their own future, are unlikely to accept any institution that may at worst condemn them even more to the role of pawns and at best remain indifferent to and independent from attempts at resolving fairly their substantive difficulties and disputes; nor, for that matter, are the big powers united enough to impose permanently such a scheme."[31]

Even if such a force could have been established, there was the danger of it leading to a world tyranny preserving an unjust status quo.[32] Because the United States dominated the nascent United Nations, the Soviets had long been suspicious of such a force, which they viewed as an instrument of the capitalists to check national liberation movements in the colonies, to keep smaller countries in line, and to crush progressive forces in their own countries.[33] "All in all," Bloomfield noted by way of summary, "a number of sobering conclusions emerge. First, on the assumption that U.N. peacekeeping will be involved in the future yet will continue to rest on a fragmented political foundation, common sense favours arrangements that do not put the existence of the organization at stake each time such a task must be undertaken. One means of achieving this decoupling lies in procedures enabling the powers to stand aside from a given operation, both physically and financially."[34]

These considerations and concerns, together with the realization that there was not one great enemy (as the framers of the charter seemed to anticipate) and that in the real world the greatest danger came from potentially uncontrolled escalation of local conflicts rather than to victim by aggressor,[35] led Secretary-General Hammarskjöld and his successor U Thant to advise against the establishment of a permanent force.[36] There was always the option of continuing with a system of ad hoc arrangements as was done in 1956.[37]

The political realities of the cold war ensured exclusion of the forces of the United States or the Soviet Union from such contingents. In 1958 Hammarskjöld, setting forth guidelines for U.N. peacekeeping operations, recommended "that they not include units from any of the permanent members of the Security Council; and not include units from any country which because of its geographical position or for other reasons might be considered as possibly having a special interest in the situation which has called for the operation. . . . These two principles . . . should be considered essential to any standby arrangements."[38]

Without a permanent force and without great power involvement the possibility for advanced planning and preparation are limited. Further, the larger the operation, the more costly it becomes and the more likely that financial assistance from the great powers will become necessary. The way to overcome these problems was seen as the earmarking of forces by appropriate nations to serve on an ad hoc basis when the United Nations called upon them. Although the original calls for earmarking forces met with little positive response, other countries have since decided to earmark forces especially for service with the United Nations. This is particularly true of the four Scandinavian/Nordic countries, which have enacted legislation enabling the training of such troops (approximately one thousand per nation) with special emphasis on riot control, communicating, and related skills.[39] This response, however, has not become the norm. United Nations Secretary-General Boutros Boutros-Ghali's renewed call in 1992 for a U.N. standby force[40] has been largely ignored. At least in the foreseeable future, troops will continue to be called together from disparate nations.

Maude Royden's Peace Army

When, in 1910, the last year of his life, William James's article "The Moral Equivalent of War" appeared, it was given wide publicity by pacifists. James believed that warlike qualities were so deeply embedded in human nature that the only hope for peace lay in simulating these warlike qualities in peaceful endeavors.[1] His proposal was in the form of a plan which "called for mankind's surplus energies to be directed, not into destructive pursuits, but into adventurous and idealistic enterprise."[2] James wrote that "as long as antimilitarists propose no substitute for war's disciplinary function, no *moral equivalent* of war . . . so long they fail to realise the full inwardness of the situation. And as a rule they do fail. The duties, penalties and sanctions pictured in the utopias they paint are all too weak and tame to touch the military-minded."[3]

Although James's plan was, perhaps, more about social values than a true harbinger of international peace, it aimed to translate what he saw as biological drives into a positive and constructive force. If, he wrote,

> there were instead of military conscription a conscription of the whole youthful population to form for a certain number of years a part of the army enlisted against *Nature,* the injustice would tend to be evened out, and numerous other goods to the commonwealth would follow. The military ideals of hardihood and discipline would be wrought into the growing fibre of the people. . . . To coal and iron mines, to freight-trains, to fishing fleets in December, to dish-washing, to clothes-washing, and window-washing, to road-building and tunnel-making, to foundries and stoke-holes, and to the frames of sky-scrapers, would our gilded youth be drafted off, according to their choice, to get the childishness knocked out of them, and to come back into society with healthier sympathies and sober ideas. They would have paid their blood-tax, done their own part in the immemorial warfare against nature.[4]

James's contentions about human innate aggressiveness are still being hotly contested,[5] and since James's era people have realized that if they win the fight against nature they could well find themselves on the losing side. Nevertheless, although nowhere did he advocate setting up an actual peace brigade, his ideas did influence the setting up of voluntary peace-camp movements and the type of peacebuilding activities that seem to be the necessary corollary of effective peacekeeping (e.g., Pierre Ceresole's Service Civil International).

In 1928 Walter Lippman, in his essay, "The Political Equivalent of War," brought the debate back to the fundamental issue of peacekeeping. He pointed out the inadequacy of James's analysis and laid a solid basis for Western thinking on nonviolent civilian defense and the concept of peace brigades. Lippman explained:

> It is not sufficient to propose an equivalent for the military virtues. It is even more important to work out an equivalent of the military methods and objectives. For the institution of war is not merely an expression of the military spirit. It is not a mere release of certain subjective impulses clamouring for expression. It is also—and, I think, primarily—one of the ways by which great human decisions are made. If that is true, then the abolition of war depends primarily upon inventing and organising other ways of deciding those issues which hither to have been decided by war.
>
> Any real programme of peace must rest on the premise that there will be causes of dispute as long as we can foresee, and that those disputes have to be decided, and that the way of deciding them must be found which is not war.[6]

The debate, however, was international, and during the late 1920s and early 1930s a new wave of pacifism was also sweeping Britain. The distance from the First World War was enough to allow dispassionate reflection on the waste, and gradually the realization began to dawn that there could be a repeat of such large-scale destruction, in the relatively near future, if action were not taken. Religious groups played a dominant part in this resurgence, and in 1934 the influential Peace Pledge Union carried on the fight against British rearmament and pushed the arguments for pacifism. By the early 1930s Gandhi, in India, had also completed fifteen years of nonviolent struggle against British imperialism. Gandhi's well-publicized Salt March to the seaside village of Dandi with a handful of followers, there to challenge the might of the Empire by contravening the unpopular salt laws, had achieved world sympathy for not only the cause of Indian independence but also for the techniques of nonviolence and their applicability in the political arena. In 1934 the publication of R. B. Gregg's book, *The Power of Non-Violence,* became a further influential popularization of the Mahatma's philosophy in action.

As Gandhi's commitments to nonviolence firmed, he spoke increasingly about nonviolence in times of war. These efforts to explain his philosophy continued during his trips abroad. For example, during a public meeting in Geneva on 10 December 1931, when he was on his way back to India after his attendance at the Second London Round Table Conference to discuss India's future, Gandhi was brutally clear about his vision of civilian defense. He was asked: "How could a disarmed neutral country allow other nations to be destroyed? But for our army which was waiting ready at our frontier during the last war we should have been ruined." Such questions were of central concern to those who opposed rearmament, and the method contained in the answer was soon to be attempted in practice.

Gandhi stated:

> At the risk of being considered a visionary or a fool I must answer this question in the only manner I know. It would be cowardly for a neutral country to allow an army to devastate a neighbouring country. But there are two ways in common between soldiers of war and soldiers of non-violence, and if I had been a citizen of Switzerland and a President of the Federal State, what I would have done would be to refuse passage to the invading army by refusing all supplies. Secondly, by re-enacting a Thermopylae in Switzerland, you would have presented a living wall of men and women and children, and inviting the invaders to walk over your corpses. You may say that such a thing is beyond human experience and endurance. I say that it is not so. . . . Imagine these men and women staying in front of an army requiring a safe passage to another country, the army would be brutal enough to walk over them you might say. I would then say, you will still have done your duty by allowing yourself to be annihilated. An army that dares to pass over the corpses of innocent men and women would not be able to repeat that experiment. You may, if you wish, refuse to believe in such courage on the part of the masses of men and women, but then you would have to admit that non-violence is made of sterner stuff. It was never conceived as a weapon of the weak, but of the stoutest hearts.[7]

During his London visit Gandhi also addressed several gatherings. He spoke with Quakers and attended their silent "prayer" meetings, addressed members of the Fellowship of Reconciliation, and stayed at Kingsley Hall, a settlement house and center of fellowship presided over by his erstwhile Ahmedabad guest Muriel Lester. Gandhi, who had been *Time* magazine's previous "Man of the Year" and who was greeted by a crowd of five thousand people on his Folkestone landing, "had now become such a world figure that he was followed everywhere by reporters and photographers, and reports of his activities appeared in hundreds of publications. . . . Everyone wanted to see him and hear him, and he was available to all."[8]

It can safely be assumed that during this period he was heard by Maude Royden, who had been an acquaintance of Gandhi's since her visit to him in India in 1928.[9] On 23 September Gandhi addressed a Guildhouse meeting chaired by Royden where he explained his mission to England and spoke on voluntary poverty. On 15 October Gandhi addressed a student meeting held at the International Students' Movement House in Russell Square. In answer to a question about the place of the police and the army in a state founded on his philosophy of nonviolence Gandhi replied, "I do not regard it as Utopian to think of a state without an army, but it requires a higher degree of courage and purity." Gandhi claimed that he could "ask people to pit non-violence against hordes of an army."[10]

A few days before the Guildhouse meeting, on 18–19 September, across the world, Japan accused China of blowing up a Manchurian railway line over which it had treaty rights. This Mukden Incident was followed by the Japanese seizure of the city of Mukden and an invasion of Manchuria. Military occupation of the region was completed rapidly, and on 18 February 1932 Japan established the puppet state of Manchukno.

In a Guildhouse sermon, shortly after the Japanese invasion, Royden proclaimed: "I would like now to enrol people who would be ready if war should break out to put their bodies unarmed between the contending forces, in whatever way it be found possible—and there are ways that you do not think of now in which it would be possible."[11]

On 17 October Gandhi again met with Royden,[12] and on 5 December she was one of several who accompanied him from London to Paris. Entries in Gandhi's diary indicate that she traveled with him throughout his continental journey.[13] The contact between the two appears to have been reasonably close—Gandhi refers in his diary to Royden merely as "Maude," and at this time he wrote to his women followers back at his ashram in India about her virtues.[14] Royden, in turn, was to keep Gandhi informed of the developments concerning the "Peace Army" she tried to establish. Although Royden explained in a sermon that the idea of interposing combatants had been around "for many years" and that the Guildhouse members, during the First World War, had "even enrolled a little band of people who have declared themselves willing to put their bodies between the opposing forces if and in what way may be found possible,"[15] it would appear that the strong influence of the Mahatma lay behind this most famous of peace army experiments.[16]

The idea of the Peace Army received little publicity until the last week of February 1932 when, following renewed Japanese aggression, Maude Royden met with the Reverend H. R. L. (Dick) Sheppard and Dr. Herbert Gray and formulated a concrete proposal. The three of them, in Royden's words, "went into retreat for a few days to ask the guidance of God on our actions with regard to the Sino-Japanese War. We longed for the League of Nations to keep its pledged word to nations attacked, but realized that, if this meant the sending of armed forces, we should fall into the old error of combating war by war."[17]

The result of this meeting was their famous letter, which appeared in the London *Daily Express* on 25 February 1932. The letter urged that "men and women who believed it to be their duty should volunteer to place themselves between the combatants. . . . We have written to the League of Nations offering ourselves for service in such a Peace Army." The army, under Sheppard's leadership, was to act as a human barrier between the combatant parties and, thus, end the fighting. Royden explained that what they wanted was "an army of pacifists who should offer themselves to the League of Nations as the 'shock troops' of peace."[18]

The operation of such an army could only come into being when "the circumstances were correct,"[19] and in this case the proposers believed that they were. Royden said: "In modern warfare, the interposition of an unarmed body of civilians of both sexes between two opposing armies will practically always be an impossibility. At that moment it was *not* impossible. China and Japan were fighting across the streets of Shanghai and Shanghai is on the sea. If the League of Nations could have gathered a Peace Army, transported it to Shanghai and landed it on the Bund or quay which was then under international control, we soldiers of peace would have been but a few hundred yards from the battle,"[20] a battle that did not involve guerrilla warfare, airplanes, or a vast front of trenches.[21] According to Royden, few of the critics of the Peace Army scheme (who charged her with preparing for the last, rather than future, wars)[22] realized this:

> The flood of correspondence which followed like a spate on the appearance of our letter in the press showed that most of the writers were hypnotised by the ideas of modern warfare that have been generated by the conduct of the last war. Certainly it might well have been believed that the opportunity for intervention of the kind we supposed could never arise. The fact remained that it had arisen. Chinese and Japanese soldiers were facing each other and firing at each other across the streets of Shanghai, and even a few thousand unarmed volunteers would have been seen, would have been effective, and could, by their acceptance of death without resistance, have stirred the conscience of the human race.[23]

The press generated by the appeal was enormous. Because of the inspirational nature of the call, it gripped the public imagination. Royden claimed that "leading articles appeared in newspapers of countries so widely different as the United States of America and Sierra Leone. Comment, even when sceptical, was friendly. We could not say that the world was ignorant of our offer."[24]

Two days after the publication of the appeal the *Manchester Guardian* summed up feelings about the proposal in a lengthy article entitled "Turning Both Cheeks." The paper noted the practical difficulties involved in bringing the "admittedly extreme" suggestion into reality: "One has to assume an adequate number of men and women with leisure and means to undertake a journey to the Far East; one has to assume that, arriving in China, they would be able to make their way between the Chinese and Japanese trenches, and that they would be suitably equipped to stay long enough in their precarious situation to make the cessation of hostilities that their presence brought about more than just a temporary lull."

The paper, however, also endorsed the idea:

> At the same time the suggestion is well worth considering, since it is seriously made by people whose good faith is beyond doubt and who have every intention of attempting to put it to the test of practice. And if on the surface it appears fantastic, is it really any more fantastic than the actual fact of war? Is it really any more fantastic for a number of civilised individuals to bear testimony to their belief in peace by risking their lives than for the same individuals to take up arms and devote themselves to slaughtering other individuals for any of the reasons commonly put forward in justification of war.[25]

But the Peace Army was never put to the test. Royden, Sheppard, and Gray sent their letter to Sir Eric Drummond, the secretary-general of the League of Nations, with the entreaty that he should not regard the plan as "fantastic." Drummond replied that he did not at all consider the idea as fantastic[26] but regretted that it was not in his constitutional power to bring the proposal before the League's Assembly. By way of consolation he, at least tacitly, encouraged them to try to bring the proposal before the Assembly, which was at that time in session, through the formal demand of one of the member states, and released the letter to the representatives of the world's press, ensuring international publicity.[27]

In her correspondence with Gandhi, Royden included copies of her exchanges with Drummond and sought the Mahatma's blessing for the project, which relegated the India question to the background because of the extreme urgency of the China/Japan situation. Gandhi approved the action, stating, "I . . . felt that you were quite right in concentrating your energy over a situation that threatened to involve bloodshed on a vast scale and that too by the adoption of the method of satyagraha."[28]

Meanwhile, volunteers enrolled for service in the Peace Army. The first was retired Irish Brigadier-General Frank Crozier, the second an engineer, and the third a Chinese Christian.[29] However, even with the worldwide publicity, barely one thousand recruits enlisted in the "army."[30] The organizers approached Sir John Simon, secretary of state for foreign affairs and head of the British delegation to the League, and the leaders of several governments represented at the Assembly with their plan, but with so few recruits "could not expect the League to take us seriously,"[31] and they received only "courteous refusals or silence."[32]

Royden later lamented, "Perhaps we should have sought to go alone. Perhaps three pacifists being killed in manner so much in the spirit of Mahatma Gandhi might have worked a miracle."[33] That, however, was not the initial plan, and an operation on the scale they envisaged was impossible to undertake on a voluntary basis. Government support was necessary for ships and finance. Without government help the plan faded. "While we were writing to Prime Ministers and Foreign Secretaries and awaiting replies," Royden recalled, "the opportunity was lost. Fighting spread over a vast front. Our project became impracticable." And she added, "It seems in the highest degree unlikely that it will ever be practicable again."[34]

Barely one month after the first flurry of excitement over the Peace Army proposal in the press, Sir John Simon, answering a question in the House of Commons regarding the reply sent to Royden et al., stated that "since there are good grounds for hoping that active hostilities are now at an end, the conditions which inspired the gallant and humanitarian offer of Miss Royden and her co-signatories will not again arise."[35]

Nevertheless, it was decided "that a permanent Peace Army should be built up for future emergencies, and for constructive peace work." The country was divided into districts and subdivided into groups where there were to be active units. The army was organized into two sections: one composed of the interposing "shock troops" and the other of war resisters who would be willing "to render constructive peace service wherever it may be required, or if not able to go themselves to help in sending others." Howard Brinton was appointed honorary international secretary and contact was attempted "with people in a number of different countries, and it is hoped that Peace Armies may eventually be established all over the world."[36]

Little, however, came of the plans in the sense of action. According to Sheppard's biographer, part of the reason the peace army idea got no further was that

Sheppard's long struggle with chronic debilitating asthma worsened in March; he came down with pleurisy and had two heart attacks.[37] Maude Royden, however, insisted that Sheppard, the "commander-in-chief," had decided to disband "the little army" because "as always he faced the facts. The opportunity had been unique but it had passed. . . . It was held better not to maintain an organisation which in these circumstances had come to seem to its leader a meaningless gesture."[38]

Periodically over the next few years there were attempts to revive the Peace Army; however, more often than not it existed only on paper or "languished as little more than a religious discussion group; earnest but negligible."[39] Eventually, a reconstituted army did see action but on such a minute scale, and in such a way, that it bore little resemblance to its original strategy. During the late 1930s some Peace Army workers lived "among Arabs and Jews in Upper Galilee and in Jerusalem, offering practical service and an attempt to understand and to promote reconciliation." A village clinic was set up and relief work undertaken. Constructive efforts in agriculture and afforestation were commenced by members in India, and in 1938 a Pacifist Service Corps was formed "to provide training and opportunity for pacifists who wished to relieve suffering but did not feel able to join Government schemes."[40] The tasks of interposition had been too great for the Peace Army, and so emphasis shifted to its second aim of peacemaking and peacebuilding.[41] Members journeyed to Palestine to undertake reconciliation work;[42] however, the 1938 effort ended in tragedy when one of the two team members, Hugh Bingham, was shot and fatally wounded.[43]

Brinton, a pacifist member of the League of Nations Union, the largest and most influential peace society in Britain after the mid-1920s,[44] produced a small book, entitled *The Peace Army*, which anticipated the Royden/Sheppard/Gray proposal in its writing but was published some months thereafter.

Brinton's book, which purports to chart the likely outcomes of intervention by peace army buffer forces, looks extremely naïve with the hindsight of more than half a century, yet it reflected the hope and belief of many pacifists in the 1930s. Brinton claimed that because hostilities do not arise in a day, "there would be ample time for preparations."[45] Before any hostilities broke out it would be announced that the Peace Army was being sent in as a precautionary measure. If the landing were opposed by force, "there would be undoubtedly an awful slaughter. But that would probably be the end of the war. The knowledge of having killed thousands of men who had made no effort to defend themselves and who were only seeking to preserve their destroyers from war and destruction would be such a ghastly sight on the conscience of any nation that it seems incredible to believe that all the innate feelings of decency of the people would not arise in revolt and lead to such a reaction against war that it would vanish forever."[46]

After an unopposed landing, "the situation would be more complex and the result a little more difficult to foresee."[47] If the Peace Army could become a buffer force between the protagonists before the outbreak of fighting, the opposing parties would have to come to some mutual agreement about what to do with this force. "The result would be protracted negotiations which would probably be fatal to the ambition of the war parties in both countries. Attention would be drawn away from the feelings of righteous hate which had been worked up, once such sentiments are allowed to die down, a war would be impossible."[48]

If fighting were to start with the Peace Army between the combatants, "it would be impossible to carry on an organized war." The problem of what to do with the unarmed force, which the combatants had not been taught to hate would lead to such chaos that "the organisation of hostilities would be bound to break down, and again delay would occur, which would probably be final."[49]

Brinton's picture of hostilities involving an unarmed buffer force may mirror Gandhi's own vision based on the fundamental goodness of humankind. It, however, was envisaged in a more innocent time, one that preceded extermination camps and the acceptance of the annihilation of civilian populations where such is considered necessary for national security. This vision was also short on logistical details; Brinton saw the Peace Army as British equipped and organized, but the reception of Royden's proposal demonstrated the lack of willingness on the part of national governments to become involved in such schemes and the practical impossibility of voluntary organizations doing so. His way of accounting for modern weapons of mass destruction in his scheme is positively Utopian. He notes that as deadly as the weapons of land warfare are, they are relatively insignificant when compared to the horrors of the airplane, and a Peace Army can do nothing to prevent air attacks (or counter the parachute dropping of troops, for that matter). Brinton was still hoping that international agreements would outlaw the use of air fleets.[50]

Brinton's efforts notwithstanding, the idea of a Peace Army gradually petered out with the approach of the Second World War, and it was not until 1960 that the idea was seriously revived in the Madariaga / Narayan proposal.

Report of the Meeting to Establish a Shanti Sena at Wardha, March 1950

About seventy-five constructive workers of different national institutions of Wardha and Sevagram met in the local Mahila Ashram on the 19th and 24th March under the presidentship of Acharya Vinoba Bhave to discuss the nature and organization of a Shanti Sena (Peace Army) which could be started in Wardha on the lines suggested by Gandhiji in his articles in *Harijan* published several years ago. Among those who attended the meetings were Acharya Kakasaheb Kalelkar, Prof. J. C. Kumarappa, Shri Shrikrishnadas Jaju, Shri Annasaheb Dastane, Shri G. Ramachandran and Shri Kanu Gandhi.

As a result of these two meetings, it was decided to start three Shanti Sena units, one in Sevagram and two in Wardha. A Joint Committee was appointed to coordinate the activities of the three units and to prepare a suitable Constitution for the Shanti Sena. It is gratifying to know that Acharya Kakasaheb Kalelkar, Prof. Kumarappa and Shri Jaju gladly enlisted their names in the Shanti Sena.

The Constitution of the Shanti Sena, as approved by the Joint Committee, is as under:

Aim

To organize collective non-violence in order to check violence in different spheres of life.

Membership

A person who believes in truth and non-violence and who is prepared to make the supreme sacrifice without malice in facing violence can be a member of the Shanti Sena (Peace Army). The membership of the Army is open to men and women, young and old. In the beginning only persons above 18 will be admitted.

Uniform

The members of the Army will be habitual wearers of *khadi*. They shall also have a badge for easy recognition.

Training

1. Physical: Exercises, drill, and regular productive labour
2. Intellectual: Serious study, according to age, of Mahatma Gandhi's ideology, brief history of modern economics and political ideologies etc. This training will be given through study circles, books and lectures.
3. Field Service: The study and practice of first-aid methods in times of communal riots, fires, floods and epidemics.
4. The study and practice of peaceful arrangements at the time of meetings, conferences and fairs.
5. Other services in emergencies.

Programme

1. The members of the Army will do at least once a week collective service of the community such as assistance to the displaced persons, service of the depressed class, every kind of sanitation, village service etc.
2. To organize collective spinning and prayers in order to create an atmosphere of peace and brotherhood.
3. To try to remove economic inequality.
4. To assist and act in times of fire, floods, labour strikes, communal riots etc.
5. To try to check corruption, black-marketing and drinking habit in order to raise the moral standard of the public.
6. Other activities relating to the constructive programme.

Organization

1. The Peace Army will keep aloof from all political parties.
2. There will be no place for secrecy in the organization of the Peace Army.
3. In the organization of the Peace Army, quality and not quantity will be emphasised. Importance will be given to character and spirit of service among the members. In this connection the eleven vows of the Ashram will have a special place.[1]
4. The members of the Army will keep maximum contact with the people of their village or locality.
5. The organization of the Army shall be decentralized. Peace Army units can be established in each village or locality of a town; but a Joint Committee could be established for mutual co-operation.
6. It will be essential to observe perfect discipline in the Peace Army.

Wardha, 6–4–'50
S. N. Agarwal[2]

The Shanti Sena Pledges

On 23 August 1957, the last day of Vinoba Bhave's Bhoodan padayatra through the state of Kerala, eight prominent Keralan Sarvodaya workers (K. Kelappan, E. Ekkanda Warriar, S. Janardan Pillai, I. K. Kumaran, A. K. Rajamma, Diwakaran Kartha, S. Govindan, and Damodaran Nayar) pledged to lay down their lives for the maintenance of peace through nonviolence in his presence, becoming the first Shanti Sainiks.[1] After making the pledge they read the following statement:

It is now ten years since India became independent, but so far we have not been able to realise Gandhiji's dream of *gram-swaraj,* village independence. There is nothing to be seen of it either in the daily constructive work carried on by Gandhiji's associates. At such a time the bhoodan movement has burst like a ray of sunlight through the all enveloping darkness. After six years of work bhoodan has made possible the auspicious programme of *gram-dan.* The more progress we make in *gram-dan* activities, the clearer becomes the picture of gram-swaraj. Today village government is no longer an empty dream; it can be demonstrated and experienced in the real world.

Today, throughout the world, society is being run into the mould of centralised government. Within that mould the full and un-hampered development of the individual is not possible. There is an all-pervading, and increasing, violence and exploitation. Some arresting, effective action has to be organised from a completely new point of view in order to liberate the individual and society, and to establish a non-violent social order on the basis of *gramdan.* Such a non-violent, non-exploiting society cannot be set up by means of constituent assemblies or governments; it can only be brought about by the people themselves.

The State and the present social order are founded upon three things: (i) the consent of the people obtained through the ballot box, which is the basis of the political strength of the State, (ii) the taxes paid by the people, which replenish the State coffers, and (iii) the army, which is the symbol of the State's power to preserve law and order by punishing the law-breaker. For the establishment of a sarvodaya order of society, non-violent equivalents have to be found for these three things. In the place of a passive vote there must be active *sampatti-dan;* and in the place of taxes there must be gifts of wealth and land; and in the place of the police and armed forces there must be a Peace Army. This experiment must be tried at once, at least in a few selected places. We must demonstrate that the power to render the people powerless is not essential for the maintenance of peace in society and that a moral popular authority cannot be set up on this basis. We must make it possible to abolish the police and the army. This is the only way to realise the dream of our great thinkers, that is to put into practice the idea of a non-violent *sarvodaya samaj.*

We are resolved to organise such a Peace Army, whose members will be ready to give their lives for the service of this ideal. The Shanti Sainiks must accept the pledge which has been drawn up for all Lok Sevaks, they must be ready to obey the orders of the Sarvodaya Mandal in respect to the Peace Army, and to face any situation in a disciplined manner. The following five pledges must be observed:

1. To observe truth, non-violence and non-possessiveness to the utmost of one's ability.
2. *Nikshan Seva,* disinterested service without desire for results.
3. Avoidance of all party politics and power politics, while endeavouring to win the utmost possible cooperation from every individual, regardless of his party affiliation.
4. Not to recognize distinctions of class or caste, and to respect all religions equally.
5. To give one's whole thought, and as much time as possible, to the Bhoo-dan movement.

Lok Sevaks are bound by these principles. The members of the Peace Army will work as Lok Sevaks in normal times and as Peace Soldiers in an emergency.

We are confident that a sarvodaya social order can be brought into being in India by the efforts of this Peace Army. This is a glorious aim, worthy to inspire every Indian. We consider ourselves fortunate to be privileged to organise this army under the inspiring guidance of Vinobaji. We appeal to our countrymen to join us in this great and sacred endeavour and we hereby offer ourselves for the task.[2]

As Vinoba expanded the idea of the Shanti Sena, the Sarva Seva Sangh began to associate with the fledgling organization. In 1958 the first committee to oversee the work of the Sena was established under the leadership of women workers headed by Marjorie Sykes. During the following year Vinoba announced the forma-

tion of the Akhil Bharat Shanti Sena Mandal with Ashadevi Aryanayakam as convener.[3] Membership of the Sena was only open to full-time Gandhian workers
who had undertaken to abide by the fivefold Lok Sevak pledge and the additional
requirement that they would be willing to go where they might be sent by the Sena
and if need be give their lives in the service of peace. The formal Lok Sevak/Shanti
Sena Pledge read:

> 1. I believe in the principles of truth, non-violence, non-possessiveness,
> bodily labour, and self-control. I will try to conduct my life on these
> principles.
> 2. I believe that the world can only know true peace when the common
> people are in direct control of their own affairs. I will, therefore, not
> take any part in party politics, but will do my best to get members of
> all political parties to help me in my work.
> 3. I will devote my whole mind to dis-interested service of the people.
> 4. I will give no place in my life to any spirit of exclusiveness in matters
> of caste, class or religion.
> 5. I will give my whole time and my best thought to the work of the
> non-violent revolution of Sarvodaya, with its practical programmes of
> *Bhoodan-yajna* and village industry.
> 6. Whenever and wherever I may be ordered to go for the work of the
> Shanti Sena, I shall be prepared to go, and also, should need arise, to
> give my life in this service.[4]

In early 1962 the discussions of the Prabhand Samiti of the Sarva Seva Sangh
focused to a large degree on the need to reorganize the Shanti Sena Mandal. It was
decided that rather than having a restricted membership the Sena should be open to
all who wished to take part. The distinction between Shanti Sahayaks and Shanti
Sainiks was to be removed. A new pledge form was tabled for discussion at the
Patna meeting on 7 April 1962. Besides reaffirming a faith in truth and nonviolence,
the proposed pledge included clauses affirming a willingness to work for peace in
the sainik's immediate surroundings and clauses restating the avoidance of involvement in party politics and of recognition of caste, class, and religious differences.
Again, the potential sainiks were to pledge willingness to lay down their lives in the
service of the Sena, but in order to make membership possible for non-full-time
Gandhian workers the clause stating readiness to do peace work in distant areas was
made optional.

At a full Sangh meeting two days later, the following revised pledge was
adopted:

> 1. I believe in the principles of truth, non-violence, non-possessiveness,
> bodily labour, and self-control. I will try to conduct my life on these
> principles.
> 2. I believe that the world can only know true peace when the common
> people are in direct control of their own affairs. I will, therefore, not
> take any part in party politics, but will do my best to get members of
> all political parties to help me in my work.

3. I will give no place in my life to any spirit of exclusiveness in matters of caste, class or religion.
4. I will consider myself responsible for the maintenance of peace in my social surroundings and will be ever prepared to work for the maintenance of peace through nonviolent means.
And in addition
5. If there is need for peace work outside my area I will be ready to go. Those who are not prepared to work outside their own area may delete this last addition and elect to remain in their own area.

With the reorganization of the Shanti Sena in mid-1962 under the presidentship of Jayaprakash Narayan, with Narayan Desai as Secretary, the pledge once again came under review. At the Madurai Prabhand Samiti meeting on 1 September, Desai reported on the version of the pledge that was accepted by the Akhil Bharat Shanti Sena Mandal at its Bombay meeting three weeks earlier. Reflecting JP's antiwar activist background and recognizing the danger of war in the world after the Cuban missile crisis, emphasis was given to war resistance as well as truth and nonviolence. The pledge was constructed in a way that, without going into deep-seated controversies, would allow the maximum number to enrol themselves as sainiks. While the pledge was simplified, care was taken to ensure that the immediate and ultimate goals of the Sena remained clear. After discussion, the following pledge, opening membership to any citizen of India above the age of eighteen years, was proposed:

I BELIEVE
1. in the establishment of a new society based on truth and non-violence;
2. that all conflicts in society can and should be solved, more so in this atomic age than ever before, by non-violent means;
3. in the fundamental unity of man;
4. that war is a crime against humanity and is a denial of a non-violent way of life

Therefore, I hereby PLEDGE that I SHALL—
1. not commit any sort of violence;
2. work for peace and be prepared, if need be, to lay down my life for it;
3. do my best to rise above the distinctions of caste, sect, colour and party because they deny the unity of man;
4. not to take part in any war and shall oppose war with all my strength;
5. help in creating the means and conditions of non-violent defence;
6. devote regularly a part of my time to the service of my fellowmen;
7. accept the discipline of the *Shanti Sena*.

A short time later, the pledge was reconsidered in view of the Indo-Chinese conflict. At the Prabhand Samiti meeting, held in Pipla on 10 November, clause one of the pledge was omitted and the section of clause four dealing with active opposi-

tion to war was deleted. By the time the pledge was finally ratified by the full Sarva
Seva Sangh meeting at Vedchhi on 12 December, clause four of the preamble had
also lost its forceful condemnation of war. With a militaristic fever sweeping the
country, and the Gandhians openly arguing about the correct attitude in a situation
where nationalism seemed to be in direct conflict with nonviolence, the final accepted pledge stated:

(Membership of the *Shanti Sena* is open to any citizen of India above 18
years of age who is prepared to take the following pledge.)

I BELIEVE
1. in the establishment of a new society based on truth and non-violence;
2. that all conflicts in society can and should be solved, more so in this
atomic age than ever before, by non-violent means;
3. in the fundamental unity of man;
4. that war blocks all human progress and is a denial of a non-violent
way of life.

Therefore, I hereby PLEDGE that I SHALL—
1. work for peace and be prepared, if need be, to lay down my life for
it;
2. do my best to rise above the distinctions of caste, sect, colour and
party because they deny the unity of man;
3. not to take part in any war;
4. help in creating the means and conditions of non-violent defence;
5. devote regularly a part of my time to the service of my fellowmen;
6. accept the discipline of the *Shanti Sena*.[5]

At the joint Sarva Seva Sangh and Shanti Sena Mandal meeting held at Kurukshetra in April 1973, it was noted that the main difference in the pledges of the Lok
Sevak and the Shanti Sainik was that the Lok Sevak was not to be a political party
member, whereas the Shanti Sainik pledge contained no such restriction. Anyone
who was willing to sacrifice him or herself for the ideal of peace could become a
sainik, but this was not qualification enough to be a full-time Gandhian Lok Sevak.
The Sevaks had to dedicate themselves to working to bring about a new type of
society based on Gandhian values. It was agreed that the pledges should remain
different.
    During the heady days of the 1970s a clause in which sainiks declared that
they would resist injustice, exploitation, and corruption was added to the pledge
form. Any citizen above the age of eighteen years who had attended a training camp
and signed the following pledge was eligible to become a Shanti Sainik:

Declaration:
a. A new society based on truth and non-violence should be formed.
b. All conflicts in the society should be settled through non-violent
means.

c. Human beings are basically one.

d. War is an obstacle in the development of humanity.

I promise that:

a. I shall devote my time for the formation of a non-violent society.

b. In the event of disturbance, I would engage myself in the task of peace-making even endangering my life.

c. I shall be always ready to give a non-violent resistance to the prevailing injustice, exploitation and corruption in the society.

d. I shall not accept the differences of caste, colour, community etc, which divide human beings.

e. I shall keep myself aloof from power and party-politics, social evils and superstitions.

f. I shall not support any fighting.

g. I shall abide by the discipline of the Shanti Sena.

The "Identity" page, containing the personal details of the applicant, that was to accompany the signed pledge and annual Re.1 membership fee, included a question about whether the sainik was "ready to go anywhere at any time if needed?"[6]

Following JP Narayan's Bihar Movement and Total Revolution campaign, the Gandhian movement split so fundamentally that it has still not recovered more than fifteen years later. In 1974 the activities of the Sarva Seva Sangh were "frozen" and as a consequence, for all intents and purposes, the Shanti Sena ceased to exist. In January 1980, without consulting the Sangh, Vinoba set up his own Shanti Sena, the Bharatiya Shanti Sena. Those who joined Vinoba's Sena pledged:

1. To have faith in truth and non-violence.

2. To have a fearless, maliceless and non-party attitude.

3. To equally treat all countries, creeds, races, castes and languages.

4. To take no part in power politics and party politics, including a determination not to vote in elections.

5. To hold no justification for war.

6. To be prepared to risk life in quelling disturbances and commotions, and

7. To observe the discipline prescribed by the Shanti Sena.[7]

Significantly, this pledge removed the clause relating to fighting injustice and so forth. (Vinoba asked who was competent to decide if another was unjust, corrupt, or exploiting),[8] and added one specifically prohibiting voting. These changes were not acceptable to the Sarva Seva Sangh leadership. Rather than face the spectacle of two rival Shanti Senas, however, the Sangh officially decided to leave its Sena dormant. Gradually, all the energies of the Bharatiya Shanti Sena were put into cow protection work. In the face of growing communal violence, in 1985 the Sarva Seva Sangh again reactivated the All-India Shanti Sena under the leadership of Acharya Ramamurti.

The new pledge stated:

1. I will work to bring about a newly constructed society which will be based on truth and nonviolence.
2. I will engage in peace work in the face of danger in times of upheaval.
3. I will immediately commence work against injustice, exploitation and corruption through nonviolent means.
4. I will not accept any differences between castes, classes, creeds, communities or the sexes.
5. I will obey the discipline of the Shanti Sena and according to the direction of the leader of the Shanti Sena I will immediately be ready to work anywhere in the district, state or nation.[9]

At the Bhopal meeting of the Sangh's Prabhand Samiti, 15–17 December 1987, after decisions taken at the newly formed National Convener Committee, to the third clause of the pledge the word *inequality* was added.[10]

Guide Lines for Shanti Sainiks in Times of Emergency

Narayan Desai

Shanti Sainiks have two jobs to do. In normal times, they contact people, render them whatever service they can and thereby spread the thought and ideals of Shanti Sena. In emergency, when peace is disrupted, they concentrate on restoring peace and mormalcy.

If there are Shanti Sainiks everywhere to serve the people disinterestedly, they can anticipate possible dangers to peace and can control the situation before it erupts. However, Shanti Sainiks are not yet spread all over the country. So a few guidelines are given below to meet emergencies.

What do we do when violence breaks out?
It has been found that generally tension prevails in an area where violence breaks out later. The Shanti Sainiks must try to remove tensions in order to prevent riots, but if this seems to be beyond their capacity, they are advised to take the following steps:
1. The Shanti Sainiks of the area should meet and discuss the situation.
2. This meeting should, as a rule, be called by the Convenor of the City Shanti Sena Samiti but, in his absence, or if he is not yet elected, or for some reason is inactive, an emergent [*sic*] meeting may be called by any other Shanti Sainik.
3. At this meeting, an immediate programme of action should be drawn up which should be communicated to the Convenor of the State Shanti Sena Mandal by telephone or telegram.
4. If necessary, requisition may be made to the State Convenor to send contingents of Shanti Sainiks from other areas.
5. Leading citizens of the city should be contacted and apprised of the situation. An appeal for peace should be issued under their signatures. Efforts should also be made to get the appeal published in the newspapers, and broadcast on the radio.

6. Efforts should be made to contact the leaders and followers of parties to the dispute.

7. Press clippings and copies of periodicals and journals containing details of the incidents should be collected to facilitate proper study and impartial reporting.

As soon as there is a riot:

No sooner the report of a violent incident reaches the Shanti Sainik, they should do the following:

1. They should reach locale of the disturbance.

2. They should give a short but unalloyed first-hand report to other Shanti Sainiks.

3. All the Shanti Sainiks should gather at a meeting and decide on an immediate programme of action.

4. They should apprise the State Shanti Sena Samiti of the situation, briefing on their programme of action, and if the situation demands, ask for the help of Shanti Sainiks from other areas.

5. They should keep in mind the following points, while working in a violent situation: (i) Let them not commit the mistake of spreading rumours, but try to dispel all rumours and counteract them by disseminating the truth. (ii) They should, if necessary, publish pamphlets for this purpose. (iii) Leaders of the parties to the dispute should be contacted immediately. (iv) Duties should be so assigned that those Shanti Sainiks, who are already well-known to the area for their service, are able to discuss matters dispassionately and intelligently and make on-the-spot decisions as the situation demands. (v) Shanti Sainiks should be posted to actual spots of violence where, even at the risk of their lives, they should carry on rescue operations while violence goes on unabated. Shanti Sainiks should be so selected that they are willing to show such courage, but in such cases, they must not be sent alone. (vi) If the situation permits, a peace procession should be organised in which citizens of the locality should be asked to participate.

Immediately after:

1. Shanti Sainiks should make it a point to take the injured persons to hospitals, or to see them there. They should also contact the families of the injured.

2. If there is any clear Sarvodaya viewpoint on the issue on which violence is alleged to have taken place, this should be explained by Shanti Sainiks. If not, they should desist from raising a controversy and keep quiet. They should only stress that no problem can be solved by violence and that peaceful methods should be adopted for its solution.

3. Talking to people and discussing with them may be useful. Much depends on how we talk. Under no circumstances should the Shanti Sainiks forget their humility and balance. They should not expose any weakness, uncertainty, ambivalence or fear. If one is afraid of this, he should rather not talk and should carry on his duties in silence.

4. The Shanti Sainiks of the city should meet at least once a day, discuss about the work and the situation, and plan the strategy of future work.

5. The Shanti Sainiks working in a city should elect a leader to deal with the circumstances and follow his instructions on immediate issues. If there is any difference of opinion, that should be ironed out later, when they meet for the day or the

following day. In no case, should they raise an open controversy on their own differences of opinion.

6. Whenever necessary, they should supply correct information about the incidents to the police, fire brigade, etc.

How to deal with the police and curfew:

In riot situations, the Shanti Sainiks naturally come in contact with the police, army personnel etc. In dealing with them, they should keep in mind the following points:

1. All the Shanti Sainiks should not try to meet and discuss with the chief police officer. This should be done only by their leader or representative. Others would rather avoid discussions with officers and police staff. If they are, however, drawn into a discussion, they should do it with utmost humility.

2. To obtain a curfew pass, they should establish contact with the President of the Akhil Bharat Shanti Sena Mandal or the Union Home Department. The State Convenor may also try to get it from local officers, if possible. There should not be separate demands from individual Shanti Sainiks for this.

3. The Shanti Sainiks should be in their simple dress, with the Shanti Sena badge and yellow band and carry their identity cards signed by the State Convenor.

4. The City Shanti Sena Samiti should have a map of the city. The strategy to be adopted for work in the disturbed area should be explained to the Shanti Sainiks with the help of the map. This will give a complete picture of the strategic points and bring home to them the extent of energy to be put in.

Shanti Sainiks from outside

1. Generally the call for Shanti Sainiks from outside is to be given by the State Convenor. They should be intimated when they should meet in the affected area.

2. They should note the full address of the local Shanti Sena Samiti and participate in the programme drawn up by it, instead of taking up any work independently.

3. They should work under the auspices of the local Samiti and follow the instructions laid down by the local leader.

4. In any case the Shanti Sainiks from outside are not aware of the existence of the local Shanti Sena Samiti, they should contact the local Sarvodaya Mandal, Sarvodaya workers, workers of the Gandhi Peace Foundation, or of Khadi Bhandars.

5. Shanti Sainiks should not go to a place unknown to them and without being called there.

Absence of Shanti Sainiks

1. When peace work is in operation, no Shanti Sainik or Sevak of the city should keep away from it.

2. Those unable to participate in the programme for some unavoidable reasons should inform in writing to the Convenor.

3. Those out of station at the time of riots should try to come back as soon as possible.

Time Schedule

In a disturbed situation, when peace work is in operation, there is no scope for individual scheduling of time and programme for Shanti Sainiks. The programme and time schedule for the day should be fixed at a meeting attended by all Shanti Sainiks and assignment of duties should also be made there, so that they are able to join their duties on time. No irregularity in this by any Shanti Sainik should be entertained.

Shanti Sena Office
The head-office of the Akhil Bharat Shanti Sena Mandal is at Rajghat, Varanasi. There are State offices almost in all States. In places where protracted work is needed, even after the quelling of riots, local offices should be set up. This office should have, besides necessary office equipment, the following things:
1. A map of the affected city;
2. A list of Shanti Sainiks and Sevaks with full address, telephone number, if any, and telegraphic address;
3. A log-book of assignments to Shanti Sainiks to be maintained daily;
4. A register containing information of absence of the Shanti Sainiks; and
5. Information about relief work, if any.

(Issued by Shri Narayan Desai, General Secretary, Akhil Bharat Shanti Sena Mandal, Varanasi).[1]

Notes

Introduction

1. See G. Myrdal, *Asian Drama: An Inquiry into the Poverty of Nations* (Harmondsworth, England: Penguin, 1968), 895–900.

2. See J. Galtung and H. Hveem, "Participants in Peacekeeping Forces," in *Essays in Peace Research,* ed. J. Galtung (Copenhagen: Christian Ejlers, 1976), vol. 2, *War, Peace and Defence,* 264–81, at p. 264.

3. In a 1994 article Wallis points out that the many new international initiatives in nonviolent intervention in war situations seem to be based on the confidence that such forms of action constitute "an idea whose time has come." Wallis, T., "Intervention from Within," *Peace News,* Jan. 1994, 10.

4. All societies have established mechanisms to maintain social control, and in modern states this control is vested in governments. By definition, states have the ability to exercise, if necessary, coercive power to maintain "peace" within their boundaries. In fact, without this ability the prevailing concept of statehood is rendered meaningless.

5. A possible exception is the "Gulf Peace Team," which placed a group of peace protesters in a desert camp in Iraq between the hostile armies during the Gulf War of January 1991. Considering the numbers involved, the vaguely worded objective ("to withstand non-violently any armed aggression by any party") appeared to be limited in practice merely to bearing silent witness to the hostilities and possibly suffering the fate of the Non-Violent Action in Vietnam initiative. Given the rapid turn of events in the Gulf, it is, perhaps, not surprising that the founding statements of the Team appear to have been drafted in a hurry and that they failed to locate the Team's effort within the historical context of such attempts. Without mentioning Gandhi, Gulf Peace Team publicity emphasized the concept of nonviolence. The same appears to be the case for the more recent Bosnian Mir Sada attempt.

1. Mainstream Peacekeeping

1. M. Harbottle, ed., *Peacekeeper's Handbook* (New York: International Peace Academy, 1978), III/4. This definition had actually been formulated some years earlier by International Peace Academy members; see I. Rikhye, M. Harbottle, and B. Egge, *The Thin Blue Line: International Peacekeeping and Its Future* (New Haven, Conn.: Yale Univ. Press, 1974), 11.

2. In fact, Peter Calvocoressi claims that the idea of international organization is itself a European idea and that Europe has been almost alone in pioneering attempts "to come to grips with the problems of international order and peace in a world divided into competitive and frequently hostile sovereignties." P. Calvocoressi, *A Time for Peace: Pacifism, Internationalism and Protest Forces in the Reduction of War* (London: Hutchinson 1987), 168–69.

3. For a brief history of these proposals and efforts to implement them, see, generally, S. J. Hemleben, *Plans for World Peace Through Six Centuries* (Chicago: Univ. of Chicago Press, 1943); J. A. R. Marriot, *Commonwealth or Anarchy? A Survey of Projects of Peace from the Sixteenth to the Twentieth Century* (London: Oxford Univ. Press, 1939); and A. C. F. Beales, *The History of Peace: A Short Account of the Organised Movement for International Peace* (London: Bell, 1931).

4. For a brief history of the efforts that culminated in the establishment of United Nations peacekeeping forces see app. A.

5. The United States proposal, adopted at the height of the Korean hostilities, limited the role of Security Council members in U.N. peacekeeping forces and allowed the General Assembly to bypass a council veto during times of crisis. See app. A.

6. UNGA 997(ES-1). For the various resolutions and commentaries see R. Higgins, *United Nations Peacekeeping 1946–1967: Documents and Commentary* (London: Oxford Univ. Press, 1969), vol. 1, *The Middle East,* 221–529.

7. UNGA 998(ES-1).

8. UNGA 1001(ES-1). Because the charter made no provision for such forces, there has been some confusion about which article was to provide the legal basis for peacekeeping operations. In relation to the United Nations Emergency Force (UNEF) see D. W. Greig, *International Law* (London: Butterworths, 1970), 576–82; and D. W. Bowett, *United Nations Forces: A Legal Study of United Nations Practice* (London: Stevens and Sons, 1964), 93–99.

9. A. James, *The Politics of Peacekeeping* (London: Chatto and Windus, 1960), 3.

10. C. C. Walker, "Peacekeeping: A Survey and an Evaluation," Appendix to L. P. Bloomfield, *The Power to Keep Peace: Today and in a World Without War* (Berkeley, Calif.: World Without War Council, 1971), 228–43, at p. 228; C. C. Walker, *Peacekeeping: 1969—A Survey and an Evaluation* (prepared for the American Friends Peace Committee, 1969), 2; and G. Evans, *Cooperating for Peace: The Global Agenda for the 1990s and Beyond* (St. Leonards, Australia: Allen and Unwin, 1993), 101–2.

11. For details of the establishment of the U.N. force that went into action in Korea and the legal ambiguity and political repercussions that surrounded the move, see app. A. Although recent developments have again encompassed peace enforcement, it is too early yet to claim that such actions can become anything approaching the norm.

12. S. Bidwell, "The Theory and Practice of Peacekeeping," *International Affairs* 54, no. 4 (1978): 635–39, at p. 639.

13. See Greig, 566–72; and Bowett, 174–82.

14. See Bowett, 249–54.

15. As Bloomfield suggested, "If one of the superpowers is adamantly opposed the UN probably should not [and almost certainly would not] be the peacekeeping instrument." See L. P. Bloomfield, "Peacekeeping and Peacemaking," *Foreign Affairs* 54, no. 4 (1966): 671–82, at p. 679.

16. See Hemleben, 16–17.

17. See Marriot, 33–51; and Hemleben, 31–40.

18. Bidwell, 635.

19. Ibid.

20. Ibid.

21. See O. Stokke, "United Nations Security Forces: A Discussion of the Problems Involved," in *Peace-Keeping: Experience and Evaluation—The Oslo Papers,* ed. P. Frydenberg (Oslo: Norwegian Institute of International Affairs, 1964), 27–67, at p. 31.

22. See D. W. Wainhouse, *International Peace Observation: A History and Forecast* (Baltimore, Md.: Johns Hopkins Univ. Press, 1966); and James, chaps. 2–4.

23. L. L. Fabian, *Soldiers Without Enemies: Preparing the United Nations for Peacekeeping* (Washington, D.C.: Brookings Institute, 1971), 3.

24. A. M. Cox, *Prospects for Peacekeeping* (Washington, D.C.: Brookings Institute, 1967), 8.

25. See James, 268, 333–34.

26. On the problems of this approach in Cambodia see Y. Moser, "UN Approach to Conflict Intervention," *Gandhi Marg* 15, no. 1 (1993): 78–86.

27. Fabian, 21.

28. Ibid., 28.

29. Cox, 6.

30. Fabian, 28–29.

31. B. E. Urquhart, "United Nations Peace-keeping in the Middle East," *The World Today* 35, no. 3 (1980): 88–93, at p. 93.

32. Fabian, 29. On the use of force generally see F. T. Liu, *United Nations Peacekeeping and the Non-Use of Force* (Boulder, Colo.: Lynne Rienner Publishers, 1992).

33. Fabian, 30.

34. See W. R. Frye, *A United Nations Peace Force* (New York: Oceana, 1957), 83–85.

35. Ibid., 88. See also S. Hoffman, "Erewhon or Lilliput: A Critical View of the Problem," in Bloomfield, *Power to Keep Peace*, 90–111, at p. 94.

36. The possible consequences of this were tragically illustrated during 1993 in the United Nations operation in Somalia. The large contingent of Pakistani peacekeepers arrived without field communication equipment, tear gas, or flak jackets. This equipment was provided by other contingents but after several poorly equipped Pakistani troops had been killed by local gunmen and after the Pakistanis, with only their firearms for riot control, fired into an angry crowd, causing casualties.

37. See Cox, 95; Frye, 85–86; and K. Skjelsbaek, "United Nations Peacekeeping: Expectations, Limitations and Results. Forty Years of Mixed Experience," in *Proceedings of the First International Symposium on Non-Violent Solutions of International Crises and Regional Conflicts, Frankfurt am Main, February 1989,* ed. E. Czempiel, L. Kiuzadjan and Z. Masoqust (Vienna: International Social Science Council, 1990), 77–90; and C. C. Moskos, *Peace Soldiers: The Sociology of a United Nations Military Force* (Chicago: Univ. of Chicago Press, 1976), 67–82.

38. Galtung and Hveem, 264.

39. Harbottle, *Peacekeeper's Handbook*, I/1.

40. Galtung and Hveem, 268.

41. Ibid., 270.

42. Ibid., 272; see also Moskos 99–115, 135.

43. Galtung and Hvecm, 279.

44. Ibid., 280.

45. I. Rikhye, "Preparation and Training of U.N. Peacekeeping Forces," in Frydenberg, ed., 183–97, at p. 197.

46. See F. P. Salstrom, "Nonviolent Peacemaking," (Philadelphia Friends Peace Committee, 1967–68; International Peace Academy, 1968–69, Manuscript); and A. I. Waskow, *Towards a Peacemakers Academy: A Proposal for a First Step Towards a United Nations Transnational Peacemaking Force* (The Hague: W. Junk, 1967).

47. J. Grønning, "Recruitment and Training," in Frydenberg, ed., 173–81, at p. 179. See also R. C. Johansen and S. H. Mendlovitz, "The Role of Enforcement of Law in the Establishment of a New International Order: A Proposal for a Transnational Police Force," *Alternatives* 6 (1980): 307–37, at p. 320.

48. Bloomfield, "Peacekeeping and Peacemaking," 677.

49. Ibid.

50. Structural violence is indirect violence built into social structures that gives rise to unequal power and, consequently, unequal life chances. See J. Galtung, "Violence, Peace and

Peace Research," *Journal of Peace Research* 6, no. 3 (1969): 167–91; and J. Galtung, "A Structural Theory of Imperialism," *Journal of Peace Research* 8, no. 2 (1971): 81–118.

51. Fabian, 20.

52. J. Galtung, "Three Approaches to Peace; Peacekeeping, Peacemaking and Peacebuilding," in *Essays in Peace Research*, vol. 2, *War, Peace and Defence*, ed. J. Galtung, 282–304, at p. 284; J. Galtung, "Three Realistic Approaches to Peace: Peacekeeping, Peacemaking, Peacebuilding," *Impact of Science on Society* 26, no. 1/2 (1976): 103–15, at p. 104; and see also J. Galtung, *The True Worlds: A Transnational Perspective* (New York: Free Press, 1980), 365.

53. K. Venkata Raman, "United Nations Peacekeeping and the Future of World Order," in *Peacekeeping: Appraisals and Proposals*, ed. H. Wiseman (New York: Pergamon, 1983), 371–401, at p. 382. See also C. Peck, "The Case for a United Nations Dispute Settlement Commission," *Interdisciplinary Peace Research* 3, no. 1 (1991): 73–87.

54. Galtung, "Three Approaches to Peace," 284–86; and Galtung, "Three Realistic Approaches to Peace," 105. Elsewhere he adds that third-party intervention is "usually only operative in a *symmetric* conflict between *underdogs*, with some topdogs appearing in the role of the third parties (typically, UN peace-keeping operations have been mainly carried out by center nations and been used to separate periphery states)." J. Galtung, "Peace, Peace Theory and an International Peace Academy," in *Papers: A Collection of Works Previously Available Only in Manuscript or Very Limited Circulation Mimeographed or Photocopied Editions*, ed. International Peace Research Institute, vol. 5, *Papers in English 1968–1972*, (International Peace Research Institute, Oslo, 1980), 51–102, at p. 82.

55. Galtung, "Three Approaches to Peace," 296.

56. Or in terms employed by John Burton, the dispute may be settled while the conflict remains unresolved. See J. Burton, *Global Conflict: The Domestic Sources of International Crisis* (London: Wheatsheaf, 1984); and especially J. Burton, "Conflict Resolution as a Political Philosophy," *Interdisciplinary Peace Research* 3, no. 1 (1990): 62–72.

57. Galtung, "Three Approaches to Peace," 297.

58. It should be noted, however, that in December 1987 the General Assembly announced (UNGA 42/161) that the United Nations would include a review of its peacekeeping operations in its provisional agenda for the forthcoming session. The resolution requested the Special Committee on Peacekeeping Operations to produce a comprehensive review of the "whole question of peacekeeping operations in all their aspects with a view to strengthening the role of the United Nations in this field." In its recommendation the Special Committee, "having in mind new opportunities for peace-keeping," considered it "useful to have further discussions, in the appropriate forums, on possible new fields for peace-keeping and on the further development of peace-keeping operations." Further, it proposed that "case studies of previous examples of peace-keeping operations should be made with a view to identifying procedural and technical problems" and that "peace-keeping operations could be used as an instrument for political confidence building, prevention of conflicts and peaceful settlement of disputes," as well as "combined with the treatment of humanitarian problems" such as refugees, prisoners of war, and technical assistance (UNGA 44/301). This evaluation may further help to overcome some of difficulties of the model and has the potential to pave the way for more frequent and effective missions for the "soldiers without enemies." For a review of the arguments about whether an unarmed peacekeeping service is best undertaken as a U.N.-oriented or non-U.N.-oriented strategy, see R. J. Magee, "Some Possible Strategies," in *Consultation on an International Peace Brigade: Working Documents and Background Papers* (n.p.: n.d., booklet), 10–15; and Moser.

59. More U.N. peacekeeping operations (fifteen) were established in the five years after the end of the cold war than in the four decades preceding it (thirteen). When U.N. peacekeepers received the Nobel Peace Prize in 1988, there were about ten thousand peacekeepers in the field. Toward the end of 1993 the number had risen to almost eighty thousand.

60. See app. A.

61. Note that Burton uses the term *interests* in the way that Galtung employs the term *goals* and *not* in the same way that Galtung uses the word *interests* (which are more akin to "ontological human needs").

62. See Burton, "Conflict Resolution," 2–3.

63. Harbottle, *What is Proper Soldiering?* (N.p.: Centre for International Peacebuilding, 1991), 3.

64. Ibid., 6.

65. Ibid., 8.

66. Ibid., 11.

2. Unarmed Peacekeeping

1. Harbottle, *Peacekeeper's Handbook,* I/1.

2. Bidwell, 637.

3. Harbottle, *Peacekeeper's Handbook,* V/20.

4. Ibid.

5. A. C. Gilpin, "Non-Violence in U.N. Peacekeeping Operations," in *Foundations of Peace and Freedom: The Ecology of a Peaceful World,* ed. T. Dunn (Swansea: Christopher Davies, 1975), 270–86, at p. 282.

6. Ibid., 283. Similarly, Major-General F. S. Carpenter, a former commandant of Canada's National Defense College and advocate of a Peacekeepers Staff College to train standby and earmarked troops for U.N. service, sees the U.N. force as earnestly trying "for an essentially nonmilitary outcome," but if necessary, "it could resort to military measures." Quoted in Walker, *Peacekeeping: 1969,* 13–14.

7. A. C. Nunn, "The Arming of an International Police," *Journal of Peace Research* 2, no. 3 (1965): 187–91, at p. 190.

8. See C. Moorehead, *Troublesome People: Enemies of War: 1916–1986* (London: Hamish Hamilton, 1987), 119–20.

9. For the argument that soldiers may be able to fulfil constabulary, as opposed to merely military, roles see Moskos, 126–29, 136–39. Moskos ends his sociological analysis of the United Nations Force in Cyprus with "what has become the unofficial motto of the U.N. soldier: 'Peacekeeping is not a soldier's job, but only a soldier can do it'."

10. Walker, "Peacekeeping: A Survey," 233; and Walker, *Peacekeeping: 1969,* 15–18.

11. Walker, "Peacekeeping: A Survey," 234.

12. Ibid., 235.

13. Ibid., 237. This threat could be exacerbated if the superpowers are on the same side, as is becoming increasingly likely, or if there is only one superpower.

14. See M. E. Hirst, *The Quakers in Peace and War* (New York: George H. Doran, 1923); R. Jones, *The Quakers in the American Colonies* (New York: Macmillan, 1911); and P. Brock, *Pacifism in the United States from the Colonial Era to the First World War* (Princeton: N.J.: Princeton Univ. Press, 1968).

15. See Hirst, 131–32.

16. See Jones, 497.

17. See J. Whitney, *John Woolman, Quaker* (London: George Harrap, 1943).

18. See D. Anet, *Pierre Ceresole: Passionate Peacemaker* (Delhi: Macmillan, 1974).

19. See, in particular, his Geneva speech, 10 Dec. 1931, *Young India,* 31 Dec. 1931, in *The Collected Works of Mahatma Gandhi* (New Delhi: Publications Division, Government of India, 1958–85 [hereafter *CWMG*]) 48: 414–21; reproduced in part in app. B.

20. For more detail on the thoughts of James and Lippman, on Gandhi's ideas of a "living wall" defense policy, and, especially, Maude Royden's Peace Army, see app. B; and T. Weber, "Gandhi's 'Living Wall' and Maude Royden's 'Peace Army,'" *Gandhi Marg* 10, no. 4 (1988): 199–212.

21. See D. A. Martin, *Pacifism: An Historical and Sociological Study* (London: Routledge and Kegan Paul, 1965), 142; and M. Ceadel, *Pacifism in Britain 1914–1945: The Defining of a Faith* (Oxford: Clarendon, 1980), 222–23.

22. Moorehead, 10, claims that the reasons for Britain's preeminence in pacifist protest and questioning of the validity of war as a method of resolving international conflicts arose "because of the nature of the British constitution [presumably, the stress on individual freedom], and because it was the country in which the dilemma was first and most clearly expressed." To this should be added the impact of Gandhi's campaigns against the British and the influence of his three-month visit to England in 1931; Moorehead, 107.

23. *Manchester Guardian,* 2 Apr. 1956; see also his earlier letter in the *Manchester Guardian,* 20 Feb. 1956; and *Peace News,* 13 Apr. 1956.

24. See S. King-Hall, *Defence in the Nuclear Age* (London: Gollancz, 1957).

25. See S. Morris, *The Arm of the Law: The United Nations and the Use of Force* (N.p.: *Peace News,* 1957, Pamphlet).

26. R. Acland, *Waging Peace: The Positive Policy We Could Pursue if We Gave Up the H-Bomb* (London: Frederick Muller, 1958).

27. Ibid., 94–95.

28. R. Bell, *Alternative to War* (London: James Clark, 1959), 69–70.

29. Ibid., 77.

30. See A. Bigelow, *The Voyage of the Golden Rule: An Experiment with Truth* (Garden City, N.Y.: Doubleday, 1959).

31. See A. Carter, "The Sahara Project Team," in *Liberation Without Violence: A Third Party Approach,* ed. A. P. Hare and H. H. Blumberg (Totowa, N.J.: Rowan and Littlefield, 1977), 126–56.

32. See B. Lyttle, *You Come With Naked Hands: The Story of the San Francisco to Moscow Walk for Peace* (Raymond, N.H.: Greenleaf, 1966); B. Deming, "San Francisco to Moscow: Why They Walk," in *Revolution and Equilibrium,* ed. B. Deming, (New York: Grossman, 1971), 51–59; and B. Deming "San Francisco to Moscow: Why the Russians Let Them In," in *Revolution and Equilibrium,* ed B. Deming (New York: Grossman, 1971), 60–72.

33. C. C. Walker, *A World Peace Guard: An Unarmed Agency for Peacekeeping* (Hyderabad (AP): Academy of Gandhian Studies, 1981), 35.

34. J. P. Narayan, "Two-fold Programme for World Peace," *Sarvodaya* 10, no. 7 (1961): 261.

35. G. Keyes, "Peacekeeping by Unarmed Buffer Forces: Precedents and Proposals," *Peace and Change* 5, no. 2/3 (1978): 3–10, at p. 8.

36. S. de Madariaga, "Towards the Ideal Federation," *The New Leader* 18, no. 25 (1960): 17–20, at p. 19.

37. When this proposal appeared later in Madariaga's article, "Blueprint for a World Commonwealth," in *Perspectives on Peace 1910–1960,* ed. Carnegie Endowment for International Peace (New York: Praeger, 1960), 47–64, at pp. 60–63, the term *White Guard* had been altered to the less racially sensitive *World Guard, Charter* had become *Additional Charter,* and the words "or by third parties" had been included in the third of the recommendations for the proposed charter.

38. Madariaga, "Towards the Ideal Federation," 20.

39. See app. B; and Weber, "Gandhi's 'Living Wall'."

40. For a report of the Gandhigram conference see *Sarvodaya* 10, (1961): 263–65.

41. Walker, *World Peace Guard,* 37.

42. T. Olson, "The World Peace Brigade: Vision and Failure," *Our Generation Against Nuclear War* 3, no. 1 (1964): 34–41, at p. 34.

43. B. Deming, "International Peace Brigade," in *Revolution and Equilibrium,* ed. B. Deming, 95.

44. Olson, 34.

45. Deming, "International Peace Brigade," 92.

46. "World Peace Brigade?" note by J. P. issued in Calcutta, 23 Dec. 1961. A. J. Muste Collection, Swarthmore College Peace Collection, Swarthmore, Pa. [hereafter, Muste Papers], Box 39, Folder 28. About one year later the All-India Shanti Sena Mandal recommended that the WPB "may recognise the Indian Shanti Sena as the Indian unit and empower it to select volunteers from India for the WPB. . . . The Indian Shanti Sena may also help in training of volunteers for WPB programs. It may also closely cooperate in any programme of non-violent action sponsored by the WPB in this region." Muste Papers, Box 41, Folder 10.

47. Ibid.

48. A. Tatum, "The World Peace Brigade: Some Specific Proposals," *The War Resister* 93, (1961): 3–6.

49. See Olson, 35; and D. Prasad, "The World Peace Brigade," *Peace News,* 6 Aug. 1971, 2–3.

50. Deming, "International Peace Brigade," 99.

51. Ibid., 98.

52. Ibid., 100.

53. "Statement of Principles and Aims of the World Peace Brigade," Muste Papers, Box 39, Folder 29.

54. Ibid.

55. Deming, "International Peace Brigade," 98.

56. "Statement of Principles and Aims," Muste Papers, Box 39, Folder 29.

57. *The World Peace Brigade . . . for Non-violent Action* (N.p.: n.d., Pamphlet), Muste Papers, Box 40, Folder 7.

58. Prasad, "World Peace Brigade," 2.

59. Olson, 36.

60. Ibid., 37.

61. C. C. Walker, "Nonviolence in Eastern Africa 1962–4: The World Peace Brigade and Zambian Independence," in *Liberation Without Violence,* eds. Hare and Blumberg, 157–77, at p. 163.

62. Four years later a similar plan for a nonviolent strategy to end the racist system in Rhodesia was published by the Reverend Bell. It called for the invasion of Rhodesia by a Commonwealth Nonviolent Expeditionary Force. Because sanctions proved a failure, the plan was again reviewed. M. P. Arthur Bottomley at the Commonwealth Relations Office asked that the proposals be seriously considered. See R. Bell, *Rhodesia: Outline of a Nonviolent Strategy to Resolve the Crisis* (London: Housmans, 1968).

63. See Walker, "Nonviolence in Eastern Africa," 163; and Olson, 36.

64. See Deming, "International Peace Brigade," 101; Walker "Nonviolence in Eastern Africa," 175; and Olson, 37–38.

65. Olson, 38.

66. Prasad, "World Peace Brigade," 2.

67. Walker, "Nonviolence in Eastern Africa," 172–73.

68. The expenditure sheets of the WPB clearly show the financial difficulties associated with the African Freedom Action Project. See Muste Papers, Box 39, Folder 31.

69. Olson, 38.

70. "Letter to the Editor," *World Peace Brigade Reports,* 7 Sep. 1963, Muste Papers, Box 39, Folder 34.

71. Olson, 38.

72. D. Prasad, "Some Thoughts on the World Peace Brigade," (War Resisters' International, 1964, Manuscript), 1.

73. Prasad, "World Peace Brigade," 2.

74. Ibid.

75. Minutes of the World Peace Brigade Council meeting, London, 30 July–2 Aug. 1962, 5, Muste Papers, Box 39, Folder 32.

76. Ibid., 7.

77. B. Deming, "Earl Reynolds: Stranger in this Country," *Liberation* 8, no. 1 (1963): 26–30, at p. 29.

78. Prasad, "World Peace Brigade," 2; and Deming, "Earl Reynolds," 29–30.

79. Muste's correspondences contain many letters attempting to solicit funds for the *Everyman III* voyage, and several of them refer to this exchange project. See, for example, Muste to Mrs. Montgomery, 16 July 1962, Muste Papers, Box 39, Folder 32.

80. Olson, 39.

81. C. C. Walker, "The World Peace Brigade: A Look at Some of its Problems," (Peace Brigades International, 1982, Manuscript).

82. Olson, 39.

83. Prasad, "World Peace Brigade," 2.

84. Olson, 39.

85. A. Scarfe and W. Scarfe, *J.P.: His Biography* (New Delhi: Orient Longman, 1975), 380.

86. Olson, 39.

87. V. Tandon, *The Social and Political Philosophy of Sarvodaya After Gandhiji* (Varanasi: Sarva Seva Sangh, 1965), 157–58. See also Muste's report of his visit to Vinoba on 26–27 Dec. 1962, Muste Papers, Box 40, Folder 12.

88. Scarfe and Scarfe, 382.

89. See memo by Muste on which Americans should join the march, 1 July 1963, *Muste Papers*, Box 40, Folder 11.

90. See minutes of the second meeting of the Asian Regional Council of the WPB, 19 Feb. 1963, Muste Papers, Box 41, Folder 10.

91. Muste Papers, Box 39, Folder 34. For the strong support among Gandhians for the war effort, see E. Lazar, "Militarism in the Land of Gandhi," *Liberation* 8, no. 3 (1963): 20–23.

92. See, for example, Charles C. Walker's reports: "From Delhi to Peking: Walking for Peace," *World Peace Brigade Reports*, July 1963; and "The Delhi-to-Peking Friendship March," *Friends Journal* 9, no. 23 (1963): 517–18.

93. See, for example, the editorial in the *Northern India Patrika*, 23 Apr. 1963; and the report of the Delhi correspondent of the *Christian Science Monitor*, 22 Mar. 1963.

94. See the letter by A. Bigelow to the editor of the *Christian Science Monitor*, 25 Apr. 1963; and the statement to the press by Siddharaj Dhadda, WPB secretary for the Asian Region, 16 Apr. 1963, Muste Papers, Box 41, Folder 6.

95. Reproduced in the Akhil Bharat Sarva Seva Sangh, ed., *Delhi-Peking Friendship March* (Varanasi, 1963, Pamphlet), 11–16.

96. See "Two Statements from China," *Peace News*, 19 Apr. 1963, 3.

97. Olson, 40.

98. Muste Papers, Box 41, Folder 3.

99. "Report from Lansbury House," n.d., Muste Papers, Box 41, Folder 6.

100. Letter from Scott to Muste, 17 May 1963, "Letters and other information from the Delhi-Peking March," (World Peace Brigade, North American Regional Council, 1963, Manuscript), 4–5, at p. 5.

101. Olson, 38.

102. Ibid., 39–40; and Walker, "Nonviolence in Eastern Africa," 174–75.

103. R. Swann and P. Salstrom, "Towards a Non-Violent Peacekeeping Corps," *Peace News*, 8 Oct. 1965, 6–7.

104. P. Arrowsmith, ed., *To Asia in Peace: The Story of a Non-Violent Action Mission to Indo China* (London: Sidgwick and Jackson, 1972), 4.

105. Ibid., 10.

106. "Northern Ireland: A Proposal for Nonviolent Intervention," *Peace News*, 10 Sep. 1971.

107. See letters by A. Vogel, *Peace News,* 24 September 1971; and N. Letchford, *Peace News,* 8 Oct. 1971.

108. See letter by B. Overy, *Peace News,* 17 Sep. 1971.

109. *Peace News,* 14 Oct. 1971.

110. See Walker, *World Peace Guard,* 82–83.

111. Ibid., 79.

112. Ibid., 88; and M. Mandal, "Unarmed Peace Keeping Force," *Vigil* 4, no. 15 (1981): 3, 9–12, at p. 3.

113. Walker, *World Peace Guard,* 88–92, at p. 89.

114. Ibid., 90–91.

115. See G. W. Choudhury, *The Last Days of United Pakistan* (Nedlands: Univ. of Western Australia Press, 1974), 210–14, 216.

116. See "Vinoba Urges UNO Sponsored P.B.," *Sarvodaya* 21, no. 3 (1971): 110–12.

117. Quoted in Walker, *World Peace Guard,* 92–94.

118. In mid-November, at a "Consultation on Peacekeeping" sponsored by the International Peace Academy, IPA Chair General Indarjit Rikhye discussed the "pre-development" work that an unarmed peace contingent on a longer assignment could undertake. As his example, he recounted the story of British students who spent a summer in Cyprus and managed to persuade some Greek and Turkish Cypriots to leave the camps and return to their abandoned villages. See C. C. Walker, "Consultation on Peacekeeping," (Haverford College, 1971, Manuscript), 3.

119. Walker, *World Peace Guard,* 79. For a complete chronology of events in the history of the Cyprus Resettlement Project see A. P. Hare, ed., *Cyprus Resettlement Project: An Instance of International Peacekeeping* (Beer Sheva: Ben Gurion Univ., 1984), 1–22.

120. A. P. Hare and F. Wilkinson, "Cyprus—Conflict and its Resolution," in Hare and Blumberg, eds., 239–47, at p. 239.

121. Hare, 4.

122. See Hare and Wilkinson, 240; Walker, "Peace Brigades as Unofficial Peacekeepers and Peacemakers," (paper prepared for Peace Brigades International, 1984, Mimeo.); and Walker, *World Peace Guard,* 79.

123. Hare, 10. Harbottle had planned a trip to the Sinai but did not find any appropriate avenue for CRP type activity, and, consequently, the idea was shelved. Personal communication from A. Paul Hare, 20 Nov. 1989.

124. Walker, "Peace Brigades," 2.

125. Ibid.

126. Walker, *World Peace Guard,* 15.

127. Mandal, "Unarmed Peace Keeping Force," 3.

128. Walker, *World Peace Guard,* 94–95. It should be noted that nongovernment attempts at peacemaking have also taken place from a non-Gandhian perspective. The loosely confederated U.S.-based Mo Tzu Project, in the early 1980s, engaged in several actions of networking and unofficial diplomacy. The aim of the Project was to send members to the world's trouble spots where they could "immerse themselves in the situations, learn about them, and then see if there was something that could be done to broker a better relationship amongst the 'partners' in conflict" (Fuller, "Better Game than War," 19). The modus operandi of the Project was to realize that behavior, including that which leads to war, "happens inside a structure of beliefs, unconscious assumptions, ingrained habits, and predispositions" (Hotchkiss, 88) and then to set out to "remodel" the structure of these "subconscious notions about who we are and how to get what we want" (ibid., 89). Project members saw that the way to enable perception of these subconscious patterns was by immersion in "someone else's conflict" because it is "the unsettling, confusing, culture-shocking differences met when grappling firsthand with a foreign culture and an alien conflict that crack open the doors of perception. Once opened, it is possible to glimpse some of the basic images on the blueprint

which need to be changed" (ibid.). See R. Fuller, "A Better Game than War: Interviews with Robert Fuller," in *Evolutionary Blues,* vol. 2, ed. D. Hoffman (Arcata, Calif.: Stiener, 1983), 7–21; M. Hotchkiss, "The Mo Tzu Project: Personal National Peace-finding," *The CoEvolution Quarterly,* Fall (1982): 82–90; and R. Fuller, "Mo Tzu in Kenya and Poland," *The CoEvolution Quarterly,* Spring (1983): 118–25.

129. Walker, *World Peace Guard,* 54.
130. Ibid., 57.
131. Ibid.
132. Ibid., 12.
133. Ibid., 13.
134. Ibid., 16–17.
135. Ibid., 19.
136. Ibid., 21.
137. Ibid., 33–34.
138. Ibid., 34–35.
139. Ibid., 34.
140. Ibid.
141. Ibid., 33.
142. Ibid.
143. Ibid., 35.
144. Ibid.
145. Ibid.
146. Walker, "Peace Brigades," 1.
147. Walker, *World Peace Guard,* 50.
148. Ibid., 35.
149. Ibid., 36.
150. Ibid., 52.
151. Ibid., 53.
152. Ibid.
153. Ibid., 54.
154. Ibid., 55.
155. One small and apparently short-lived effort, the World Peace Army founded by New York Quakers, hoped to avoid governments and international bodies, which it identified as the agents responsible for war. See M. Shepard, "Peace Brigades," *Fellowship* July/Aug., (1982): 9–10, at p. 10. The WPA issued a few "Peace Army Reports" in 1981, indicating their commitment to Gandhi's satyagraha and outlining a few proposed WPB emulating actions. See E. Cattell, "Peace Army Progress," *Peace Army Reports* 1, no. 2 (1981): 1.
156. M. Shepard, "Peace Brigades," *World Encyclopedia of Peace* (Oxford: Pergamon, 1986), vol. 2, 178–80, at p. 180. This tradition continues. During December 1991 at an "International NGO Conference on Peace and Security in the Middle East" a workshop, "Non-armed Non-violent United Nations Peace Teams," was conducted. The workshop called for the establishment of an "Organismo di Interposizione Nonviolenta di Pace" and for the United Nations to place the proposed organization "under its protection and to press governments of Member States to authorise the participation of volunteers in this body." In 1992 "A Discussion Paper for the New Democratic Party's Task Force on the Reform of the United Nations" proposed the creation of a professional, unarmed, gender-equal Canadian peace corps: "The Peace Corps is to be established at the national level, be composed of men and women trained in unarmed peace-making and peace-keeping and be placed in whole or in part at the service of the United Nations." H. Sinn, "United Nations Reform and a Professional Peace Corps" (1992, Manuscript).
157. M. Shepard, "Ray Magee, Peaceworker" (n.d., Manuscript).
158. See "Consultation on an International Peace Brigade," minutes of the Grindstone

Island (Portland, Ontario) meeting, 31 Aug.–4 Sep. 1981; and Shepard, "Peace Brigades," 1986, 179.

159. P. Dijkstra, "Peace Brigades International," *Gandhi Marg* 8, no. 7 (1986): 391–406, at p. 406.

160. Shepard, "Peace Brigades," 1986, 179.

161. Ibid.

162. D. N. Clark, "Transnational Action for Peace: The Peace Brigades International," *Transnational Perspectives* 9, no. 4 (1983): 7–11, at p. 10; and Dijkstra, "Peace Brigades International," 404–5. For an earlier proposed list of qualifications for prospective PBI volunteers see Mandal, "Unarmed Peace Keeping Force," 10–12.

163. Dijkstra, "Peace Brigades International," 403.

164. See D. N. Clark, "Transnational Action." At The Trier (West Germany) International Council Meeting of PBI interest was expressed in shifting emphasis from Central America to other parts of the globe. See H. Sinn, "International Conference in Trier," *Peace Brigades* 7, no. 1 (1990): 1.

165. Walker, "Peace Brigades," 3.

166. Dijkstra, "Peace Brigades International," 403; C. C. Walker, "Report of Meetings of Peace Brigades International," *Gandhi Marg* 8, no. 12 (1987): 764–66, at p. 765; see also the extensive reports in the annual report of PBI's Central America Project 1989, *Nonviolence at Work in Central America;* and for a description of PBI's escort work, P. Coy, "Protective Accompanyment: How Peace Brigades International Secures Political Space and Human Rights Nonviolently," in *Nonviolence: Social and Psychological Issues,* ed. V. K. Kool (Lanham, Md.: Univ. of America Press, 1993), 235–45.

167. Walker, "Peace Brigades," 3; Dijkstra, "Peace Brigades International," 403–4.

168. At present restricted to escort duties. See minutes of PBI Directorate Meeting, 9–13 Apr. 1990, at Bradford, England, especially minute 32.1 on p. 14; and N. Bowen, "PBI Called to Sri Lanka," *Peace Brigades* 7, no. 1 (1990): 1, 3.

169. Dijkstra, "Peace Brigades International," 404.

170. PBI Directorate Minutes (minute no. 39), 18; and A. Mager, "Israeli-Palestine Project Plans Future," *Peace Brigades* 7, no. 1 (1990): 4.

171. One of the few substantive published articles on the Gulf Peace Team is R. Burrowes, "The Gulf War and the Gulf Peace Team," *Social Alternatives* 10, no. 2 (1991): 35–39.

172. See R. Burrowes, "Life in the Gulf Peace Camp," *Issues* 15, May (1991): 56–60.

173. Gulf Peace Team "Constitution," 1990, 1.

174. Gulf Peace Team "Summary of meeting," 4 Nov. 1990, 3.

175. *Baghdad Observer,* 17 Dec. 1990.

176. *Baghdad Observer,* 11 Dec. 1990.

177. Letter dated 13 Nov. 1990, signed by Jean Dreze and Mohamed Sidek Ahmad on behalf of the GPT.

178. *News Release,* 7 Dec. 1990. On the same day a letter was sent to Iraq's Prime Minister Ramadhan, announcing that "we are now arranging for about 100 volunteers to fly to Iraq on 17 December—the first wave of several hundred volunteers from many countries waiting to join the camp." On 11 Dec. 1990 a GPT organizer, Jean Dreze, told a London press conference that the Team expected five thousand volunteers in the desert. The following day the Iraqi press ran the report with a headline, "Peace Camp to Attract Thousands, Says Activist," *Baghdad Observer,* 12 Dec. 1990.

179. H. Clark, "Civilian Intervention—It Doesn't Hurt to Try," *Peace News,* Oct. (1992): 2.

180. B. Lyttle, "Solidarity for Peace in Sarajevo," *Midwest Pacifist Commentator* 8, no. 1 (1993): 1–8, 10; C. Schweitzer, "Intervening in Sarajevo: Hopes and Realities," *Peace News,* Feb. 1993, 2.

181. C. Schweitzer, "We Divide One Peace . . . ," *Peace News,* Sep. (1993): 8–9, at p. 8.

182. For discussions of the Mir Sada action see Schweitzer, "We Divide One Peace"; B. Lyttle "Mir Sada/We Share One Peace" (1993, Manuscript); and E. Gulcher, "Sarajevo 1993 622: If You Do Not Come Back I Will Come and Get You," (19, Aug. 1993, manuscript posted on PeaceNet Conference "Yugo. antiwar," 2 Sept. 1993).

183. Schweitzer, "We Divine One Peace," 9.

184. See Gulcher. At the time of writing, the activists who made it into Sarajevo, now calling themselves Harmonie International, plan to fulfil a promise they made to the mayor of the city to return and celebrate Christmas with the inhabitants, and another group of activists is also planning an action that will take them to Mostar. Drawing on the experience of recent attempts, in Dec. 1993, Sjeme Mir ("Seeds of Peace") plans to take two hundred committed peace activists to Split and walk to the Hercegovinan capital. They plan to place themselves in areas controlled by all three warring factions.

185. Galtung, "Peace Theory," 82.

186. Ibid.

187. See Wallis, 10.

188. Besides PBI, one of the leading attempts at this type of action has been undertaken by the American Christian Nicaragua-focused Witness for Peace. Exploratory teams, which went to Nicaragua in 1983 to ascertain for themselves what was really happening in the country, noticed that their presence stopped Contra attacks on villages (it would have been bad politics for the Contras to use U.S.-supplied weapons to kill U.S. citizens). This realization lead to a permanent presence in border areas, providing deterrence through nonviolent interventions. See E. Griffin-Nolan, *Witness for Peace* (Louisville, Ky.: Westminster/John Knox Press (1991); R. Sider, *Exploring the Limits of Non-Violence: A Call for Action* (London: Spire, 1988); and R. Taylor, "Witness for Peace and the Pledge of Resistance," *Nonviolent Sanctions,* Spring/Summer (1990): 16–17. For a description of peace "monitor" actions by Christian church organizations in South Africa see K. Roep, " 'You Never Know the Effect': An Experience in International Monitoring," *Reconciliation International,* Autumn (1993): 7–8.

189. See T. Weber, "From Maude Royden's Peace Army to the Gulf Peace Team: An Assessment of Unarmed Interpositionary Peace Forces," *Journal of Peace Research* 30, no. 1 (1993): 45–64.

190. See "Consultation on an International Peace Brigade"; and M. Shepard, "Tooling up for Peace: The Launching of Peace Brigades International" (paper, n.d.), 13–17.

191. Muste Papers, Box 39, Folder 28.

192. For an elaboration on the objectives of a "third party" see G. R. S. Rao, "The Concept of a Third Force in Conflict Resolution," *Gandhi Marg* 12, no. 4 (1968): 421–30; and O. R. Young, *The Intermediaries: Third Parties in International Crises* (Princeton, N.J.: Princeton Univ. Press, 1967).

193. F. Blum, "Non-Violence and the Establishment of a Peace Brigade," Muste Papers, Box 39, Folder 28.

194. Muste Papers, Box 39, Folder 28.

195. Of course, there is no guarantee that it would not remain limited in scope even if taken up by the United Nations.

3. The Historical Gandhian Background

1. *Indian Opinion,* 3 May 1913, *CWMG* 12: 52–53.

2. *Young India,* 24 Nov. 1921, *CWMG* 21: 477–79.

3. See Gandhi's speech at the Congress session in Ahmedabad on 28 Dec. 1921, *Young India,* 19 Jan. 1922, *CWMG* 22: 99–104.

4. *Young India,* 22 Dec. 1921, *CWMG* 22: 63–64.

5. A. G. Khan, *My Life and Struggle: The Autobiography of Badshah Khan* (Delhi: Hind Pocket Books, 1969), 97. Khan pointed out that his community was faction ridden and constantly feuding, that its members "were inclined to be violent," and that "one of their worst characteristics was their habit of taking revenge" (96–97). See also D. G. Tendulkar, *Abdul Ghaffar Khan: Faith is a Battle* (New Delhi: Gandhi Peace Foundation, 1967), 59.

6. Khan, 97.

7. Quoted in Pyarelal, *Thrown to the Wolves: Abdul Ghaffar* (Calcutta: Eastlight Book House, 1966), 135.

8. See J. V. Bondurant, *Conquest of Violence: The Gandhian Philosophy of Conflict* (Berkeley: Univ. of California Press, 1967), 138.

9. Pyarelal, *A Pilgrimage for Peace: Gandhi and Frontier Gandhi among N.W.F. Pathans* (Ahmedabad: Navajivan, 1950), 37.

10. See Tendulkar, *Abdul Ghaffar Khan,* 75.

11. See, for example, the front-page story in the *Bombay Chronicle,* 17 Mar. 1930; and Nehru's letter to Gandhi 13 Mar. 1930, in S. Gopal, ed., *Selected Works of Jawaharlal Nehru,* (New Delhi: Jawaharlal Nehru Memorial Fund, Orient Longman, 1973), vol. 4, 292–93.

12. A photostat of the play is in the collection of the Sabarmati Harijan Ashram, Ahmedabad: *Sabarmati Nidhi* [Trust] SN no. P16852.

13. See Gandhi's letter to M. Desai 25 Apr. 1930, *CWMG* 43: 321–22; his speech at Chharwada on 26 Apr. 1930, *CWMG* 43: 330–34; and Gandhi's interview with the *Bombay Chronicle,* 24 Apr. 1930, *CWMG* 43: 349–50. For the Dharasana struggle see I. E. Desai, *Dharasanani Shauryagatha* (Surat: Swatantra Itihas, Samiti Jilla Panchayat Surat, 1973); J. Gandhi, *Dharasanano Jung* (Gandhinagar: Information Department Gujarat Government, 1978); Gujarat Provincial Congress Committee, *The Black Regime at Dharasana (A Brief Survey of the "Dharasana Raid")* (Ahmedabad, 1930); and G. Sharp, *Gandhi Wields the Weapon of Moral Power (Three Case Histories)* (Ahmedabad: Navajivan, 1960), 132–51.

14. See Web Miller's eyewitness account in W. Miller, *I Found No Peace: The Journal of a Foreign Correspondent* (Harmondsworth, England: Penguin, 1940), 134–37; and those of George Slocombe in the *Daily Herald,* 19 May 1930.

15. Quoted in D. Hogg, *Memories for Tomorrow* (London: Regency Press, 1981), 60.

16. *Harijan,* 26 Mar. 1938, *CWMG* 66: 406–7.

17. Cf. n. 8 chap. 4.

18. *Harijan,* 18 June 1938, *CWMG* 67: 125–27.

19. Ibid.

20. *Harijan,* 21 July 1940, *CWMG* 72: 272.

21. *Harijan,* 11 Aug. 1940, *CWMG* 72: 363.

22. *Harijan,* 15 Sep. 1940, *CWMG* 72: 455–56.

23. *CWMG* 74: 64.

24. *National Herald,* 24 Jan. 1942, *CWMG* 75: 250.

25. For example, Gandhi claimed that "if we would improve our status through the help and cooperation of the British, it is our duty to win their help by standing by them in their hour of need," and "I thought that England's need should not be turned into our opportunity, and that it was more becoming and farsighted not to press our demands while the war lasted." M. K. Gandhi, *An Autobiography or The Story of My Experiments With Truth* (Ahmedabad: Navajivan, 1927), 290.

26. *Harijan,* 26 Nov. 1938, *CWMG* 67: 138.

27. *Harijan,* 15 Mar. 1942, *CWMG* 75: 395. Gandhi adds that "Hitlerism will never be defeated by counter-Hitlerism. It can only breed superior Hitlerism raised to the *nth* degree." *Harijan,* 26 June 1940, *CWMG* 72: 187.

28. N. K. Bose, "Gandhian Approach to Social Conflict and War," in *Gandhi, India and the World,* ed. S. Ray (Melbourne: Hawthorn Press, 1970), 261–69, at p. 268.

29. Immediately exploitation has ceased "armaments will be felt as a positively unbear-

able burden." *Harijan,* 12 Nov. 1938, quoted in A. T. Hingorani and G. A. Hingorani, eds., *The Encyclopedia of Gandhian Thoughts* (New Delhi: AICC(I), 1985), 82.

30. "A non-violent man or society does not anticipate or provide for attackers from without. On the contrary, such a person or society firmly believes that nobody is going to disturb them." *Harijan,* 13 Apr. 1940, *CWMG* 71: 407. Further, in his "Draft Resolution for the Working Committee," Gandhi makes the point that "if India were free and independent without an army she would have no fear of external aggression. The best defence that free India can put up . . . would be to cultivate friendliness with the whole world." *CWMG* 50: 241.

31. For a general introduction to the notion of civilian defence see T. K. Mahadevan, A. Roberts, and G. Sharp, eds., *Civilian Defence: An Introduction* (New Delhi: Gandhi Peace Foundation, 1967).

32. *Harijan,* 13 Apr. 1940, *CWMG* 71: 406–8.

33. Ibid. For a criticism of the "living wall" method of resistance to an invading army see A. Roberts, "Civilian Defence Strategy," in *The Strategy of Civilian Defence: Non-Violent Resistance to Aggression,* ed. A. Roberts (London: Faber, 1967), 215–54, at pp. 238–40.

34. *Harijan,* 17 Dec. 1938, *CWMG* 68: 192.

35. Mira Behn [Madeleine Slade], *The Spirit's Pilgrimage* (London: Longmans, 1960), 230; see also Mirabehn's letter to Gandhi on this subject, and Gandhi's reply, quoted in Pyarelal, *Mahatma Gandhi: The Last Phase* (Ahmedabad: Navajivan, 1958), vol. 2, 815–18.

36. T. A. Raman, *What Does Gandhi Want?* (London: Oxford Univ. Press, 1943), 99. At this time Gandhi noted that "men can slaughter one another for years in the heat of battle, for then it seems to be the case of kill or be killed. But if there is no danger of being killed yourself by those you slay, you cannot go on killing defenseless and unprotesting people endlessly. You must put down your gun in self-disgust." Quoted in Pyarelal, *Mahatma Gandhi,* vol. 2, 815.

37. N. K. Bose, *Studies in Gandhism* (Ahmedabad: Navajivan, 1972), 112; see also the interview, appearing under the title "Can India be Defended?" that Gandhi gave to the American journal *Liberty,* Aug. 1940, during which he expounded on the actions that a hypothetically free India would undertake in the face of invasion. Gandhi declared that "the representatives of the free Indian State would let the invader in without opposition. But they would tell the invader and all his forces at the frontier that the Indian people would refuse to cooperate in any work in any undertaking. They would refuse to obey orders despite all threats and despite all punishments inflicted upon them." Quoted in Pyarelal, *Mahatma Gandhi,* vol. 2, 814.

38. See *Harijan,* 22 Mar. 1942, *CWMG* 75: 409–10; and *Harijan,* 12 Apr. 1942, *CWMG* 76: 12–13.

39. Bose, *Studies in Gandhism,* 113.

40. Ibid. The difficulty of achieving the unanimity of purpose to accomplish this, however, even when the defenders are all committed to the peace movement, was graphically illustrated by the 1965 Grindstone Island sociodrama that ended with several of the "defenders" being "killed" and the "attackers" not de-roled. See T. Olson and G. Christiansen, *Thirty-One Hours: The Grindstone Experiment* (Toronto: Canadian Friends Service Committee, 1968).

41. See M. Skodvin, "Non-Violent Resistance During the German Occupation," in A. Roberts, 136–53; J. Bennett, "The Resistance Against German Occupation of Denmark," in A. Roberts, 154–72; J. J. Lanza Del Vasto, *Warriors of Peace: Writings on the Technique of Nonviolence* (New York: Alfred A. Knopf, 1974), 194–221; R. B. Gregg, *The Power of Non-Violence* (Ahmedabad: Navajivan, 1960), 3–39; and G. Sharp, *The Politics of Nonviolent Action,* pt. 1, "Power and Struggle" (Boston: Porter Sargent, 1973), 63–105.

42. Orwell, for example, notes, "It is difficult to see how Gandhi's methods could be applied in a country where opponents of the regime disappear in the middle of the night and are never heard of again. Without a free press and the right of assembly, it is impossible not

merely to appeal to outside opinion, but to bring a mass movement into being, or even to make your intentions known to your adversary." "Reflections on Gandhi," in G. Orwell, *The Collected Essays, Journalism and Letters of George Orwell,* vol. 4, *In Front of Your Nose,* (Harmondsworth, England: Penguin, 1970), 523–31, at p. 529.

43. *Harijan,* 15 Oct. 1938, *CWMG* 67: 405.

44. Ibid.

45. *Harijan,* 5 May 1946, *CWMG* 84: 66.

46. Ibid.

47. See Gandhi's speeches at prayer meetings in Calcutta on 6 Sep. 1947, *Harijan,* 21 Sep. 1947, *CWMG* 89: 158; and 7 Sep. 1947, *Amrita Bazar Patrika,* 8 Sep. 1947, *CWMG* 89: 161.

48. See Gandhi's speech at a prayer meeting in New Delhi on 26 Oct. 1947, *CWMG* 89: 412–16.

49. Reproduced in *The Hindustan Standard,* 7 Sep. 1947, *CWMG* 89: 156.

50. P. F. Power, *Gandhi on World Affairs* (London: Allen and Unwin, 1961), 129.

51. See, for example, his comments in "Question Box," *Harijan,* 9 Aug. 1942, *CWMG* 76: 350–51.

52. Quoted in D. G. Tendulkar, *Mahatma: Life of Mohandas Karamchand Gandhi* (New Delhi: Publications Division, Ministry of Information and Broadcasting, Government of India, 1961), vol. 6, 150.

53. Dated 28 July 1942, *CWMG* 76: 341.

54. *The Bombay Chronicle,* 18 Apr. 1945, *CWMG* 79: 390.

55. Quoted in B. N. Sharga, *Gandhi: His Life and Teachings* (Lucknow: Upper India Publishing House, 1950), 389–90.

56. *Harijan,* 22 Aug. 1948.

57. *Harijan,* 13 Feb. 1949.

58. *Harijan,* 5 Feb. 1950.

59. *Harijan,* 19 Feb. 1950.

60. Ibid. See also A. J. Muste, "Aims and Objects of Satyagraha Units," *Harijan,* 12 Mar. 1950.

61. W. R. Miller, *Nonviolence: A Christian Interpretation* (London: Allen and Unwin, 1964), 119.

4. The Philosophical Gandhian Background

1. Quoted in R. Iyer, *The Moral and Political Thought of Mahatma Gandhi* (New York: Oxford Univ. Press, 1973), 156.

2. The Sanskrit word *satya* means more than the narrow interpretation that is accorded the English word *truth:* it includes the connotations "real, sincere, existent, pure, good, effectual, valid." Monier-Williams, *Sanskrit-English Dictionary* (Oxford: Clarendon, 1899), quoted in Iyer, 150.

3. *Harijan,* 21 Sep. 1934, *CWMG* 59: 43.

4. Quoted in M. Desai, *The Diary of Mahadev Desai* (Ahmedabad: Navajivan, 1953), 249.

5. *Young India,* 31 Dec. 1931, *CWMG,* 47: 404.

6. Letter to P. G. Mathew, 9 July 1932, *CWMG* 50: 175.

7. Iyer, 157.

8. Although Gandhi often spoke of the necessity of a belief in God for the practice of satyagraha (e.g., "Satyagraha is . . . based on an unquestionable faith in God and His justice" [*Harijan,* 18 Feb. 1926, *CWMG* 30: 25]; a satyagrahi's [one practicing satyagraha] "strength comes from within, from his reliance on God" [*Harijan,* 3 June 1939, *CWMG* 69: 273]; "Satyagrahis must cultivate a living faith in God" [*Harijan,* 3 June 1939, *CWMG* 69: 76]; and

"Satyagraha presupposes the living presence and guidance of God" [*Younq India*, 2 Aug. 1928, *CWMG* 37: 113]) a closer examination of his writings, even taking into account his many references to God as a person, can establish that in reality for him God is "an undefinable and universal Power that cannot be conceived apart from humanity or from the whole of nature" (Iyer, 94). On many occasions Gandhi even repudiated the notion of a personal God: "God is not a person. . . . God is the force. He is the essence of life. He is pure and undefiled consciousness." *Harijan*, 22 June 1947, *CWMG* 88: 148; and "I don't believe God to be a personal being in the sense that we are personal beings." Quoted in C. Shukla, *Conversations of Gandhiji* (Bombay: Vora, 1949), 36. He noted that one's concept of God is limited and subjective: each person should "think of Him as best appears to him, provided that the conception is pure and uplifting." *Harijan*, 18 Aug. 1946, *CWMG* 85: 145. In short, Gandhi realized that God could be viewed in many different ways: "God is Truth and Love; God is ethics and morality; God is fearlessness. God is the source of Light and Life and yet He is above and beyond all these. God is conscience. He is even the atheism of the atheist. . . . He transcends speech and reason. . . . He is a personal God to those who need his personal presence. He is embodied to those who need His touch," *Young India* 5 Mar. 1925, *CWMG* 26: 224.

9. "I believe in the essential unity of man and for that matter of all that lives." *Young India*, 4 Dec. 1924, *CWMG* 25: 390.

10. Gandhi, *Autobiography*, xi.

11. *Young India*, 31 Dec. 1931, quoted in R. K. Prabhu and U. R. Rao, eds., *The Mind of Mahatma Gandhi* (Ahmedabad: Navajivan, 1967), 42.

12. *Harijan*, 24 Nov. 1933 *CWMG* 56: 216.

13. See *Harijan*, 23 June 1946, *CWMG* 84: 229.

14. The committee was set up under the chairmanship of Lord Hunter to investigate the disturbances in the Punjab that culminated in the massacre of hundreds of Indian civilians by troops under the direction of General Dyer at Jallianwalla Bagh in Amritsar on 13 Apr. 1919.

15. Quoted in Tendulkar, *Mahatma*, vol. 1, 282.

16. M. K. Gandhi, *From Yeravda Mandir* (Ahmedabad: Navajivan, 1932), 6.

17. See F. Fanon, *The Wretched of the Earth* (Harmondsworth, England: Penguin, 1967), 94; and Sartre's preface to the book, especially p. 18.

18. *Young India*, 11 Aug. 1920, *CWMG* 18: 132.

19. Gandhi did, however, realize the possible need for physical violence directed at other humans in the rare cases of the defense of third parties; see *Young India*, 11 Aug. 1920, *CWMG* 18: 132; 4 Nov. 1926, *CWMG* 31: 544–47; and 11 Oct. 1928, *CWMG* 37: 337

20. *Harijan*, 5 Sept. 1936, *CWMG* 63: 262.

21. *Young India*, 25 Aug. 1920, *CWMG* 18: 195; cf. W. R. Miller, 24–25, where the author claims that in the classical scriptures *ahimsa* is not equated with love, has no positive content as such, merely connoting abstention.

22. *Harijan*, 29 Apr. 1939, *CWMG* 69: 41. Gandhi further warns that one must "hate the sin and not the sinner." Gandhi, *Autobiography*, 230.

23. *Harijan*, 25 Mar. 1939, *CWMG* 69: 69.

24. See M. Buber, *I and Thou: A New Translation*, trans. W. Kaufmann (Edinburgh: T. and T. Clark, 1970).

25. V. V. Ramana Murti, "Buber's Dialogue and Gandhi's Satyagraha," *The Journal of the History of Ideas* 29, no. 4 (1968): 605–13, at p. 608.

26. W. Eteki-Mboumoua, in T. K. Mahadevan, ed., *Truth and Nonviolence: A UNESCO Symposium on Gandhi* (New Delhi: Gandhi Peace Foundation, 1970), 135.

27. J. Bowker, *Problems of Suffering in Religions of the World* (Cambridge: Cambridge Univ. Press, 1970), 211. And it is by this unity, rather than the body, that the self is defined.

28. According to Gandhi, "Those who die unresistingly are likely to still the fury of violence by their wholly innocent sacrifice. But this truly non-violent action is not possible

unless it springs from a heart belief that he whom you fear and regard as a robber, dacoit or worse, and you are one, and that therefore, it is better that you die at his hands than that he, your ignorant brother, should die at yours." *Harijan*, 29 June 1940, *CWMG* 72: 200.

29. Toward the end of his life, when spelling out his vision of the Shanti Sena, Gandhi noted that the sainik will "allow himself, if need be, to be killed and thereby live through his victory over death." *Harijan*, 5 May 1946, *CWMG* 84: 67.

30. A. Naess, *Gandhi and the Nuclear Age* (Totowa, N.J.: Bedminster Press, 1965), 28–33. For a more detailed version of this formula see A. Naess, *Gandhi and Group Conflict: An Exploration of Satyagraha* (Oslo: Universitetsforlaget, 1974), 54.

31. Naess, *Gandhi and Group Conflict*, 55. This line of reasoning was adopted by Vinoba Bhave. See M. W. Sonnleitner, *Vinoba Bhave on Self-Rule & Representative Democracy* (New Delhi: Promilla, 1988), 13–42. It seems to have meant little to Jayaprakash Narayan (see, generally, chap. 8, this volume).

32. Quoted in Tendulkar, *Mahatma*, vol. 6, 88.

33. *Harijan*, 1 June 1947, quoted in Prabhu and Rao, 146.

34. *Harijan*, 20 Oct. 1940, *CWMG* 73: 108.

35. Sharp, *Politics of Nonviolent Action*, pt. 3, "Dynamics of Nonviolent Action," 709.

36. M. Chatterjee, *Gandhi's Religious Thought* (Notre Dame, Ind.: Univ. of Notre Dame Press, 1983), 76.

37. Bondurant, *Conquest of Violence*, 228.

38. *Young India*, 19 Mar. 1925, *CWMG* 16: 271.

39. Quoted in Sharp, *Politics of Nonviolent Action*, pt. 3, "Dynamics of Nonviolent Action," 709.

40. *Young India*, 4 Aug. 1920, *CWMG* 18: 118.

41. *Harijan*, 10 June 1939, *CWMG* 69: 275; see also the evaluation by early Gandhian scholar Richard B. Gregg when he claimed that for the operation of Gandhian nonviolence, although it is not necessary to believe with Rousseau that all persons are inherently good from the beginning of their lives, it is impossible to believe with Calvin that people are inherently bad and continuously sinful with only sporadic attempts at goodness. It is enough, he claims, to take as the starting point that "each person has inherently all the time both capacities, for good and for evil, and that both potentialities are plastic"; Gregg, *Power of Non-Violence*, 131.

42. *Harijan*, 18 June 1938, *CWMG* 62: 175.

43. From Gandhi's paraphrase of Ruskin's *Unto This Last*, in *The Selected Works of Mahatma Gandhi*, ed. S. Narayan, vol. 4, The Basic Works, 37–80, at p. 46.

44. *Harijan*, 11 Aug. 1940, *CWMG* 72: 350.

45. *Harijan*, 5 May 1946, *CWMG* 84: 62.

46. Bondurant, *Conquest of Violence*, 194.

47. See *Harijan*, 22 Feb. 1942, *CWMG* 75: 295.

48. L. H. Pelton, *The Psychology of Non-Violence* (New York: Pergamon Press, 1974), 143.

49. For an analysis of the way that self-suffering aids the process of conversion see Sharp, *Politics of Nonviolent Action*, pt. 3, "Dynamics of Nonviolent Action," 717–31.

50. Naess, *Gandhi and Group Conflict*, 85.

51. Quoted in G. N. Dhawan, *The Political Philosophy of Mahatma Gandhi* (Bombay: Popular Book Depot, 1957), 143.

52. Ibid.

53. *Harijan*, 15 Apr. 1939, quoted in Dhawan, 143.

54. *Young India*, 8 Oct. 1925, *CWMG* 28: 305.

55. It would seem that this scenario is at least possible; there is surely some psychological cost in being disliked by associates. At its most optimistic, in the case of tyrants, this may work by touching the heart of the many who support them through cooperation, thus isolating them: "Then, if all the satyagrahis die in the defence of their cause without any visible effect

upon the aggressor, that very act of sacrifice will awaken the conscience of the world, and the satyagrahis will have done all that it is possible for them to do." N. K. Bose "The Theory and Practice of Sarvodaya," in *The Meanings of Gandhi,* ed. P. F. Power (Honolulu: East-West Center, Univ. Press of Hawaii, 1971), 79–89, at p. 83.

56. *Young India,* 19 Mar. 1925, *CWMG* 26: 327; and see also *Young India,* 8 Aug. 1929, *CWMG* 41: 204.

57. For the argument that conversion of an opponent through self-suffering can occur, albeit via a less direct route than Gandhi and Gregg suggest, see T. Weber, "The Marchers Simply Walked Forward Until Struck Down: Nonviolent Suffering and Conversion," *Peace and Change* 18, no. 3 (1993): 267–89.

58. See Gandhi, *Autobiography,* 266; and M. K. Gandhi, *Satyagraha in South Africa* (Madras: Ganesan, 1928), 175.

59. See Gregg, *Power of Non-Violence,* passim.

60. See K. Shridharani, *War Without Violence* (Bombay: Bharatiya Vidya Bhavan, 1962).

61. See E. H. Erikson, *Gandhi's Truth: On the Origins of Militant Nonviolence* (New York: Norton, 1969).

62. *Young India,* 23 Mar. 1921, *CWMG* 19: 466.

63. Gandhi, *Autobiography,* 266.

64. Ibid.

65. B. Kumarappa, Foreword in M. K. Gandhi *Non-Violent Resistance* (New York: Schocken, 1961), iii.

66. M. Deutsch, "Conflicts: Productive and Destructive," *Journal of Social Issues* 25, no. 1 (1969): 7–41, at p. 10.

67. Ibid.

68. B. Deming, "On Revolution and Equilibrium," in *Revolution and Equilibrium,* ed. B. Deming, 211.

69. Gregg, *Power of Non-Violence,* 109.

70. Satyagraha will not always be successful. As with all other methods of conflict resolution it will have its share of failures; however, Gandhi firmly believed that the greater the degree of nonviolence exhibited by the practitioner of nonviolence, the greater the chances of success. In the case of the theoretically totally nonviolent person it would invariably succeed "with no rancour left behind, and in the end the enemies . . . converted into friends." *Harijan,* 12 Nov. 1938, *CWMG* 68: 30.

71. R. R. Diwakar, *Saga of Satyagraha* (New Delhi: Gandhi Peace Foundation, 1969), 25.

72. Bondurant, *Conquest of Violence,* vi-vii.

73. Ibid., 192.

74. Ibid., 195.

75. H. J. N. Horsburgh, *Non-Violence and Aggression: A Study of Gandhi's Moral Equivalent of War* (London: Oxford Univ. Press, 1968), 161.

76. H. J. N. Horsburgh, *Mahatma Gandhi* (London: Lutterworth Press, 1972), 36.

77. Adapted from Naess, *Gandhi and Group Conflict,* 70–84.

78. Ibid., 70. Gandhi states that "It is never the intention of a *satyagrahi* to embarrass the wrong-doer. The appeal is never to his fear; it is, must be always to his heart" (*Harijan,* 25 Mar. 1939, *CWMG* 69: 69).

79. Naess, *Gandhi and Group Conflict,* 71.

80. Ibid.

81. Ibid., 75. Gandhi spelled this out when he commented that "immediately we begin to think of things as our opponent thinks of them we shall be able to do them full justice. I know that this requires a detached state of mind, and it is a state very difficult to reach. Nevertheless for a satyagrahi it is absolutely essential. Three fourths of the miseries and

misunderstandings in the world will disappear, if we step into the shoes of our adversaries and understand their standpoint. We will then agree with our adversaries quickly or think of them charitably" (*Young India* 19 Mar. 1925, *CWMG* 66: 271).

82. Naess, *Gandhi and Group Conflict*, 79.

83. Ibid. Gandhi claimed, "I believe in trusting. Trust begets trust. Suspicion is foetid and only stinks. He who trusts has never yet lost in the world" (*Young India*, 4 June 1925, *CWMG* 27: 195); and "It is true that I have often been let down. Many have deceived me and many have been found wanting. But I do not repent of my association with them. . . . The most practical, the most dignified way of going in the world is to take people at their word, when you have no positive reason to the contrary" (*Young India*, 26 Dec. 1924, *CWMG* 25: 450).

84. Naess, *Gandhi and Group Conflict*, 81. Although Bondurant correctly points out that satyagraha is a process of synthesis rather than compromise (Bondurant, *Conquest of Violence*, 197), Gandhi made it clear that although "eternal principles" were to be defended unto death (*Harijan*, 5 Sep. 1936, *CWMG* 63: 256), "A satyagrahi never misses, can never miss, a chance of compromise on honourable terms." *Young India*, 16 Apr. 1931, *CWMG* 46: 7. Gandhi claimed that he himself was essentially a man of compromise "because I can never be sure that I am right." Quoted in L. Fischer, *A Week with Gandhi* (London: Allen and Unwin, 1943), 102.

85. Naess, *Gandhi and Group Conflict*, 81, 104.

86. Ibid., 81.

87. Ibid., 84, 104. Gandhi maintains that "in a pure fight the fighters would never go beyond the objective fixed when the fight began even if they received an accession to their strength in the course of the fighting, and on the other hand they could not give up their objective if they found their strength dwindling away." Gandhi, *Satyagraha in South Africa*, 412–13.

88. Adapted from Naess, *Gandhi and the Nuclear Age*, 60–62.

89. Bondurant, *Conquest of Violence*, 11.

90. Gregg, *Power of Non-Violence*, 41.

91. Ibid.

92. *Young India*, 8 Oct. 1925, *CWMG* 28: 306.

93. The Mahatma's statements on this point have included: "There is no such thing as compulsion in the scheme of non-violence. Reliance has to be placed upon the ability to reach the intellect and the heart" (*Harijan*, 23 July 1938, *CWMG* 67: 195); "non-violence is never a method of coercion, it is one of conversion" (*Harijan*, 8 July 1939, *CWMG* 69: 392); and "coercion is an offspring of violence. Conversion is the fruit of non-violence and love." *Young India*, 26 Nov. 1931, quoted in Hingorani, 55.

94. See C. M. Case, *Non-Violent Coercion: A Study in Social Pressure* (New York: Century, 1923).

95. It is in this way that Gandhi attempted to use his much-publicized "fasts unto death"; see "Fasting in Satyagraha," in Bose, *Studies in Gandhism*, 119–21.

96. *The Pioneer*, 2 Aug. 1934, *CWMG* 58: 248.

97. *Young India*, 19 Sep. 1929, *CWMG* 41: 374.

98. *Harijan*, 1 June 1947; quoted in Prabhu and Rao, 327.

99. *Harijan*, 2 Jan. 1937; *CWMG* 64: 192.

100. The Indian National Congress was the main nationalist organization whose office bearers were elected annually. Although he rarely occupied an official position in Congress, Gandhi was the ultimate power holder.

101. *Harijan*, 15 Feb. 1948, *CWMG* 90: 526–28.

102. See J. W. Gould, "Gandhi's Contribution to the Practice of the Law of Love in International Relations," *Gandhi Marg* 1, no. 7 (1979): 436–51, at p. 448.

103. *Harijan*, 28 July 1940, *CWMG* 72: 306.

104. R. B. Gregg, *A Discipline for Non-Violence* (Ahmedabad: Navajivan, 1941), 13.

105. See M. K. Gandhi, "Constructive Programme: Its Meaning and Place," in *The Selected Work of Mahatma Gandhi*, ed. S. Narayan: 335.

106. It will be apparent from this list that the Constructive Program is somewhat different from the type of technical assistance work that aims to tackle the "problems" caused by "underdevelopment." Here, rather, the emphasis is on "uplift."

107. Gregg, *Discipline*, 5.

108. Horsburgh, *Non-Violence and Aggression*, 67.

109. M. K. Gandhi, *Hind Swaraj or Indian Home Rule* (Ahmedabad: Navajivan, 1939), 30.

110. For example: "Training for military revolt means learning the use of arms ending perhaps in the atomic bomb. For civil disobedience it means the Constructive Programme" (Gandhi, *Constructive Programme*, 336); and "Constructive work . . . is for a non-violent army what drilling etc. is for an army designed for bloody warfare." *Young India*, 9 June 1930, quoted in J. P. Chander, ed., *Teachings of Mahatma Gandhi* (Lahore: Indian Printing Works, 1947), 122.

111. For example, "Civil Disobedience, mass or individual, is an aid to constructive effort and is a full substitute for armed revolt." *Gandhi Constructive Programme*, 336.

112. Ibid., 369.

113. Ibid., 370.

114. For example, Gandhi has claimed, "Unaccompanied by the spirit of service, courting imprisonment, and inviting beating and lathi charges, becomes a species of violence." *Harijan*, 25 Mar. 1939, *CWMG* 69: 8. See also H. J. N. Horsburgh "Nonviolence and Impatience," *Gandhi Marg* 12, no. 4 (1968): 355–61, at p. 359.

115. Gregg, *Discipline*, 5.

116. *Harijan*, 12 Apr. 1942 *CWMG* 86: 6.

117. See Gandhi, *Satyagraha in South Africa*, 174–81; *Harijan*, 31 Aug. 1947, *CWMG* 89: 62; and prayer meeting speech, *CWMG* 88: 274.

118. Quoted as an appendix to Gandhi, "Constructive Programme: It's Meaning and Place," 372.

119. *Young India*, 6 Aug. 1931, *CWMG* 47: 246.

120. *Harijan*, 1 June 1940, *CWMG* 72: 105.

121. *Harijan*, 21 July 1940, quoted in M. K. Gandhi, *Non-Violence in Peace and War* (Ahmedabad: Navajivan, 1942), vol. 1, 308.

5. A History of the Shanti Sena

1. S. Narayan, *Vinoba: His Life and Work* (Bombay: Popular, 1970), 168.

2. *Harijan*, 4 Apr. 1948.

3. Ibid. "Singing parties" refers to the frequent gatherings in village India to sing devotional songs (*bhajans*).

4. S. Narayan, *Vinoba*, 174.

5. *Harijan*, 6 May 1950. See app. C for the complete text of S. N. Agarwal's report of the meeting.

6. The word *Sarvodaya* literally means the welfare or "rising" of all, not merely the majority. Sarvodaya is the term used in India for the social philosophy of Mahatma Gandhi, and Sarvodaya workers are, in effect, Gandhian social workers.

7. V. Tandon, *Sarvodaya ki Aur* (Delhi: Atmaram, 1968), 74.

8. *Harijan*, 13 May 1950. Kalelkar notes that the uniform consisted of "a blue button on the Gandhi cap, and a piece of blue scarfe made of *khadi*." See K. S. Kalelkar, "Non-violent Army for Peace," *Fellowship* May (1956): 13–15, at p. 15.

9. *Harijan*, 22 July 1950.

10. Formed in 1949 as a confederation of the All-India Spinners' Association, All-India Village Industries Association, Hindustani Talimi Sangh, Go Seva Sangh, and Hindustani Prachar Sabha; all constructive work organizations founded by Gandhi.

11. See Resolution No. 16 in the minutes of the Sarva Seva Sangh conference held at Wardha, 13 July 1950. All references to the discussions held by the Sarva Seva Sangh (hereafter SSS) and the Sangh's Prabhand Samiti (executive committee, hereafter SSSPS) are taken from the Sangh's minutes books held at the Sarva Seva Sangh headquarters in Sevagram, near Wardha. Where there is more readily obtainable English language documentation available, it is used in preference to my own translations of the minutes.

12. G. Ostergaard and M. Currel, *The Gentle Anarchists: A Study of the Leaders of the Sarvodaya Movement for Non-Violent Revolution in India* (Oxford: Clarendon Press, 1971), 59.

13. V. Bhave, *Swaraj Sastra* [*The Principles of a Non-Violent Political Order*], (Varanasi: Sarva Seva Sangh, 1973), 79.

14. See SSS minutes of conference at Shivarampalli, 7 Apr. 1951, Resolution No. 15.

15. S. Ram, *Vinoba and His Mission* [*Being an Account of the Rise and Growth of the Bhoodan Yajna Movement*], (Varanasi: Akhil Bharat Sarva Seva Sangh, 1962), 51.

16. V. Bhave, *Shanti Sena* (Varanasi: Sarva Seva Sangh, 1963), 10.

17. See SSS minutes of meeting at Bajajwadi, Wardha, 6 July 1951, Resolution No. 79.

18. See R. Church, "Vinoba and the Origins of Bhoodan," *Gandhi Marg* 5, no. 8/9 (1983): 469–91.

19. The figure is 7,500, according to Tandon, but this appears to be a typographical error. The intended figure was probably 75,000. See V. Tandon, "The Bhoodan-Gramdan Movement, 1951–74—A Review," *Gandhi Marg* 5, no. 8/9 (1983): 492–500, at p. 493. Vinoba biographer Kanti Shah puts the figure at 40,000 miles (65,000 kilometers approximately), whereas Vinoba's close associate, Nirmala Deshpande, claims that the distance was "more than 80,000 kms." See K. Shah, *Vinoba: Life and Mission (An Introductory Study)* (Varanasi: Sarva Seva Sangh, 1979), 64; and N. Deshpande, "Vinoba Wisdom," *Gandhi Marg* 5, no. 8/9 (1983): 630–33, at p. 631.

20. See Tandon, "Bhoodan-Gramdan Movement."

21. Ibid., 499.

22. Ibid., 493.

23. V. Nargolkar, *The Creed of Saint Vinoba* (Bombay: Bharatiya Vidya Bhavan, 1963), 211–12.

24. Ram, 204.

25. Ibid., 205, 212; Bhave, *Shanti Sena*, 1963, 23.

26. Bhave, *Shanti Sena*, 1963, 12; Ram, 206; and Nargolkar, *Creed of Saint Vinoba*, 212. Vinoba himself enrolled as a Shanti Sainik and took the pledge (see Ostergaard and Currel, 371). For a note on the Shanti Sena pledges generally and the text of the specific pledge taken by the initial eight Shanti Sainiks see app. D.

27. Bhave, *Shanti Sena*, 1963, 13–14.

28. Ram, 212; Bhave, *Shanti Sena*, 1963, 30.

29. See app. D.

30. The Sarvodaya Patra system had been announced in 1955 at the annual Sarvodaya conference held at Pandharpur. See Ram, 497–99, at p. 498. It was renamed the Shanti Patra by a resolution of the Shanti Sena Mandal during August 1961. See SSSPS minutes of meeting at Varanasi, 13 August 1961; N. Desai, *Shanti Sena in India* (Varanasi: Sarva Seva Sangh, 1969), 23; and A. D. Aryanayakam, "Shanti Sena: The Peace Army of India," *The War Resister* 92 (1961): 11–12, at p. 12.

31. Nargolkar, *The Creed of Saint Vinoba*, 216–17.

32. Bhave, *Shanti Sena*, 1963, 53–54.

33. Nargolkar, *Creed of Saint Vinoba*, 217.

34. Interview with Jagdishbhai Lakhia, Gujarat Shanti Sena coordinator during the 1960s, 20 Nov. 1988, at Mangrol.

35. *Sarva Seva Sangh (Monthly Newsletter)* 2, no. 1 (1968): 51.

36. Desai, *Shanti Sena in India,* 1969, 23.

37. *Sarva Seva Sangh (Monthly Newsletter)* 1, no. 4 (1967): 45.

38. Bhave, *Shanti Sena,* 1963, 75.

39. Desai, *Shanti Sena in India,* 1969, 7.

40. See Bhave, *Shanti Sena,* 1963, 136–49.

41. Ram, 252–53.

42. Bhave, *Shanti Sena,* 1963, 56.

43. Ibid., 71–73.

44. Ibid., 93, 101, 129–30.

45. Ibid., 100. Vinoba made the point that a sainik must work for *both* peace and a nonviolent transformation of society that amounted to a social revolution; see V. Bhave, "The Shanti Sainik: His Duties and Responsibilities," *Bhoodan* 5, no. 25 (1960): 196–97.

46. Bhave, *Shanti Sena,* 1963, 108.

47. Ashadevi Aryanayakam had been one of Rabindranath Tagore's students and Gandhi's co-worker. With her husband she founded the education center at Sevagram.

48. Ram, 265.

49. See Vinoba's Pathankot speech, Bhave, *Shanti Sena,* 1963, 73–74.

50. Ibid., 128.

51. See SSSPS minutes of meeting at Varanasi, 10 May 1960.

52. See SSSPS minutes of meeting at Indore, 17 Aug. 1960.

53. See SSS minutes of meeting at Bangalore, 29 Oct. 1960.

54. "Shanti-Sena in India," *Bhoodan* 6, no. 36 (1963): 285.

55. See SSSPS minutes of meeting at Varanasi, 2 Nov. 1961.

56. N. Desai, *Shanti Sena in India* (Varanasi: Sarva Seva Sangh, 1962), 9; and Bhave, *Shanti Sena,* 1963, 159. See also N. Desai, *A Report of the All India Shanti Sena (August 1957 to July 1962)* (Varanasi: Akhil Bharat Shanti Sena Mandal, 1962).

57. N. Desai, *Towards a Non-Violent Revolution* (Varanasi: Sarva Seva Sangh, 1972), 12, 68.

58. Desai, *Shanti Sena in India,* 1969, 24.

59. Ibid.

60. For the revised pledge see app. D.

61. "Broadcasting the Shanti Sena," *Bhoodan* 7, no. 2 (1962): 2.

62. Ibid.

63. See the comments of Jugatram Dave, SSSPS minutes of meeting at Kapri, 30 March 1964; and SSS minutes of meeting at Vaighai, 17 Nov. 1964.

64. See report of the SSS half-yearly session at Nakodar, 16–18 May 1972, 94.

65. To a large extent the Tatpar Shanti Sena was defeated by logistics. Most sainiks did not have telephones, and no efficient means of communication could be devised. It could take up to four days to reach riot-affected areas if they were in distant parts of the country. Interview with Chunibhai Vaidya, SSS secretary, 30 Nov. 1988, at Sabarmati Ashram, Ahmedabad.

66. See SSS minutes of meeting at Patna, 9 Apr. 1962; and "Broadcasting the Shanti Sena," 2.

67. See SSSPS minutes of meeting at Patna, 17 June 1962.

68. Interview with Narayan Desai on 25 Nov. 1988, at Vedchhi.

69. For the often strained relationship between JP and Vinoba see R. Church, "Vinoba Bhave, Jayaprakash Narayan and Indian Democracy," *Gandhian Perspectives* 2, no. 2 (1980): 89–129; and for their differences over the appropriate response to Chinese incursion see T. Weber, "Peacekeeping, the Shanti Sena and Divisions in the Gandhian Movement During the Border War with China," *South Asia* 13, no. 2 (1990): 65–78.

70. J. P. Narayan, *The Dual Revolution* (Tanjore: Sarvodaya Prachuralaya, 1963), 25–27. JP reiterated this interpretation at the inaugural speech of the War Resisters' International conference at Gandhigram at the end of 1960; see J. P. Narayan, *A Picture of Sarvodaya Social Order* (Tiruchirapalli: Sarvodaya Prachuralaya, 1961), 161–76, at p. 171.

71. Goa was a small Portuguese colony on the west coast of India. From the mid-1950s onward satyagrahis attempted several nonviolent "invasions" in an effort to liberate Goa; however, the task was finally achieved by the Indian army in Dec. 1961.

72. J. P. Narayan, "Why a World Peace Guard," *Vigil* 12, no. 48/49 (1962): 771–72; and J. P. Narayan, "Thoughts on Goa," *Bhoodan* 6, no. 37 (1961): 300.

73. Bhave, *Shanti Sena,* 1963, 94–96, at p. 94.

74. Bhave, *Shanti Sena,* 1963, 118–20.

75. The Sangh's stance on the tensions of the Indo-Chinese border had already been discussed at a SSSPS meeting held in Varanasi on 29 Oct. 1959 and at a meeting of the full SSS at Sevagram 20–27 Mar. 1960. At the earlier meeting, just two months after the Longju Incident, the first border skirmish between India and China, JP was anxious for the Sangh to formulate an attitude to the situation. Although some argued for satyagraha on the border, it was agreed that the role for Shanti Sainiks and Sahayaks was to create a national atmosphere conducive to nonviolence that would help the idea of popular self-defense gain momentum. JP, Shankarrao Deo, and Vallabh Swami were deputed to prepare a statement on the issue. To a large degree the statement was a criticism of the attitude of China. Much of the sixth day of the Sevagram conference was taken up with heated debate on this statement. There was heavy criticism of the drafters for issuing it without first consulting the Sangh membership or having it endorsed by Vinoba. A resolution clarifying the Sangh's position was drafted. It stated that in the nuclear age the use of force had become obsolete and that the border clash had become a challenge to believers in nonviolence and provided an opportunity to seek out nonviolent alternatives to war. The Sangh, further, declared that its duty was to strengthen the forces of nonviolence because national defense through military means does nothing about poverty, unemployment, and internal peace. For real national security, gramswaraj and the Shanti Sena were declared essential. The resolution reiterated the need for maintaining love for opponents and Gandhi's message of the way of conversion. It concluded with a call to create conditions in the country that would make such an approach possible and a pledge that Sangh members would, if the country were attacked, die if necessary but would refuse to use violence against, or to submit to, the enemy. See also S. Dhadda, "Aggression and Non-Violence," *Bhoodan* 4, no. 32 (1959): 249–50.

76. Nargolkar, *Creed of Saint Vinoba,* 250–51.

77. Ibid., 252.

78. Ibid., 253.

79. V. Bhave, "The Present Crisis in India: Appeal to Countrymen," *Sarvodaya* 12, no. 6 (1962): 204–5, at p. 205.

80. S. Narayan, *Vinoba,* 300.

81. Ibid.

82. Ibid.

83. J. Bristol, "Lessons from the India-China Conflict," *Bhoodan* 8, no. 14 (1963): 107–8, at p. 108. See also P. Brock, *The Mahatma and Mother India (Essays on Gandhi's Non-Violence and Nationalism)* (Ahmedabad: Navajivan, 1983), 81; and P. Brock, *Twentieth-Century Pacifism* (New York: Van Nostrand Reinhold, 1970), 221. See app. D for the text of the pledges.

84. A. Scarfe and W. Scarfe, *J. P.: His Biography* (New Delhi: Orient Longman, 1975), 380.

85. Ibid. For JP's summary of the arguments at the Vedchhi conference see J. P. Narayan, "The Unresolved Question," *Sarvodaya* 13, no. 7 (1964): 273–78, at p. 276.

86. Although this is the "official" Indian version of events, it is not necessarily supported by the available facts. See N. Maxwell, *India's China War* (Harmondsworth, England: Penguin, 1972).

87. Bhave, *Shanti Sena,* 1963, 154–57. This was the intention of Sarvodaya workers Vasant and Kusum Nargolkar who had received permission from Nehru to go to the troubled North East Frontier Agency to "propagate ideas of *gramdan* and non-violent resistance." Vinoba, however, taking care to ensure that the Shanti Sena was not embroiled in controversy, gave their "very small scale . . . experiment in organising non-violent resistance by the villagers, in case of a repeated Chinese attack in September or October 1963" a relatively lukewarm blessing: "It is good that you are going to NEFA as individuals. . . . You are striving in your own small way to find out the non-violent alternative to violent resistance or to war. If you achieve even a limited success in your attempt to offer non-violent resistance in some village, it should be considered as a victory for the Sarvodaya movement. If you fail in it, you should be inclined to look upon it as your personal failure." K. Nargolkar, *In the Wake of the Chinese Thrust* (Bombay: Popular, 1965), 1, 3.

88. Scarfe and Scarfe, 380. JP's writings on war and national defense at this time were a restatement of Gandhi's sentiments about the efficacy of a "living wall" approach and the belief that soldiers could not continue killing nonresisting nonthreatening civilians forever. See J. P. Narayan, "India, China and Peace," *Liberation* 8, no. 7 (1963): 21–24.

89. Scarfe and Scarfe, 380. See also letter from American Delhi to Peking marcher Ed Lazar to A. J. Muste, 3 May 1963, Muste Papers, Box 41, Folder 1.

90. The Sarva Seva Sangh made it clear that the responsibility for the march lay with the World Peace Brigade and that the Shanti Sena Mandal was merely the host. While endorsing the objects of the march and congratulating the marchers on their effort, the Sangh cautioned that although members were free to express their views, those views should not be too controversial. See SSS minutes of the Sarva Seva Sangh conference at Arambagh, 23 Apr. 1963.

91. J. P. Narayan, "Unresolved Question," 277.

92. Ibid., 277–78; and Scarfe and Scarfe, 381.

93. Quoted in V. Tandon, ed., *Selections from Vinoba* (Varanasi: Sarva Seva Sangh, 1981), 203.

94. Ostergaard and Currel, 256. Bristol notes that there was confusion about what positive resistance action could be taken by sainiks: fighting nonviolently beside the Indian army or placing themselves between the contesting forces without "opposing one army more than another"? And what if the Indian Army did not let them reach the border? What if they blocked the path of the advancing Chinese troops, who, in turn, merely drove off the road and around them? He concludes, "These questions, however, remained academic since no action was taken." J. E. Bristol, *Non-violence and India Today* (Philadelphia: Peace Education Division of the American Friend's Service Committee, 1963), 4.

95. Narayan, "Unresolved Question," 277; and Scarfe and Scarfe, 381.

96. Ostergaard and Currel, 256.

97. Interview with Thakurdas Bang, 2 Feb. 1989, at Gopuri.

98. Narayan, "Unresolved Question," 278.

99. Scarfe and Scarfe, 381.

100. Ostergaard and Currel, 256.

101. Tandon, *Social and Political Philosophy,* 156.

102. Ostergaard and Currel, 254.

103. Tandon, *Social and Political Philosophy,* 156. Kalelkar had already expressed this sentiment when in 1950 he maintained that premature steps toward nonviolence by government that did not command public support would result in the fall of the government and its replacement with one less favorable to nonviolence. See V. Tandon, "Present-day Sarvodaya Thinkers and War," *Gandhi Marg* 15, no. 1 (1971): 64–72, at p. 65. During 1959, the previous period of high border tension, Vinoba had apparently declared that the sending of Shanti Sainiks to the affected areas was itself a "violent approach." See Dhadda, 250.

104. Ostergaard and Currel, 254. The authors add that arguments such as Prasad's,

quoting Gandhi that violence is superior to cowardice, "often conveniently omitted to mention [Gandhi's] view that the practice of non-violence is always superior to the use of violence." Marjorie Sykes was already making this point in early 1963; see M. Sykes, "Shanti Sena and the Government," *Sarvodaya* 12, no. 9 (1963): 337–41, and ibid. 12, no. 10 (1963): 387–88, 393. See also Lazar, 20–23.

105. Tandon, *Social and Political Philosophy,* 157.

106. Ibid., v.

107. See Sykes, "Shanti Sena and the Government"; and A. J. Muste, *Report on the Indian Crisis* (Varanasi: World Peace Brigade, Asia Region, 1963), 6. Bristol correctly indicates that the following three points should be kept in mind when discussing the attitude of Gandhians to India's war effort with China: (1) Gandhi's nonviolent movement was a nationalist movement and those in the government were in the movement as old comrades in suffering with the Gandhians. (2) The towering personality of Nehru ensured that no one wished to embarrass him. (3) Vinoba was venerated in the Gandhian movement, and his blessing was required for any action. J. Bristol, "Lessons from the India-China Conflict," *Bhoodan* 8, no. 13 (1963): 99–102, at p. 99. Although Vinoba had not personally met Nehru until the 1948 Sevagram conference, there Vinoba stated, "I do not look on Pandit Jawaharlal Nehru as a representative of the Government; I regard him as a member of the Gandhian family," and "Gandhiji had reiterated several times that Pandit Nehru would be his successor. We can, therefore, lay claim to his guidance at this difficult hour." They were to meet several more times before Nehru's death in 1964, and Nehru often sought Vinoba's advice on difficult matters. See Narayan, *Vinoba,* 170–71, 302–14; and V. Tandon, "Nehru and Vinoba," *Gandhi Marg* 10, no. 8/9 (1988): 570–78. Further, Ostergaard claims that Vinoba considered Nehru his "brother" and believed that he "was earnestly trying to carry on Gandhi's work." See G. Ostergaard, "Vinoba's 'Gradualist' Versus Western 'Immediatist' Anarchism," *Gandhi Marg* 5, no. 8/9 (1983): 509–30, at p. 523.

108. Ostergaard and Currel, 256–57.

109. Ibid., 374.

110. K. Nargolkar, *Wake of the Chinese Thrust,* 9–10.

111. Ibid., 272.

112. Ibid., 271.

113. See SSSPS minutes of Meeting at Raipur, 22 Dec. 1963.

114. *Bhoodan* 8, no. 38/39 (1964): 299.

115. Ostergaard and Currel, 11.

116. J. P. Narayan, "The Urgency for Shanti Sena," *Sarvodaya* 14, no. 4 (1964): 153–57, at p. 156; and J. P. Narayan, *Towards Total Revolution,* ed. Brahmanand (Bombay: Popular, 1978), vol. 2, 292. See also N. Desai, "While the Hearts Were Scorched," in *A Time to Speak (An Appeal for Rethinking our Communal Disturbances)* (pamphlet, "Only for private circulation," issued by the Sarva Seva Sangh, 1964), 19–24, at pp. 19–21.

117. Narayan, "Urgency for Shanti Sena," 158.

118. Ibid.

119. Ibid., 156–57.

120. *Bhoodan* 5, no. 5 (1960): 39.

121. *Bhoodan* 8, no. 38/39 (1964): 299.

122. At SSS meeting at Vaighai on 17 November 1964 it was resolved that all Shanti Sainiks should be associated with a local kendra, that kendras should be introduced in Gramdan villages, and that khadi kendras should have shanti kendras attached.

123. Desai, *Shanti Sena in India,* 1969, 25–26.

124. N. Desai, *A Handbook for Shanti Sainiks* (Varanasi: Sarva Seva Sangh, 1963), 13; see also N. Desai, *A Hand Book for Shanti Sena Instructors* (Varanasi: Akhil Bharat Shanti Sena Mandal, n.d.), 12–17, for advice about "Initiating and Running a Shanti Kendra."

125. C. C. Walker, *Organizing for Nonviolent Direct Action* (Cheney, Pa.: author, 1961).

126. Desai, *Handbook for Shanti Sainiks,* 1.

127. "Training in Shanti Sena," *Bhoodan* 6, no. 40 (1962): 332.

128. Desai, *Towards a Non-Violent Revolution,* 102.

129. Ibid., 103.

130. Ibid.

131. Ibid., 105.

132. K. Kumar, "A Report on the Balia Sarvodaya Conference," *Gandhi Marg* 10, no. 3 (1966): 246–48, at p. 248.

133. During the Nakodar session of the SSS, Rawat and Gangaprasad Agarwal were named co-conveners of the Sena under the convenership of Narayan Desai. See SSSPS minutes of meeting at Nakodar, 14–20 May 1972.

134. S. Patel and I. Rawat, *Shanti Sena Margdarshika* (Vedchhi: Gujarat Vidyapith, 1970).

135. See N. Radhakrishnan, *Gandhi and Youth: The Shanti Sena of GRI* (Gandhigram: Gandhigram Rural Institute, 1990); N. Radhakrishnan, "Training in Peace Education: An Indian Perspective," *Gandhi Marg* 6, no. 4/5 (1984): 331–43; N. Radhakrishnan, "The Shanti-sena in Gandhigram" (N.d., Manuscript); and N. Radhakrishnan, "Shanti Sena: Concept and Practice," *Non-violent Revolution* 8, no. 6 (1990): 2–4.

136. See Vinoba's speech at the Raipur SSS conference, 23 December 1963.

137. N. Radhakrishna and N. Desai, "Indo-Pakistan Conflict and our Duty," *Sarvodaya* 15, no. 5 (1965): 224–26.

138. See SSS minutes of conference at Sevagram, 8 Aug. 1963, and see SSS minutes of conference at Vaighai, 17 Nov. 1964.

139. Desai, *Shanti Sena in India,* 1969, 26.

140. Ibid., 27. At the Shanti Sena Mandal meeting at Pattikalayana (Harayana), 30–31 Mar. 1967, presided over by JP, it was decided that all Shanti Sainiks should renew their pledge yearly by sending a letter to the central office during the week of Gandhi's death anniversary. Those who failed to renew their pledge "either by writing or by reading it in a group, should be deleted from the Shanti Sena Register." See "The Strengthening of Shanti Sena Movement," *Peace Newsletter* (published by the Gandhi Peace Foundation) 1, no. 19 (1967): 3–5.

141. See SSS minutes of conference at Shivarampalli, 25 Apr. 1967. At the "Consultation on an International Peace Brigade" held on Grindstone Island, Ontario, 31 Aug.–4 Sept. 1981, in answer to the question "How many Shanti Sainiks are there?" Narayan Desai answered, "In the 1960s a gross figure was 12,000 potential volunteers nationwide, but after screening, a net figure of circa 6,000." See minutes, 5.

142. See SSS minutes of conference at Shivarampalli, 25 Apr. 1967.

143. T. Bang, *The Next Step* (N.p.: Sarva Seva Sangh, n.d.), 13.

144. Ibid., 14.

145. See report of the SSS half-yearly conference at Nasik, 5–8 May 1971, 14.

146. See report of the SSS half-yearly conference at Nakodar, in the Punjab, 16–18 May 1972, 94; and minutes of the joint SSSPS and Shanti Sena Mandal meeting at Kurukshetra, 6–14 Apr. 1973, especially the speeches by R. K. Patil and Gangaprasad Agarwal. Badriprasad Swami added that work was not progressing effectively owing to financial difficulties. At the SSS Prabhand Samiti meeting at Sarnath, near Varanasi, 12–14 July 1973, the Shanti Sena Mandal reported a budget shortfall in excess of Rs.42,300.

147. Desai, *Towards a Non-Violent Revolution,* 90; and see also N. Desai "The Making and Bearing of the Youth Peace Corps" (N.d., Mimeo.).

148. Desai, *Towards a Non-Violent Revolution,* 90; and Akhil Bharat Shanti Sena Mandal, *Youth Peace Corps (Tarun Shanti Sena)* (Varanasi, n.d., Booklet), 3.

149. J. P. Narayan, "The Philosophy of Peace," *Interdiscipline* 5, no. 1/2 (1968): 98–103, at pp. 101–102.

150. S. K. Mishra, "A Search for a Peaceful Revolution, A Challenge for the Indian Youth," *People's Action* 8, no. 8 (1973): 9–16, at p. 11.

151. J. P. Narayan, "Indian Youth Peace Corps," *Sarvodaya* 17, no. 9 (1968): 393–95, at p. 393.

152. Desai, *Hand Book for Shanti Sena Instructors,* 1.

153. Desai, *Towards a Non-Violent Revolution,* 92.

154. Ibid., 93.

155. Akhil Bharat Shanti Sena Mandal, *Youth Peace Corps,* 5.

156. Mishra, 12.

157. Ibid., 7–8.

158. See the report by Thakurdas Bang at the joint SSS / Shanti Sena Mandal meeting at Kurukshetra, 6–14 Apr. 1973, where he detailed the content of his talks with leading Tarun Shanti Sainiks. He declared that the youth agreed with the work of the Sarvodaya movement but wanted their own separate identity while keeping contact with the movement.

159. Interview with Ashok Bang, a leading Tarun Shanti Sena worker, and son of Professor Thakurdas Bang, 4 Feb. 1989, at Gopuri.

160. G. Ostergaard, *Nonviolent Revolution in India* (New Delhi: Gandhi Peace Foundation, 1985), 153, 294–98.

161. See N. Desai, *Handbook for Satyagrahis* (New Delhi: Gandhi Peace Foundation, 1980), 39–41; and N. Desai, *A Hand-Book for a Satyagrahi* (Varanasi: National People's Committee, n.d.), 48–50.

162. Interview with Ashok Bhargava, 16 Nov. 1988, at Mangrol.

163. Interview with Arun Kumar, leading Tarun Shanti Sainik and Bihar movement activist, 21 Jan. 1989, at Rajghat, Varanasi.

164. In Desai's words, the Tarun Shanti Sena was finally disbanded because "there was nobody who was willing to give full time to it." N. Desai, "Narayan Desai: Nonviolent Revolutionary—A Diary of a Gandhian Educator," ed. A. Paul Hare (1979, Manuscript), 87.

165. Interview with Ashok Bang, 4 Feb. 1989, Gopuri.

166. See comments by Abhey Bang, Acharya Ramamurti, Manmohan Choudhuri, and Narayan Desai.

167. Interview with Ashok Bang, 4 Feb. 1989, Gopuri.

168. For a detailed description of the later history of the Gandhian movement see especially Ostergaard, *Nonviolent Revolution;* and also Church, "Bhave, Narayan and Indian Democracy"; M. Shepard, *Since Gandhi* (Weare, N. H.: Greenleaf Books, 1984); and I. Harris, "Sarvodaya in Crisis: The Gandhian Movement in India Today," *Asian Survey* 27, no. 9 (1987): 1036–52.

169. See J. P. Narayan, "Face to Face," in J. P. Narayan, *Towards Total Revolution,* ed. Brahmanand (Bombay: Popular, 1978), vol. 1, 231–53.

170. For a somewhat more positive assessment of the outcome of the Musahari experiment see R. C. Pradhan, "Musahari: A Gandhian Experiment in Peace Action and Peace Education," *Bulletin of Peace Proposals* 15, no. 2 (1984): 125–33.

171. Leading Sarvodaya worker Kanti Shah implied that many of the difficulties of the next few years resulted from Vinoba's becoming a de facto captive of the views of his closest followers after his withdrawal from the world: "Vinoba's contact with the outer-world had diminished. So, he had to rely on information received through others. All the workers could not meet him regularly. Many colleagues regarded as close to him were, I feel, no longer healthy or detached in their outlook." Shah, *Vinoba: Life and Mission,* 131.

172. See J. P. Narayan, *Total Revolution* (Varanasi: Sarva Seva Sangh, 1975).

173. See V. Nargolkar, *JP's Crusade for Revolution* (New Delhi: Chand, 1975), 110–14.

174. For a detailed description of this historic meeting see Ostergaard, *Nonviolent Revolution,* 95–111.

175. Ibid., 167–81.

176. V. Bhave "Dissolution of the Sarva Seva Sangh," *Sansthakul* 4, no. 10 (1976): 8–9.

177. Amarnath Mishra had left university in 1954 to join the Bhoodan movement; in 1962 Narayan Desai invited him to join the Shanti Vidyalaya at Rajghat.

178. See SSSPS minutes of meeting at Sevagram, 23 July 1978. The next year the budget for the Sena was still an extremely low Rs.45,000. See SSSPS minutes of meeting at Ferozpur, 19 July 1979.

179. See report of the SSS meeting at Ferozpur, 17–19 July 1979, 39.

180. As early as 1958, while not expressly outlawing the casting of ballots by Shanti Sainiks, Vinoba, whose word was law in the Gandhian movement, answered the question, "May a Shanti Sainik vote in elections?" in such a way as to make his feelings on the matter quite clear. He stated, "Every person has a right to vote, but all the same it would be better that a Shanti Sainik should keep clear of these affairs." Bhave, *Shanti Sena*, 1963, 94.

181. Interview with Manmohan Choudhury, 3 Jan. 1989, at Rajghat, New Delhi; and Amarnath Mishra, 17 Jan. 1989, at Rajghat, Varanasi.

182. Interview with Achyut Deshpande, 16 Feb. 1989, at Ghatkopar, Bombay.

183. See SSSPS minutes of meeting at Bhopal, 25 Oct. 1971; "Vinoba Urges UNO Sponsored P. B.," 110–12; and *Sarvodaya* 23, no. 2 (1973): 64.

184. See "Vinoba's Answers to Acharyakul Questions," *Sansthakul* 9, no. 10 (1981): 4–7, at p. 5. The figure seven hundred thousand would have given approximately Vinoba's ideal of one sainik for every five thousand people in the world. The one hundred thousand figure that was to make up India's contribution, came about "because India's population is one seventh of the world's population," *Sarvodaya* 23, no. 2 (1973): 64.

185. See Ostergaard, *Nonviolent Revolution*, 324.

186. Interview with Narayan Desai, 25 Nov. 1988, at Vedchhi.

187. Sarva Seva Sangh, *Sarva Seva Sangh Work Report, July 1979-April 1981, from Ferozpur to Ujain* (Varanasi: Sarva Seva Sangh, 1981), 21–22.

188. Interview with Chunibhai Vaidya, 30 Nov. 1988, Harijan Ashram, Ahmedabad.

189. Quoted in Ostergaard, *Nonviolent Revolution*, 324.

190. See *Sarva Seva Sangh Work Report*, 22.

191. He later made it clear that they should not vote even for independent candidates. See Tandon, *Selections from Vinoba*, 334.

192. Ibid., 333–34.

193. See SSSPS minutes of meeting at Khadagpur, 31 May-6 June 1980; and report of SSS conference held at Khadagpur, 1–3 June 1980, 16–18; and *Vigil* 2, no. 44/45 (1980): 20.

194. See SSSPS minutes of meeting at Nadiad, 27 Oct. 1980.

195. Report of the SSS conference at Shrimangeshi, Goa, 1–3 Mar. 1981, 18–19.

196. "Bharatiya Shanti Sena," *Sansthakul* 10, no. 10 (1982): 5–8 at p. 7.

197. *Sansthakul* 10, no. 9 (1981): 1–6 at p. 1.

198. "Bharatiya Shanti Sena," 7.

199. Ibid.

200. *Sansthakul* 10, no. 9 (1981): 1–6, at p. 6.

201. See report of the SSS meeting at Jaganathpuri, Orissa, 28–30 Nov. 1981, 53.

202. See SSSPS minutes of meeting at Jaganathpuri, 27–30 Nov. 1981.

203. Interview with Acharya Ramamurti, 7 Jan. 1989, at Khadigram.

204. Gujarat remained an anomaly. Deshpande had appointed Rawat state convener, and Rawat and Patel recommenced running their Shanti Sena camps—the only venue for such camps during the lean years in the history of the Shanti Sena. Fifteen hundred enrollments were taken (although Rawat admits that many were sainiks in little but name), and Gujarat become the only truly functioning state in the Bharatiya Shanti Sena fold. When the SSS decided to reactivate its national Sena, it decided against working in Gujarat. As the Gujarat Sena also began to show signs of decline (Rawat stopped recruitment when the Sangh reorga-

nized its Sena), the Sangh was ready to reconsider this concession, but as its energies went increasingly into fighting the government of Rajiv Gandhi, no action was taken. Because of this inaction, Rawat has recently threatened to revive his own recruitment campaign. Interviews with Indrasingh Rawat, 10 Nov. 1988 and 13 Feb. 1989, at Karadi.

205. See SSSPS minutes of meeting at Sevagram, 29–30 Aug. 1984.

206. See SSSPS minutes of meeting at Delhi, 14–15 Sep. 1985.

207. *Vigil* 7, no. 46 (1985): 6.

208. See SSSPS minutes of meeting at Ranipatra, 4–7 Mar. 1986.

209. Ramamurti, "The Next Thirteen Years in India: A Nonviolent Perspective," *Vigil* 9, no. 9 (1987): 3–7, 15–16, at p. 7.

210. See SSSPS minutes of meeting at Khadigram, 24–26 June 1987.

211. See SSSPS minutes of meeting at Bhopal, 15 Sep. 1987; and app. D for the text of the revised pledge.

212. In 1987 Ramamurti made his feelings clear when he stated that since the coming to office of the Rajiv government, and as its direct consequence, the country has been moving away from the Gandhian path faster than before, and that now both the polity and the economy are irretrievably set on a totally un-Gandhian path. See Ramamurti, "Next Thirteen Years."

213. See SSSPS minutes of meeting at Borivilli, Bombay, 23–29 Dec. 1987.

214. See SSSPS minutes of meeting at Sevagram, 13 Apr. 1988.

215. See SSSPS minutes of meeting at Trivandrum, 8 Dec. 1988.

216. Interview with Badriprasad Swami, 18 Jan. 1989, at Rajghat, Varanasi.

217. Ibid.

218. Interview with Dr. K. Arunachalam, chairman of the Gandhi Smarak Nidhi, 5 Sep. 1990, at Melbourne.

219. Personal communication from Badriprasad Swami, dated 21 Sep. 1990. See also references to the "Challenge of Gandhi" campaign in *Sansthakul* 20, no. 3 (1990): 21–22; and *Sansthakul* 20, no. 4 (1990): 23–24. The program states that "Shanti Sena organised in every village with the concurrence of Gram Sabhas should take up the task of establishing peace and justice," *Sansthakul* 20, no. 7 (1990): 6–12, at p. 11.

220. The only mention of the Shanti Sena in the resolutions of the Sarva Seva Sangh, adopted at a meeting immediately preceding the Sarvodaya sammelan, was in a general call to workers to help propagate "programmes related to Gramswaraj," which included, inter alia, the Shanti Sena. See *Sansthakul* 20, no. 4 (1990): 21–22, especially p. 22.

6. Peacekeeping and the Shanti Sena

1. Charles Walker, for example, states that it was the Indian Shanti Sena who "sent a team to try to negotiate a cease-fire." Walker, "Peace Brigades," 3.

2. See Ostergaard and Currel, 278, 281.

3. For a history of the Naga conflict see M. Aram, *Peace in Nagaland—Eight Year Story: 1964–1972* (New Delhi: Arnold-Heineman, 1974), 81–88; and J. P. Narayan, "Peacemaking in Nagaland," in J. P. Narayan, *Nation Building in India*, ed. Brahmanand (Varanasi: Navachetna, n.d.), 361–73.

4. Quoted in Aram, *Peace in Nagaland,* 83. By way of contrast, according to Naga leader A. Z. Phizo, Gandhi hoped that the Nagas would wish to join the Union of India while insisting that nobody had the right to force them to do so. See D. Prasad, "Gandhi's Concept of Freedom," *Gandhi Marg* 11, no. 3 (1989): 327–32, at p. 330.

5. Aram, *Peace in Nagaland,* 84.

6. Scarfe and Scarfe, 386.

7. A. Bhattacharjea, *Jayaprakash Narayan: A Political Biography* (New Delhi: Vikas, 1975), 130–31.

8. Scarfe and Scarfe, 386.

9. Narayan, *Nation Building in India,* 337–38.

10. Narayan, "Peacemaking in Nagaland", 372.

11. Narayan, *Nation Building in India,* 359.

12. Scarfe and Scarfe, 389.

13. Ibid. See also SSSPS minutes of meeting at Kapri, 30 Mar. 1964.

14. B. B. Ghosh, *History of Nagaland* (New Delhi: S. Chand, n.d.), 183. The Baptist church leaders knew that it was important to include someone in the Peace Mission "who could be a spokesman of the underground Nagas and this could be none else but Michael Scott." C. Singh, *Political Evolution of Nagaland* (New Delhi: Lancer, 1981), 101.

15. Singh, 102; A. Yonuo, *The Rising Nagas: A Historical and Political Study* (Delhi: Vivek, 1974), 257.

16. Narayan, "Peacemaking in Nagaland," 370.

17. Ibid., 365.

18. On this point see the account of the peace negotiations by head of the Indian Government delegation, Y. D. Gundevia, *War and Peace in Nagaland* (Dehra Dun: Palit and Palit, 1975).

19. Scarfe and Scarfe, 389.

20. Narayan, *Nation Building in India,* 323.

21. M. Aram, "Peace Action in Nagaland: Some Aspects of Modus Operandi," in Seminar Report *Peace Research for Peace Action* (New Delhi: Gandhi Peace Foundation/Gandhian Institute of Studies, 1972), 65–70, at p. 69.

22. Scarfe and Scarfe, 388.

23. Ibid., 390–91.

24. See Singh, 129–30; and also Ghosh, 184; Aram, *Peace in Nagaland,* 71; Scarfe and Scarfe, 390; and Yonuo, 258–59.

25. Some writers state quite bluntly that at this stage "the Indian side felt that Scott was a little too inclined towards the rebels, the latter felt that Jayaprakash Narayan tended to lean towards New Delhi." N. Nibedon, *Nagaland: The Night of the Guerrillas* (New Delhi: Lancer, 1978), 126; and see also 137, 147.

26. See the reports by Sykes and JP at the SSSPS meeting at Jayaprakashnagar (in Nagaland), 5 July 1966. At the Prabhand Samiti meeting held three weeks earlier in Bangalore, Rs.15,000 was sanctioned for the center.

27. See SSSPS minutes of meeting at Gopuri, 6 May 1965.

28. Aram, "Peace Action in Nagaland," 69.

29. Ibid.

30. Singh, 145–46.

31. Its most "enthusiastic proponents" being "the 'peace makers' who got a lot of mileage out of it" according to a review in one of India's leading political journals. "What is the 'Shillong Agreement'?" *Economic and Political Weekly* 13, no. 21 (1978): 859–60.

32. M. Aram, "Nagaland Peace Mission and North East India," in *Women's Pilgrimage to Spiritual Freedom Conference Paunar: Souvenir,* ed. S. Ranade (Paunar, 1980), 28–30, at p. 29.

33. For an account of Maharaj's life and work see *Earthen Lamps* (New Delhi: Sahitya Akademi, 1979), by Gujarat's major literary figure of the first half of this century, Jhaverchand Meghani; and D. Hardiman, *Peasant Nationalists of Gujarat: Kheda District 1917–1934* (Delhi: Oxford Univ. Press, 1981), 174–76.

34. For the historical and sociological background to dacoity in the Chambal area see generally B. N. Juyal, S. Kumari, and S. Sundaram, "The Taming of Chambal" (report on "Peace Intervention in Complex Crime Situations: Case Study of the Second Sarvodaya Peace Mission with Chambal Dacoits" by the Gandhian Institute of Studies, Varanasi, 1978); and V. Nargolkar, *Crime and Non-violence* (Poona: Sulabha Rashtriya Granthamala Trust, 1974), 49–78.

35. Quoted in Nargolkar, *Crime and Non-violence,* 83.

36. For the text of the letter see ibid., 87–89.

37. For the details of the surrender see generally S. D. Bhatta, . . . *And They Gave Up Dacoity* (Varanasi: Akhil Bharat Sarva Seva Sangh, 1962); Juyal et al., 335–50; and Nargolkar, *Crime and Non-violence,* 105–16.

38. Quoted in Bhatta, 288.

39. From J.P.'s forward to R. P. Garg, *Dacoit Problem in Chambal Valley: A Sociological Study* (Varanasi: Gandhian Institute of Studies, 1965), iii.

40. Nargolkar, *Crime and Non-violence,* 143.

41. S. Narayan, *Vinoba,* 283.

42. Personal communication from Narayan Desai, Nov. 1989.

43. See Juyal et al., 356–58.

44. Ibid., 359–62.

45. Ibid., 363.

46. Ibid.

47. Ibid., 366.

48. Ibid.

49. Ibid. And see also Nargolkar, *Crime and Non-violence,* 147–49.

50. Nargolkar, *Crime and Non-violence,* 152. The account of the lead-up to the surrender is based largely on the account in Juyal et al., 369–72.

51. Interview with Indrasingh Rawat and Sombhai Patel, the Shanti Sainiks responsible for "bringing in" the dacoit gang of Makan Singh, 13 Feb. 1989, at Karadi.

52. Juyal et al., 371.

53. Ibid., 372.

54. See Nargolkar, *Crime and Non-violence,* 159–66.

55. The rehabilitation scheme that had been negotiated carried with it some of the deficiencies that are inherent in deals in which different actors have varying degrees of bargaining power. The more powerful dacoits, generally those with more family resources to start with, by and large received a more favorable rehabilitation package than lowly dacoits, who were often in greater need. This led to some disenchantment among low-ranking dacoits. See Juyal et al., 388–93.

56. Juyal et al., 388–93.

57. For a description of Mungawali prison see Juyal et al., 411–15; and Nargolkar, *Crime and Non-violence,* 191–93, and 196–97.

58. Juyal et al., 415.

59. Ibid., 416.

60. Ibid., 417.

61. Ibid., 414.

62. Ibid., 425.

63. Interview with B. N. Juyal, 24 Jan. 1989, at Rajghat, Varanasi.

64. Juyal et al., 438.

65. Ibid., 445–46.

66. Ibid.

67. Nargolkar, *Crime and Non-violence,* 189.

68. Juyal et al., 459.

69. See SSSPS minutes of meeting at Ferozpur, 16 July 1979.

70. B. N. Juyal, "Ill Omens in Chambal Valley," *Everyman's Weekly,* 1 June 1975, 5.

71. See generally Pyarelal, *Mahatma Gandhi: The Last Phase,* vol. 1, book 2 (Ahmedabad: Navajivan, 1956).

72. See Desai, *Handbook for Satyagrahis,* 38–39.

73. N. Desai, "Guide Lines for Shanti Sainiks in Times of Emergency," *People's Action* 4, no. 4 (1970): 23–24. For the complete text of the "Guide Lines" see app. E. See also the chapter on the Shanti Sena in M. Shepard, *Gandhi Today: A Report on Mahatma Gandhi's Successors* (Arcata, Calif.: Simple Productions, 1987), 40–63, especially, 45–50.

74. Desai, "Guide Lines for Shanti Sainiks," 23.

75. Personal communication from Narayan Desai, Nov. 1989.

76. N. Desai, "The Role of the Shanti Sena in Conflict Resolution," *Interdiscipline* 11, no. 2 (1974): 166–68 at p. 167.

77. N. Desai, "Role of the Shanti Sena," 166–68. See also M. Shepard, "Shanti Sena: Peace Keeper," *Peace News,* 29 May 1981, 10–11; and Shepard, "Peace Brigades," 1982, 9–10.

78. *Bhoodan* 5, no. 5 (1960): 39; and see also SSSPS minutes of meeting, Varanasi, 10 May 1960.

79. *Bhoodan* 5, no. 5 (1960): 39.

80. Desai, *Towards a Non-Violent Revolution,* 27.

81. *Bhoodan* 9, no. 2 (1964): 12.

82. *Peace Newsletter* 1, no. 3 (1968): 3–4.

83. Interview with Indrasingh Rawat, 11 Nov. 1988, at Karadi.

84. Ibid.

85. In 1982–83 Nirmala Deshpande organized the first such march by the Bharatiya Shanti Sena. See Harris, "Sarvodaya in Crisis," 1051. Other marches were undertaken by SSS stalwarts such as Yashpal Mithal, Thakurdas Bang, and Radhakrishna Bajaj at intervals from 1986 (interviews with Narayan Desai, 26 Nov. 1988, at Vedchhi, and Nirmalbhai Chandra, 24 Dec. 1988, at the Gandhi Peace Foundation, New Delhi).

86. Because the Shanti Sena had grown out of the Bhoodan movement, most sainiks were rural workers. There were only 175 Shanti Sainiks in Calcutta, most of them only active on a part-time basis. The small numbers limited Sena work to a few selected localities. The impact of the Sena on the Calcutta killing was, therefore, relatively insignificant. See Desai, "While the Hearts Were Scorched," 24.

87. This description is largely based on the account in B. B. Chatterjee, P. N. Singh, and G. R. S. Rao, *Riots in Rourkela: A Psychological Study* (New Delhi: Gandhian Institute of Studies/Popular Book Services, 1967), 32–36; M. M. Choudhuri, "A Report on the Disturbances in Rourkela and the Sundergarh District," in *A Time to Speak (An Appeal for Rethinking Our Communal Disturbances)* (N.p.: Sarva Seva Sangh, 1964), 11–18; and an interview with Manmohan Choudhuri, 3 Jan. 1989, at Rajghat Colony, New Delhi.

88. Chatterjee et al., 32; and Choudhuri, "Report on the Disturbances," 12.

89. When news of the riots in Jamshedpur and Rourkela reached Cuttack, tension quickly mounted there also. A small but influential band of sainiks made house-to-house contacts in the tensest areas with the support of all major political parties and leading citizens. Overt violence did not break out in the city. See Desai, "While the Hearts Were Scorched", 24.

90. Choudhuri, "Report on the Disturbances," 11.

91. Ibid., 14.

92. Desai, "While the Hearts Were Scorched," 22.

93. J. P. Narayan, "Flames of Jamshedpur," in *Communal Violence: (A Perspective),* ed. Sarva Seva Sangh (Varanasi: Sarva Seva Sangh, 1964), 27–35, at pp. 28–29. Choudhuri adds that a few weeks after the rioting in one village, some people had asked a government official why the government had not yet paid them the promised Rs.1,000 for every Muslim killed. Choudhuri, "Report on the Disturbances," 11.

94. Choudhuri, "Report on the Disturbances," 18.

95. Interview with Manmohan Choudhuri, 3 Jan. 1989, at Rajghat Colony, New Delhi.

96. Desai, "While the Hearts Were Scorched," 23; and interview with Manmohan Choudhuri, 3 Jan. 1989, at Rajghat Colony, New Delhi.

97. Desai, "While the Hearts Were Scorched," 19.

98. Desai, *Towards a Non-Violent Revolution,* 29.

99. Ibid., 30.

100. See N. Desai, "Peace at Last in Ahmedabad," *People's Action* 4, no. 3 (1970): 21–23, at p. 21.

101. Desai, *Towards a Non-Violent Revolution*, 31.

102. Desai says that one of Ahmedabad's leading papers carried a banner headline announcing that women's breasts had been cut off in a predominantly Muslim area. The following day the government compelled the paper to provide proof or publish a denial of the story. The retraction occurred "in a small corner" on the fifth page. But by that time Muslim women were being molested by "members of wild mobs" and several hundred Muslims lay dead. See Desai, *Towards a Non-Violent Revolution*, 31; and Shepard, *Gandhi Today*, 48.

103. Interview with Jagdishbhai Lakhia, Gujarat Shanti Sena coordinator during the 1960s, 20 Nov. 1988, at Mangrol.

104. Desai, "Peace at Last," 21; and N. Desai, "Shanti Sena work in Ahmedabad," *Sarvodaya* 19, no. 10 (1970): 428–31, at p. 428.

105. Desai, *Towards a Non-Violent Revolution*, 33.

106. Desai, "Peace at Last," 22; and Desai "Shanti Sena Work in Ahmedabad," 428.

107. Desai, "Shanti Sena Work in Ahmedabad," 428.

108. Ibid., 430; and Desai, "Peace at Last," 22.

109. Desai, "Peace at Last," 22–23.

110. Desai, *Towards a Non-Violent Revolution*, 37.

111. J. R. Wood, "Reservations in Doubt: The Backlash Against Affirmative Action in Gujarat, India," *Pacific Affairs* 60, no. 3 (1987): 408–30, at p. 421.

112. N. Desai, "Peace-makers role in Gujarat," *Indian Express,* 7 May 1981.

113. For an account of this riot see Wood, "Reservations in Doubt."

114. Ibid., 425.

115. Desai, *Towards a Non-Violent Revolution*, 56.

116. Ibid., 59.

117. Ibid., 60.

118. See the report of the SSS half-yearly session, held at Nakodar in the Punjab, 16–18 May 1972, 89.

119. Desai, *Towards a Non-Violent Revolution*, 61. And see also N. Desai, mimeographed paper (no title) on the Shanti Sena, 27 June 1987, 3.

120. Desai, *Towards a Non-Violent Revolution*, 61.

121. Ibid., 62–63; Desai, mimeographed paper, 3.

122. Interview with Narayan Desai, 25 Nov. 1988, at Vedchhi.

123. See Desai, mimeographed paper, 3. When peace work in NEFA was commencing, Desai wrote that "work in the border area will be (1) Building up the moral of the people, (2) Preparing the people for non-violent action in the case of aggression, (3) Non-violent action in the case of injustice, (4) Constructive work, and (5) Awakening the sense of community"; Desai, *Handbook for Shanti Sainiks,* 3. See also Desai's comments at the Kurukshetra SSSPS meeting, in Apr. 1973, where the objectives of the peace work in NEFA were listed as national unity, service for the people, nonviolent resistance, and world peace.

124. N. Desai, "Shanti Sena Centres in NEFA" (N.d., manuscript,), 2.

125. Desai, *Towards a Non-Violent Revolution*, 75.

126. Ibid.

127. Ibid.

128. Ibid., 79.

129. See, for example, the section on the Muri Shanti Kendra in N. Desai, "Problems before Social Workers in the Eastern Himalaya," in *Social Work in the Himalaya: Proceedings of the Seminar on Social Work in the Himalayas,* ed. R. Rahul (Delhi: Delhi School of Social Work, Univ. of Delhi, 1969), 74–85, at p. 80, that was omitted when the article was reprinted in Desai, *Towards a Non-Violent Revolution,* pp. 71–78.

130. Interview with Narayan Desai, 25 Nov. 1988, at Vedchhi.

131. M. Mandal, "Nonviolent Experiment in Cyprus," *People's Action* 8, no. 4 (1974): 33–34, at p. 34.

132. C. C. Walker, "Peace Brigades," 2.

133. Personal communication from A. Paul Hare, 20 Nov. 1989.

134. Interview with Nachiketa Desai, 2 Dec. 1988, at Ahmedabad.

135. Interview with Jagdishbhai Lakhia, 16 Nov. 1988, at Mangrol.

136. Interview with Nachiketa Desai, 2 Dec. 1988, at Ahmedabad.

137. Ibid. Walker adds, "Some of the more difficult matters might have been helped by discussions at the outset, but this is dubious: for example, sex in protracted projects," quoted in Hare, 32–33.

138. Interview with Jagdishbhai Lakhia, 16 Nov. 1988, at Mangrol.

139. Interview with Arunbhai Bhatt, 12 Dec. 1988, at Bhavnagar.

140. Ibid.

141. Interview with Amarnath Mishra, 17 January 1989, at Rajghat, Varanasi. The views were echoed by Jagdishbhai Lakhia when he made the point that there is no use in sending sainiks to the front in times of war unless they are trained for what is to come, something that had not been achieved at the time of the Chinese invasion of India and was still not the case. Effective constructive work in the villages means, ipso facto, that a defense scheme has been set up and *then* there is a role for the sainik. Sainiks, in Jagdishbhai's view, can only be effective in areas where they have worked and are known. Interview with Jagdishbhai Lakhia, 20 Nov. 1988, at Mangrol.

142. Interview with Narayan Desai, 28 Nov. 1988, at Vedchhi.

143. Desai, *Hand Book for Shanti Sena Instructors,* i.

144. At this camp the basis of the Sena, the pledge of the Shanti Sainik, and the general direction and field of work of the fledgling organization were discussed.

145. See M. Sykes, "Appendix III: Report of the Shanti Sainik Camp Held at Sevagram from October 14 to 22, 1958," in Bhave, *Shanti Sena,* 1963, 136–49.

146. Akhil Bharat Shanti Sena Mandal, *Youth Peace Corps,* 8.

147. Desai, *Hand Book for Shanti Sena Instructors,* 1.

148. Akhil Bharat Shanti Sena Mandal, *Youth Peace Corps,* 8.

149. Desai, *A Hand Book for Shanti Sena Instructors,* 2–6.

150. Ibid., 6.

151. Ibid., 7.

152. Ibid., 8–9.

153. Ibid., 10.

154. Ibid.

155. Desai, *Towards a Non-Violent Revolution,* 107.

156. Ibid., 108–9.

157. Ibid., 115.

158. Ibid., 116.

7. The Ideological Basis of the Shanti Sena

1. Akhil Bharat Sarva Seva Sangh, *Planning for Sarvodaya* (Varanasi: Sarva Seva Sangh, 1957), 117.

2. *Bhoodan Yajna,* 7 February 1958, quoted in V. Tandon "Vinoba and Satyagraha," *Gandhi Marg* 2, no. 7 (1980): 385–94, at p. 387.

3. V. Bhave, *Democratic Values* (Varanasi: Sarva Seva Sangh, 1962), 13–14.

4. See Ostergaard, " 'Gradualist' Versus 'Immediatist' Anarchism," 517.

5. Although ideally the circumstances should make no difference to the practice of satyagraha, Vinoba often criticized Gandhi indirectly when he contrasted their differing use of satyagraha: "It is . . . mistaken to imagine that the negative Satyagraha of pre-independence days will find much scope . . . in a popular democratic set-up" (quoted in Tandon, *Selections from Vinoba,* 279) and that "in a democracy Satyagraha can never take the form of the exercise of pressure" but must rely on "the change of heart" (ibid., 280). For Vinoba's views on satyagraha in a democracy see generally Bhave, *Democratic Values,* 152–59.

6. Tandon, *Selections from Vinoba*, 392.

7. Ibid. It should be noted, however, that others, such as Nargolkar, claim that the failure to achieve a nonviolent revolution is at least partly the fault of Vinoba, who refused to sanction the use of satyagraha. See V. Nargolkar, "Vinoba and Satyagraha," *Gandhi Marg* 2, no. 12 (1981): 661–72.

8. Quoted in Tandon, *Selections from Vinoba*, 281.

9. *Harijan*, 7 July 1951.

10. K. Shah, ed., *Vinoba on Gandhi* (Varanasi: Sarva Seva Sangh, 1985), 52.

11. Bhave, *Democratic Values*, 78.

12. Ibid., 64.

13. V. Bhave, *Swaraj Sastra*, 19.

14. Ibid., 47. Vinoba was careful to make the point that the ultimate ideal of Sarvodaya was a society free *from* government, not *devoid of* government, because "governments are also absent in societies where chaos reigns." Quoted in Tandon, *Selections from Vinoba*, 158. See also A. H. Doctor, *Sarvodaya: A Political and Economic Study* (Bombay: Asia, 1967), 149–77; and A. H. Doctor, *Anarchist Thought in India* (London: Asia, 1964), 55–70.

15. Shah, *Vinoba: Life and Mission*, 135.

16. Ibid., 137.

17. Bhave, *Democratic Values*, 67.

18. In 1981, after the collapse of the Janata government, Vinoba was asked to spell out his objections to the casting of votes. He explained that "party means a part," and so voting for one party will result in the division of the country. To emphasize his point he added that the people "gave one party both votes and notes [money], but it fell. Hence let it be realized that non-voting is the best." From the context of the interview it was clear that this "advice" was mandatory for Bharatiya Shanti Sena members. See the interview with Vinoba at his Shanti Sena conference at Paunar, 17–18 Oct. 1981, *Sansthakul* 9, no. 9 (1981): 1–6, at p. 3.

19. V. Bhave, *Bhoodan Yagna* (Ahmedabad: Navajivan, 1957), 87.

20. See Shah, *Vinoba: Life and Mission*, 135.

21. See Tandon, *Selections from Vinoba*, 91.

22. *Harijan*, 8 December 1951; see also V. Bhave, *Third Power* (Varanasi: Sarva Seva Sangh, 1972), 68.

23. Bhave, *Third Power*, 71. Although admitting that the collection of only four million acres of Bhoodan land, instead of the target fifty million was a "poor achievement indeed," Vinoba still termed Bhoodan a success in bringing about a change in attitudes through feelings of guilt: "The pride of ownership has gone away altogether. When I go to a village I often find that the big landholders have left their homes for the day. . . . I have got a hold on their heart." V. Bhave, "Wherein Lies Real Revolution," *Sarvodaya* 13, no. 4 (1963): 126–29, at p. 129.

24. V. Bhave, *Shanti Sena*, comp. J. Natarajan and D. G. Groom (Tanjore: Sarvodaya Prachuralaya, 1958), 14. See also Weber, "Peacekeeping, the Shanti Sena and Divisions in the Gandhian Movement."

25. Shah, *Vinoba on Gandhi*, 64.

26. Bhave, *Shanti Sena*, 1958, 32.

27. Interview with Arunbhai Bhatt, 12 Dec. 1988, at Bhavnagar.

28. Shah, *Vinoba on Gandhi*, 65.

29. Quoted in Tandon, *Selections from Vinoba*, 196.

30. See Tandon, *Social and Political Philosophy*, 195.

31. *Sarvodaya* 23, no. 2 (1973): 64; and see also "Vinoba Urges UNO Sponsored P.B.," *Sarvodaya* 21, no. 3 (1971): 110–12; and V. Bhave, "The Task before Shanti Sainiks," *Sarvodaya* 20, no. 1 (1970): 9–12.

32. See Tandon, *Selections from Vinoba*, 191.

33. Shah, *Vinoba on Gandhi*, 76.

34. See his speech at the Annual Sarvodaya Conference in Pandharpur, May 1958, quoted in Ram, 499; and Bhave, *Shanti Sena*, 1958, 37–38.

35. Gandhi's statements in this regard include the following: "If a single satyagrahi holds out to the end, victory is absolutely certain" (Gandhi, *Satyagraha in South Africa*, 5); "If there is one individual who is almost completely nonviolent, he can put out the conflagration" (*Harijan*, 8 Sep. 1940 *CWMG* 72: 437); if a lone individual cannot neutralize violence "you must take it that he is not a true representative of ahimsa" (*Harijan*, 14 Mar. 1936, *CWMG* 62: 200); and "If there is *one* true Satyagrahi it would be enough. I am trying to be that true Satyagrahi" (*Harijan*, 20 Jan. 1940, *CWMG* 71: 99).

36. Shah, *Vinoba on Gandhi*, 77.

37. "Sarvodaya Social Order," in J. P. Narayan, *Towards Revolution*, (New Delhi: Arnold-Heinemann, n.d.), 74–85, at p. 83.

38. Quoted in Nargolkar, "Vinoba and Satyagraha," 669.

39. J. P. Narayan, *Towards Total Revolution*, vol. 1, 229.

40. See J. P. Narayan, "Face to Face," 246. One writer has argued that this "reformulation" of JP's concept of Sarvodaya was contributed to by his post-Musahari world trip to seek aid for war-torn Bangladesh where he came "into close contact with the students' movement abroad." See D. Kantowsky, *Sarvodaya: The Other Development* (New Delhi: Vikas, 1980), 33.

41. J. P. Narayan, *Prison Diary* (Bombay: Popular, 1977), 21–22. At the time Nargolkar had summarized the position thus: "So far as Vinobaji's theory on non-violent revolution is concerned, it may be granted for the sake of argument, that it is impeccable. But in practice, it failed to deliver the goods in terms of revolutionary changes in the present social and economic structure . . . the gramdan-gram-swarajya programme never rose to the pitch of a mass-movement. Later, it degenerated into a hopelessly local activity sustained with tremendous effort by a few dedicated workers, who were constantly goaded by Vinobaji. There was no enthusiastic participation by the people. There was no involvement of the people in gramdani villages in the difficult task of promoting Sarvodaya ideals in their individual and collective lives." Nargolkar, *JP's Crusade*, 86–87.

42. Narayan, *Prison Diary*, 22. At times he was even more blunt when contrasting Vinoba's gentle / gentler approach with peaceful people's struggle for revolutionary changes by claiming that he could not "understand Vinobaji on this point," adding that Vinoba had not demonstrated in practice just how the desired progression could be made; see J. P. Narayan, *Towards Total Revolution*, vol. 4, 187.

43. Narayan, *Prison Diary*, 30.

44. See, for example, Narayan, *Total Revolution*, 92–95.

45. Gandhi is quoted as having said, "I know . . . that if I survive the struggle for freedom, I might have to give non-violent battle to my own countrymen which may be as stubborn as that in which I am now engaged." *Young India*, 30 Jan. 1930, *CWMG* 42: 436–37. This quotation from Gandhi is not particularly well known. It is probable that, rather than having read Gandhi's 1930 newspaper articles with great care, JP picked up this legitimizing assertion from Tandon's book on the Sarvodaya movement where it is reproduced and for which he wrote the foreword. See Tandon, *Social and Political Philosophy*, 27.

46. Narayan, *Total Revolution*, 60–61. JP repeats a version of this statement in his 1975 introduction to a collection of his writings on total revolution: "How prophetic Mahatma Gandhi was when he foresaw as far back as 1930 that if he survived the freedom struggle, he would have to fight many a non-violent battle as stubbornly as the one in which he was engaged against the British!" Narayan, *Towards Revolution*, 12.

47. *Free Press Journal*, 5 Aug. 1953, quoted in Brahmanand, "Introduction," in Narayan, *Towards Total Revolution*, vol. 1, xcvii.

48. JP came to the conclusion that although Vinoba's aim was change through complete nonviolence "the observance of complete non-violence was not possible in a mass movement"; consequently, he declared his objective to be a little less ambitious, "social change through peaceful people's power." See "Why Total Revolution," in J. P. Narayan, *Towards Total Revolution*, ed. Brahamanand vol. 4, (Bombay: Popular, 1978), 115–17, at p. 115.

49. See "Reconstruction of the Indian Polity," in *Socialism, Sarvodaya and Democracy: Selected Works of Jayaprakash Narayan,* ed. B. Prasad (Bombay: Asia, 1964), 192–239.

50. JP readily admits that he has no knowledge of things spiritual in terms of religion or metaphysics. See Narayan, *Towards Total Revolution,* vol. 1, 96–97. According to JP's friends and biographers, Allan and Wendy Scarfe, by the early 1960s Bhoodan was for JP primarily a way of alleviating the existing problems of landlessness in the quickest way possible rather than a means to raise the moral tenor of society that might, at some future time, help solve problems of landlessness and rural poverty. Interview with Allan and Wendy Scarfe, 20 Nov. 1989, at Warrnambool, Victoria.

51. JP did, however, admit that "though all my energies would be bent towards developing *lokniti* [politics of the people], I shall not shut my eyes to what happens in the sphere of *rajniti* [politics of the state]." J. P. Narayan, *From Socialism to Sarvodaya* (Varanasi, Sarva Seva Sangh, 1958), 49.

52. Ibid., 48.

53. *Gramsamkalpa* (the creation of community determination to accept the Gandhian way of life) was the part of the Gramdan process that was to follow *grambhavana* (consciousness and collective will among the village people) and that was, in turn, to lead to *lok shakti* (people's power) and eventually to *lokniti* (people's polity). See A. B. Bharadwaj, *Living Non-Violence* (Delhi: Gandhi-in-Action, 1986) 22; and S. Dasgupta, *A Great Society of Small Communities: The Story of India's Land Gift Movement* (Varanasi: Sarva Seva Sangh, 1968), 10.

54. Narayan, *Towards Total Revolution,* vol. 2, 251–56, at p. 256.

55. See the report of JP's "Presidential Address" at the Thirteenth All-India Sarvodaya Sammelan at Sarvodayapuram, in West Godavary, Andhra Pradesh, 18–20 Apr. 1961, 21. For the argument that Gandhians should "consciously choose to participate in politics and take up positions of authority and power in State administration" to bring about a Sarvodaya social order see T. K. Oommen, "Rethinking Gandhian Approach," *Gandhi Marg* 1, no. 7 (1979): 416–23.

56. See A. Bhattacharjea, *Jayaprakash Narayan,* 120; and J. P. Narayan, "The Revolt Against the System," in *Towards Total Revolution,* vol. 4, 121–32, at p. 122.

57. During a press club statement in October 1974 he admitted that this would not lead to a partyless democracy "but to a democracy which has parties. But these parties will be much better controlled by people themselves." *Sarvodaya* 24, no. 5 (1974): 176–77. Elsewhere during this same period, JP noted that partyless democracy is "an ideal," "something for the future," that may come into existence "in the far distance"; see Narayan, *Towards Total Revolution,* vol. 4, 79, 90.

58. Narayan, *Prison Diary,* 57.

59. J. P. Narayan, "The Path of Revolution," in Narayan, *Towards Total Revolution,* vol. 4, 80–95, at p. 94.

60. V. Bhave, "Task Before Shanti Sainiks," *Sarvodaya* 20, no. 1 (1970): 9–12. See also Weber, "Peacekeeping, the Shanti Sena and Divisions in the Gandhian Movement."

61. J. P. Narayan, *Sarvodaya Answer to Chinese Aggression* (Tanjore: Sarvodaya Prachuralaya, 1963), 27.

62. Narayan, "Peace Army," 287. At around the time JP and Narayan Desai took over the organization of the Shanti Sena, in consultation with Muste, JP suggested the deployment of a protest boat, manned entirely by an Indian crew, to the U.S. Pacific nuclear testing zone; see SSSPS minutes of meeting at Patna, 17 June 1962.

63. See the reports of the sixth day of the War Resisters' International conference at Gandhigram, 26 Dec. 1961, *Sarvodaya* 10, no. 8 (1961): 352.

64. V. Bhave, "First Steps for World Peace Brigade," *Sarvodaya* 10, no. 9 (1961): 344–48.

65. See N. Desai, "Gramdan and Shanti Sena," *War Resistance* 2, no. 28/29 (1969): 26–27. Interestingly, the article focuses on constructive work and a third-party approach to

conflict when noting the role of the Shanti Sena; however, when listing examples of work undertaken by sainiks (successful "satyagrahas" against the eviction of peasants from their land by government officials, demonstrations against injustices in rural society, and organizing the people to fight against corruption), it emphasizes the second-party approach to conflict situations that was to characterize the thinking of JP in his later years.

66. Desai, *A Handbook for Shanti Sainiks,* 3; and Desai, *Shanti Sena in India,* 1969, 4.
67. Narayan, "Philosophy of Peace," 101.
68. Ostergaard, " 'Gradualist' Versus 'Immediatist' Anarchism," 524.
69. Ibid., 528.
70. Quoted in Tandon, *Social and Political Philosophy,* 204.
71. Shah, *Vinoba: Life and Mission,* 109.
72. Ibid., 110.
73. Ibid., 121.
74. Ibid., 150.
75. M. Zachariah, *Revolution Through Reform: A Comparison of Sarvodaya and Conscientization* (New York: Praeger, 1986), 126.
76. See Ostergaard, *Nonviolent Revolution,* 367–68; and T. Bang, "An Experiment in People's Candidates," *Vigil* 12, no. 7 (1990): 7–9.
77. On this matter a "Consultation" was called by SSS at Katol on 8–10 June 1989 to determine the policy to be adopted at the approaching general election. It was unanimously decided that "methods adopted should be in keeping with the principles of truth and nonviolence," that "the casting of votes will be our most effective instrument of bringing about change," and that voter education, the setting up of "voters' councils," and the setting up of "people's candidates" were important tasks before Sarvodaya workers. See "Sarva Seva Sangh, Consultation, Katol," *Gandhi Marg* 11, no. 1 (1989): 124.
78. Interview with Indrasingh Rawat, 10 Nov. 1988, at Karadi.
79. Interview with Arunbhai Bhatt, 12 Dec. 1988, at Bhavnagar.
80. Interview with Achyut Deshpande, 16 Feb. 1989, at Ghatkopar, Bombay.
81. Interview with Jagdishbhai Lakhia, 16 Nov. 1988, at Mangrol.
82. Almost two hundred people were killed as a result of a riot that grew out of tensions after pro and anti demonstrations when it was declared that Urdu would become the second official language of Bihar; see P. Brass, *Language, Religion and Politics in North India* (London: Cambridge Univ. Press, 1974), 260–61, 264–67.
83. Interview with Nirmalbhai Chandra, 24 Dec. 1988, at New Delhi.
84. See Vinoba's introduction to K. G. Mashruwala, *Gandhi and Marx* (Ahmedabad: Navajivan, 1951), 12.
85. See Brahmanand, "Jayaprakash Narayan's Views on Peace: A Documentation Article," *Interdiscipline* 5, no. 1/2 (1968): 78–96, at p. 87.
86. Ostergaard and Currel, 257.
87. Ibid.
88. Narayan, *Sarvodaya Answer to Chinese Aggression,* 5.
89. See SSSPS minutes of meeting at Ranipatra, 4 Mar. 1988.
90. Interview with Nirmalbhai Chandra, 24 Dec. 1988, at New Delhi.
91. Personal communication from Badriprasad Swami, 21 Sep. 1990.
92. Interview with Acharya Ramamurti, 7 Jan. 1989, at Khadigram.
93. Ibid.
94. Ibid.
95. Ibid.
96. Ibid.
97. Ramamurti, *Shanti Sena: Keyon, Kaise, Kisliye?* (Varanasi: Sarva Seva Sangh, 1986), 15.
98. Interview with Acharya Ramamurti, 7 Jan. 1989, at Khadigram.
99. Interview with Hemnath Singh, Ramamurti's secretary, 6 Jan. 1989, at Khadigram.

100. See SSSPS minutes of meeting at Ranipatra, 4 Mar. 1986.
101. Interview with Chunibhai Vaidya, 29 Nov. 1988, at the Sabarmati Ashram, Ahmedabad.
102. Interview with Narayan Desai, 28 Nov. 1988, at Vedchhi.
103. Ramamurti, *Shanti Sena,* 10–11.
104. Ibid., 12–14; A few years earlier, when laying down the rules for his Bihar Shanti Sena, Ramamurti made it clear that he expected the type of discipline from sainiks that would have them obeying their leaders promptly and without question. See Ramamurti, *Himsa ki Pelti Ag se Mukti Kaise?* (Varanasi: Sarva Seva Sangh, 1983), 23–24.
105. See SSSPS minutes of meeting at Ranipatra; and interview with Thakurdas Bang on 2 Feb. 1989, at Gopuri.
106. Ramamurti, *Shanti Sena,* 21–22.
107. Ibid., 8–9, 15–16.
108. Interviews with Amarnath Mishra, 17 and 18 January 1989, at Rajghat, Varanasi; and Badriprasad Swami, 18 Jan. 1989, at Rajghat, Varanasi. In the words of Manmohan Choudhuri the Shanti Sena is to be a "general purpose corps devoted to the cause of bringing about a nonviolent social revolution"; see M. M. Choudhuri, "Shanti Sena," *Vigil* 10, no. 1 1988: 1–2.
109. Interview with Badriprasad Swami, 18 Jan. 1989, at Rajghat, Varanasi.
110. See the Sarva Seva Sangh's *Draft Manifesto of the Sarvodaya Movement* (Varanasi: Sarva Seva Sangh, 1972), 58–60; and the final version of the draft that appeared under the title *What Sarvodaya Stands For: A Manifesto* (Varanasi: Sarva Seva Sangh, 1973), 61–62.
111. Interview with Chunibhai Vaidya, 30 Nov. 1988, at the Sabarmati Ashram in Ahmedabad.
112. The one notable exception is Thakurdas Bang, the main proponent of the move to send sainiks to the border in 1962. He acknowledges that the government would prevent them from going to an area of battle and that today they are not in a position to take any effective action; however, his views have changed little. He realizes that sainiks who defy the government would end up languishing in jail but notes that even this may have some value and that such symbolic steps should be taken. Interview with Thakurdas Bang, 2 Feb. 1989, at Gopuri.
113. For example, besides involvement with the World Peace Brigade, at SSSPS meeting at Patikaliana, 7 Nov. 1963, the possibility of joint Shanti Sena and Civil Service International camps was mooted.
114. Interview with Amarnath Mishra, 18 Jan. 1989, at Rajghat, Varanasi.
115. I. Harris, "The Spiritual Dimension of Vinoba Bhave's Thought," *Gandhi Marg* 5, no. 8/9 (1983): 435–53, at pp. 444–45. On this see generally R. Church, "Banning Cow Slaughter in India: The Roots of State Politics" (Department of Politics, Brock Univ., Ontario, 1980, Manuscript) for the genesis of Vinoba's position see 24–26; and A. Deshpande, "Cow-Slaughter Ban Movement," *Sansthakul* 20, no. 1 (1992): 14–16.
116. Interview with Indrasingh Rawat, 13 Feb. 1989, at Karadi.
117. Interview with Achyut Deshpande, 16 Feb. 1989, at Ghatkopar, Bombay.
118. Interview with Arunbhai Bhatt, 12 Dec. 1988, at Bhavnagar.
119. *Sansthakul* 10, no. 9 (1981): 1–6 at p. 6.
120. Ibid.
121. Interview with Dilkhushbai Divanji, 8 Feb. 1989, at Matwad.
122. Interview with Achyut Deshpande, 16 Feb. 1989, at Ghatkopar, Bombay; see also A. Bhatt and S. Das comps., *Cow Protection: An Imperative for Survival* (Paunar: Paramdham Prakashan, 1990).
123. See speech by Justice Alladi Kuppuswami, "Acharyakul Seminar on Cow Protection," *Sansthakul* 20, no. 6 (1990): 6–11; and generally Church "Banning Cow Slaughter in India."
124. Interview with Achyut Deshpande, 16 Feb. 1989, at Ghatkopar, Bombay.

8. Lessons From the Shanti Sena

1. Interview with Acharya Ramamurti, 7 Jan. 1989, at Khadigram.

2. Interview with Jagdishbhai Lakhia, 16 Nov. 1988, at Mangrol.

3. This is not to say that the question of structural violence is to be ignored. Even some leading Bharatiya Shanti Sainiks have partially distanced themselves from Vinoba's gentle/gentler ideal on this question. Arunbhai Bhatt, for instance, maintains that in conditions of unpeace it is the function of the Shanti Sainik to create peace; however, where the peace is unjust, it is no peace for the oppressed, and the sainik should create conflict. The real question is "peace for whom?" Interview with Arunbhai Bhatt, 12 Dec. 1988, at Bhavnagar.

4. Interview with Acharya Ramamurti, 7 Jan. 1989, at Khadigram.

5. Interview with Indrasingh Rawat, 10 Nov. 1988, at Karadi

6. See Galtung, "Peace, Peace Theory," 83.

7. The question of where nongovernmental oppressors fit into this scheme is a little more problematic. As I suggest in the section below, it will depend on whether one follows Gandhi's actions or ideals.

8. Interview with Jagdishbhai Lakhia, 16 Nov. 1988, at Mangrol.

9. Harris, "Sarvodaya in Crisis," 1042.

10. Horsburgh, *Mahatma Gandhi,* 58.

11. Gregg, *Discipline,* 4.

12. Ibid.

13. Horsburgh, "Nonviolence and Impatience," 359.

14. Ibid., 360.

15. Several of the various versions of the Shanti Sena pledge refer explicitly to the "unity of man." See app. D.

16. See Prasad, "Shanti Sena aur Himsaka Pratikar," (Hindi) *Gandhi Marg* Sep.–Oct. (1984): 42–62, at pp. 56–57.

17. For a Western interpretation of the Shanti Sena almost entirely in terms of international peace see Muste, *Report on the Indian Crisis,* 9.

18. Quoted in Shah, *Vinoba: Life and Mission,* 1.

19. Critic of the Sarvodaya movement Adi H. Doctor argues that the vision of a Sarvodaya order, of which the Shanti Sena was to be an integral component, is a vision doomed to nonrealization. See Doctor, *Anarchist Thought,* 84–108; and Doctor, *Sarvodaya,* 149–77. If this analysis is correct, it is unrealistic to expect the Shanti Sena to operate in any way other than as an ad hoc peacekeeping force as it did during its years of most visible operation.

20. Prasad, "Shanti Sena," 57–58. And this, of course, overcomes the problems observed by Galtung where outside peacekeepers come to dislike the population they are working with, preventing the type of interaction that facilitates peacemaking and peacebuilding.

21. On this point see Radhakrishna's reply to Prasad's article, "Shanti Sena ek Seha-Chintan," (Hindi) *Gandhi Marg* Feb. (1985): 35–38, at p. 38.

22. M. Sen, *Gandhian Way and the Bhoodan Movement* (Varanasi: Sarva Seva Sangh, 1964), 44. In this paraphrase of Vinoba's views Sen is echoing Max Weber's contrasting notions of *authority* (which a Shanti Sena with the attributes described will possess) and *power* (which is probably all a riot-controlling police force can exercise).

23. Although Arlo Tatum realized that the recruitment of brigade members solely for service in far-off places would not be feasible, he merely envisaged that the initial training of potential brigadiers would be undertaken locally. Those who had proven themselves in constructive work in their own communities would then be eligible for selection for an international force. See A. Tatum, "World Peace Brigade," in *A Search for Alternatives to War and Violence,* ed. T. Dunn (London: James Clark, 1963), 129–34, at p. 132.

24. Young maintains that although independence and impartiality may be strengths of

nongovernmental organizations attempting a third-party role in international conflict, such groups lack too many important attributes and resources (such as "salience" to give them relevance and respect in the eyes of the conflicting parties, access to necessary physical resources such as communication facilities, transport, information-processing equipment, and high mobility). This may be another reason for looking toward the United Nations to fill the need. See Young.

25. Interview with Dilkhushbhai Divanji, 7 Nov. 1988, at Matwad.

26. Interview with Indrasingh Rawat, 10 Nov. 1988, at Karadi.

27. Interview with Narayan Desai, 28 Nov. 1988, at Vedchhi. He adds that in any case no central body *can* be formed at present because there is no one on the horizon with the stature of the past great leaders who could undertake such a centralization.

28. It should be pointed out that peacemaking and peacebuilding are processes and peacekeeping is a specific short-term task that must at times be carried out so that the all-important processes can be undertaken. See L. N. Tiwary, "Peace-Keeping Tasks of the U.N.O.," *Sarva Seva Sangh (Monthly Newsletter)* 2, no. 1 (1968): 24–25.

29. As Maude Royden and others have found, the international community has a great deal of resistance to actively assisting unarmed peacekeeping operations not directly under its control. Madariaga and JP and, more recently, Ray Magee and other PBI leaders also have found that the United Nations has shown relatively little interest in investigating the possibility of establishing its own broadly defined unarmed peacekeeping force.

30. Myrdal, 66.

31. Ibid., 891.

32. Ibid., 899.

33. See report of the half-yearly Sarva Seva Sangh conference at Ernakulam, 19 Dec. 1972, 7.

34. For an articulation of this complaint from the Gandhian point of view see M. Choudhuri, *Threats to Liberty* (Varanasi: Sarva Seva Sangh, 1983), 24–27.

35. Harris adds that because both Sarvodaya and the government have the same clients (villagers), there is a real tussle over a conflict in values. The government has a vision of a high-technology future for the country, whereas the Gandhians oppose the technological revolution. The plans they have for rural development and their strong views about the operation of the industrial sector are incompatible. One is concerned with "development," measured in terms of economic achievement, the other with a more spiritual concept of "uplift," the changing of the moral values of the people through work at the grass-roots level. Harris, "Sarvodaya in Crisis," 1044.

36. N. Desai, "While the Hearts Were Scorched," 24.

37. Interview with Chunibhai Vaidya, 30 Nov. 1988, at the Sabarmati Ashram in Ahmedabad. It should be noted that the same appears true for the international unarmed peacekeeping groups that have taken to the field. While there are armies and a functioning U.N. peacekeeping force, it will be difficult to raise sufficient finances for an effective level of operation.

38. E. Linton, *Fragments of a Vision: A Journey Through India's Gramdan Villages* (Varanasi: Sarva Seva Sangh, 1971), 112.

39. Here the debate seems to mirror the one engaged in by Western alternative seekers between those who opt out of corporate society and its political processes to live a life of example and those who see this approach as essentially escapist given that meaningful changes can only come about quickly enough in a rapidly deteriorating world through explicit involvement in the political arena where direct battles must be fought.

40. R. Niebuhr, *Moral Man and Immoral Society: A Study in Ethics and Politics* (New York: Scribner's, 1932), 243.

41. For a contrary opinion see Devdutt, "Vinoba and the Gandhian Tradition," *Gandhi Marg* 5, no. 8/9 (1983): 600–615.

42. Doctor, *Anarchist Thought*, 36–54.

43. Devdutt claims that even before Gandhi's death, the Socialist JP sided with the Mahatma on fundamental political issues more frequently than Nehru; see Devdutt, "Gandhi's Technique of Social Change and Jayaprakash Narayan," *Gandhi Marg* 2, no. 7 (1980): 361–73. Further, JP's secretary, Brahmanand, claims that whereas Nehru turned to constitutional and parliamentary methods to fight the British and remained an adherent of this avenue to bring about change, JP, like the nonconstitutionalist and revolutionary Gandhi, chose the method of people's struggle to achieve a more just social order; see Brahmanand, "Introduction," in Narayan, *Towards Total Revolution*, vol. 1, xxxix, 1xix, 1xxxv–1xxxvi.

44. Devdutt, "Gandhi's Technique of Social Change," 371; and Devdutt, "Vinoba and the Gandhian Tradition," 610.

45. S. Verma, *Metaphysical Foundation of Mahatma Gandhi's Thought* (New Delhi: Orient Longman, 1970), 10, and see also, 20, 134.

46. Perhaps Socialist political colleague of JP, Madhu Limaye, summed up the situation best when he stated, "It was [the] 'inconsistency' and the mighty 'negative' movements that [Gandhi] launched that created a new consciousness among the people, fearlessness and self-reliance, real *loka-shakti*." M. Limaye, *The Age of Hope: Phases of the Socialist Movement* (Delhi: Atma Ram, 1986), 204. For an analysis favoring satyagraha as a system of gradation, rather than one rent by contradiction see the perceptive essay by M. W. Sonnleitner, "Gandhian Satyagraha and Swaraj: A Hierarchical Perspective," *Peace and Change* 14, no. 1 (1989): 3–24.

47. G. Sharp, "A Study of the Meaning of Nonviolence," in *Gandhi: His Relevance for Our Times,* ed. G. Ramachandran and T. K. Mahadevan (Berkeley, Calif.: World Without War, 1971), 21–66.

48. See his tables, ibid., 64–66.

49. Ibid., 29.

50. Ibid.

51. J. Galtung, "Gandhi and Conflictology," in *Papers,* ed. International Peace Research Insitute, 107–158, at p. 116.

52. In an insightful article, philosopher Smith argues that there is an ambiguity in nonviolence being seen both as an appeal to moral principle and as an effective practical device for achieving a given goal. He adds, "Those who practice nonviolence are forced to oscillate between these two poles. On the one hand, nonviolence as a form of response is adopted because it is dictated by a principle, the principle that violence is always to be avoided because in itself it is 'wrong' and perpetuates the very divisiveness we are trying to overcome. On the other hand, nonviolence is not chosen for this reason alone. It is chosen because, as a matter of actual fact derived from past experience, this method has been shown to be more *effective* than violence in accomplishing certain objectives." J. E. Smith, "The Inescapable Ambiguity of Nonviolence," *Philosophy East and West* 19, no. 2 (1969): 155–58, at p. 157.

53. I. Tikekar, *Integral Revolution (An Analytical Study of Gandhian Thought)* (Varanasi: Sarva Seva Sangh, 1970), 6. Tikekar stresses that according to Gandhi we can know only our present physical lives and so should concern ourselves with our present life rather than with questions concerning the hereafter; see Tikekar, 142.

54. Galtung, *Gandhi and Conflictology,* 116.

55. Galtung, *Gandhi and Conflictology,* 126. And the results of research seem to imply that something like this ideal either occurs in practice or Gandhians at least believe that it does. When Nakhre asked his sample of satyagrahis. "Whom do you think satyagraha affects the most?" 37.5 percent (and nine out of fourteen satyagrahi leaders) replied that the "greatest impact was on the satyagrahis themselves." One leader added that whatever the effect on the opponent, "more importantly it creates a new man out of the satyagrahi himself." A. Nakhre, "Meaning of Nonviolence: A Study of Satyagrahi Attitudes," *Journal of Peace Research* 13, no. 3 (1976): 185–96, at p. 206.

56. Tikekar, 7.

57. For Vinoba's views on *moksha,* "the complete destruction of the ego, and becoming one with society and God-personified universe" being the "noblest fruit of life" see Tandon, *Social and Political Philosophy,* 51. Some Sarvodaya thinkers, for example, K. G. Mushruwala, have criticized this ideal because it "has encouraged escapism and differentiation between worldly and other-worldly"; ibid., 52.

58. Even JP saw Vinoba as "first and last a man of God" rather than as politician, social reformer, or revolutionary. He noted that for Vinoba "service of man is . . . nothing but an effort to unite with God." He gave no indication, however, that he considered this reason for service more important than social reform or revolution. J. P. Narayan, "Acharya Vinobha Bhave," in *Sri Jayaprakash Narayan Sixtyfirst Birth Day Celebrations: Commemorative Volume* (Madras: Sri Jayaprakash Narayan Sixty-first Birthday Celebrations Committee, 1963), 90–92, at p. 90.

59. Tikekar, 213; and see also Galtung, *Gandhi and Conflictology,* 139.

60. Tandon notes that the "very conception of Sarvodaya denotes going beyond the seeming conflicts of interests to a spiritual view of life. It strikes a happy mean between old 'spiritualism' which derided life and the prevailing materialism which totally rejects the spiritual." Tandon, *Social and Political Philosophy,* 202. However, he provides no evidence to demonstrate that this "happy mean" has been, or even can be, achieved.

61. The best example of this occurred after Gandhi's Rajkot fast when he admitted that "to my discredit I have been guilty of playing what may be called a double game. . . . This method I admit is wholly inconsistent with ahimsa." *Harijan,* 20 May 1939, *CWMG* 69: 270. Shortly after he added: "I was weighed in my own scales at Rajkot and found wanting. . . . For me to rely on the Viceroy instead of God, or in addition to God, to act upon the Thakore Sahib, was an act of pure violence." *Harijan,* 24 June 1939, *CWMG* 69: 360. Gandhi biographer Nanda explains that Gandhi's appeal to the viceroy to intervene in a dispute that, ostensibly, was aimed at bringing about the local ruler's conversion, "had vitiated the spiritual value of the fast and was thus a lapse from the high ideal of non-violence which he set before himself." This led him to stiffen "his demands upon would-be Satyagrahis; they had to be truly non-violent in action, as well as in thought." See B. R. Nanda, *Mahatma Gandhi: A Biography* (Delhi: Oxford Univ. Press, 1981), 418, 420.

62. *Harijan,* 2 Mar. 1940, quoted in Prabhu and Rao, 26.

63. For an uncomplimentary analysis of Gandhi's fasts, see Raman, 107–13.

64. Bondurant, *Conquest of Violence,* 9.

65. Case, 379. In this line of argument the test of nonviolence depends less on reality as experienced by the coerced and more on the state of mind of the person attempting to bring about change in the opponent. Where there is a total commitment to conversion and absence of even a subconscious desire to humiliate the act of coercion can be classified as nonviolent.

66. K. Shridharani, *War Without Violence* (Bombay: Bharatiya Vidya Bhavan, 1962), 264.

67. Ibid., 263.

68. Naess, *Gandhi and Group Conflict,* 92. Sonnleitner, "Gandhian Satyagraha," 7, uses the term *compulsion* rather than *coercion* in this context.

69. *Young India,* 8 Aug. 1929, *CWMG,* 41: 204.

70. In the words of Horsburgh, "Violence aims to coerce; non-violence may coerce, but it hopes to convert rather than to enforce submission." Horsburgh, "Nonviolence and Impatience," 357. This is probably how satyagraha in fact operates most of the time, but a mere hope of conversion is not only far from consistent with the stated ideal but also paves the way for non-Gandhian compromises of principle.

71. See T. Weber, "The Lesson from the Disciples: Is There a Contradiction in Gandhi's Philosophy of Action?" *Modern Asian Studies* 28, no. 1 (1994): 195–214.

72. Vinoba's disinclination to follow his mentor with regard to the employment of aggressive satyagraha may have resulted from a stronger will or, perhaps, his rejection of its

use reflected, as Nargolkar convincingly points out, the differing temperaments of the two: "The nonviolent struggle for Indian independence was led by a Mahatma who happened to be a political activist, while the post-Independence movement for the establishment of a more egalitarian social order through Bhoodan, Gramdan, and Gram-swarajya was conceived and guided by a saint, who, apart from being deeply spiritual, was . . . by temperament a teacher, disinclined to action." Nargolkar, "Vinoba and Satyagraha," 667; and see also Nargolkar, *JP's Crusade,* 87.

73. Devi Prasad summed up the dilemma accurately when he remarked that the psychology of the attraction to politics is understandable: it is a way of seeming to be doing *something,* even though at some deep level it may be contradictory to the ultimate aims of the Shanti Sena. Interview with Devi Prasad, 22 Dec. 1988, in New Delhi.

74. Rao, 428. However, Michael Scott's second party leanings hampered the operation of the Mission by earning the mistrust of the government. In this example Galtung appears to have been proved right. The problems associated with neutrality in a vertical conflict, therefore, remain.

75. Interestingly, Narayan Desai, while maintaining that if "your heart is pure, this will become known and your neutrality will be accepted," nevertheless believes that credibility on the part of the sainik is more important than nonpartisanship. He cites Gandhi as an implacable opponent of the British, who maintained credibility. Interview with Narayan Desai, 26 Nov. 1988, at Vedchhi.

76. Interview with Indrasingh Rawat, 11 Nov. 1988, at Karadi.

77. Interview with Narayan Desai, 26 Nov. 1988, at Vedchhi.

78. Desai, mimeographed paper, 5.

79. Nakhre, 194.

80. Interview with Jagdishbhai Lakhia, 16 Nov. 1988, at Mangrol.

81. J. Galtung, *The Way is the Goal: Gandhi Today* (Ahmedabad: Gujarat Vidyapith, 1992), 73.

82. Ibid., 147.

83. For an analysis of the Quaker approach to international conciliation see C. H. M. Yarrow, *Quaker Experiences in International Conciliation* (New Haven, Conn.: Yale Univ. Press, 1978).

84. Galtung and Hveem, 280.

85. Interview with Acharya Ramamurti, 7 Jan. 1989, at Khadigram.

86. K. L. Schonborn, *Dealing with Violence: The Challenge Faced by Police and Other Peacekeepers* (Springfield, Ill.: Charles C. Thomas, 1975). In his Ph.D. dissertation, on which this book is based, Schonborn used the terms *violent* and *nonviolent* for *authoritarian* and *humanitarian,* respectively. See K. L. Schonborn "Response to Social Conflict: Violent and Non-Violent Third Party Intervention" (Ph.D. diss., Univ. of Pennsylvania, 1971).

87. Schonborn, *Dealing With Violence,* 179–80, 185–89; Schonborn, "Response to Social Conflict," 270–71, 274, 277, 448.

88. Schonborn, *Dealing with Violence,* 180–81, 189–90; Schonborn, "Response to Social Conflict," 282.

89. Schonborn, *Dealing with Violence,* 183–84, 190–94; Schonborn, "Response to Social Conflict," 286.

90. Schonborn, *Dealing with Violence,* 181–83, 190; Schonborn, "Response to Social Conflict," 263, 282.

91. Schonborn, "Response to Social Conflict," 20; Schonborn, *Dealing with Violence,* 306.

92. Schonborn, "Response to Social Conflict," 263, 296, 448.

93. G. Zahn, "The Ethics of Martyrdom," *Gandhi Marg* 10, no. 4 (1966): 291–94, at p. 291.

94. A. Huxley, *Ends and Means: An Inquiry into the Nature of Ideals and into the Methods Employed for Their Realization* (Edinburgh: Readers' Union and Chatto and Windus, 1938), 9.

95. Gandhi, *Hind Swaraj,* 71.

96. *Young India,* 17 July 1924, *CWMG* 24: 396.

97. *Harijan,* 11 Feb. 1939, *CWMG* 67: 390.

98. But then again, perhaps this argument loses its validity where the sacrifice is undertaken *for* God or the believer sees a connection between the level of sacrifice and the probability of salvation, hence, the long tradition of, for example, Christian charity work.

99. This is not to say that no sainiks suffer from a belief in the "illusion" of duality, but they are steeped in a tradition that takes nonduality more or less for granted, perhaps providing another reason, in addition to the purely historical one, why there were so few Muslim sainiks.

100. Gandhi, *Satyagraha in South Africa,* 508.

101. Gandhi has often been described as the archetypal karma yogin—one who practices *nishkam karma,* the yoga of unselfish action in the world without attachment to results.

102. M. K. Gandhi, "Ethical Religion," in *The Selected Works of Mahatma Gandhi,* ed. S. Narayan, vol. 4, 1–35, at p. 33.

103. Ibid., 32.

104. Ibid., 7.

105. *Harijan,* 14 Mar. 1936, *CWMG* 62: 201.

106. "Intrinsic good" is that which is right because of the very order of things in the Gandhian belief system. Perhaps the word *intrinsic* can be substituted by *instrumental* if the latter is used at a far deeper and more abstract level than the narrow cost/benefit analysis that this term usually attracts. In other words, nonviolence may be instrumental in the quest for self-realization.

107. Interview with Indrasingh Rawat, 11 Nov. 1988, at Karadi.

108. Interview with Narayan Desai, 28 Nov. 1988, at Vedchhi.

109. Gandhian theorist, Joan Bondurant, noted that a life of ideals requires a great deal of self-discipline. After her observation of some of Gandhi's disciples, she concluded that those who have mastered such a life, which enabled them to act constructively, may find, as the Gandhians had, "a sense of becoming, or realization of self that makes the demanding tasks required not only tolerable but also attractive." J. V. Bondurant, "The Search for a Theory of Conflict" in *Conflict: Violence and Non-Violence,* ed. J. V. Bondurant (Chicago : Aldine-Atherton, 1971), 1–25, at p. 22.

110. In 1990 Krishnaswamy became secretary of the Gandhi Peace Foundation.

111. See *Keesing's Contemporary Archives,* vol. 10 (1955–56): 14,401–402.

112. F. Watson and H. Tennyson, *Talking of Gandhi* (New Delhi: Orient Longman, 1976), 155–56.

113. But they would have reflected Gandhi's early conceptions and conformed to his "living wall" strategy of national defense. See app. B.

114. But note Geoffrey Ostergaard's important point that the claim of the Gandhians that they unite "instrumental" with "expressive" action is easier to make than sustain. When faced with an apparent lack of instrumental success, they tend to fall back to the position that they are, nevertheless, expressing the truth. Ostergaard notes that despite Gandhi's talk of "experiments with truth" this is a closed system in that it is not falsifiable: "Failures are always ascribed to the practitioners' weaknesses, lack of purity etc. and not to the philosophy, since by definition satyagraha is grounded in truth and therefore can never fail." Personal communication, 1 Aug. 1988. A similar point is made by W. Borman in his *Gandhi and Non-Violence* (Albany: State Univ. of New York Press, 1986).

Appendix A. The Establishment of United Nations Peacekeeping Forces

1. A summary of some of the arguments presented in this appendix have been published in T. Weber, "The Problems of Peacekeeping," *Interdisciplinary Peace Research* 1, no. 2 (1989): 3–26.

2. As called for by the Moscow conference in its "Declaration of Four Nations [U.S., U.K., U.S.S.R., and China] on General Security" in Nov. 1943. See R. B. Russell, *A History of the United Nations Charter: The Role of the United States 1940–1945* (Washington, D.C.: Brookings Institute, 1959), 977.

3. From the preamble to the charter of the United Nations.

4. Increased to fifteen by amendment in 1963.

5. Fabian, 14.

6. Frye, 52.

7. Article 43 sets out the procedures for the establishment of the force by asking all members to "undertake to make available to the Security Council, on its call and in accordance with a special agreement or agreements, armed forces, assistance, and facilities, including rights of passage, necessary for the purpose of maintaining international peace and security." These agreements were to "govern the number and types of forces, their degree of readiness and general location, and the nature of the facilities and assistance to be provided" (Art. 43 [2]).

8. See B. G. Lall, "Peacekeeping at the UN," *Bulletin of the Atomic Scientists* Oct. (1966): 43–45; Bowett, 12–18; E. Luard, "United Nations Peace Forces," in *The Evolution of International Organizations,* ed. E. Luard (London: Thames and Hudson, 1966), 138–76, at p. 140; and Frye, 53.

9. Fabian, 14.

10. See L. Goodrich, "Efforts to Establish an International Police Force Down to 1950," app. to Frye, 172–94.

11. J. L. Brierly, *The Law of Nations: An Introduction to the International Law of Peace* (Oxford: Oxford Univ. Press, 1949), 282.

12. Quoted in A. W. Cordier, W. Foote, and M. Harrelson, eds., *Public Papers of the Secretaries-General of the United Nations,* vol. 1, *Trygve Lie 1946–1953* (New York: Columbia Univ. Press, 1969) 240.

13. See Higgins, vol. 2, 153–312.

14. See Greig, 545–47; and Bowett, 32–36.

15. Article 39 states, "The Security Council shall determine the existence of any threats to the peace, breach of the peace, or act of aggression and shall make recommendations, or decide what measures shall be taken in accordance with Articles 41 and 42, to maintain or restore international peace and security." Those articles, in turn, provide sanctions, both economic and diplomatic in the case of Article 41 and, if that is inadequate, "such action by air, sea, or land forces as may be necessary to maintain or restore international peace and security. Such action may include demonstrations, blockade, and other operations by air, sea, or land forces of Members of the United Nations" (Art. 42).

16. This may no longer be the case. Since the ending of the cold war, the possibilities for united Security Council actions of this kind are again being contemplated. The unanimous Security Council decision to blockade Iraq after its invasion of neighboring Kuwait may be the start of a new enforcement role for the council.

17. UNGA 5/377A(V).

18. "Earmarked" units are ones that have been singled out for service with the United Nations and can be available for active duty within two to eight weeks of an appropriate request. By contrast, "standby" units are available on notice of one week.

19. See Frye, 60–61.

20. For Trygve Lie's proposals see Cordier et al., eds., 131–35, 166–77, 472–76; see also S. M. Schwebel, "A United Nations 'Guard' and a United Nations 'Legion'," app. to Frye, 195–216.

21. See Frye, 1–31.

22. G. Clark and L. B. Sohn, *World Peace Through World Law* (Cambridge, Mass.: Harvard Univ. Press, 1966), xxix. For the history of the evolution of this plan see H. B.

Hollins, A. L. Powers, and M. Sommer, *The Conquest of War: Alternative Strategies for Global Security* (Boulder, Colo.: Westview Press, 1989), 38–47.

23. For example, their 1966 figures put the required strength at between 200,000 and 400,000 men. See Clark and Sohn, xiv, 314, 468.

24. Bloomfield, *Power to Keep Peace*, 16.

25. Frye, 75–78.

26. Johansen and Mendlovitz attempt to provide answers to these questions with their more recent proposal for a small, gradually introduced, transnational police force. See Johansen and Mendlovitz. They hoped that their proposal would be acted upon during the 1980s. Although this has not been the case, the rapid change in political alliances may see it being taken more seriously during the 1990s.

27. Frye, 80.

28. See Hoffman, 100.

29. Ibid., 102.

30. Bloomfield, *Power to Keep Peace*, 51.

31. Hoffman, 105.

32. Bloomfield, *Power to Keep Peace*, 20.

33. Ibid., 38–45.

34. Bloomfield, "Peacekeeping and Peacemaking," 679.

35. Bloomfield, *Power to Keep Peace*, 50.

36. See D. Hammarskjöld's report, "Summary study of the Experience Derived from the Establishment and Operation of the United Nations Emergency Force," in Cordier et al., vol. 4, 230–92; and U Thant's Address to the Harvard Alumni Association, "A United Nations Stand-by Peace Force," ibid. vol. 6, 354–63.

37. Secretary-General Hammarskjöld, after initiating the setting up of that UN Force, subsequently declared, "I believe . . . that the Secretary-General should . . . help in filling any vacuum that may appear in the system which the Charter and traditional diplomacy provide for the safeguarding of peace and security." Quoted in Cordier et al., eds., vol. 3, 665.

38. Ibid. vol. 4, 282.

39. See app. in Frydenberg, 313–32, for details of the various enactments.

40. B. Boutros-Ghali, *An Agenda for Peace: Preventive Diplomacy, Peacemaking and Peacekeeping* (New York: United Nations, 1992), 25.

Appendix B. Maude Royden's Peace Army

1. See I. L. Horowitz, *War and Peace in Contemporary Social and Philosophical Theory* (London: Souvenir Press, 1973), 159.

2. P. Mayer, ed., *The Pacifist Conscience* (Harmondsworth, England: Penguin, 1966), 179.

3. Quoted in Mayer, 179–90, at pp. 185–86.

4. Ibid., 188.

5. Compare, for example, K. Lorenz, *On Aggression* (London: Methuen, 1966), with A. Montagu, *The Nature of Human Aggression* (Oxford: Oxford Univ. Press, 1976), and the papers in A. Montagu, ed., *Man and Aggression* (Oxford: Oxford Univ. Press, 1973). For a thorough review of the literature in this area see S. D. Nelson, "Nature/Nurture Revisited 1: A Review of the Biological Bases of *Conflict*," *Journal of Conflict Resolution* 18, no. 2 (1974) : 285–335.

6. *Atlantic Monthly,* Aug. 1928, 181–82.

7. *Young India,* 31 Dec. 1931; *CWMG* 48: 420.

8. J. D. Hunt, *Gandhi in London* (New Delhi: Promilla, 1978), 192.

9. See the note by Gandhi to his secretary, 17 Dec. 1928, which indicated that he was expecting her to call in later that day (*CWMG* 38: 235).

10. *CWMG* 48: 158.

11. "Reminder to Youth," in *The New World,* Nov. 1931, 7. The journal states that the extracts are "from a sermon recently delivered."

12. See *CWMG* 48: 460.

13. See entries for 5 Dec. 1931 and 12 Dec. 1931 in *CWMG* 48: 459–68, at pp. 465, 466.

14. On 30 Jan. 1932, *CWMG* 49: 53.

15. *The Peace Army: A Sermon by A. Maude Royden, C.H., D.D., preached at the Guildhouse, Eccleston Square S.W.1, on Sunday evening, February 1932.* (N.p.: n.d.), 5. From the leaflet it appears that they were defeated by the logistics of getting the volunteers to the front. The Peace Army papers referred to can be found in the Swarthmore College Peace Collection, Swarthmore.

16. It is of course quite possible that the idea originated with Royden and that Gandhi got it from her.

17. A. M. Royden, "The Peacemaker," in *Dick Sheppard: An Apostle of Brotherhood,* ed. W. Paxton et al. (London: Chapman and Hall, 1938), 73–81, at p. 76.

18. A. M. Royden, "Master Christian?" in *Gandhi Memorial Peace Number,* ed. K. Roy (Shantiniketan: Visva-Bharati Quarterly, 1949), 130–34, at p. 132. The offer of "troops" to the League would have overcome the problems associated with transporting and equipping such "soldiers of peace." See *Peace Army: A Sermon.*

19. Royden, "Peacemaker," 76.

20. Royden, "Master Christian," 132.

21. Royden "Peacemaker," 77.

22. See Ceadel, 97.

23. Royden, "Peacemaker," 77.

24. Royden, "Master Christian?" 133.

25. *Manchester Guardian,* 27 Feb. 1932.

26. This response was made much of in Peace Army propaganda for years to come. The pamphlet referred to in n. 41, this appendix, for example, had the words "Not a Fantastic Proposal" printed prominently on its cover, and, in 1935 when the "Army" addressed letters to the secretary-general of the League of Nations and to several delegations pointing out that a Peace Army "could have been sent to Abyssinia" after the Italian invasion, again Drummond's words were featured heavily.

27. See the leaflet, *The Peace Army: Being a Letter to the General-Secretary of the League of Nations and His Reply* (N.p., n.d.); Royden, "Master Christians," 133; and Royden, "Peacemaker," 78.

28. Gandhi to Royden, 26 Apr. 1932, *CWMG* 49: 371. It should be noted that even if Royden had succeeded in landing her force in Shanghai and had actually prevented hostilities as planned through physical interposition, it might have been self-defeating in terms of the Gandhian nonviolence she was advocating and the Mahatma was endorsing. I thank Theodore Olson for pointing out the *objectively* coercive elements in Royden's attempt. The deaths of many unarmed *British* volunteers in Shanghai at the hands of the Japanese would have constituted a grave *political* (in addition to moral) hazard to the Japanese. And this element of political coercion is not the basis on which she would have hoped that her attempt proved "effective."

29. Royden, "Master Christians," 133; and Royden, "Peacemaker," 78.

30. Royden, "Master Christian," 133.

31. See *Peace Army: Being a Letter;* and Royden, "Peacemaker," 78.

32. Royden, "Master Christian," 133.

33. Ibid.

34. Ibid.

35. 23 Mar. 1932, vol. 263, House of Commons Debates, col. 1013; see also 16 Mar. 1932, col. 258.

36. This information was repeated in numerous Peace Army leaflets, often with the same title but slightly different wording. See, for example the leaflets *Peace Army: An Explanation* (N.p., n.d.); and *The Peace Army: Queries and Answers,* (N.p., n.d.); the newsletters "The Peace Army," (N.p., n.d.) and "What is the Peace Army?" April 1932; and the supplement to the July/Aug. 1932, edition of *The Peace Review* entitled "The New Agencies of Peace."

37. R. E. Roberts, *H. R. L. Sheppard: Life and Letters* (London: John Murray, 1942), 217–18.

38. Royden, "Peacemaker," 79.

39. Keyes, 4. The Peace Army's newsletter no. 14, November 1938, still lists Royden as "President" as does a letter addressed to supporters dated November 1939. Looking at the organization's leaflets and correspondences for the years of the middle and later 1930s, it is clear, however, that she is little more than a figurehead. With the coming of the Second World War Royden lost her faith in Pacifism (see Royden, "Master Christian," 132–34), and although the Peace Army was still issuing news-sheets in early 1940, it finally petered out during the war.

40. *The Peace Army* (N.p., 1940, leaflet).

41. The aims of the "army" were now explained as "belief that Peace Armies should be sent to the world's danger spots before actual strife breaks out; their presence should serve to create peace and this would be their aim—but if fighting should begin, they would be there on the spot and could offer the final service of standing unarmed between the combatants." See the leaflet *Peacemaking—and Palestine,* (N.p., n.d.).

42. Ibid. See also the leaflet *Peacemaking—and Palestine* (Leaflet no. 2).

43. See the Peace Army leaflet *In Memoriam, Hugh Bingham, Soldier of Peace, Jerusalem, 1939;* and Ceadel, 96.

44. Ceadel, 317.

45. H. Brinton, *The Peace Army* (London: Williams and Norgate, 1932), 73.

46. Ibid., 73–74.

47. Ibid., 74.

48. Ibid.

49. Ibid., 74–75.

50. Ibid., 76–77.

Appendix C. Report of the Meeting to Establish a Shanti Sena at Wardha, March 1950

1. The eleven vows are, Truth, Non-violence, Fearlessness, Self-control, Control over palate, Non-possession, Non-thieving, Physical labour, Non-untouchability, Equal regard for all religions and Swadeshi, all in the spirit of humility.

2. S. N. Agarwal, "Shanti Sena, Wardha," *Harijan,* 6 May 1950.

Appendix D. The Shanti Sena Pledges

1. Ram, 206. Although others had previously taken on the title of Shanti Sainik as early as 1950 (see app. C), this was the first recruitment for the operational Shanti Sena.

2. Quoted in Bhave, *Shanti Sena,* 1963, 133–35.

3. For the early history of the Shanti Sena see Desai, *Shanti Sena in India,* 1969.

4. Quoted in Bhave, *Shanti Sena,* 1963, 131–32. For a slightly different translation of the Lok Sevak pledge see Ram, 511.

5. Quoted in Bhave, *Shanti Sena,* 1963, 160.

6. This pledge translation can be found in a small pamphlet, Akhil Bharat Shanti Sena Mandal, *Shanti-Sena: Organization and Programme* (Varanasi: Akhil Bharat Shanti Sena Mandal, n.d.), 4–5.

7. "Bharatiya Shanti Sena," *Sansthakul* 10, no. 10 (1982): 5–8, at p. 5; and for an earlier and different translation see *Sansthakul* 9, no. 1 (1980): 6.

8. See Prabhand Samiti meeting at Khadagpur, West Bengal, 31 May-6 June 1980.

9. Ramamurti, *Shanti Sena,* 39.

10. For an expanded version of this appendix see T. Weber, "A Brief History of the Shanti Sena as Seen Through the Changing Pledges of the Shanti Sainik," *Gandhi Marg* 13, no. 3 (1991): 316–26.

Appendix E. Guide Lines for Shanti Sainiks in Times of Emergency

1. *People's Action* 4, no. 4 (1970): 23–24.

Bibliography

Acland, R. *Waging Peace: The Positive Policy We Could Pursue if We Gave Up the H-Bomb.* London: Frederick Muller, 1958.

Agarwal, S. N. "Shanti Sena, Wardha." *Harijan,* 6 May 1950.

Akhil Bharat Sarva Seva Sangh, ed. *Delhi-Peking Friendship March.* Varanasi: Akhil Bharat Sarva Seva Sangh, 1963.

————. *Planning for Sarvodaya.* Varanasi: Akhil Bharat Sarva Seva Sangh, 1957.

Akhil Bharat Shanti Sena Mandal. *Shanti-Sena: Organisation and Programme.* Varanasi: Akhil Bharat Shanti Sena Mandal, n.d.

————. *Youth Peace Corps (Tarun Shanti Sena).* Varanasi: Akhil Bharat Shanti Sena Mandal, n.d. Pamphlet.

Anet, D. *Pierre Ceresole: Passionate Peacemaker.* Delhi: Macmillan, 1974.

Aram, M. "Nagaland Peace Mission and North East India." In *Women's Pilgrimage to Spiritual Freedom Conference Paunar: Souvenir,* edited by S. Ranade, 28–30. Paunar: S. Ranade, 1980.

————. "Peace Action in Nagaland: Some Aspects of Modus Operandi." In Seminar Report, *Peace Research for Peace Action,* 65–70. New Delhi: Gandhi Peace Foundation/Gandhian Institute of Studies, 1972.

————. *Peace in Nagaland—Eight Year Story: 1964–1972.* New Delhi: Arnold-Heineman, 1974.

Arrowsmith, P., ed. *To Asia in Peace: The Story of a Non-Violent Action Mission to Indo China.* London: Sidgwick and Jackson, 1972.

Aryanayakam, A. D. "Shanti Sena: The Peace Army of India." *The War Resister* 92 (1961): 11–12.

Bang, T. "An Experiment in People's Candidates." *Vigil* 12, no. 7 (1990): 7–9.

————. *The Next Step.* N.p.: Sarva Seva Sangh, n.d.

Beales, A. C. F. *The History of Peace: A Short Account of the Organised Movement for International Peace.* London: Bell, 1931.

Bell, R. *Alternative to War.* London: James Clark, 1959.

————. *Rhodesia: Outline of a Nonviolent Strategy to Resolve the Crisis.* London: Housmans, 1968.

Bennett, J. "The Resistance Against German Occupation of Denmark." In *The Strategy of Civilian Defence; Non-Violent Resistance to Aggression,* edited by A. Roberts, 154–72. London: Faber, 1967.

Bharadwaj, A. B. *Living Non-Violence.* Delhi: Gandhi-in-Action, 1986.

"Bharatiya Shanti Sena." *Sansthakul* 10, no. 10 (1982): 5–8.

Bhatt, A., and S. Das, comps. *Cow Protection: An Imperative for Survival.* Paunar: Paramdham Prakashan, 1990

Bhatta, S. D. . . . *And They Gave Up Dacoity.* Varanasi: Akhil Bharat Sarva Seva Sangh, 1962.

Bhattacharjea, A. *Jayaprakash Narayan: A Political Biography.* New Delhi: Vikas, 1975.

Bhave, V. *Bhoodan Yagna.* Ahmedabad: Navajivan, 1957.

———. *Democratic Values.* Varanasi: Sarva Seva Sangh, 1962.

———. "Dissolution of the Sarva Seva Sangh." *Sansthakul* 4, no. 10 (1976): 8–9.

———. "First Steps for World Peace Brigade." *Sarvodaya* 10, no. 9 (1961): 344–48.

———. "The Present Crisis in India: Appeal to Countrymen." *Sarvodaya* 12, no. 6 (1962): 204–5.

———. "The Shanti Sainik: His Duties and Responsibilities." *Bhoodan* 5, no. 25 (1960): 196–97.

———. *Shanti Sena.* Varanasi: Sarva Seva Sangh, 1963.

———. *Shanti Sena.* Compiled by J. Natarajan and D. G. Groom. Tanjore: Sarvodaya Prachuralaya, 1958.

———. "The Sino-Indian Conflict." *Gandhi Marg* 7, no. 1 (1963): 1–4.

———. *Swaraj Sastra* [*The Principles of a Non-Violent Political Order*]. Varanasi: Sarva Seva Sangh, 1973.

———. "The Task Before Shanti Sainiks." *Sarvodaya* 20, no. 1 (1970): 9–12.

———. *Third Power.* Varanasi: Sarva Seva Sangh, 1972.

———. "Vinoba's Answers to Acharyakul Questions." *Sansthakul* 9, no. 10 (1981): 4–7.

———. "Wherein Lies Real Revolution." *Sarvodaya* 13, no. 4 (1963): 126–29.

Bidwell, S. "The Theory and Practice of Peacekeeping." *International Affairs* 54, no. 4 (1978): 635–39.

Bigelow, A. *The Voyage of the Golden Rule: An Experiment with Truth.* Garden City, N.Y.: Doubleday, 1959.

Bloomfield, L. P. "Peacekeeping and Peacemaking." *Foreign Affairs* 54, no. 4 (1966): 671–82.

———. *The Power to Keep Peace: Today and in a World Without War.* Berkeley, Calif.: World Without War Council, 1971.

Bondurant, J. V. *Conquest of Violence: The Gandhian Philosophy of Conflict.* Berkeley: Univ. of California Press, 1967.

———. "The Search for a Theory of Conflict." In *Conflict: Violence and Non-Violence,* edited by J. V. Bondurant, 1–25. Chicago: Aldine-Atherton, 1971.

Borman, W. *Gandhi and Non-Violence.* Albany: State Univ. of New York Press, 1986.

Bose, N. K. "Gandhian Approach to Social Conflict and War." In *Gandhi, India and the World,* edited by S. Ray, 261–69. Melbourne: Hawthorn Press, 1970.

———. *Studies in Gandhism.* Ahmedabad: Navajivan, 1972.

————. "The Theory and Practice of Sarvodaya." In *The Meanings of Gandhi,* edited by P. F. Power, 79–89. Honolulu: East-West Center, Univ. Press of Hawaii, 1971.

Boutros-Ghali, B. *An Agenda for Peace: Preventive Diplomacy, Peacemaking and Peace-keeping.* New York: United Nations, 1992.

Bowen, N. "PBI Called to Sri Lanka." *Peace Brigades* 7, no. 1 (1990): 1, 3.

Bowett, D. W. *United Nations Forces: A Legal Study of United Nations Practice.* London: Stevens and Sons, 1964.

Bowker, J. *Problems of Suffering in Religions of the World.* Cambridge: Cambridge Univ. Press, 1970.

Brahmanand. "Jayaprakash Narayan's Views on Peace: A Documentation Article." *Interdiscipline* 5, no. 1/2 (1968): 78–96.

————. "Introduction." In J. P. Narayan, *Towards Total Revolution.* Vol. 1, *Search for an Ideology,* edited by Brahmanand, xii–cli. Varanasi: Navachetna, n.d.

Brass, P. *Language, Religion and Politics in North India.* London: Cambridge Univ. Press, 1974.

Brierly, J. L. *The Law of Nations: An Introduction to the International Law of Peace.* Oxford: Oxford Univ. Press, 1949.

Brinton, H. *The Peace Army.* London: Williams and Norgate, 1932.

Bristol, J. "Lessons from the India-China Conflict." *Bhoodan* 8, no. 13 (1963): 99–102; 8, no. 14 (1963): 107–8.

————. *Non-violence and India Today.* Philadelphia: Peace Education Division of the American Friend's Service Committee, 1963.

————. "Non-Violence in India Reassessed." *Sarvodaya* 13, no. 4 (1963): 148–49.

"Broadcasting the Shanti Sena." *Bhoodan* 7, no. 2 (1962): 2.

Brock, P. *The Mahatma and Mother India (Essays on Gandhi's Non-Violence and Nationalism).* Ahmedabad: Navajivan, 1983.

————. *Pacifism in the United States from the Colonial Era to the First World War.* Princeton, N. J: Princeton Univ. Press, 1968.

————. *Twentieth-Century Pacifism.* New York: Van Nostrand Reinhold, 1970.

Buber, M. *I and Thou: A New Translation.* Translated by W. Kaufmann. Edinburgh: T. and T. Clark, 1970.

Burrowes, R. "The Gulf War and the Gulf Peace Team." *Social Alternatives* 10, no. 2 (1991): 35–39.

————. "Life in the Gulf Peace Camp." *Issues* 15, May (1991): 56–60.

Burton, J. "Conflict Resolution as a Political Philosophy." *Interdisciplinary Peace Research* 3, no. 1 (1990): 62–72.

————. *Global Conflict: The Domestic Sources of International Crisis.* London, Wheatsheaf, 1984.

Calvocoressi, P. *A Time for Peace: Pacifism, Internationalism and Protest Forces in the Reduction of War.* London: Hutchinson, 1987.

Carter, A. "The Sahara Project Team." In *Liberation Without Violence: A Third Party Approach,* edited by A. P. Hare and H. H. Blumberg, 126–56. Totowa, N.J.: Rowan and Littlefield, 1977.

Case, C. M. *Non-violent Coercion: A Study in Methods of Social Pressure.* New York: Century, 1923.

Cattell, E. "Peace Army Progress." *Peace Army Reports* 1, no. 2 (1981): 1.

Ceadel, M. *Pacifism in Britain 1914–1945: The Defining of a Faith*. Oxford: Clarendon Press, 1980.

Chander, J. P., ed. *Teachings of Mahatma Gandhi*. Lahore: Indian Printing Works, 1947.

Chatterjee, B. B., P. N. Singh, and G. R. S. Rao. *Riots in Rourkela: A Psychological Study*. New Delhi: Gandhian Institute of Studies/Popular Book Services, 1967.

Chatterjee, M. *Gandhi's Religious Thought*. Notre Dame, Ind.: Univ. of Notre Dame Press, 1983.

Choudhuri, M. M. "A Report on the Disturbances in Rourkela and the Sundergarh District." In *A Time to Speak (An Appeal for Rethinking our Communal Disturbances)*. 11–18. N.p.: Sarva Seva Sangh, 1964. Small pamphlet "only for private circulation."

——. "Shanti Sena." *Vigil* 10, no. 1 (1988): 1–2.

——. *Threats to Liberty*. Varanasi: Sarva Seva Sangh, 1983.

Choudhury, G. W. *The Last Days of United Pakistan*. Nedlands: Univ. of Western Australia Press, 1974.

Church, R. "Banning Cow Slaughter in India: The Roots of State Politics." Department of Politics, Brock Univ., 1980. Manuscript.

——. "Vinoba and the Origins of Bhoodan." *Gandhi Marg* 5, no. 8/9 (1983): 469–91.

——. "Vinoba Bhave, Jayaprakash Narayan and Indian Democracy." *Gandhian Perspectives* 2, no. 2 (1980): 89–129.

Clark, D. N. "Transnational Action for Peace: The Peace Brigades International." *Transnational Perspectives* 9 no. 4 (1983): 7–11.

Clark, G., and L. B. Sohn. *World Peace Through World Law*. Cambridge, Mass.: Harvard Univ. Press, 1966.

Clark, H. "Civilian Intervention—It Doesn't Hurt to Try." *Peace News* Oct. (1992): 2.

"Consultation on an International Peace Brigade." Minutes of the Grindstone Island (Portland, Ontario) meeting, 31 Aug.-4 Sept. 1981.

Cordier, A. W., W. Foote, and M. Havrelson, eds. *Public Papers of the Secretaries-General of the United Nations*. Vol. 1, *Trygve Lie 1946–1953;* vol. 3, *Dag Hammarskjöld 1956–1957;* vol. 4, *Dag Hammarskjöld 1958–1960;* and vol. 6, *U Thant 1961–1964*. New York: Columbia Univ. Press, 1969.

Cox, A. M. *Prospects for Peacekeeping*. Washington, D.C.: Brookings Institute, 1967.

Coy, P. "Protective Accompanyment: How Peace Brigades International Secures Political Space and Human Rights Nonviolently." In *Nonviolence: Social and Psychological Issues,* edited by V. K. Kool, 235–45. Lanham, Md: Univ. Press of America, 1993.

Dasgupta, S. *A Great Society of Small Communities: The Story of India's Land Gift Movement*. Varanasi: Sarva Seva Sangh, 1968.

Deming, B. "Earl Reynolds: Stranger in this Country." *Liberation* 8, no. 1 (1963): 26–30.

——. "International Peace Brigade." In *Revolution and Equilibrium,* edited by B. Deming, 92–101. New York: Grossman, 1971.

——. "On Revolution and Equilibrium." In *Revolution and Equilibrium,* edited by B. Deming, 194–221. New York: Grossman, 1971.

————. "San Francisco to Moscow: Why the Russians Let Them In." In *Revolution and Equilibrium,* edited by B. Deming, 60–72. New York: Grossman, 1971.

————. "San Francisco to Moscow: Why They Walk." In *Revolution and Equilibrium,* edited by B. Deming, 51–59. New York: Grossman, 1971.

Desai, I. E. *Dharasana ni Shauryagatha.* Surat: Swatantra Itihas, Samiti Jilla Panchayat Surat, 1973.

Desai, M. *The Diary of Mahadev Desai.* Ahmedabad: Navajivan, 1953.

Desai, N. "Gramdan and Shanti Sena." *War Resistance* 2, no. 28/29 (1969): 26–27.

————. "Guide Lines for Shanti Sainiks in Times of Emergency." *People's Action* 4, no. 4 (1970): 23–24.

————. *A Hand-Book for a Satyagrahi.* Varanasi: National People's Committee, n.d.

————. *Handbook for Satyagrahis.* New Delhi: Gandhi Peace Foundation, 1980.

————. *A Handbook for Shanti Sainiks.* Varanasi: Sarva Seva Sangh, 1963.

————. *A Hand Book for Shanti Sena Instructors.* Varanasi: Akhil Bharat Shanti Sena Mandal, n.d.

————. "The Making and Bearing of the Youth Peace Corps." N.d. Mimeo.

————. Mimeographed paper (no title) on the Shanti Sena, 27 June 1987.

————. "Narayan Desai: Nonviolent Revolutionary—A Diary of a Gandhian Educator," edited by A. Paul Hare. 1979. Manuscript.

————. "Peace at Last in Ahmedabad." *People's Action* 4, no. 3 (1970): 21–23.

————. "Peace-makers' Role in Gujarat." *Indian Express,* 7 May 1981.

————. "Problems Before Social Workers in the Eastern Himalaya." In *Social Work in the Himalaya: Proceedings of the Seminar on Social Work in the Himalayas,* edited by R. Rahul, 74–85. New Delhi: Delhi School of Social Work, Univ. of Delhi, 1969.

————. *A Report of the All India Shanti Sena (August 1957 to July 1962).* Varanasi: Akhil Bharat Shanti Sena Mandal, 1962.

————. "The Role of the Shanti Sena in Conflict Resolution." *Interdiscipline* 11, no. 12 (1974): 166–68.

————. "Shanti Sena Centres in NEFA." N.d. Manuscript.

————. *Shanti Sena in India.* Varanasi: Sarva Seva Sangh, 1962.

————. *Shanti Sena in India.* Varanasi: Sarva Seva Sangh, 1969.

————. "Shanti Sena Work in Ahmedabad." *Sarvodaya* 19, no. 10 (1970): 428–31.

————. "Some Points for Consideration at the Consultation on an International Peace Brigade." In *Consultation on an International Peace Brigade: Working Documents and Background Papers,* 3–9. N.p., n.d. Booklet.

————. *Towards a Non-Violent Revolution.* Varanasi: Sarva Seva Sangh, 1972.

————. "Unarmed Peacekeeping." *The Hindusthan Times,* 4 August 1974.

————. "While the Hearts Were Scorched." In *A Time to Speak (An Appeal for Rethinking our Communal Disturbances),* 19–24. N.p.; Sarva Seva Sangh, 1964. A small pamphlet "only for private circulation."

Deshpande, A. "Cow-Slaughter Ban Movement." *Sansthakul* 20, no. 1 (1992): 14–16.

————. "Vinoba Wisdom." *Gandhi Marg* 5, no. 8/9 (1983): 630–33.

Deutsch, M. "Conflicts: Productive and Destructive." *Journal of Social Issues* 25, no. 1 (1969): 7–41.

Devdutt, "Gandhi's Technique of Social Change and Jayaprakash Narayan." *Gandhi Marg* 2, no. 7 (1980): 361–73.

————. "Vinoba and the Gandhian Tradition." *Gandhi Marg* 5, no. 8/9 (1983): 600–615.

Dhadda, S. "Aggression and Non-Violence." *Bhoodan* 4, no. 32 (1959): 249–50.

Dhawan, G. N. *The Political Philosophy of Mahatma Gandhi.* Bombay: Popular Book Depot, 1957.

Dijkstra, P. "Nonviolence in Practice." *Gandhi Marg* 14, no. 1 (1992): 247–52.

————. "Peace Brigades International." *Gandhi Marg* 8, no. 7 (1986): 391–406.

Diwakar, R. R. *Saga of Satyagraha.* New Delhi: Gandhi Peace Foundation, 1969.

Doctor, A. H. *Anarchist Thought in India.* London: Asia, 1964.

————. *Sarvodaya: A Political and Economic Study.* Bombay: Asia, 1967.

Erikson, E. H. *Gandhi's Truth: On the Origins of Militant Nonviolence.* New York: Norton, 1969.

Evans, G. *Cooperating for Peace: The Global Agenda for the 1990s and Beyond.* St. Leonards, Australia: Allen and Unwin, 1993.

Fabian, L. *Soldiers Without Enemies: Preparing the United Nations for Peacekeeping.* Washington, D.C.: Brookings Institute, 1971.

Fanon, F. *The Wretched of the Earth.* Harmondsworth, England: Penguin, 1967.

Fischer, L. *A Week with Gandhi.* London: Allen and Unwin, 1943.

Frydenberg, P., ed. *Peace-Keeping: Experience and Evaluation—The Oslo Papers.* Oslo: Norwegian Institute of International Affairs, 1964.

Frye, W. R. *A United Nations Peace Force.* New York: Oceana, 1957.

Fuller, R. "A Better Game than War: Interviews with Robert Fuller." In vol. 2 of *Evolutionary Blues,* edited by D. Hoffman, 7–21. Arcata, Calif.: Stiener, 1983.

————. "Mo Tzu in Kenya and Poland." *The CoEvolution Quarterly,* Spring 1983: 118–25.

Galtung, J. "Gandhi and Conflictology." In *Papers: A Collection of Works Previously Available Only in Manuscript or Very Limited Circulation Mimeographed or Photocopied Editions.* Vol. 5, *Papers in English 1968–1972,* edited by the International Peace Research Institute, 107–58. Oslo: International Peace Research Institute, 1980.

————. "A Gandhian Theory of Conflict." In *In Theory and in Practice: Essays on the Politics of Jayaprakash Narayan,* edited by D. Selbourne, 95–110. Delhi: Oxford Univ. Press, 1985.

————. "Peace, Peace Theory and an International Peace Academy." In *Papers: A Collection of Works Previously Available Only in Manuscript or Very Limited Circulation Mimeographed or Photocopied Editions.* Vol. 5, *Papers in English 1968–1972,* edited by the International Peace Research Institute, 51–102. Oslo: International Peace Research Institute, 1980.

————. "A Structural Theory of Imperialism." *Journal of Peace Research* 8, no. 2 (1971): 81–118.

————. "Three Approaches to Peace: Peacekeeping, Peacemaking and Peacebuilding." In *Essays in Peace Research.* Vol. 2, *War, Peace and Defence,* edited by J. Galtung, 282–304. Copenhagen: Christian Ejlers, 1976.

————. "Three Realistic Approaches to Peace: Peacekeeping, Peacemaking, Peacebuilding." *Impact of Science on Society* 26, no. 1/2 (1976): 103–15

————. *The True Worlds: A Transnational Perspective.* New York: Free Press, 1980.

————. "Violence, Peace and Peace Research." *Journal of Peace Research* 6, no. 3 (1969): 167–91.

————. *The Way is the Goal: Gandhi Today*. Ahmedabad: Gujarat Vidyapith, 1992.

Galtung, J., and H. Hveem, "Participants in Peacekeeping Forces." In *Essays in Peace Research*. Vol. 2, *War, Peace and Defence,* edited by J. Galtung, 264–81. Copenhagen: Christian Ejlers, 1976.

Gandhi, J. *Dharasanano Jung*. Gandhinagar: Information Department, Gujarat Government, 1978.

Gandhi, M. K. *An Autobiography or the Story of My Experiments with Truth*. Ahmedabad: Navajivan, 1927.

————. *The Collected Works of Mahatma Gandhi*. Vols. 1–90, 1958–1985. New Delhi: Publications Division, Government of India.

————. "Constructive Programme: Its Meaning and Place." In *The Selected Works of Mahatma Gandhi*. Vol. 4, *The Basic Works,* edited by S. Narayan, 333–74. Ahmedabad: Navajivan, 1968.

————. "Ethical Religion." In *The Selected Works of Mahatma Gandhi*. Vol. 4, *The Basic Works,* edited by S. Narayan, 1–35. Ahmedabad: Navajivan, 1968.

————. *From Yeravda Mandir*. Ahmedabad: Navajivan, 1932.

————. *Hind Swaraj or Indian Home Rule*. Ahmedabad: Navajivan, 1939.

————. *Non-Violence in Peace and War*. Vol. 1. Ahmedabad: Navajivan, 1942.

————. *Non-Violent Resistance*. New York: Schocken, 1961.

————. *Satyagraha in South Africa*. Madras: Ganesan, 1928.

————. "Unto This Last: A Paraphrase." In *The Selected Works of Mahatma Gandhi*. Vol. 4, *The Basic Works,* edited by S. Narayan, 37–80 Ahmedabad: Navajivan, 1968.

"Gandhi's Challenge." *Sansthakul* 20, no. 7 (1990): 6–12.

Garg, R. P. *Dacoit Problem in Chambal Valley: A Sociological Study*. Varanasi: Gandhian Institute of Studies, 1965.

Ghosh, B. B. *History of Nagaland*. New Delhi: S. Chand, n.d.

Gilpin, A. C. "Non-Violence in U.N. Peacekeeping Operations." In *Foundations of Peace and Freedom: The Ecology of a Peaceful World,* edited by T. Dunn, 270–86. Swansea: Christopher Davies, 1975.

Goodrich, L. "Efforts to Establish an International Police Force down to 1950." Appendix to W. R. Frye, *A United Nations Peace Force,* 172–94. New York: Oceana, 1957.

Gopal, S., ed. *Selected Works of Jawaharlal Nehru*. Vol. 4. New Delhi: Jawaharlal Nehru Memorial Fund, Orient Longman, 1973.

Gould, J. W. "Gandhi's Contribution to the Practice of the Law of Love in International Relations." *Gandhi Marg* 1, no. 7 (1979): 436–51.

Gregg, R. B. *A Discipline for Non-Violence*. Ahmedabad: Navajivan, 1941.

————. *The Power of Non-Violence*. Ahmedabad: Navajivan, 1960.

Greig, D. W. *International Law*. London: Butterworths, 1970.

Griffin-Nolan, E. *Witness for Peace*. Louisville, Ky. Westminster/John Knox Press, 1991.

Grønning, J. "Recruitment and Training." In *Peace-Keeping: Experience and Evaluation—The Oslo Papers,* edited by P. Frydenberg, 173–81. Oslo: Norwegian Institute of International Affairs, 1964.

Gujarat Provincial Congress Committee. *The Black Regime at Dharasana (A Brief Survey of the "Dharasana Raid")*. Ahmedabad, 1930.

Gulcher, E. "Sarajevo 1993: If You Do Not Come Back I Will Come and Get You"

19 Aug. 1993. Manuscript, posted on PeaceNet Conference "Yugo. antiwar," 2 Sept. 1993.

Gundevia, Y. D. *War and Peace in Nagaland.* Dehra Dun: Palit and Palit, 1975.

Harbottle, M., ed. *Peacekeeper's Handbook.* New York: International Peace Academy, 1978.

———. *What is Proper Soldiering?* N.p.: Centre for International Peacebuilding, 1991.

Hardiman, D. *Peasant Nationalists of Gujarat: Kheda District 1917–1934.* Delhi: Oxford Univ. Press, 1981.

Hare, A. P., ed. *Cyprus Resettlement Project: An Instance of International Peacemaking.* Beer Sheva: Ben Gurion Univ., 1984.

Hare, A. P., and E. Wilkinson. "Cyprus—Conflict and Its Resolution." In *Liberation Without Violence: A Third Party Approach,* edited by A. P. Hare and H. H. Blumberg, 239–47. Totowa, N.J.: Rowan and Littlefield, 1977.

Harris, I. "Sarvodaya in Crisis: The Gandhian Movement in India Today." *Asian Survey* 27, no. 9 (1987): 1036–52.

———. "The Spiritual Dimension of Vinoba Bhave's Thought." *Gandhi Marg* 5, no. 8/9 (1983): 435–53.

Hemleben, S. J. *Plans for World Peace Throuqh Six Centuries.* Chicago: Univ. of Chicago Press, 1943.

Higgins, R. *United Nations Peacekeeping 1946–1967; Documents and Commentary.* Vol. 1, *The Middle East,* and vol. 2, Asia. London: Oxford Univ. Press. 1969.

Hingorani, A. T., and G. A. Hingorani, eds. *The Encyclopedia of Gandhian Thoughts.* New Delhi: AICC(I), 1985.

Hirst, M. E. *The Quakers in Peace and War.* New York: George H. Doran, 1923.

Hoffman, S. "Erewhon or Lilliput: A Critical View of the Problem." In L. P. Bloomfield, *The Power to Keep Peace: Today and in a World Without War,* 90–111. Berkeley: World Without War Council, 1971.

Hogg, D. *Memories for Tomorrow.* London: Regency Press, 1981.

Hollins, H. B., A. L. Powers, and M. Sommer. *The Conquest of War: Alternative Strategies for Global Security.* Boulder, Colo.: Westview Press, 1989.

Horowitz, I. L. *War and Peace in Contemporary Social and Philosophical Theory.* London: Souvenir Press, 1973.

Horsburgh, H. J. N. *Mahatma Gandhi.* London: Lutterworth Press, 1972.

———. *Non-Violence and Aggression: A Study of Gandhi's Moral Equivalent of War.* London: Oxford Univ. Press, 1968.

———. "Nonviolence and Impatience." *Gandhi Marg* 12, no. 4 (1968): 355–61.

Hotchkiss, M. "The Mo Tzu Project: Personal National Peace-finding." *The Co-Evolution Quarterly,* Fall (1982): 82–90.

Hunt, J. D. *Gandhi in London.* New Delhi: Promilla, 1978.

Huxley, A. *Ends and Means: An Inquiry into the Nature of Ideals and into the Methods Employed for Their Realization.* Edinburgh: Readers' Union and Chatto and Windus, 1938.

Iyer, R. *The Moral and Political Thought of Mahatma Gandhi.* New York: Oxford Univ. Press, 1973.

James, A. *The Politics of Peacekeepinq.* London: Chatto and Windus, 1960.

James, W. "The Moral Equivalent of War." In *The Pacifist Conscience,* edited by P. Mayer, 179–90. Harmondsworth, England: Penguin, 1966.

Johansen, R. C., and S. H. Mendlovitz. "The Role of Enforcement of Law in the Establishment of a New International Order: A Proposal for a Transnational Police Force." *Alternatives* 6 (1980): 307–37.

Jones, R. *The Quakers in the American Colonies.* New York: Macmillan, 1911.

Juyal, B. N. "Ill Omens in Chambal Valley." *Everyman's Weekly,* 1 June 1975, 5.

Juyal, B. N., S. Kumari, and S. Sundaram. "The Taming of Chambal." Report on "Peace Intervention in Complex Crime Situations: Case Study of the Second Sarvodaya Peace Mission with Chambal Dacoits" by the Gandhian Institute of Studies, Varanasi, 1978.

Kalelkar, K. S. "Non-violent Army for Peace." *Fellowship* May (1956): 13–15.

Kantowsky, D. *Sarvodaya: The Other Development.* New Delhi: Vikas, 1980.

Keesing's Contemporary Archives. Vol. 10 (1955–56): 14, 401–2

Keyes: G. "Peacekeeping by Unarmed Buffer Forces: Precedents and Proposals." *Peace and Change* 5, no. 2/3 (1978): 3–10.

Khan, A. G. *My Life and Struggle: The Autobiography of Badshah Khan.* Delhi: Hind Pocket Books, 1969.

King-Hall, S. *Defence in the Nuclear Age.* London: Gollancz, 1957.

Kumar, K. "A Report on the Balia Sarvodaya Conference." *Gandhi Marg* 10, no. 4 (1966): 246–48.

Kumarappa, B. "Editor's Note." In M. K. Gandhi, *Non-Violent Resistance,* iii–vi. New York: Schocken, 1961.

Kuppuswami, Justice A. "Acharyakul Seminar on Cow Protection." *Sansthakul* 20, no. 6 (1990): 6–11.

Lall, B. G. "Peacekeeping at the UN." *Bulletin of the Atomic Scientists* Oct. (1966): 43–45.

Lanza Del Vasto, J. J. *Warriors of Peace: Writings on the Technigue of Nonviolence.* New York: Alfred A. Knopf, 1974.

Lazar, E. "Militarism in the Land of Gandhi." *Liberation* 8, no. 3 (1963): 20–23.

"Letters and other information from the Delhi-Peking March." World Peace Brigade, North American Regional Council, 1963. Manuscript.

Limaye, M. *The Age of Hope: Phases of the Socialist Movement.* Delhi: Atma Ram, 1986.

Linton, E. *Fragments of a Vision: A Journey Through India's Gramdan Villages.* Varanasi: Sarva Seva Sangh, 1971.

Lippman, W. "The Political Equivalent of War." *Atlantic Monthly* Aug. (1928): 181–82.

Liu, F. T. *United Nations Peacekeeping and the Non-Use of Force.* Boulder, Colo.: Lynne Rienner Publishers, 1992.

Lorenz, K. *On Aggression.* London: Methuen, 1966.

Luard, E. "United Nations Peace Forces." In *The Evolution of International Organisations,* edited by E. Luard, 138–76. London: Thames and Hudson, 1966.

Lyttle, B. "Mir Sada / We Share One Peace." August 1993. Manuscript.

———. "Solidarity for Peace in Sarajevo." *Midwest Pacifist Commentator* 8, no. 1 (1993): 1–8, 10.

———. *You Come with Naked Hands: The Story of the San Francisco to Moscow Walk for Peace.* Raymond, N.H.: Greenleaf, 1966.

Madariaga, S. de. "Blueprint for a World Commonwealth." In *Perspectives on Peace*

1910–1960, edited by the Carnegie Endowment for International Peace, 47–64. New York: Praeger, 1960.

———. "Towards the Ideal Federation." *The New Leader* 18, no. 25 (1960): 17–20.

Magee, R. J. "Some Possible Strategies." In *Consultation on an International Peace Brigade: Working Documents and Background Papers,* 10–15. N.p.: n.d. Booklet.

Mager, A. "Israeli-Palestine Project Plans Future." *Peace Brigades* 7, no. 1 (1990): 4.

Mahadevan, T. K., ed. *Truth and Nonviolence: A UNESCO Symposium on Gandhi.* New Delhi: Gandhi Peace Foundation, 1970.

Mahadevan, T. K., A. Roberts, and G. Sharp, eds. *Civilian Defence: An Introduction.* New Delhi: Gandhi Peace Foundation, 1967.

Mandal, M. "Nonviolent Experiment in Cyprus." *People's Action* 8, no. 4 (1974): 33–34.

———. "Unarmed Peace Keeping Force." *Vigil* 4, no. 15 (1981): 3, 9–12.

Marriot, J. A. R. *Commonwealth or Anarchy? A Survey of Projects of Peace from the Sixteenth to the Twentieth Century.* London: Oxford Univ. Press, 1939.

Martin, D. A. *Pacifism: An Historical and Sociological Study.* London: Routledge and Kegan Paul, 1965.

Mashruwala, K. G. *Gandhi and Marx.* Ahmedabad: Navajivan, 1951.

Maxwell, N. *India's China War.* Harmondsworth, England: Penguin, 1972.

Mayer, P., ed. *The Pacifist Conscience.* Harmondsworth, England: Penguin, 1961.

Meghani, J. *Earthen Lamps.* New Delhi: Sahitya Akademi, 1979.

Miller, W. *I Found No Peace: The Journal of a Foreign Correspondent.* Harmondsworth, England: Penguin, 1940.

Miller, W. R. *Nonviolence: A Christian Interpretation.* London: Allen and Unwin, 1964.

Ministry of Education, *Gandhian Outlook and Techniques.* A verbatim report of the proceedings of the seminar, Contribution of Gandhian Outlook and Techniques to the Solution of Tensions Between and Within Nations, New Delhi, 5–17 Jan. 1953. New Delhi: Ministry of Education, Government of India, 1953.

Mira Behn [Madeleine Slade]. *The Spirit's Pilgrimage.* London: Longmans, 1960.

Mishra, S. K. "A Search for a Peaceful Revolution, A Challenge for the Indian Youth." *People's Action* 8, no. 8 (1973): 9–16.

Montagu, A., ed. *Man and Aggression.* Oxford: Oxford Univ. Press, 1973.

———. *The Nature of Human Aggression.* Oxford: Oxford Univ. Press, 1976.

Moorehead, C. *Troublesome People: Enemies of War: 1916–1986.* London: Hamish Hamilton, 1987.

Morris, S. *The Arm of the Law: The United Nations and the Use of Force. Peace News,* 1957. Pamphlet.

Moser, Y. "UN Approach to Conflict Intervention." *Gandhi Marg* 15, no. 1 (1993): 78–86.

Moskos, C. C. *Peace Soldiers: The Sociology of a United Nations Military Force.* Chicago: Univ. of Chicago Press, 1976.

Muste, A. J. "Aims and Objects of Satyagraha Units." *Harijan,* 12 March 1950.

———. "On the Indian Crisis 1962–3." *Bhoodan* 7, no. 44 (1963): 349–50, 355.

———. *Report on the Indian Crisis.* Varanasi: World Peace Brigade (Asia Region), 1963.

Muste Papers. A. J. Muste Collection, Swarthmore College Peace Collection, Swarthmore, Pennsylvania.

Myrdal, G. *Asian Drama: An Inquiry into the Poverty of Nations.* Harmondsworth, England: Penguin, 1968.

Naess, A. *Gandhi and Group Conflict: An Exploration of Satyagraha.* Oslo: Universitetsforlaget, 1974.

―――. *Gandhi and the Nuclear Age.* Totowa, N.J.: Bedminster Press, 1965.

Nakhre, A. "Meaning of Nonviolence: A Study of Satyagrahi Attitudes." *Journal of Peace Research* 13, no. 3 (1976): 185–96.

Nanda, B. R. *Mahatma Gandhi: A Biography.* Delhi: Oxford Univ. Press, 1981.

Narayan, J. P. "Acharya Vinobha Bhave" *Sri Jayaprakash Narayan Sixtyfirst Birth Day Celebrations: Commemorative Volume.* Madras: Sri Jayaprakash Narayan Sixty-First Birthday Celebrations Committee, 1963.

―――. *The Dual Revolution.* Tanjore: Sarvodaya Prachuralaya, 1963.

―――. "Face to Face." In *Towards Total Revolution.* Vol. 1, *Search for an Ideology,* edited by Brahmanand, 231–52. Bombay: Popular, 1978.

―――. "Flames of Jamshedpur." In *Communal Violence: (A Perspective),* edited by the Sarva Seva Sangh, 27–35. Varanasi: Sarva Seva Sangh, 1964.

―――. *From Socialism to Sarvodaya.* Varanasi: Sarva Seva Sangh, 1958.

―――. "India, China and Peace." *Liberation* 8, no. 7 (1963): 21–24.

―――. "Indian Youth Peace Corps." *Sarvodaya* 17, no. 9 (1968): 393–95.

―――. "The Path of Revolution." In *Towards Total Revolution.* Vol. 4, *Total Revolution,* edited by Brahmanand, 80–95. Bombay: Popular, 1978.

―――. "Peace Army." *Bhoodan* 6, no. 36 (1961): 287.

―――. "Peacemaking in Nagaland" In *Nation Building in India,* edited by Brahmanand, 361–73. Varanasi: Navachetna, n.d.

―――. "The Philosophy of Peace." *Interdiscipline* 5, no. 1/2 (1968): 98–103

―――. *A Picture of Sarvodaya Social Order.* Tiruchirapalli: Sarvodaya Prachuralaya, 1961.

―――. *Prison Diary.* Bombay: Popular, 1977

―――. "Reconstruction of the Indian Polity." In *Socialism, Sarvodaya and Democracy: Selected Works of Jayaprakash Narayan,* edited by B. Prasad, 192–239. Bombay: Asia, 1964.

―――. "The Revolt Against the System." In *Towards Total Revolution.* Vol. 4, *Total Revolution,* edited by Brahmanand, 121–132. Bombay: Popular, 1978.

―――. *Sarvodaya Answer to Chinese Aggression.* Tanjore: Sarvodaya Prachuralaya, 1963.

―――. "Thoughts on Goa." *Bhoodan* 6, no. 37 (1961): 300.

―――. *Total Revolution.* Varanasi: Sarva Seva Sangh, 1975.

―――. *Towards Revolution.* New Delhi: Arnold-Heinemann, n.d.

―――. *Towards Total Revolution.* Vol. 1, *Search for an Ideology,* edited by Brahmanand. Bombay: Popular, 1978.

―――. *Towards Total Revolution.* Vol. 2, *Politics in India,* edited by Brahmanand. Bombay: Popular, 1978.

―――. *Towards Total Revolution.* Vol. 4, *Total Revolution,* edited by Brahmanand. Bombay : Popular, 1978.

―――. "Two-fold Programme for World Peace." *Sarvodaya* 10, no. 7 (1961): 261.

―――. "The Unresolved Question." *Sarvodaya* 13, no. 7 (1964) 273–78.

―――. "The Urgency for Shanti Sena." *Sarvodaya* 14, no. 4 (1964): 153–157.

―――. "Why a World Peace Guard." *Vigil* 12, no. 48/9 (1961): 771–72.

Narayan, S. *Vinoba: His Life and Work*. Bombay: Popular, 1970.

Nargolkar, K. *In the Wake of the Chinese Thrust*. Bombay: Popular, 1965.

Nargolkar, V. *The Creed of Saint Vinoba*. Bombay: Bharatiya Vidya Bhavan, 1963.

————. *Crime and Non-violence*. Poona: Sulabha Rashtriya Granthamala Trust, 1974.

————. *JP's Crusade for Revolution*. New Delhi: Chand, 1975.

————. "Vinoba and Satyagraha." *Gandhi Marg* 2, no. 12 (1981): 661–72.

Nelson, S. D. "Nature/Nurture Revisited 1: A Review of the Biological Bases of Conflict." *Journal of Conflict Resolution* 18, no. 2 (1974): 285–335.

Nibedon, N. *Nagaland: The Night of the Guerrillas*. New Delhi: Lancer, 1978.

Niebuhr, R. *Moral Man and Immoral Society: A Study in Ethics and Politics*. New York: Scribner's, 1932.

Nonviolence at Work in Central America. Peace Brigades International. Annual Report of the Central America Project, 1989.

"Northern Ireland: A Proposal for Nonviolent Intervention." *Peace News,* 10 September 1971.

Nunn, A. C. "The Arming of an International Police." *Journal of Peace Research* 2, no. 3 (1965): 187–91.

Olson, T. "The World Peace Brigade: Vision and Failure." *Our Generation Against Nuclear War* 3, no. 1 (1964): 34–41.

Olson, T., and G. Christiansen. *Thirty-One Hours: The Grindstone Experiment*. Toronto: Canadian Friends Service Committee, 1968.

Oommen, T. K. *Charisma, Stability and Change: An Analysis of Bhoodan-Gramdan Movement in India*. New Delhi: Thompson, 1972.

————. "Rethinking Gandhian Approach." *Gandhi Marg* 1, no. 7 (1979): 416–23.

Orwell, G. "Reflections on Gandhi." In *The Collected Essays, Journalism and Letters of George Orwell*. Vol. 4, *In Front of Your Nose*, 523–31. Harmondsworth, England: Penguin, 1970.

Ostergaard, G. *Nonviolent Revolution in India*. New Delhi: Gandhi Peace Foundation, 1985.

————. "Vinoba's 'Gradualist' Versus Western 'Immediatist' Anarchism." *Gandhi Marg* 5, no. 8/9 (1983): 509–30.

Ostergaard, G., and M. Currel. *The Gentle Anarchists: A Study of the Leaders of the Sarvodaya Movement for Non-Violent Revolution in India*. Oxford: Clarendon Press, 1971.

Patel, S., and I. Rawat, *Shanti Sena Margdarshika*. Vedchhi: Gujarat Vidyapith, 1970.

Peace Army leaflets and newsletters, Swarthmore College Peace Collection, Swarthmore, Pa.

Peck, C. "The Case for a United Nations Dispute Settlement Commission." *Interdisciplinary Peace Research* 3, no. 1 (1991): 73–87.

Pelton, L. H. *The Psychology of Non-Violence*. New York: Pergamon, 1974.

Power, P. F. *Gandhi on World Affairs*. London: Allen and Unwin, 1961.

Prabhu, R. K., and U. R. Rao, eds. *The Mind of Mahatma Gandhi*. Ahmedabad, Navajivan, 1967.

Pradhan, R. C. "Musahari: A Gandhian Experiment in Peace Action and Peace Education." *Bulletin of Peace Proposals* 15, no. 2 (1984): 125–33.

Prasad, B., ed. *A Revolutionary's Quest: Selected Writings of Jayaprakash Narayan*. Delhi: Oxford Univ. Press, 1980.

Prasad, D. "Gandhi's Concept of Freedom." *Gandhi Marg* 11, no. 3 (1989): 327–32.

————. "Shanti Sena aur Himsaka Pratikar" (Hindi). *Gandhi Marg* Sep.-Oct. (1984): 42–62.

————. "Some Thoughts on the World Peace Brigade." War Resisters' International, 1964. Manuscript.

————. "The World Peace Brigade." *Peace News,* 6 August 1971, 2–3.

Pyarelal. *Mahatma Gandhi: The Last Phase.* Vol. 1. Ahmedabad: Navajivan, 1956.

————. *Mahatma Gandhi: The Last Phase.* Vol. 2. Ahmedabad: Navajivan, 1958.

————. *A Pilgrimage for Peace: Gandhi and Frontier Gandhi among N.W.F. Pathans.* Ahmedabad: Navajivan, 1950.

————. *Thrown to the Wolves: Abdul Ghaffar.* Calcutta: Eastlight Book House, 1966.

Radhakrishna. "Shanti Sena ek Saha-Chintan" (Hindi). *Gandhi Marg,* Feb. (1985): 35–38.

Radhakrishna, and N. Desai, "Indo-Pakistan Conflict and Our Duty." *Sarvodaya* 15, no. 5 (1965): 224–26.

Radhakrishnan, N. *Gandhi and Youth: The Shanti Sena of GRI.* Gandhigram: Gandhigram Rural Institute, 1990.

————. "Shanti Sena: Concept and Practice." *Non-violent Revolution* 8, no. 6 (1990): 2–4.

————. "Shantisena in Gandhigram." N.d. Manuscript.

————. "Training in Peace Education: An Indian Perspective." *Gandhi Marg* 6, no. 4/5 (1984): 331–43.

Ram, S. *Vinoba and His Mission (Being an Account of the Rise and Growth of the Bhoodan Yajna Movement).* Varanasi: Akhil Bharat Sarva Seva Sangh, 1962.

Raman, T. A. *What Does Gandhi Want?* London: Oxford Univ. Press, 1943.

Ramamurti. *Himsa ki Pelti Ag se Mukti Kaise?* Varanasi: Sarva Seva Sangh, 1983.

————. "The Next Thirteen Years in India: A Nonviolent Perspective." *Vigil* 9, no. 9 (1987): 3–7, 15–16.

————. *Shanti Sena: Keyon, Kaise, Kislive?* Varanasi: Sarva Seva Sangh, 1986.

Ramana Murti, V. V. "Buber's Dialogue and Gandhi's Satyagraha." *Journal of the History of Ideas* 29, no. 4 (1968): 605–13.

Rao, G. R. S. "The Concept of a Third Force in Conflict Resolution." *Gandhi Marg* 12, no. 4 (1968): 421–30.

Rikhye, I. "Preparation and Training of U.N. Peacekeeping Forces." In *Peace-Keeping: Experience and Evaluation—The Oslo Papers,* edited by P. Frydenberg, 183–97. Oslo: Norwegian Institute of International Affairs, 1964.

Rikhye, I., M. Harbottle, and B. Egge. *The Thin Blue Line: International Peacekeeping and Its Future.* New Haven, Conn.: Yale Univ. Press, 1974.

Roberts, A. "Civilian Defence Strategy." In *The Strategy of Civilian Defence; Non-Violent Resistance to Aggression,* edited by A. Roberts, 215–54. London: Faber, 1967.

Roberts, R. E. *H. R. L. Sheppard: Life and Letters.* London: John Murray, 1942.

Roep, K. "hair 'You Never Know the Effect': An Experience in International Monitoring." *Reconciliation International,* Autumn (1993), 7–8.

Royden, A. M. "Master Christian?" In *Gandhi Memorial Peace Number,* edited by K. Roy, 130–34. Shantiniketan: Visva-Bharati Quarterly, 1949.

————. "The Peacemaker." In W. Paxton et al., *Dick Sheppard: An Apostle of Brotherhood,* 73–81. London: Chapman and Hall, 1938.

————. "Reminder to Youth." *The New World,* November 1931, 7.

Russell, R. R. *A History of the United Nations Charter: The Role of the United States 1940–1945*. Washington, D.C.: Brookings Institute, 1959.

Salstrom, F. P. "Nonviolent Peacemaking." Philadelphia Friends Peace Committee, 1967–68; International Peace Academy, 1968–69. Manuscript.

"Sarva Seva Sangh, Consultation, Katol," *Gandhi Marg* 11, no. 1 (1989): 124.

Sarva Seva Sangh. *Draft Manifesto of the Sarvodaya Movement*. Varanasi,1972.

———. *Sarva Seva Sangh Work Report, July 1979-April 1981, from Ferozpur to Ujain*. Varanasi, 1981.

———. *What Sarvodaya Stands For: A Manifesto*. Varanasi, 1973.

Sarva Seva Sangh and Sarva Seva Sangh Prabhand Samiti Meeting Minutes. Sarva Seva Sangh minutes books and session reports, Sarva Seva Sangh headquarters, Sevagram.

Scarfe, A., and W. Scarfe. *J. P.: His Bioqraphy*. New Delhi: Orient Longman, 1975.

Schonborn, K. L. *Dealing with Violence: The Challenge Faced by Police and Other Peacekeepers*. Springfield, Ill.: Charles C. Thomas, 1975.

———. "Response to Social Conflict: Violent and Non-Violent Third-Party Intervention." Ph.D. diss., Univ. of Pennsylvania, 1971.

Schwebel, S. M. "A United Nations 'Guard' and a United Nations 'Legion'." Appendix, W. R. Frye, *A United Nations Peace Force*, 195–216. New York: Oceana, 1957.

Schweitzer, C. "Intervening in Sarajevo: Hopes and Realities." *Peace News*, February 1993, 2.

———. "We Divide One Peace . . ." *Peace News*, September 1993, 8–9.

Sen, M. *Gandhian Way and the Bhoodan Movement*. Varanasi: Sarva Seva Sangh, 1964.

Shah, K. *Vinoba: Life and Mission [An Introductory Study]*. Varanasi: Sarva Seva Sangh, 1979.

Shah, K., ed. *Vinoba on Gandhi*. Varanasi: Sarva Seva Sangh, 1985.

"Shanti-Sena in India." *Bhoodan* 6, no. 36 (1961): 285.

Sharga, B. N. *Gandhi: His Life and Teachinqs*. Lucknow: Upper India Publishing House, 1950.

Sharp, G. *Gandhi Wields the Weapon of Moral Power (Three Case Histories)*. Ahmedabad: Navajivan, 1960.

———. *The Politics of Nonviolent Action*. Pt. 1, "Power and Struggle," and pt. 3, "The Dynamics of Nonviolent Action". Boston: Porter Sargent, 1973.

———. "A Study of the Meaning of Nonviolence." In *Gandhi: His Relevance for our Times,* edited by G. Ramachandran and T. K. Mahadevan, 21–66. Berkeley, Calif.: World Without War, 1971.

Shepard, M. *Gandhi Today: A Report on Mahatma Gandhi's Successors*. Arcata, Calif.: Simple Productions, 1987.

———. "Peace Brigades." *Fellowship,* July/Aug. 1982, 9–10.

———. "Peace Brigades" *World Encyclopedia of Peace*. Vol. 2, 178–80. Oxford: Pergamon, 1986.

———. "Ray Magee, Peaceworker." N.d. Manuscript.

———. "Shanti Sena: Peace Keeper." *Peace News: For Nonviolent Revolution* 29 May 1981, 10–11.

————. *Since Gandhi*. Weare, N.H.: Greenleaf Books, 1984.

————. "Tooling up for Peace: The Launching of Peace Brigades International." N.d. Manuscript.

Shridharani, K. *War Without Violence*. Bombay: Bharatiya Viduya Bhavan, 1962.

Shukla, C. *Conversations of Gandhiji*. Bombay: Vora, 1949.

Sider, R. *Exploring the Limits of Non-Violence: A Call for Action*. London: Spire, 1988.

Singh, C. *Political Evolution of Nagaland*. New Delhi: Lancer, 1981.

Sinn, H. "International Conference in Trier." *Peace Brigade* 7, no. 1 (1990): 1.

————. "United Nations Reform and a Professional Peace Corps." Discussion Paper for the New Democratic Party's Task Force on the Reform of the United Nations, 1992. Mimeo.

Skjelsbaek, K. "United Nations Peacekeeping: Expectations, Limitations and Results. Forty Years of Mixed Experience." In *Proceedings of the First International Symposium on Non-Violent Solutions of International Crises and Regional Conflicts, Frankfurt am Main, February 1989*, edited by E. Czempiel, L. Kiuzadjan, and Z. Masoqust, 77–90. Vienna: International Social Science Council, 1990.

Skodvin, M. "Non-Violent Resistance During the German Occupation." In *The Strategy of Civilian Defence; Non-Violent Resistance to Aggression*, edited by A. Roberts, 136–53. London: Faber, 1967.

Smith, J. E. "The Inescapable Ambiguity of Nonviolence." *Philosophy East and West* 19, no. 2 (1969): 155–58.

Sonnleitner, M. W. "Gandhian Satyagraha and Swaraj: A Hierarchical Perspective." *Peace and Change* 14, no. 1 (1989): 3–24.

————. *Vinoba Bhave on Self-Rule & Representative Democracy*. New Delhi: Promilla, 1988.

Stokke, O. "United Nations Security Forces: A Discussion of the Problems Involved." In *Peace-Keeping: Experience and Evaluation—The Oslo Papers*, edited by P. Frydenberg, 27–67. Oslo: Norwegian Institute of International Affairs, 1964.

Swann, R., and P. Salstrom. "Towards a Non-Violent Peacekeeping Corps." *Peace News*, 8 October 1965, 6–7.

Sykes, M. "Report of the Shanti Sainik Camp Held at Sevagram from October 14 to 22, 1958." Appendix to V. Bhave, *Shanti Sena*, 136–49. Varanasi: Sarva Seva Sangh, 1963.

————. "Shanti Sena and the Government." *Sarvodaya* 12, no. 9 (1963): 337–41; 12, no. 10 (1963): 387–88, 393.

Tandon, V. "The Bhoodan-Gramdan Movement (1951–74)—A Review." *Gandhi Marg* 5, no. 8/9 (1983): 492–500.

————. "Nehru and Vinoba." *Gandhi Marg* 10, no. 8/9 (1988): 570–78.

————. "Present-day Sarvodaya Thinkers and War." *Gandhi Marg* 15, no. 1 (1971): 64–72.

————. *Sarvodaya ki Aur*. Delhi: Atmaram, 1968.

————. ed. *Selections from Vinoba*. Varanasi: Sarva Seva Sangh, 1981.

————. *The Social and Political Philosophy of Sarvodaya after Gandhi*. Varanasi: Sarva Seva Sangh, 1965.

————. "Vinoba and Satyagraha." *Gandhi Marg* 2, no. 7 (1980): 385–94.

Tatum, A. "World Peace Brigade." In *A Search for Alternatives to War and Violence,* edited by T. Dunn, 129–34. London: James Clark, 1963.

———. "The World Peace Brigade: Some Specific Proposals." *The War Resister* 93 (1961): 3–6.

Taylor, R. "Witness for Peace and the Pledge of Resistance." *Nonviolent Sanctions,* Spring/Summer (1990): 16–17.

Tendulkar, D. G. *Abdul Ghaffar Khan: Faith Is a Battle.* New Delhi: Gandhi Peace Foundation, 1967.

———. *Mahatma: Life of Mohandas Karamchand Gandhi.* 8 vols. New Delhi: Publications Division, Ministry of Information and Broadcasting, Government of India, 1961.

The Peace Army: A Sermon by A. Maude Royden, C.H., D.D., Preached at the Guildhouse, Eccleston Square S.W.1, on Sunday evening, February 1932. n.p.: n.d., leaflet.

"The Strengthening of Shanti Sena Movement." *Peace Newsletter* 1, no. 9 (1967): 3–5.

Tikekar, I. *Integral Revolution (An Analytical Study of Gandhian Thought).* Varanasi: Sarva Seva Sangh, 1970.

Tiwary, L. N. "Peace-Keeping Tasks of the U.N.O." *Sarva Seva Sangh* (monthly newsletter) 2, no. 1 (1968): 24–25.

"Training in Shanti Sena." *Bhoodan* 6, no. 40 (1962): 332.

"Turning Both Cheeks." *Manchester Guardian,* 27 February 1932.

"Two Statements from China." *Peace News,* 19 April 1963.

Urquhart, B. E. "United Nations Peace-keeping in the Middle East." *World Today* 36, no. 3 (1980): 88–93.

Venkata Raman, K. "United Nations Peacekeeping and the Future of World Order." In *Peacekeeping: Appraisals and Proposals,* edited by H. Wiseman, 371–401. New York, Pergamon, 1983.

Verma, S. *Metaphysical Foundation of Mahatma Gandhi's Thought.* New Delhi: Orient Longman, 1970.

"Vinoba Urges UNO Sponsored P. B." *Sarvodaya* 21, no. 3 (1971): 110–12.

Wainhouse, D. W. *International Peace Observation: A History and Forecast.* Baltimore, Md.: Johns Hopkins Univ. Press, 1966.

Walker, C. C. "Consultation on Peacekeeping." Haverford College, 1971. Manuscript.

———. "The Delhi-to-Peking Friendship March." *Friends Journal* 9, no. 23 (1963): 517–18.

———. "From Delhi to Peking: Walking for Peace." *World Peace Brigade Reports,* July 1963.

———. "Nonviolence in Eastern Africa 1962–4: The World Peace Brigade and Zambian Independence." In *Liberation Without Violence: A Third Party Approach,* edited by A. P. Hare and H. H. Blumberg, 157–77. Totowa, N.J.: Rowan and Littlefield, 1977.

———. *Organizing for Nonviolent Direct Action.* Cheney, Pa.: author, 1961.

———. "Peace Brigades as Unofficial Peacekeepers and Peacemakers." Paper prepared for Peace Brigades International, 1984. Mimeo.

———. "Peacekeeping: A Survey and an Evaluation." In L. P. Bloomfield, *The*

Power to Keep Peace: Today and in a World Without War, 228–43. Berkeley, Calif.: World Without War Council, 1971.

———. *Peacekeeping: 1969—A Survey and an Evaluation.* Monograph prepared for the American Friends Peace Committee, 1969.

———. "A Proposal for a Transnational, Nonmilitary Agency for Peacekeeping." In *Consultation on an International Peace Brigade: Working Documents and Background Papers,* 16–19. N.p.: n.d. Booklet.

———. "Report of Meetings of Peace Brigades International." *Gandhi Marg* 8, no. 12 (1987): 764–66.

———. "The World Peace Brigade: A Look at Some of Its Problems." Peace Brigades International, 1982. Manuscript.

———. *A World Peace Guard: An Unarmed Agency for Peacekeeping.* Hyderabad (AP): Academy of Gandhian Studies, 1981.

Wallis, T. "Intervention from Within." *Peace News,* January 1994, 10.

Waskow, A. I. *Towards a Peacemakers Academy: A Proposal for a First Step Towards a United Nations Transnational Peacemaking Force.* The Hague: W. Junk, 1967.

Watson, F., and H. Tennyson. *Talking of Gandhi.* New Delhi: Orient Longman, 1976.

Weber, T. "A Brief History of the Shanti Sena as Seen Through the Changing Pledges of the Shanti Sainik." *Gandhi Marg* 13, no. 3 (1991): 316–26.

———. *Conflict Resolution and Gandhian Ethics.* New Delhi: Gandhi Peace Foundation, 1991.

———. "From Maude Royden's Peace Army to the Gulf Peace Team: An Assessment of Unarmed Interpositionary Peace Forces." *Journal of Peace Research* 30, no. 1 (1993): 45–64.

———. "Gandhi's 'Living Wall' and Maude Royden's 'Peace Army'." *Gandhi Marg* 10, no. 4 (1988): 199–212.

———. "The Lesson from the Disciples: Is There a Contradiction in Gandhi's Philosophy of Action?" *Modern Asian Studies* 28, no. 1 (1994): 195–214.

———. "The Marchers Simply Walked Forward Until Struck Down: Nonviolent Suffering and Conversion." *Peace and Change* 18, no. 3 (1993): 267–89.

———. "Peacekeeping, the Shanti Sena and the Divisions in the Gandhian Movement During the Border War with China." *South Asia* 13, no. 2 (1990); 65–78.

———. "The Problems of Peacekeeping." *Interdisciplinary Peace Research* 1, no. 2 (1989): 3–26.

———. "The Satyagrahi as Heroic Idea." *Gandhi Marg* 11, no. 5 (1989): 133–53.

"What is the 'Shillong Agreement'?" *Economic and Political Weekly* 13, no. 21 (1978): 859–60.

Whitney, J. *John Woolman, Quaker.* London: George Harrap, 1943.

Winter, J. M., ed. *War and Economic Development.* Cambridge, Cambridge Univ. Press, 1975.

Wood, J. R. "Reservations in Doubt: The Backlash Against Affirmative Action in Gujarat, India." *Pacific Affairs* 60, no. 3 (1987): 408–30.

Yarrow, C. H. M. *Quaker Experiences in International Conciliation.* New Haven, Conn. Yale Univ. Press, 1978.

Yonuo, A. *The Rising Nagas: A Historical and Political Study*. Delhi: Vivek, 1974.

Young, O. R. *The Intermediaries: Third Parties in International Crises*. Princeton, N.J.: Princeton Univ. Press, 1967.

Zachariah, M. *Revolution Through Reform: A Comparison of Sarvodaya and Conscientization*. New York: Praeger, 1986.

Zahn, G. "The Ethics of Martyrdom." *Gandhi Marg* 10, no. 4 (1966): 291–94.

Index

Acland, Sir Richard, 15, 40
Agarwal, G., 102
Ahimsa. *See* Nonviolence
Akhil Bharat Shanti Sena. *See* Shanti
   Sena
Aram, M., 105, 108
Arrowsmith, P., 36
Aryanayakam, A., 76–78, 207
Asian Drama (Myrdal), 167
Azad, P., 97

Bang, A., 91
Bang, T., 82, 89, 95, 99
Bangladesh war, 28, 104, 126–28
Beati i Costruttori di Pace, 38–39
Bell, R., 15–16, 40, 223n. 62
Bharatiya Shanti Sena: and aggressive
   satyagraha, 157; and cow
   protection, 99–100, 157–59, 210;
   Deshpande becomes leader of, 99;
   founded, 97; in Gujarat, 244n. 204;
   members, 99–100; pledge, 210; and
   Sarva Seva Sangh, 98–99; and
   voting, 151. *See also* Cow
   protection; Shanti Sena
Bhargava, A., 91
Bhatt, A., 130–33, 158
Bhave, V. *See* Vinoba

Bhoodan, 71–73, 89, 92–93, 141–42,
   144, 146, 152, 205; JP's assessment
   of, 145
Bidwell, S., 3–4
Bigelow, A., 16
Bihar Movement, 94, 140–41, 146–
   47, 154. *See also* Total Revolution;
   JP Movement
Bingham, H., 201
Bloomfield, L., 7, 192–93
Blum, F., 40–41, 137, 178
Bondurant, J. V., 60, 63, 175
Bosnian war, 38–39
Boutros-Ghali, Boutros, 194
Brinton, H., 17, 200–202
Buber, M., 58
Burton, J., 9

Case, C. M., 175
Ceresole, P., 12, 14, 40, 66, 196
Chaliha, B. P., 106
Chambal Valley Peace Mission, 108–
   15, 137; assessment of, 114–15;
   background to, 108; and JP, 110–
   11, 114; rehabilitation work
   during, 112–14; and Vinoba, 108–
   10
Chatra Yuva Sangharsh Vahini, 91–92

Syracuse Studies on Peace and Conflict Resolution
Harriet Hyman Alonso, Charles Chatfield, and Louis Kriesberg, Series Editors

A series devoted to readable books on the history of peace movements, the lives of peace advocates, and the search for ways to mitigate conflict, both domestic and international. At a time when profound and exciting political and social developments are happening around the world, this series seeks to stimulate a wider awareness and appreciation of the search for peaceful resolution to strife in all its forms and to promote linkages among theorists, practitioners, social scientists, and humanists engaged in this work throughout the world.

Other titles in the series include:

An American Ordeal: The Antiwar Movement of the Vietnam Era. Charles DeBenedetti; Charles Chatfield, assisting author

Building a Global Civic Culture: Education for an Interdependent World. Elise Boulding

Cooperative Security: Reducing Third World Wars. I. William Zartman and Victor A. Kremenyuk, eds.

The Eagle and the Dove: The American Peace Movement and United States Foreign Policy, 1900–1922. John Whiteclay Chambers II

From Warfare to Party Politics: The Critical Transition to Civilian Control. Ralph M. Goldman

Gender and the Israeli-Palestinian Conflict: The Politics of Women's Resistance. Simona Sharoni

The Genoa Conference: European Diplomacy, 1921–1922. Carole Fink

Give Peace a Chance: Exploring the Vietnam Antiwar Movement. Melvin Small and William D. Hoover, eds.

Intractable Conflicts and Their Transformation. Louis Kriesberg, Terrell A. Northrup, and Stuart J. Thorson, eds.

Israeli Pacifist: The Life of Joseph Abileah. Anthony Bing

Mark Twain's Weapons of Satire: Anti-imperialist Writings on the Philippine-American War. Mark Twain; Jim Zwick, ed.

One Woman's Passion for Peace and Freedom: The Life of Mildred Scott Olmsted. Margaret Hope Bacon

Organizing for Peace: Neutrality, the Test Ban, and the Freeze. Robert Kleidman

Peace as a Women's Issue: A History of the U.S. Movement for World Peace and Women's Rights. Harriet Hyman Alonso

Peace/Mir: An Anthology of Historic Alternatives to War. Charles Chatfield and Ruzanna Ilukhina, volume editors

Plowing My Own Furrow. Howard W. Moore

Polite Protesters: The American Peace Movement of the 1980s. John Lofland

Preparing for Peace: Conflict Transformation Across Cultures. John Paul Lederach

The Road to Greenham Common: Feminism and Anti-Militarism in Britain since 1820. Jill Liddington

Timing the De-escalation of International Conflicts. Louis Kriesberg and Stuart Thorson, eds.

Virginia Woolf and War: Fiction, Reality, and Myth. Mark Hussey, ed.

The Women and the Warriors: The United States Section of the Women's International League for Peace and Freedom, 1915–1946. Carrie Foster